Harold's Cross

A HISTORY

Harold's Cross

A HISTORY

JOE CURTIS

Front cover image: Bread being handed-out outside Our Lady's Hospice in the 1940s. (Courtesy of Sisters of Charity)

First published 2016

The History Press Ireland
50 City Quay
Dublin 2
Ireland
www.thehistorypress.ie

The History Press Ireland is a member of Publishing Ireland,
the Irish book publishers' association.

© Joe Curtis, 2016

British Library Cataloguing in Publication Data.
A catalogue record for this book is available from the British Library.

ISBN 978 1 84588 238 9

Typesetting and origination by The History Press
Printed in Malta, by Melita Press

CONTENTS

Acknowledgements   6

1.   Historical Sketch   7
2.   The Earl of Meath   13
3.   The Park (The Green)   20
4.   Orphanages   28
5.   Mount Jerome Cemetery   41
6.   Religion   46
7.   Education   72
8.   Our Lady's Hospice   95
9.   Mount Argus   114
10.   Mills   123
11.   Business   137
12.   Canal, Rivers and Transport   160
13.   Housing   168
14.   Barracks   179
15.   Famous People   207

Selected Sources   216
Index   219

ACKNOWLEDGEMENTS

Thanks to the National Archives, National Library, National Museum, Irish Architectural Archive, Valuation Office, Dublin City Library and Archives, Sisters of Charity, Sisters of St Clare, Passionist Fathers, Holy Rosary Church, Anglican Church, Russian Orthodox Church, Carmelite Monastery in Delgany, Religious Society of Friends, Lord Meath, Trinity College Map Library, Griffith College, Cathal Brugha Barracks, Military Archives, RCB Library, Diocesan Archives.

Numerous individuals assisted me, including David Williams (British Hydropower Association), Donal S. Blake, Sarah Kenny (Scoil Íosagáin), Joe Miller, Marie Corbett (Our Lady's Hospice), Alan Massey (Mount Jerome), Teresa Whittington (Central Catholic Library), Kevin Kennedy (Cathal Brugha Barracks), Sibeil Doolan, Fr Gerry Kane.

1

HISTORICAL SKETCH

Historians believe that Harold's Cross derived its name from an ancient cross that marked the boundary between the lands owned by the Archbishop of Dublin and the lands of the Harold family. That family was based at Harold's Grange in Rathfarnham from about 1250 to 1540, up until St Mary's Abbey was dissolved by King Henry VIII. But the Harolds still occupied the land as tenants until the 1641 Rebellion. Thereafter, the land was owned by the Taylors (Taylor's Grange), and then by the famous Huguenot banking family of La Touché. Nowadays, the land is part of Marley Park. Over the centuries, the Harold property extended to the edge of Harold's Cross, and the Harold clan often attacked adjoining property under the control of the archbishop, until 1350 when peace was restored. The boundary cross was probably just south of the present Kenilworth traffic lights, at the boundary of the Liberty of St Sepulchre (also called the Archbishop's Liberty). William Duncan is known for his map of Dublin, dated 1821, but he also produced a map in 1814, which shows an ecclesiastical cross just south of the turn-off for Rathgar Lane (now Avenue). We do not know the size or material used, but a stone cross would have been appropriate. Until recently, there was a very old house behind Deveney's shop, called Cruz del Campo, which is Spanish for 'Cross in the Field'. The archbishop maintained a gallows (gibbet) on the green, roughly opposite the present cemetery entrance, where criminals were hanged, and which also acted as a deterrent to encroachment by the Harolds. Later on, a maypole replaced the gallows, and was the centre of much merriment and dancing every May, until the middle of the nineteenth century. The maypole dancing was re-enacted on 2 May 2010, and hopefully will prove to be a popular annual event.

There are two surviving Church of Ireland maps for Harold's Cross, dated 1717 and 1782, showing part of the farm of St Sepulchre let by the archbishop to the Usher family, but extending only to the present Greenmount Lane (called Mill Lane in 1782) and the present old stone wall on the south side of St Clare's Primary School driveway. The latter map also shows a 'brook' – the original line of the River Poddle.

From the sixth to the ninth century, there were four main roads radiating from Dublin: Slige Mor to Connaught, Slige Dala to Munster, Slige Midluachra to Ulster, and Slige Chualann to Leinster, the latter passing through Harold's Cross.

Old deeds refer to Harold's Cross Road as the Great Road, or 'Common of Harrolds Crofs', or the High Road.

In the William Petty (Down) Survey of 1654–1658, which recorded the land forfeited after the Cromwellian Wars, Harold's Cross was in the Barony of Newcastle and Uppercross, which in turn was subdivided into parishes. St Kevin's Parish included Acres Cross, which is referred to as the 'alias for Harrolds Cross'. The survey recorded three big landowners for the area (as at 1641), being Sir Adam Loftus, Sir William Usher, and the Earl of Meath. Adam Loftus was a descendant of the Protestant archbishop of Dublin and lord chancellor of the same name, who had built Rathfarnham Castle in 1583. A map produced by the Earl of Meath around 1836 shows land to the west of Harold's Cross (towards Dolphin's Barn) in the ownership of Sir Compton Domville, whose main estate was in Santry. The reference to acres is intriguing, because it could have been a family surname; certainly there was a Richard Acres, merchant, living in Dublin during the latter part of the seventeenth century, and this surname still survives.

Watson's Almanac of 1734 records that the coach fare from Dublin to 'Harrolds Crofs' was 1s 1d. In 1743, the almanac notes that Edmond Weld of 'Harrolds Crofs' was a member of the Common Council of Dublin (the Welds occupied land around the present Mount Argus area).

Rocque's map of 1760 shows 'Harrolds Crofs', including Mount Jerome House, Chicken Lane (also called Hen and Chicken Lane and later Mount Drummond Avenue), Corn Mill (Loader Park), and a scattering of different houses.

Taylor's map of 1816 shows Greenmount Mill, Mount Jerome House, Mount Tallant House, Cruz del Campo, Rose Grove (beside the unlisted

St Clare's Convent), a horse barracks (now called Cathal Brugha Barracks), a kiln near the present canal, and the Tongue and City Water Course (part of the River Poddle).

The census for 1821 records 144 houses, 223 families, and a population of 1,049 for the village of Harold's Cross. Fifty-seven people were employed in agriculture, ninety-four in trade and manufacture, and 170 in other occupations (321 people employed).

The Tithe Applotment Books were prepared in the 1820s and '30s, listing the occupiers and acreage of farms, in order to calculate the 'tithes' to be paid annually to the Anglican Church. St Catherine's Parish (generally the west side of Harold's Cross), included the following:

Rathland	Joseph Byrne	17.5 acres
Rathland	Peter Farrell	22.5 acres
Rathland	Kavanagh	18.5 acres
Mount Jerome	Keogh	25.5 acres
Harolds Crofs	Joseph Pim	25 acres

St Peter's Parish (generally the east side of Harold's Cross) included:

Harold's Cross Road	Michael Buckley	13.5 acres
Harold's Cross Road	William Gibton	21 acres
Harold's Cross Road	Bryan	37 acres
Kimmage Road	Thomas Magin	11.5 acres
Kimmage Road	John Byrne	16.5 acres
Kimmage Road	Mrs Byrne	11.5 acres
Kimmage Road	Laurence Murray	16.5 acres

Lewis, in 1837, describes Harold's Cross as having a population of 1,101 people, and 157 houses. Pims Cotton Factory at Greenmount employed 150 people. The house Mount Argus was owned by J. Byrne, and the house Greenmount was owned by J. Webb. There was a paper mill (later called Loader Park), and a flour mill (later called Harold's Cross Laundry). There was a national school, and the Convent of St Clare, in addition to a monastery of Discalced Carmelites opposite St Clare's. These figures were based on the 1831 Census, which included the information that eighty-two people were employed in retail trade or handicraft, seventy-four were female servants, and seventy-five were 'capitalists, bankers, professional and other educated men'.

The Rathmines township was formed in 1847 by the Rathmines Improvement Act, and comprised part of the parish of St Peter in the barony of Uppercross, which included the east side of Harold's Cross. That act listed the first Commissioners, who would serve for a term of three years – Terence Thomas Dolan, Frederick Jackson, Christopher Edward Wall, John Holmes, John Butler, William Todd, Andrew Gill, Frederick Stokes, John Connor (of Harold's Cross), Edward Galavan, John Scally, John Hawker Evans (of Mount Harold), Thomas McEniry, Patrick Palmer Bacon, Henry Read, John Sibthorpe, Alexander Parker, and John Purser. The Rathmines and Rathgar Improvement Act 1862 extended the area to include Rathgar. The Rathmines, Rathgar and St Catherine's Improvement Act 1866 added Cherry Orchard in the Parish of St Nicholas (the present Harmsworth offices), Argos, Mount Jerome, Rathland East and Rathland West in the Parish of St Catherine. The township was substantially independent from Dublin Corporation and provided most of its own services – roads, drains, water, street lighting, street cleaning and so on, recouping the cost by way

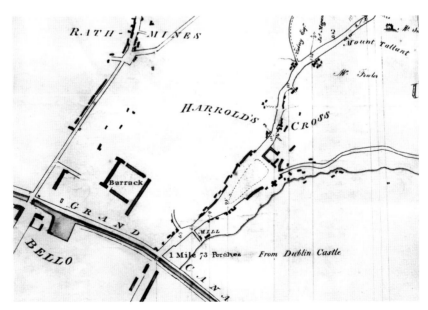

1814 Duncan map of Harold's Cross. Note the church property boundary cross just south of the junction with Rathgar Avenue. (Courtesy of National Archives)

of 'rates' on each property in the locality. In 1897, the Commissioners built their new town hall in Rathmines, including the landmark red sandstone clock tower, and in 1899, the Rathmines and Rathgar Urban District Council was formed. In 1930, Dublin Corporation took over when the township was dissolved, and the Harold's Cross region was designated Dublin SW7, later Dublin 6, and now it is partly designated Dublin 6W and Dublin 12. A low-level stone with bronze insert is positioned at the corner of Harold's Cross Road and Tivoli Avenue, with the date 1847 and the words 'Rathmines Township' inscribed. Most cast-iron street lamps in Brighton Square, and some in Kenilworth Square, date from the Rathmines township days, and their ornate design reflects a more leisurely era.

Thom's Directory of 1875 lists the following interesting occupations of Haroldians – soap and candle dealer, land engineering and geodesic surveyor, post office letter receiver, coal factor, locksmith and bell hanger, and three car owners (a horse-drawn cab or taxi). There is also reference to some tenements (the forerunner of bedsits and flats). The same directory in 1900 refers to a chimney curer and a malster.

Harold's Cross was (and still is) much higher than the city, and small hillocks came to be called mounts, so the various villas and big houses were called, for example, Mount Argos, Mount Jerome, Mount Harold, Mount Tallant, Mount Drummond, Greenmount (later, Our Lady's Mount), and so on.

In the eighteenth and nineteenth centuries, Harold's Cross was renowned for its 'fresh air' and healthy environment, not forgetting extensive orchards, but it is thought that the opening of the Mount Jerome Cemetery in 1836 halted the development of the area.

The National Museum has three prehistoric artefacts, which were found in the Harold's Cross locality. The first is a 250mm-long (10 inches), finely polished black-limestone axe head dating from around 3000 BC, found in 1874 in the back garden of 19 Harold's Cross (now 87 Harold's Cross Road, once part of St Clare's Convent). The second is a 150mm-long (6 inches), flanged and stop-ridge bronze palstave (axe head), dating from around 1500 BC, found in 1950 in the back garden of 23 Kenilworth Park. The third item is a tiny 21mm (¾ inch) cream-coloured barbed-and-tanged flint arrowhead, dating from around 2300 BC, found in the back garden of 16 Westfield Road, near Mount Argus. Thus the neighbourhood can lay claim to both Stone Age

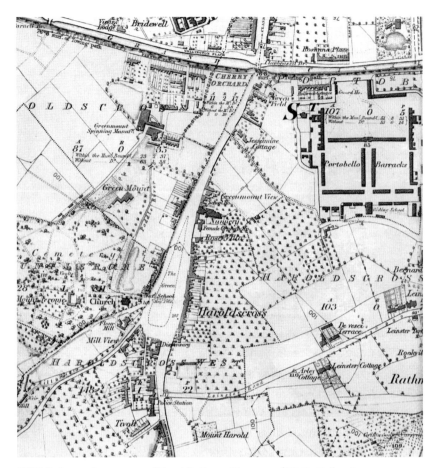

1837 Ordnance Survey map of Harold's Cross. (Courtesy of Trinity College)

and Bronze Age connections, when axes were used as tools (cutting down trees and tilling the land), and arrows were employed to kill animals for food. Up to recent times, lands in the Mount Argus area were known as Rathlands, and the 'Rath' may be referring to Bronze Age fortified housing or farms – usually a mound of earth surrounded by a ditch.

2

THE EARL OF MEATH

William Brabazon came to Ireland in 1534, from Leicestershire in England, after being appointed under treasurer and receiver general of Ireland (vice-treasurer in 1536).

The Abbey of St Thomas was established in 1177, just to the south of the present-day St Catherine's church in Thomas Street, and named after St Thomas-à-Becket, the archbishop who had been murdered in Canterbury Cathedral in 1170. The abbey was founded by William FitzAldelm, the deputy of King Henry II in Ireland, and was entrusted to the Canons of the Congregation of St Victor. They were granted land in Donore (west side of Harold's Cross) in 1178, and land in Bray in 1180. In 1305, the abbey was granted judicial power, and hence a court was built. Thereafter, the name 'Abbey of Thomas Court and Donore' was used. Around 1539, King Henry VIII ordered the dissolution of the monasteries in Ireland and England, but the abbots were given titles and generous pensions in compensation, including £42 per annum to (Sir) Henry Duff, abbot of Thomas Court and Donore, at that stage the Order of St Augustin. The Dublin properties and landholdings of Thomas Court and Donore were granted by the king to William Brabazon in 1544, for good and faithful service to the Crown, by way of letters patent (royal decrees or orders). William died in 1552, and is buried in the crypt under St Catherine's church in Thomas Street. His descendants acquired the title Baron Ardee in 1616, and Earl of Meath in 1627.

The Abbey of Thomas Court and Donore included most of the present Coombe area of Dublin, and extended through the west side of Harold's Cross as far as Sundrive Road. Other landholdings on the east side of Harold's Cross were acquired by succeeding generations of Brabazons, these being originally owned by the Archbishop of Dublin.

In 1618 Sir William Brabazon was granted extensive lands in Wicklow, especially around Bray, these also being part of the original Abbey of Thomas Court in Dublin, but the family continued to reside in Dublin until the middle of the seventeenth century. Killruddery House, outside Bray, then became (and still is) the seat of the Brabazons.

The Coombe area of Dublin has for many centuries been called 'The Liberties'. A liberty was an area of private jurisdiction outside the walled area of Dublin City, and both the Earl of Meath and the Archbishop of Dublin owned and controlled separate areas in the Coombe, Harold's Cross and beyond. Thus Charles Brooking's map of 1728 shows and refers to the Archbishop's Liberty and the Earl of Meath's Liberty. Even when Mount Argus was sold in 1858, the Landed Estates Court described it as being in the Earl of Meath's Liberty. 'Riding the franchises' became a custom, whereby every year the city councillors would ride around on horseback, along the exact boundary between the city and the independent liberties.

The Report from the Commission on Municipal Corporations in Ireland 1836 gives a very good description of the five manorial jurisdictions or liberties of Dublin, namely St Sepulchre (Archbishop's), Thomas Court and Donore, Deanery of St Patrick, Kilmainham, and Glasnevin/Grangegorman/Christchurch. There was formerly a sixth, St Mary's Abbey. The first three were popularly called 'The Liberties', a nickname that continues to this day. These five liberties were independent of the city of Dublin, and were self-governing. The Liberty of St Sepulchre was further subdivided into eight manors: St Sepulchre, Tallaght, Rathcoole/Clondalkin, Shankill, Ballymore-Eustace, Castlekevin (Wicklow), Swords (including Rush, Lusk, Clonmelkin), and Finglas. The manor of St Sepulchre derived its powers from a royal charter during the reign of King Charles I, dated 1636, which referred to an original charter in the reign of King John (1199–1216). It was usual to delineate the boundary of the archbishop's liberties by means of crosses.

The manor of St Sepulchre stretched from Bishop Street to Harcourt Street, Hatch Street, Donnybrook, Milltown, along the River Dodder by Rathgar Lane (now called Orwell Road and Rathgar Avenue) to Rathfarnham Road (now Kenilworth traffic lights) which it crosses, then to Kimmage Road (possibly the present driveway into Mount Argus), where it meets the Liberty of Donore, then down Harold's Cross to New Street, Francis Street, Bull

Alley, Kevin Street, and back to Bishop Street. The Liberty of the Deanery of St Patrick is contained within these boundaries, comprising just over 5 acres, but became a haven for bad debtors, because of its vague status.

The Liberty of Thomas Court and Donore is described in detail, comprising most of the streets and alleys in the present Liberties/Coombe area, but extending through the west side of Harold's Cross as far as the present Sundrive Road (comprising the Hospice, Mount Jerome and Mount Argus). For example, the manor of Thomas Court included part of Thomas Street, Meath Street, part of the Coombe, Pimlico, part of Marrowbone Lane, School Street, Bond Street and so on. The adjoining manor of Donore included part of the Coombe, part of Skinners Alley, part of Brabazon Street, part of Ardee Street, part of New Market, part of Tanners Row, part of Blackpitts, part of Weavers Square, part of Love Lane, part of Cork Street, and then the west side of Harold's Cross. The street names reflected family names of the Earl of Meath (Brabazon, Ardee, Meath), and also the occupations of many residents.

Therefore, up to the middle of the nineteenth century, Harold's Cross was in two different Liberties – St Sepulchre, and Thomas Court and Donore. St Sepulchre was controlled by a seneschal appointed by the archbishop, and likewise, the seneschal for Thomas Court and Donore was appointed by the Earl of Meath. The seneschal was a judge (usually a barrister) who presided over the civil court, generally for bad debts. Joseph Radcliffe was the seneschal in 1836 for St Sepulchre, while Thomas L. Kelly was responsible for Thomas Court and Donore. Other staff included a marshal (keeper of gaol or marshalsea), coroner, weighmaster and so on. A Grand Jury (similar to present City Councillors) sat twice a year to decide on policy and Grand Jury cess (tax).

The Earl of Meath built many of the houses and cottages in the Coombe area, mostly for renting, but he subdivided and let large parcels of his land in Harold's Cross, leaving the new tenants to build houses and other properties, usually for renting. Thus the Earl of Meath can claim credit for the layout of much of Harold's Cross.

Each large parcel of land was let by the Earl of Meath to a tenant for the duration of the lives of three named people, with a 'covenant for perpetual renewal', at a stipulated fixed yearly rent. As each of the three people died, a new name was inserted in the lease, and an extra year's rent was paid as a 'fine' to the Earl of Meath. Thus a lease could extend forever. However, the Renewable Leasehold Conversion Act 1849 gave these tenants the right to obtain a fee farm grant from the landlord, with the old rent being slightly increased to allow for the loss of periodic 'fines' at renewal stage. As a result, most of the leases from the Earl of Meath were converted to fee farm grants in the 1850s, although the earl still retained the freehold until the Landlord and Tenant (Ground Rent) Act 1967 was introduced to allow long leaseholders to purchase the freehold. Some people think that their houses were built in the same year as the fee farm grant, but usually the houses are much older.

The following is a brief history of the early development of the Earl of Meath's property in Harold's Cross.

EXAMPLE OF EARLY DEED

In a lease of 1688, the Earl of Meath leased a large tract of land to John Edkins for forty-four years, comprising 'mount jerrom, rathlands, the Blackberry parks and the wood parks, with usual covenants except that of grinding at ye mills'.

BARBERS LAND (ALSO CALLED BARBERSTOWNLAND)

Barbers Land stretches from Mount Drummond Avenue to Park View Avenue and includes St Clare's Convent and the Greyhound Stadium. Sir William Usher once owned the land to the south of this parcel. The northern portion of St Clare's Convent was originally owned by the Archbishop of Dublin, being part of the farm of St Sepulchre, and the high stone boundary wall is still to be seen today, separating the former convent from the primary school driveway. All of Barbers Land was leased by the Earl of Meath to Daniel Faulkner from 1700, and the fee farm grant was acquired by John Galloway in 1853. John Galloway agreed (as was common in leases of the time) to 'grind all corn meal and other grist that shall be used on the said granted premises at one or more of the mills in the said Manor and Liberty belonging to the said Earl ... and at no other mill or mills whatsoever'. 'Lives' listed in 1822 were Mary Taylor, Marmaduke Coghill Cramer Roberts and Skeffington Connor. Francis Stith was the occupier before 1700.

HATHLAND

Hathland stretches from No. 44 to No. 156 Harold's Cross Road, and includes the front field of the hospice. It was leased by the Earl of Meath to Hobart Barry from 1703 at £18 per annum, and had previously been occupied by John Browne, and before him by John Holmes. Elizabeth Carruthers was the leasehold owner from 1828, and after she married Launcelot Watson, they obtained the fee farm grant in 1857 from the Earl of Meath. 'Lives' of Richard and William Kellett mentioned in 1850.

THE DOUBLE MILL FIELDS

The Double Mill Fields were leased by the Earl of Meath to James Horan from 1783, and comprised most of the old houses on Parnell Road, and the new student accommodation in the present Griffith College on the north bank of the Grand Canal. The college land (former Richmond Bridewell) was leased by the Earl of Meath to Jacob Poole from 1750.

THE WOOD MILLS (CORN MILLS)

Now the Greenmount Industrial Estate, the Wood Mills were leased by the Earl of Meath to George Spence from 1691, and then to Frederick Falkiner from 1760, Lydia Bolton from 1802, and Joshua Fayle from 1830. In 1850, the following 'lives' were listed – Leonard Greenham, Queen Victoria and Prince George of Cumberland. William Harvey Pim obtained the fee farm grant from the Earl of Meath in 1855. The Greenmount Oil Co. land and adjoining Cherry Orchard (now Nos 2–42 Harold's Cross Road) were owned by the Archbishop of Dublin, and a Mr Choppin is shown as occupier on a 1717 Church of Ireland map as tenant of William Usher.

HEMPTHORNS LAND

This is now part of the hospice, and also Parnell Road from Applegreen Garage to 44 Parnell Road, including Arbutus Avenue and the ESB Depot. The plot includes the site of the National Stadium on the South Circular Road. It was leased by the Earl of Meath to John Robins in 1763. S. Winter and others obtained a fee farm grant in 1858.

BLACKBERRY PARKS

Now part of hospice, Blackberry Parks were leased by the Earl of Meath to George Cuppaidge from 1748.

SMITH'S LAND

Now part of Clogher Road, Scoil Íosagáin etc., Smith's Land was once occupied by Patrick Andrews and was known as Sally Park – hence the nickname Sally's Bridge for Parnell Bridge. It was also called Alderman Flanagan's Land around 1900 – he was a farmer/market gardener who lived in Portmahon House on South Circular Road near Rialto Bridge. It was leased by the Earl of Meath to Roger Roberts from 1694. Part of it was acquired by Dublin Corporation for housing in 1941.

PORTOBELLO BARRACKS

Now called Cathal Brugha Barracks, the south-west part of Portobello Barracks was leased by the Earl of Meath to Edward Edwards from 1720, and the north-west part was leased to Thomas Taylor and Henry Curran from 1753. Major Charles Henry Sirr acquired an interest in the nineteenth century.

MOUNT JEROME

The east part (along with Blackberry Parks) of Mount Jerome was leased to George Cuppaidge from 1748. It was previously leased by Elizabeth Richardson, and before that by Joseph Leeson. Cemetery Co. acquired it in 1840. The west part was leased to John Gaffney from 1752, and sold to Cemetery Co. in 1909 (21 acres).

RATHLANDS (PART OF)

A substantial part of Mount Argus (also known as Argos) was contained in the very large parcel of land known as Rathlands. The Earl of Meath leased it to Hester Kerr (a widow) from 1749 at a yearly rent of £32 9s 8d. Joseph Byrne was the tenant by 1838. The 'lives' were Patrick Kenna, Thomas Kenna, and the Marquis of Kildare.

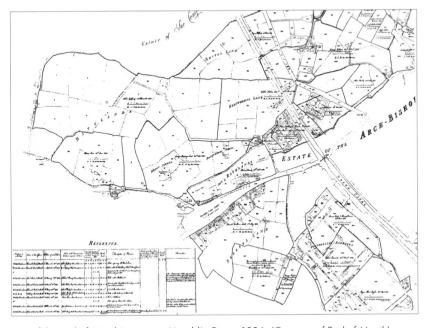

Part of the Earl of Meath's estate in Harold's Cross, 1836. (Courtesy of Earl of Meath)

3

THE PARK (THE GREEN)

The triangular Green, with a handful of small cabins around it, was the focal point of the locality for hundreds of years, and was the scene of many faction fights between different families and gangs. The land was commonage, and in the past, the locals used this for grazing their animals. A newspaper reported in 1883 that on Sunday evenings, after the pubs closed at 7 p.m., crowds of men assembled on the Green to wrestle!

A newspaper notice in 1861 advised that the 1st Infantry Brigade, consisting of 1st Battalion Grenadier Guards, 26th Cameronians, and 96th Regiment, would assemble on Harold's Cross Green at 10.30 a.m., under Major General Bloomfield, for the purpose of route marching.

In 1885, there was a mass meeting on the Green of the Robert Emmet Branch of the Irish National League – their office was at 84 Harold's Cross.

On 6 March 1887, 500 unemployed men from all over Dublin staged a protest meeting on the Green.

In 1890, the Harold's Cross Improvement Association was formed, comprising Phillip McDonnell, William Fanagan TC (town commissioner), Ed Ball, Very Reverend Dominic O'Neill, James Ellis TC, Dr John Keys, R. Cassels, Robert Bordman, W.B. Ellis, Thomas Keogh, James Dignam, George C. Murphy, W. Maher and T.N. Smith TC. They persuaded the Rathmines and Rathgar Commissioners to purchase the 3-acre Green (3 acres, 1 rood and 5 perches to be exact) from the Irish Land Commission for 5 shillings in 1893. Various businesses contributed £500 towards a new park, including James Talbot Power (the whiskey family), John Jameson (another whiskey family), Laurence Malone, Mr Pim, Mr Eason and Lord Ardilaun (Guinness family). The famous landscape gardener William Sheppard, who was responsible for St Stephen's Green and Palmerston Park, designed the new park, including a feature 'dripping pool' (a man-made waterfall). The entire area was surrounded by railings, and opened in 1894 with great celebrations.

Dublin Corporation superseded the Rathmines and Rathgar Urban District Council in 1930, and took over responsibility for the park in 1934. They built the public toilets opposite the entrance to Mount Jerome in 1943, and this little building was recently converted into a café. The corporation also re-arranged the railings at the top of the park, so that one large tree was left outside the park, and this was provided with a concrete seat around the base, thus encouraging people to sit and chat. Thereafter, the tree became known locally as the Tree of Knowledge! In recent years, the tree was cut down. In the early years, the park became very neglected and it wasn't until the 1960s that the Parks Department of Dublin Corporation set to work, laying out flower and rose beds, lawns and shrubs. They also built the children's playground at that time, which comprised swings, a see-saw, a merry-go-round, a monkey puzzle and so on. After recent refurbishment, the playground is a colourful showpiece, and there are bark shavings to protect young knees, and although the merry-go-round has gone, there are many new attractions. Around the park, there are plenty of fixed wooden seats, and even two brick-built summerhouses near the upper end. The numerous trees planted over 120 years ago are now mature and leafy, providing much colour and shelter all year round.

In the 1960s, brass bands played on Sunday evenings during the summer months, and youngsters could fish for 'pinkeens' in the pond, and watch frogs leap. Locals will remember different park rangers, including Joey and 'Masher'. Before the advent of the automatic drinking water font, you could quench your thirst by using the bell-shaped bronze cup suspended on a chain.

Trinity College Dublin started its College Garden on the campus in 1687. From 1794 to 1803, Professor Edward Hill from Trinity College Dublin tried to operate a College Garden from Harold's Cross (calling it the Harold's Cross Botanical Gardens), but amid some controversy, the college relocated the gardens to Ballsbridge (the modern Jurys Hotel site) in 1806, and then to Trinity Hall in Dartry in 1968, where they still flourish behind the new halls of residence. The exact location of the garden in Harold's Cross is not known, being described only as 6 acres leased from Samuel

1972 view of the roads from Kimmage and Terenure converging at the bottom of the Green. Note Carroll's Lantern Inn on the left. (Courtesy of Dublin City Library and Archives)

Stephens. In the past, such gardens were often referred to as 'physic gardens', because of their main association with medicine. Professor Hill, who was also president of the College of Physicians, referred to Harold's Cross as the best location in Europe for a botanical garden. Coincidentally, the National Botanical Gardens in Glasnevin started in 1795. Dublin City Council's gardeners are still carrying on this great tradition in the Harold's Cross Park.

HIGH CROSS

The well-known limestone high cross at the northern end of the Park (the bottom end) was erected by the surviving members of the 4th Battalion, Dublin No. 1 Brigade of the IRA (formerly called the Irish Volunteers), in the Marian year, 1954, in honour of their members who served since 1916. Previously there was a horse trough at this junction.

Eamon de Valera was the outgoing taoiseach when the fourteenth Dail was dissolved on 24 April 1954. The new high cross was unveiled on Sunday 25 April by President Sean T. O'Ceallaigh, and blessed by the new parish priest of the Holy Rosary church, Very Revd Kevin Brady, assisted by curate Father Flood. Earlier, the 4th Battalion had attended a special mass in the Holy Rosary church. A guard of honour was formed by the 26th

Battalion of the FCA, and amongst the huge attendance was Lord Mayor B. Butler, former members of Cumann na nBan and the Irish Citizen Army. Many fine speeches were made on the day, and the Army No. 1 Band played the Last Post and Reveille, and of course, the national anthem. That evening, a variety concert was held in the National Stadium on the South Circular Road, with acts by Kathleen Watkins (now Gay Byrne's wife) on the harp, Joe Lynch (tenor), Paddy Crosby and Noel Purcell (comedians), Eugene Lambert (ventriloquist), Harry Brogan, and the Rowsome Pipe Quartet.

The 16½ foot high cross weights 6 tonnes, and the single block of limestone which is the main part of the cross was cut and carved by Eamon Crowe, who was working for the famous Harrisons in 178 Pearse Street. In fact, Pearse's father (who was English) worked initially as a stonemason for Harrison's, before starting his own similar business in the same street. The high cross project cost £2,000, collected by donations and concerts, organised by the 4th Battalion, from its offices at 14 Thomas Street.

In its early days, the 4th Battalion catchment area extended from Portobello Bridge, along the canal to Clondalkin, across to Tallaght and Glencree, back to Rathfarnham, down along the Dodder to Milltown, and back to Portobello. Until October 1920, there were nine companies in the 4th Battalion (A – I), with Rathmines, Rathgar and Terenure comprising 'A' Company, while Harold's Cross was in 'C' Company. After 1920, 'A' Company comprised Rathgar, Terenure, part of Harold's Cross, and Crumlin, while 'C' Company contained Rathmines, another part of Harold's Cross, and Kimmage.

The headquarters of 'A' Company was a disused mill at Larkfield, Sundrive Road, Kimmage, owned by Count George Noble Plunkett. George became a count of the Holy Roman Empire, in recognition of his financial assistance to the Blue Nuns in setting up a convent in Rome. He was director of the National Museum from 1907 to 1916, although he lost that position because of his family's involvement in the 1916 Rising. The extended Plunkett family (especially the Crannies) were house builders and developers, and built many of the fine houses around Belgrave Road and Palmerston Road, both in Rathmines, in addition to parts of Ballsbridge and Donnybrook, most of which they rented to well-to-do families. Countess Plunkett took a keen interest in managing the sixty-five properties, and liked acquiring additional assets. She bought Larkfield Mills around 1912 for investment purposes, while most of the Plunkett family lived in 26 Upper Fitzwilliam Street. Joseph Mary Plunkett was living in another of their properties, 17 Marlborough Road, Donnybrook, and decided to move into the detached house which was part of Larkfield Mills. The following year, 'A' Company started using the two-storey mill for training, employing the first floor as a drill hall and the ground floor as a miniature rifle range. The adjoining field was also put to good use. The Volunteers were later joined by men who had returned from England and who used the large premises for living quarters, calling it Larkfield Garrison. Joseph Mary Plunkett, one of the leaders of the Easter Rising, was living in Larkfield when he became engaged to Grace Gifford of 8 Temple Villas, Palmerston Road, Rathmines, on 2 December 1915. Grace became a Catholic shortly afterwards, and then married Joseph Mary in Kilmainham Gaol the day before his execution for taking part in the 1916 Rising. Another signatory of the 1916 Proclamation, Thomas McDonagh, had married Grace's sister, Muriel, a few years previously. Larkfield is now the Supervalu Shopping Centre on Sundrive Road, and a plaque commemorates the Plunkett family. Down in the centre of Harold's Cross, the Greenmount Oil Co. (now the site of blocks of apartments) had a rifle club for its staff, including a miniature rifle range, which was also used by 'A' Company at weekends before the 1916 Rising.

A large framed roll of honour listing all the members of the battalion was recently on display in the Pearse Museum, St Enda's Park, Rathfarnham, as was a 1915 photograph of the Volunteers practising in Larkfield Drill Hall – they are now hanging in Kilmainham Jail. The leading members of the 4th Battalion were Padraig Pearse, Willie Pearse, Eamon Ceannt (Kent), Con Colbert, Joseph Mary Plunkett, and Cathal Brugha. Padraig Pearse, Eamon Ceannt and Joseph Plunkett were signatories of the 1916 Proclamation. During the 1916 Easter Rising, Eamon Ceannt was the commandant of the 4th Battalion, based in the South Dublin Union (a dreaded workhouse for destitute people, later called St Kevin's Hospital, and now called St James's Hospital), with some men on duty in nearby Jamesons Whiskey Distillery on Marrowbone Lane. Immediately after the 1916 Rising, thousands of arrests were made in Dublin and around the country (especially Galway and Wexford). Around thirty men from Harold's Cross, including ten men from Larkfield Garrison, were deported (via Richmond Barracks, Inchicore) to Knutsford and Stafford prisons in

Members of the South Dublin Union, Marrowbone Lane, and Roe's Distillery 1916 Garrisons, April 1966. From left to right, back row: Sean Harbourne, Seamas O'Flaherty, Frank Holland, Joe Doyle, Patrick Ward, Dan Horan, Patrick Egan, Seamas McCochlain, Patrick J. Dunne, Sean O'Shaughnessy, Liam O'Flaherty, Gerald Doyle, Francis Byrne, Patrick Harbourne. Fourth row: James Byrne, Joe Clarke, Patrick Mason, George Nolan, Frank Kelly, James Corrigan, Sean Treacy, Thomas Graham, Arthur Power, Padraig O'Broin, Liam McCabe, Edward Merriman. Third row: Michael Cunningham, James J. Burke, John Saul, Peter Ward, Patrick O'Loughlin, Joe Corcoran (Br Louis OSF), Thomas Kavanagh, Thomas J. Doyle, Patrick J. Rigney, Joseph O'Connell, Patrick Byrne, Seamas O'Murchadha. Second row: Sean McGlynn, George Byrne, Mrs Winifred Somerville (*née* Byrne), Mrs Rose Farrelly (*née* Mulally), Mrs Emly Handley (*née* O'Keefe), Mrs May Doyle (*née* Byrne), Mrs Maura Clince (nee Quigley), Mrs Pricilla Kavanagh (*née* Quigley), Mrs Josephine McNamara (*née* O'Keefe), Mrs Eileen Harbourne (nee Cooney), Mrs Sheila Lynch (*née* O'Hanlon), Mrs Margaret Timmons (*née* O'Flaherty), Patrick J. Bailey. Front row: Joseph Doolan, Joseph Kennedy, Joseph O'Neill, Joseph Byrne, Henry Pender, John Adams, Patrick J. Young, Christopher McEvoy, Thomas J. Boylan. (Courtesy of Sibeil Doolan)

England, and after a few weeks, most were sent to an internment camp in Frongoch, North Wales, and then released just before Christmas.

After the 1916 Rising, the Thomas Davis branch of the Gaelic League in Rathmines acted as a cover for the 4th Battalion. The sacristan of Rathmines Catholic church (Our Lady of Refuge) was a member of 'A' Company, and he arranged for some officers to sleep in the church while 'on the run'. Arms and ammunition for the Volunteers were also stored in the vaults, and these miraculously escaped a huge fire on 26 January 1920, which started because

Every Easter, a wreath is secretly laid at the cross, which was erected by the surviving members of the 4th Battalion of the Dublin No. 1 Brigade of the Volunteers in 1954.

In 2016, a wreath was laid by the government at St James' Hospital, in memory of the members of the 4th Battalion who fought here (then called the South Dublin Union or Workhouse) in 1916.

of a fault in the electrical fuseboard, and virtually destroyed the church, although the arms and ammunition were brought to safety.

Very few women were arrested, although many were very active in the following years, especially in 'behind-the-scenes' operations, often carrying messages and guns. During the Civil War, 1922–1923, their important role was recognised: hundreds were imprisoned in Kilmainham Jail, including five from Harold's Cross, and soon afterwards transferred to the North Dublin Union (Grangegorman). The two Robinson sisters, who were originally from Skerries, operated a tobacconist called O'Dalys, beside the present Delaney's Cycles at Emmet Bridge. Sinead and Eilis were arrested on 6 February 1923, and transferred to the North Dublin Union on 27 April 1923. On 7 May 1923, Eilis and two others escaped, and Eilis walked the long journey home through the dark night. Sinead was released on 28 September 1923, and continued to run the shop in Harold's Cross until 1971.

In later decades, the 4th Battalion continued its association with Harold's Cross, holding its annual mass on Easter Sunday in the Holy Rosary Church, after marching up Harold's Cross Road. IRA notes published in the *Evening Press* in the 1950s refer to the 'National Association, Old Fianna, Fourth Battalion'.

The 2016 centenary commemorations of the 1916 Rising included the laying of a wreath in St James's Hospital, outside one of the original workhouse buildings (now used by Trinity College Dublin). Various former workhouse buildings are still in use today, especially on the east side of the complex, recognisable by the grey limestone structures, although some are partly obscured by modern extensions. Near the James's Street entrance there is a plaque on a stone pillar, remembering the 1916 Rising, and also a small nearby headstone in memory of the victims of the 1845–50 Famine.

4

ORPHANAGES

ST CLARE'S CONVENT

St Clare's Convent, in the past referred to as the Poor Clares, was originally an enclosed order of contemplative nuns. Clare of Assisi was strongly influenced by Francis of Assisi, and started the order in Italy in 1212.

Cicely Dillon from Ireland was professed in 1622 in Holland, and was sent to Dublin (Cook Street) in 1629 as mother abbess to start an Irish branch of the nuns. However, the authorities ordered them to leave, and they settled near Athlone, on the shores of Lough Ree (Bethlehem). In 1712, a further attempt to open a convent in Dublin was made (in Channel Row), but they were forced to close it in 1728, and move to North King Street. In passing, it should be noted that the Dominican nuns immediately took over the Channel Row premises and stayed until about 1808. By 1751, the Poor Clare nuns had split over a dispute concerning a confessor/priest, and the abbess and nine nuns moved to Dorset Street, which was then called Drumcondra Lane.

The wealthy religious patron Maria O'Brien was overseeing a lay orphanage for girls in Hendrick Street and she persuaded the Poor Clares to build an orphanage in Harold's Cross, largely funded by John Corballis, a wealthy Catholic. In fact, the orphanage in Hendrick Street had been founded in 1801 by three laymen – Patrick Quarterman, James Auger and George Poland, but funded and managed by Maria O'Brien, daughter of wealthy businessman Denis O'Brien – hence the name Maria Female Orphans. Maria joined the Presentation Nuns in Rahan, County Offaly, in 1822 (aged 57) but died in 1827. Twelve Poor Clare nuns under Mother Elizabeth Clare Byrne moved from Dorset Street to Harold's Cross in 1804 to start a girls' orphanage, initially staying for twelve years in an end-of-terrace house (the present No. 87). Almost immediately, the nuns and their generous sponsors acquired an adjoining building with land, and that building was later converted into a school and extended over the years. A new L-shaped three-storey orphanage was built in record time, and opened in 1806, when the girls were transferred here from the lay orphanage in Hendrick Street. An old photo shows a brick rear facade (probably yellow brick), which was later plastered over. It seems that a yard separated the original convent house from the new orphanage, with side doors located in both buildings to provide easy access. When the yard was filled in with a new house (the present No. 89) in the 1830s, the interconnecting doors were blocked up, but part of the doorway between No. 89 and the orphanage can still be seen, as can a 13ft-high very old stone boundary wall in the back garden.

A new convent followed in 1816, costing £7,000, and a new chapel in 1819. The fabulous carved marble altar dates from 1910. Rooms were provided above and below the chapel to give it the outwards appearance of a ballroom, so as not to attract the attention of the authorities, before Catholic emancipation was achieved in Ireland in 1829. Even the chapel bell was hidden in a chimney stack at roof level, in the same position as the present bellcote. Prior to 1817, the nuns wore ordinary clothes, and had no habit, and were addressed as missus. They later wore a brown habit, which trailed along the ground, and included a white bib, a white-lined brown veil, and white forehead-board, so that only the face was visible.

The nuns supported themselves by subscriptions and with an annual charity sermon, in addition to the income from the sale of the orphans' needlework. The chapel was open to the public, with a plate (collection) at each mass. Furthermore, each new novice brought a dowry, usually a large sum of money, or property provided by her family. Girls without a dowry usually became 'lay sisters'. However, from the very beginning, the nuns had very generous and powerful benefactors, especially the Corballis family, in addition to Maria O'Brien and Mrs Anna Maria O'Brien (*née* Ball), who also contributed to the Sisters of Charity and the Loreto nuns. The O'Brien and Ball families were connected by marriage, since Maria's brother, John, married Anna Maria Ball (whose sister, Fanny, founded the Irish branch of the Loreto nuns). The Corballis family of Roebuck in Clonskeagh also had ties with the Balls, since two daughters were nuns in the Loreto order.

These three wealthy Catholic families, in conjunction with Archbishop Daniel Murray, were instrumental in founding most of the nuns' orders in Dublin in the first half of the nineteenth century.

A committee of governesses effectively controlled the convent. Its members at various times included the Countess of Fingal, Hon. Mrs Caddel, Hon. Mrs Preston (Gormanston Castle), Hon. Mrs Southwell, Lady Bellew of Barmeath (County Louth), Lady Bellew of Mountbellew (Galway), Mrs Sweetman of Booterstown, Mrs Sweetman of Kingstown (now called Dún Laoghaire), Mrs S. Hussey, Mrs John Corballis, Miss Dease, Mrs John Ennis, Lady Killeen, and Mrs Verschoyle.

In 1821, the annual sermon was preached in Francis Street Chapel by the Most Revd Murray (later Archbishop of Dublin) in aid of the seventy-five female orphans. At that stage, Fr Henry Young was the chaplain, Mrs Mary Francis Xavier Bacon was the abbess, and there were fifteen professed choir nuns, one novice and two lay sisters. In those years, there was an average of fifty charity sermons a year, in aid of different causes.

Lewis records that in 1837 there were an abbess, seventeen professed nuns and lay sisters, and ninety children. The 1836 Catholic Directory refers to two dormitories, each with fifty beds.

In 1849, the nuns built themselves burial vaults in a small mortuary or chapel, at a cost of £406, and the very thick walls contain the coffins. There are now ninety-three plaques on the inside walls, commemorating the deceased, the first one dating from 1819 and belonging to Sister Mary Elizabeth (Catherine Coppinger). There is currently space for seven more coffins, but the nuns also have a plot in Glasnevin Cemetery. This building is some distance from the convent, to the east of the original Greenmount View (now Nos 75–77), on a small site which the nuns originally used as a graveyard.

The 1881 Census recorded fifty-eight orphans and twenty-one nuns. The 1901 Census recorded sixty-three girls, mostly 9 to 12 years old. Most of them were born in various parts of Ireland, but four were from India, eleven from England, one from Malta, and one from Gibraltar. The matron was Australian, and there were twenty-seven nuns at that time. Such diversity reflects the fact that the orphans were by this stage mostly from ex-servicemen's families, and received financial support from the British Government of the time. By 1911, there were sixty-four orphans and nineteen nuns. By the mid-1950s, there were nineteen nuns and fifty-six orphan girls.

In 1866, the nuns increased the size of their estate by buying up land immediately to the north, comprising 5 acres, 3 roods and 25 perches, paying £53 4s 9d initially, and a rent of £27 4s per annum. This land was part of the farm of St Sepulchre and was sold by Lord Archbishop of Dublin Richard Chenevix Trench. The nuns then purchased the freehold in 1875 for £680 from the Commissioners of Church Temporalities. Another interesting transaction occurred in 1907 when the nuns (Elizabeth O'Loughlin, Margaret Walsh, Bridget Doyle and Mary Maxwell) bought Grosvenor Gardens (previously called Mount Drummond), comprising 3 acres, 3 roods and 15 perches, for £722, in order to prevent a building company (presumably the Dublin Artisan Dwellings Co.) from acquiring the land and erecting small cottages, because it was feared that the chimney smoke would become a nuisance to the orphans. The Smith family were tenants on the land at that stage, as fruit-and-market gardeners. The nuns sold on the land again in 1917 for £700 to a more suitable person. In 1938, Dublin Corporation bought 2 acres, 1 rood and 17 perches from the nuns for £925, by way of compulsory purchase order, and they also bought Grosvenor Gardens, in order to build the houses in Mount Drummond Square and Avenue.

Over the years, the nuns were bequeathed various houses by admirers, which they then sold as long leaseholds, thereby receiving a ground-rent income as well as capital. For example, Mrs Clarke owned Nos 127–134, Harold's Cross Road (now Nos 66–80), and let them on short-term leases to various tenants. When she died, she left all the property to the nuns in her will. The nuns continued the letting arrangements for a few years, but in 1920 they sold the houses as 999-year leaseholds, in eight lots, realising £3,025, and thereafter continued to collect the annual ground rents. However, in recent years, the ground rents have been sold to investors, or bought out by the householders.

In the 1960s, the nuns were still an enclosed order. Their beautiful small chapel was always open to the public for Sunday mass at 10 a.m. and weekday mass at 7.30 a.m. The nuns were never seen at mass, but body outlines could be vaguely observed behind a wooden latticed screen off the left-hand side of the main altar, most of which was draped with a black curtain, and the priest always gave Holy Communion through a small hatch here, with the nuns lining up two by two. In fact, there was a private chapel/choir behind the screen, with wooden pews, stained-glass windows and the stations of the cross. The floor above the nuns' private chapel was used as an infirmary for the sick nuns, with a restricted view of the altar in the public chapel below. The public chapel had a beautiful carved Carrara marble altar (dating from 1910), and wonderful stained-glass windows in the side walls, especially the south wall. Mayer of Munich was responsible for the south-east stained-glass window. There is a large gallery at the rear of the chapel where the organ was located, but originally this area was reserved only for the orphan girls, who didn't mingle with the public, only coming down for Holy Communion.

In 1973, the Poor Clares throughout Ireland reorganised themselves into two separate groups – the Sisters of St Clare and the Poor Clares. The latter still lived in contemplative, enclosed convents, while the former were more community-orientated. In 1975, the Harold's Cross nuns joined the Sisters of St Clare, and thereafter their brown habits were frequently seen on the streets, although sometimes partly obscured by ordinary clothes.

Up until the mid-1970s, the nuns had a good-sized farm, and kept their own herd of cows. The land now occupied by the primary school and generalate was called 'the Haggard field'.

In the mid-1970s, the nuns built a new single-storey co-educational primary school parallel to Mount Drummond Avenue and closed down the old primary school, but retained it for its recent use as the novitiate house and national headquarters of the Secular Order of Franciscans (Third Order), which held monthly meetings here. This order is a lay religious grouping of men and women, with about 10,000 members throughout the thirty-two counties.

The girls' orphanage closed in 1981, and around 1984 was converted to its recent use as a students' hostel and conference centre. Before closing the original orphanage, the nuns bought two local houses for small groups of boys and girls, one called La Verna at 76 Harold's Cross Road, and the other on 43 Kenilworth Park (not to be confused with 53/54 Kenilworth Square, which was occupied by the Faithful Companions of Jesus Sisters). Since 1997, the nuns no longer catered for orphans, and concentrated on mission work in El Salvador.

Although the history of the buildings is interesting, of more importance is the story of the hundreds of orphan girls who resided here over its 200 years' history. Most people think of orphans as young children who have lost both parents, possibly because of a road accident or ill health. In fact, many orphans had lost only one parent, which left a father or mother to look after a large family of children. Perhaps parents had separated, leaving a big burden on one adult. Other children born 'out of wedlock' were taken in charge by Church and State, as were some children from large poor families, even where both parents were alive. Most of the orphanages in Ireland were State-funded and called industrial schools, and were very often confused with reformatory schools for young offenders (frequently for minor misdemeanours). The Department of Education was responsible for all these establishments. However, some orphanages were privately operated, and not subject to any controls or inspections. St Clare's in Harold's Cross was private, receiving fees from family/relations, whereas their other girl's orphanage, St Joseph's in Cavan town, was State-funded. The moving story of the Cavan orphanage is told by Mavis Arnold in her book, *The Children of the Poor Clares*, including the terrible tragedy of a fire in 1943, which killed thirty-five orphans and one lay woman. Various other books and official reports in relation to Irish orphanages in general make interesting but very sad reading, and one wonders if St Clare's in Harold's Cross was any different. We do not know if there were any interchanges between the orphanages in Harold's Cross and Cavan, either of nuns or girls having holidays.

The Poor Clares had many other convents and schools around Ireland, but the most famous during the latter half of the nineteenth century was Kenmare in County Kerry. From here, 'the Nun of Kenmare', wrote many books on Home Rule and social reform. The nun in question was Sister Mary Francis Clare (Margaret Anna Cusack), who was baptised an Episcopalian in Coolock, County Dublin, joined an Anglican convent in London, converted to Catholicism, and finally joined the Poor Clares in Newry in 1859 at the age of 30. She earned a handsome income for the Poor Clares from her books and pamphlets, but their content caused consternation amongst the bishops and politicians, forcing her to move to Knock, County Mayo in 1881. In December of that year, Harold's Cross convent achieved notoriety when the nuns obeyed the unpopular Archbishop McCabe and 'evicted' the Nun of Kenmare, who stopped over en-route from Newry. She emigrated to England, and founded the Sisters of Saint Joseph of Peace in 1884, in Nottingham, before setting out for America. She finally died a poor spinster back in Warwickshire, in England, in 1899. Her order still flourishes in America. For a period in the 1990s, the order used the house at 43 Kenilworth Park in Dublin (previously employed for some orphans), which recently closed. St Clare's Convent is now the forwarding address for any post. The Nun of Kenmare is commemorated by a large bronze plaque on the wall at the corner of York Street and Mercer Street in Dublin, erected by the Royal College of Surgeons of Ireland in 1998 – furthermore, Dublin Corporation renamed this junction as 'Cusack Corner'.

The Voters Register for 2004 listed thirteen nuns in St Clare's Convent plus eleven in Bethany House and three in Bethlehem, including a chaplain.

In the same field as the modern primary school, a new generalate, including offices and an oratory, was built in 1990 (called Bethlehem, 63 Harolds Cross Road) to accommodate the mother superior and seven nuns. Twenty years later, in 2010, the nuns demolished this new convent and built themselves a modern three-storey one after closing the original old chapel. The new convent is about 23,000 square feet in size, with twenty-three en-suite bedrooms and eighteen car spaces, providing more than enough space for the many visitors on holiday from their other convents, especially Newry in Northern Ireland. The building has lounges, parlours, dining room, kitchen, stores, prayer room, offices, laundry, and separate staff accommodation. The old chapel has now been listed by Dublin City Council, but they were too late to prevent the nuns removing the beautiful stained-glass windows and fabulous marble altar. One stained-glass window from the private chapel off the main altar, dedicated to St Clare, has been re-erected in the entrance hall of the new convent and backlit by a bulb. Other windows have been sent to their convent in Newry. The nuns in Harold's Cross now have a modern chapel in their new convent, featuring the beautiful diamond-encrusted gold tabernacle from the old chapel, and new stained-glass windows were commissioned.

Within the past few years, the nuns sold the old convent, chapel, school, orphanage and most of the land, but retained the mortuary and the adjoining orchard. Hundreds of new apartments are currently planned for the large site, while the old buildings will mostly be converted into apartments.

PROTESTANT ORPHANAGE

Many people are probably unaware of a very interesting three-storey red-bricked building, set back from the main road, beside the former Healy's grocery shop, which still retains a front lawn! No. 201 Harold's Cross Road (previously No. 57) is probably mid-eighteenth century, and it seems to be included on Rocques 1760 map. At one time it was the summer house/holiday home of the Allen family. Edward and Ellen Allen married in 1798 in a Quaker meeting house in Sycamore Alley in the city centre, and lived at 22 Upper Bridge Street, also operating their wholesale linen drapery business from there. Their son Richard was born at their holiday home in Harold's Cross in 1803, the fourth child in a family of fifteen. Richard is said to have seen the Great Comet of 1811 while on holiday in the Harold's Cross house. He led a very busy life, being involved in temperance work, the anti-slavery crusade, the Dublin Statistical Society, and the Mechanics Institute. He died in 1886 at his home, Brooklawn, in Blackrock. His father, Edward, died in 1848, aged 83, and his flat headstone can still be seen inside the gate of the Quaker burial ground, at 104 Cork Street, opposite Bru Caoimhin (now a home for the aged), which was previously Cork Street Fever Hospital (a Quaker hospital). Nowadays the name Allen is still common in Quaker circles, such as Darina and Myrtle Allen, famous in the food business.

By the 1860s, the house had been converted into a Protestant orphanage and school for girls. Around 1890, the orphanage was enlarged by rebuilding No. 56 (now 199), comprising a shop on the ground floor, and a large open-plan room at first-floor level, in addition to an extension onto the north side of the main building.

The orphanage was run as a charity by a voluntary group of lay people who belonged to the Plymouth Brethren. The matron and children attended church in nearby Grosvenor Hall, Grosvenor Road, which was built in 1859 by Baptists, but which came into the hands of the Brethren around 1865. The Brethren had its origins in Plymouth, England, and then Dublin in the 1820s. They practise a simplified form of Christianity. They have no priests or ministers, but select elders to lead them. The elders wear civilian clothes (no robes), and give talks about the Bible. Some women still wear bonnets or simple hats. Members are baptised as teenagers or even adults, on similar lines to Baptists. Each hall is completely independent, but has loose ties with the other halls.

The 1881 Census records that ten orphans worshiped at Grosvenor Hall, presumably the girls from Harold's Cross.

The 1901 Census for Harold's Cross lists a Miss Sophie Bailey as the matron of the orphanage, with Brethren as her religion. Mary Jane Redpath (a Presbyterian) was the teacher, and there were sixteen girls ranging in age from 2 to 15 years.

The 1911 Census lists Mary Rutledge (Church of Ireland) as the matron, but the religion of the ten children is described as 'in Brethren Orphanage'.

Starting in the 1860s, the various matrons at Harold's Cross were Miss Kirkland, Miss Myers, Miss Nidd, Miss Bailey, Miss Rutledge, Miss Jago, and Miss Anwyl.

The girls in Harold's Cross probably came into contact with Henry Figgis, who conducted the services in Grosvenor Hall in the 1890s, since he was actively involved in the Children's Special Services Mission (CSSM), now called the Scripture Union. This Christian organisation started in London in 1867, and is now worldwide. Summer camps with a religious theme were organised for children, and this tradition is still carried on in Ireland, with outings to Avoca Manor and Greystones, both in Wicklow. Henry Figgis lived in a splendid 1860s architectural gem at 26 Temple Road, Dartry (also called 'The Chalet'), and even arranged for a carved biblical inscription on the outside of his rear oriel window – 'Thou Lord Alone Makest Me To Dwell In Safety'. Ironically, his daughter, Hilda, died after falling out of an upstairs window in The Chalet. In later years, Revd Bertie Neill (father of the recent Anglican Archbishop of Dublin) was actively involved in the Scripture Union, and was also the rector of the former Harold's Cross Anglican church, beside Mount Jerome.

By the late 1930s, the orphanage (only four girls at this stage) had moved to Kimberley, La Touche Road, Greystones, and 22-year-old Adeline Mathers from Portadown became the 'temporary' matron. In 1955, they moved to 'Mayil', Burnaby Road, but again moved in 1968 to 'Westbank', New Road, Greystones, comprising a large detached house and assembly hall, with plenty of garden space. The £8,000 received from the sale of 'Mayil' helped to defray the £12,000 cost of 'Westbank'. In recent years, fostering and adoption have taken over from orphanages, and even before that, boys, as well as girls, were catered for at Westbank. Following a High Court determination in 1984, a new trust was set up with six trustees, and the Brethren doctrine is set out in detail. The trust is now called the Protestant Orphanage Charity. 'Westbank' was empty for some time, before being sold in recent years.

The home was financially well-provided for by anonymous individuals and companies, and so the children were sent to good schools, both in Greystones and elsewhere in Ireland. Throughout this period, the orphans always worshipped with the Brethren in Florence Road, Bray, although the Hillside Evangelical Church in Greystones was used for weddings and large funerals.

Even after leaving Harold's Cross in the 1930s, the trustees of the orphanage retained the two buildings (Nos 199–201) for an income. No. 201 was subdivided into six apartments, while No. 199 had a ground-floor shop, an apartment overhead, and a two-storey (second and third floor) rear apartment. Healy's shop bought the buildings in 1977, though leasing the shop only, from 1948. Interestingly enough, the 1929 Trust Deed for the orphanage refers to Midleton Evans Perry, possibly a Quaker, as the lessor of the property. Some of the trustees in

The ground-floor corridor of
St Clare's Convent in 1997.

Anne-Marie Bevan in the parlour
of St Clare's Convent in 2004.

The nun's refectory under the chapel in St Clare's Convent in 2004.

the past included Bindon Scott, Vera Ward Brown, George Palmer Baxter, Cecil Benjamin George Lewis, Charles Eric Barington, and George Ivan Morris. Dr Richard H. Nightingale from Leonards Corner also had some involvement in the building.

The people of Harold's Cross referred to the Protestant orphanage as 'The Bird's Nest'. However, it is interesting to note that an Anglican orphanage at 19–20 York Road, Dún Laoghaire was officially called The Bird's Nest or Mrs Smyly's Home, having been built in 1862 for infant boys and girls. Mrs Smyly started looking after orphans in 1852, and when she died in 1901, she left behind seven homes and four day schools. Other Smyly ladies carried on the tradition, which is still going strong, although the large building in York Road was sold in 1977.

The annals for the hospice comment on 'The Bird's Nest' in the opening decades of the twentieth century, including mention of 'mothers and babies', and proselytising on behalf of Protestants.

Some of the residents of Harold's Cross remember the girls in the 1930s being escorted on walks through the Park, and their familiar outfits consisted of navy-blue gym slips, red blouse, navy cardigan, navy-blue winter coats with red collar trim, and navy-blue hats. The girls in Westbank, Greystones, had a different uniform.

The Brethren are still active in Irishtown Gospel Hall, South Hill Evangelical Church in Booterstown, the Christian Assembly Evangelical Church in Florence Road, Bray, and the Gospel Hall at 178 Upper Rathmines Road. The Brethren should not be confused with the former Moravian Church at Lower Kevin Street (1746–1980), who were called United Brethren. Just to confuse matters more, Freemasons (a lay charitable and social organisation), also call each other brethren.

ST TERESA'S MONASTERY

Although not an orphanage, this order of nuns is included here for convenience. The Carmelite nuns were originally at Arran Quay, then moved to Ranelagh, and around 1813 some went to Warrenmount School to teach. In 1892, they decided to give up teaching and resume the contemplative life, so they handed over teaching at Warrenmount to the Presentation Sisters and moved to Harold's Cross, although a smaller group had left to set up a monastery in Delgany in 1844.

The premises in Harold's Cross was a Georgian house called Mount Tallant in Mount Tallant Avenue, a two-storey-over-basement, with two big bow windows at the front. They built a chapel in 1894, together with a chapter room and choir.

Being an enclosed order of contemplative nuns, they were never seen in public. One of their occupations was the making of altar breads for the Holy Rosary church (and probably many other churches). When the altar boy from the Rosary church called to collect the breads, an ingenious device was used, so that there was no physical or visual contact between the two parties. A revolving polished hardwood drum, about 750mm high and 450mm in diameter, had a vertical opening in one side. The bowl of breads was placed in the drum on the nun's side and revolved through 180 degrees so the altar boy could remove the breads on his side. A similar device is still in use in the convent at Roebuck in Clonskeagh.

In 1925, the nuns sold two distinct parcels of land to Dublin Corporation, one for Harold's Cross National School (Clareville Road School), which was completed in 1937, and the other for local authority houses on Mount Tallant Avenue, built in 1937–38 by G & T Crampton using mass concrete.

These should not be confused with the Guinness Estate built in 1949, comprising 192 houses on Corrib Road, twenty-four on Derravaragh Road and twenty-two on Melvin Road.

In 1972, St Teresa's Monastery was sold to the Franciscan Missionaries of Mary, and the Carmelites joined their fellow sisters in Delgany.

The Franciscan Missionaries of Mary, a French order of nuns, started in Loughglynn in County Roscommon in 1903. They are a truly international order, with 8,500 sisters of seventy nationalities in seventy-seven countries. St Teresa's Monastery was too big for their needs, so they sold the land to a developer, who built 100 houses in 1975–1977, appropriately called The Cloisters, with the nuns retaining two linked houses at the far end of the estate as their convent. At the beginning of the twentieth century, the nuns in Roscommon specialised in butter making on their farm, but later sold their famous recipe to Mitchelstown Creameries.

Besides The Cloisters there are two other modern estates of houses at the lower end of Mount Tallant Avenue, one called Cedar Court (with lovely old cedar trees on the green) replacing a house called Mount Saville, and the other called Cherry Court, replacing the Rathgar Tennis Grounds and the Mayfield Tennis Grounds.

MOUNT JEROME CEMETERY

Mount Jerome House probably dates from the early part of the eighteenth century, and the name may be attributed to St Jerome, translator of the Old Testament from Aramaic and Greek into Latin. The Wilkinson family occupied the house for many decades in the early days.

The most famous occupant of the house at the end of the eighteenth and beginning of the nineteenth century was John Keogh, who was very active in Catholic emancipation, and who was a friend of Wolfe Tone. John Keogh died in 1817.

The General Cemetery Co. of Dublin, whose major shareholder was Robert Shaw (of Bushy Park), purchased the house and extensive grounds in 1836, laid it out as a cemetery and built extensive burial vaults in the same year. For many years, dividends were paid to the shareholders out of the company profits. Around 1909, a further 21 acres to the west was acquired. Up until the 1920s, most of the burials were Protestants, and Glasnevin Cemetery was used by Catholics. The three-storey-over-basement house was used as offices, although around the 1940–'50s the top two storeys were removed. Rom Massey, funeral undertakers, purchased the cemetery in 1984, and converted the ground floor of the old house into a lovely spacious coffee shop, and the basement is now used as the offices. Alan Massey is now the owner, and has done a wonderful job of clearing away every bit of ivy and weeds throughout the cemetery, with the result that many people are erecting new headstones over old graves.

The 47 acres provide a huge variety of walking opportunities, both around the perimeter and through a labyrinth of internal roads and paths. Most of the paths have names, such as Guinness Walk, Nuns

Walk, Hawthorn Walk, Yew Walk, Archbishops Walk, and there is even a Kavanagh Corner, many of them obviously lined with mature trees. Upon entering the gates, there is a quaint two-storey-over-basement gate lodge built around 1860, which was once occupied by different families, including the Bovenizers, although with time it became semi-derelict. In recent years, the lodge was extended and restored as a residence. Immediately past the lodge was a nice timber-framed waiting room, followed by toilets and a bicycle shed, but all of these have now been demolished. Further up the avenue on the left-hand side is a stonemason's workshop and large yard, producing headstones. At the top of the avenue is a fine mortuary chapel with vaults underneath, built in 1847 to a design by William Atkins, and to the left of this is the old Mount Jerome House. Behind the house was a walled garden, which in the last two decades has been filled with modern graves, and the wall itself demolished in 1998. The original stables behind the house have recently received a new lease of life, since in 2002 Massey converted one section into two mortuary chapels (the Garden Chapel and the Angels' Chapel), and then another section was restored as stables for four black horses, following the reintroduction of horse-drawn hearses for special occasions. Massey also introduced Victorian-style ushers, dressed in black tailcoats and top hats.

The fountain to the left of the mortuary has been dry for a long time, and likewise two other fountains. Most of the area surrounding the chapel comprises the old part, filled with monumental headstones, catacombs and private mausoleums. This could easily be regarded as a museum of miniature Classical architecture, because the stonework and statuary is superb, and a testament to the artistry and craftsmanship of a more meticulous and leisurely bygone age. Many a famous or wealthy (or both) citizen is buried here. In random locations, graves are surmounted by broken columns, usually indicating the burial place of a young person.

Immediately behind the main chapel is a state-of-the-art new crematorium (which replaces the original detached building opened in 2000), for those who favour the expression 'dust thou art, and into dust thou shalt return'. The practice of cremation has given rise to a new phrase – the Columbarium Wall. The urns containing the ashes are placed in pockets/holes in a wall, and covered with a plaque in memory of the deceased. The main chapel has been beautifully restored, and provided with carpeting and comfortable seating. The walls are adorned with a large number of stone plaques in memory of the dead. Every September, a mass for the dead is celebrated here.

The cemetery is the final resting place of a large number of famous people, such as Thomas Davis (writer and founder of Young Ireland), J.M. Synge (playwright, famous for *The Playboy of the Western World*), George Russell (Æ) (writer and poet), Jack B. Yeats (artist), Walter Osborne (painter), Mairtin Ó Cadhain (author of novels in Irish), Arthur Guinness II (brewing family), Thomas Drummond (under-secretary of Ireland), Joseph Sheridan Le Fanu (writer), George Petrie (artist), Sir William Wilde (ophthalmic surgeon and father of the writer Oscar Wilde), Alexander Thom (famous for his directories), Alex Findlater (grocery shops), Sarah Purser (one of the founders of An Tur Gloinne stained-glass studios), Detective David Nelligan (one of Michael Collins's spies in Dublin Castle), John Skipton Mulvany (architect), Thomas Kirk (sculptor), Jacob Owen (architect), Sir Richard Griffith (Griffith's Valuations), Sir William Rowan Hamilton (mathematician and astronomer), Archbishop Plunkett (archbishop) and Jerome Connor (sculptor who created the statue of Robert Emmet in St Stephens Green), to name but a few. The National Library has a photo of the Thomas Davis statue when it stood inside the mortuary chapel, although it is now in City Hall.

The infant Pollock twins were the first to be buried in this cemetery on 14 September 1836, and their impressive tomb is dwarfed by their father's adjoining one – Matthew Pollock of Oatlands House, Stillorgan, of Ferrier Pollock fame (wholesale drapers, who once owned Powerscourt House in South William Street). Oatlands is now a Christian Brothers School. The twins' plot, size 10ft by 10ft, was purchased by their father for £25, with a perpetual right of burial. Other infants were buried in the same plot in 1839, 1856, 1862 and 1863.

The first vault in the cemetery was opened in 1836 by John Purser of Rathmines Castle just behind the mortuary chapel. The first Harold's Cross person to be buried on, 1 November 1836, was Anna Day, aged 1, who died of 'consumption', also known as tuberculosis (TB).

The Huguenots (French Protestants) have their own plot, which was transferred here in 1968 from Peter Street (opposite the present National Archives), and the burials date from 1713 to 1830. The Muslims have a separate section opposite the entrance to the Monumental Works, which was used only between 1968 and 1991.

One of the saddest memorials is the one erected in 1859 in Orphans Walk, which is a big plot for Protestant orphans, all of whom are nameless and came from the Female Orphan House, North Circular Road.

Halfway down Yew Walk, there is a small headstone erected by the Protestant Girls' Orphanage in Harold's Cross. Although there are no names given, the records show that the grave contains the remains of Louisa Graham, who died in 1916 aged 5½, and Alice McGinley, who died in 1929 aged 84. Nearby is the large Protestant plot of the Home for Aged Governesses and Respectable Single Females, which was recently in Harcourt Terrace – they in fact own the orphan grave, and have another large plot in Orphans Walk.

There are some interesting communal plots in Laburnum Walk, such as the former Old Men's Asylum in Northbrook Road, Molyneux Asylum for the Blind (it was in Leeson Park, beside Christ Church), and the Mageough Home in Cowper Road, Rathmines (still thriving).

The Dublin Metropolitan Police (DMP) purchased a plot in 1884 for members who died in poor financial circumstances. The Royal Irish Constabulary (RIC) also have a plot.

In recent years, the Bethany Home plot was discovered, and a headstone was erected, with the 219 names of deceased members. Bethany was a Protestant home for single women and their babies, based in 112–116 Orwell Road in Rathgar from 1934 to 1972, and from 1921 at 23–25 Blackhall Place in Stoneybatter.

The Gresham vault brings to life one of the fears of bygone days, when medicine was fairly rudimentary – the fear of being buried alive if the doctors made a mistake. A lady buried there took no chances, and pre-arranged for an external bell to be positioned on the top of her vault, linked to a chain inside, so that she could sound the alarm if she woke up in a tiny dark room!

The Mount Jerome Monumental Works inside the cemetery still makes headstones, and has been operated by the Doyle family for over fifty years. Another famous stonemason's name to be seen on many headstones is Crowe, and various members of this family had workshops in the Coombe area. In fact, the Crowe family still have a Signed and Sealed Apprenticeship

Indenture for one of their forebears, covering the period 1907–1914. In those days, the pay was 1*d* per hour in year one, rising to 6*d* per hour in the seventh year (final year). The apprentice stonecutter entered into a very stringent master/pupil relationship, and Master (Major) Gamble at that time had great power. Robins Bros had a yard and workshop opposite the Holy Rosary church from 1950 to 1975, and until recent years, Broe Headstones had a yard at the corner of St Clare's Avenue beside Siopa Linn. Nowadays the letters and figures on headstones are no longer handcut, but instead compressed air guns with sand do the hard work, assisted by computer-generated templates.

Sundays bring a riot of colour to the gates of Mount Jerome, as hundreds of people flock to visit the graves of their loved ones, laden down with fresh flowers sold by the street traders, and Flynn's florist. The traders pay the city council €150 yearly, and work a seven-day week.

The Passionists in Mount Argus have their own simple graveyard beside their church, but there are also some more ornate headstones there for lay people, presumably relations of the priests/brothers, or associated with the monastery. Having once been an enclosed order, the Poor Clares have their own private vaults near the convent.

The Sisters of Charity from the hospice have their own private cemetery in Donnybrook, which they acquired in 1837 (the castle was built in 1798). However, the first six nuns to die were buried in James's Street Cemetery (behind the redundant Protestant church), and the next five, including Mary Aikenhead's sister, Anne (d. 1828), were laid to rest in the vaults in the basement of the pro-cathedral. Unfortunately, the small number of vaults is reserved for the wealthy, and most of the thousand or so other coffins are sadly neglected and in disarray throughout the basement corridors, with many falling asunder and displaying lead lining. In Donnybrook, most of the graves are represented by simple cast-iron crosses about 450mm high. The various mother superiors have either a stone high cross or a statue. The main high cross, with vault underneath, represents Mary Aikenhead and was donated by John H. Parker of Harold's Cross.

6

RELIGION

CATHOLIC CHURCH

Adjacent to the right-hand side of the entrance to Mount Jerome Cemetery is a single-storey building, recently used as a lighting showroom. In 1798, a cottage here was leased (free) to the Catholic Church by John Corballis, a wealthy Catholic, and immediately converted into a chapel. It is clearly shown as such on one of the Earl of Meath's maps. This building continued in use as a church until it was converted into a national school in 1833.

The Harold's Cross and Rathmines area became a separate parish in 1823, having previously been part of the Parish of St Nicholas Without (Francis Street). The new parish was called St Mary and St Peter of Milltown and Harold's Cross. Up to then, people went to mass in the small chapel beside Mount Jerome, in St Clare's Convent, in Milltown Church, or in the Carmelite Convent in Ranelagh. Rathmines had no church because of its small population, whereas Harold's Cross and Milltown were full of mill workers. Between 1823 and 1830, Rathmines Catholics went to Sunday mass in the parish priest's flat in Portobello Place (he later lived in Charlemont Mall). The first church in Rathmines was built in 1830 on Earl of Meath property, and in fact Lord Brabazon laid the foundation stone in 1824 and waived the first year's rent of 30 guineas. The present Our Lady of Refuge in Rathmines was built in 1856 (while the original smaller church continued its activities inside the shell of the new building), but was substantially rebuilt after a disastrous fire in January 1920. When the church beside Mount Jerome closed in 1833, it was recorded that St Clare's Convent had two Sunday masses, with two plates (collections), making it difficult for the church at Mount Jerome to survive financially. The church possessions, including a pair of silver cruets and tray presented by Mrs Draper in 1812, were transferred to Rathmines.

Harold's Cross remained part of the parish of Rathmines until 1935, when it acquired independent parish status. In preparation for this, the clergy bought Mount Harold House (a four-storey Georgian residence) in 1931, comprising two stores, a kitchen and a toilet in the basement, a reception room on the ground floor, a bedroom, sitting room, toilet and bathroom on each of the first and second floors, and three maids' rooms, toilet and bathroom on the third floor.

When Foxrock Parish was building a new church at the top of Kill Avenue, their 1907 timber-framed and corrugated-steel-sheeted church, based in Torquay Road, was dismantled and re-erected in the grounds of Mount Harold House in 1935, much closer to the road than the present church. This held about 400 people, and had a wooden altar but no pulpit. The first parish priest was Very Revd P. McGough. A report in 1937 noted that most of the standard furniture and fixtures were present, for example three blessed altar cloths, six candlesticks, two altar covers, a tabernacle safe lined with wood and white silk, two gold and purple reversible tabernacle veils, and so on. The altar breads were obtained from the Carmelite Convent in Mount Tallant Avenue, and the altar wine from T.W. & J. Kelly Ltd. The tin church was later dismantled and moved to Merrion Road for another church-building project.

The present church of Our Lady of the Rosary was built in 1938 by Murphy of Castlewood Avenue in Rathmines. It is a fine ashlar-granite structure, very spacious and airy inside, utilising bright-yellow colour schemes, with a capacity of about 1,250 people. The distinctive patterned rubber in the aisles has worn well, and likewise the pitch-pine flooring in the seating areas. The Communion rail is 116 feet long. The big pipe organ has been on the rear gallery since 1947, having been built by a dentist, Mr Rabson, at his surgery in 43 Heytesbury Street, but reassembled by Meads, the organ builders. All the windows have plain glass, and it wasn't until 1996 that a beautiful stained-glass window was provided by the Abbey Stained Glass Studios for the north elevation, in the existing window over the altar. Our Lady is depicted holding a set of rosary beads, and the use of grey glass for the face and hands is now very appropriate in our multicultural society.

In December 2003, a pleasing set of four large wool tapestries by Mary Moriarty was hung on the north wall of the sanctuary, although it needs to be viewed from close quarters for the visitor to appreciate the details.

Some of the priests lived in Mount Harold House up until the mid-1970s, when the upper storeys were demolished, and two new houses built in the rear orchard, well known to altar boys who were fond of 'boxing the fox' – robbing the apples. A rear vehicular entrance from Leinster Road West was provided at the same time.

In the 1950s and '60s, May processions around the village were an annual event, including the crowning of Our Lady, not forgetting the annual Corpus Christi procession. Sometimes the processions extended down to Mount Drummond Avenue, and once or twice mass or benediction was celebrated at the high cross at the bottom of the park, with bunting and streamers adorning many houses.

Memories of the church in the 1960s include the men's and boys' sodalities, with plaques on upright timber poles held in brass rings at the end of each row of seats, indicating the different guilds. Roaring retreats, sometimes called 'missions', from visiting priests and missionaries, were the order of the day, especially during Lent.

Father Brown was in charge of the altar boys (there were no altar girls up to the 1990s), and sometimes he organised 'hops' for the young people of the parish. Father Purcell was a bit of a character, since he was always late for mass, but finished well ahead of time because of his 'speed reading'.

Billy Prendergast was a popular and efficient sacristan from about 1940 to 1980, and his work now is done by hordes of lay helpers.

There are four side altars, and sometimes in the past there were two masses being said at the same time, one at the main altar and another at a side altar, each with its own following.

The various parish priests were Percy McGough (1935), Kevin Brady (1954), Patrick Crowe (1973), Kevin McDowell (1981), Desmond Begg (1985), Desmond Dockery (1998), Ron Neville (1999) and Gerry Kane (2008).

The present single-storey pastoral centre beside the church was built within the last two years, and sits on the site of the old Mount Harold House.

The parish hall and sports ground was called Rosary Hall, and was located a few hundred yards up from the church, just past Kenilworth Motors. The clergy bought Westfield Park at auction in 1954. It was an early Georgian two-storey house of three bays, with big gardens attached. A concert hall, with corrugated-asbestos cement roof, was added on the west side, and the original house was used as the changing rooms. The gardens were laid out as football pitches. The altar boys' annual party was held in the hall around Christmas time, when a box of chocolates was presented to the 'altar boy of the year'. In the mid-1990s, most of the land was sold off for town houses, now called Kenilworth Manor, but the rear of the site was retained for one football pitch and a new community centre, with a youth club on the ground floor and a hall/meeting room at first-floor level.

Many concerts were held in Rosary Hall over the years, mostly mounted by the Harold's Cross Musical Society. The initial group comprised former members of St Gabriel's Youth Club in Loader Park, Mount Argus, who had performed in musicals for years before. May Spinks had been involved in the youth club since 1951, and she started the Harold's Cross Musical Society in 1967.

Her first show in 1968 was *Rose Maria*, and was held in the Marist Convent Hall, Clogher Road. Later venues included the Archbishop Byrne Hall in the city centre, Marianella Hall in Rathgar, and then the Rosary Hall in Harold's Cross. In 1982, the society moved to the John Player Theatre on the South Circular Road, near Sally's Bridge. Many members will have fond memories of some rehearsals in May Spinks' front parlour at 31 Westfield Road, which was in fact the headquarters of the society. She also found time to teach music for many years in the Junior School of Our Lady's, Templeogue.

Altar boys in the Holy Rosary church, 1953. The sacristan, Billy Prendergast, is on the extreme right. (Courtesy of Joe Miller)

While the Holy Rosary church was being renovated in 2004, the adjacent Parish Centre was used for the sacraments – this room was the only remains of the old Mount Harold House.

Other shows over the years included *Maid of the Mountains*, *Belle of New York*, *Merry Widow*, *Student Prince*, *Lilac Time*, *Oklahoma*, *The Golden Years*, *White Horse Inn*, *New Moon*, *Hearts a Wonder*, *Fiddler on the Roof*, *The Desert Song*, *Oliver*, *Sweethearts*, *My Fair Lady*, *Mikado*, *Showboat* and *Calamity Jane*, and obviously the most popular were performed on more than one occasion.

Members of different societies moved around a lot, performing in different venues, and over the years the Harold's Cross Musical Society forged strong links with the Tallaght Musical Society, so when the Rosary Hall closed in the early 1990s most of the members transferred to Tallaght.

ANGLICAN CHURCH

Prior to 1903, the west side of Harold's Cross was in St Catherine's Parish, the east side in Rathmines Parish, and the area south of Tivoli Avenue was in Rathfarnham Parish. Rathmines only achieved separate parish status in 1883, because even when the Holy Trinity church was built in 1826, it was merely a chapel-of-ease in St Peter's Parish (centred on Aungiers Street).

St Catherine's Parish, centred on St Catherine's church, Thomas Street, extended to Harold's Cross, taking in the hospice area, Mount Jerome and Mount Argus. The boundaries in fact corresponded exactly with part of the Earl of Meath estate, and the earl had civil and ecclesiastical jurisdiction in the parish, including appointing the vicar.

Prior to the Disestablishment of the Church of Ireland Act 1869, the Protestant Church and State were inextricably linked, with the former performing the civil function of collecting Grand Jury cess (local-authority rates) in addition to parish cess (tax or tithes, equal to one-tenth of your income) from all property owners (even Catholics), in order to maintain the Protestant Church and clergy. After the Act of 1869, the Protestants had to fend for themselves, and were no longer called 'The Established Church'.

In the first half of the nineteenth century, the English clergy, especially people like Revd Alex Dallas, aspired to gaining more Protestant converts in Ireland, and spearheaded what was effectively a second Reformation, especially in the west of Ireland where soup kitchens were used as bribes. In 1822, William Magee, the Protestant Archbishop of Dublin, declared religious war on the Catholic Church.

Trustee or proprietary chapels were built under the terms of An Act for the Encouragement of Building Churches and Chapels in Ireland 1836. These chapels were not provided for by the State (through tithes), but were built and maintained by private subscription, especially thanks to rich lay people who favoured the conversion of Catholics to Protestantism. Therefore, these chapels were free to preach a different form of Christianity, which was not to be heard in the ordinary parishes. Known evangelists could not obtain appointments in the more important parishes, so they operated from the proprietary chapels, which were also nicknamed 'preaching houses'. Evangelists were ardent gospel preachers, often of the 'bible thumping, hell, fire and damnation' variety. The most famous proprietary chapels in Dublin were the Bethesda Chapel in Dorset Street, Trinity Church in Lower Gardiner Street (recently a Labour Exchange), Leeson Park, Sandford Park, and Zion in Rathgar. Evangelists became 'respectable' when they started becoming archbishops, and the first such Archbishop of Dublin was William Cunningham (Lord Plunkett), who founded the Kildare Place Training College and was buried in Mount Jerome in 1897.

While the 'second Reformation' was taking place in Ireland, the Irish Catholic Church was sending missionaries from Maynooth and All Hallows' College to India, China, Africa and other countries to gain converts, and to administer to the spiritual and educational needs of the British Empire.

With the closure of the Catholic chapel beside Mount Jerome in 1833, Harold's Cross was chosen as a good location for a proprietary chapel, and John D. Hastings, the vicar of St Catherine's Parish, laid the foundation stone in 1838 for the Harold's Cross Episcopal church, which was built by R. and W. Tough to a design by John Louche. The church was paid for by weekly subscriptions and generous donations, including £400 from the Right Honourable Countess Dowager of Rosse. The first trustees were John D. Hastings, Very Revd R.H. Dawson (Dean of St Patrick's), Arthur Guinness, Thomas Kingston (Vicar of St James's), A.T. Burroughs, Vice-Admiral R.D. Oliver, T.M. Mason, W.C. Hogan, and J.H. Singer.

The first chaplain/incumbent was Robert James McGhee, who was known to be very abrasive and antagonistic towards the Catholic Church and 'papists'. His religious career started in the tiny church on Lord Powerscourt's Estate in Enniskerry, County Wicklow, progressing to meetings in a building at Brighton Terrace, Bray, for disillusioned parishioners from St Paul's church, also in Bray. This led to the building of an independent trustee chapel at Crinken (near Bray) in 1840, but in the meantime McGhee had accepted the post in Harold's Cross. However, he remained a trustee of St James's, Crinken, until his departure from Ireland in 1846. Some of his sermons in Harold's Cross were printed, and can be consulted in the National Library, as can one given by Revd Mortimer O'Sullivan on 10 September 1843, seeking donations to clear the church-building debt of £900.

While the Harold's Cross Episcopal church was gaining converts, the Catholic Church encouraged the Passionists, also well-known preachers, to move into a farmhouse at nearby Mount Argus (part of the Earl of Meath's Estate) in 1856, and build a small chapel. However, it was not until after the Disestablishment of the Church of Ireland Act 1869, that the Passionists could build a giant church to dwarf the Episcopal church beside Mount Jerome.

One of the trustees of the Harold's Cross Episcopal Church was Revd Thomas Kingston, who was the vicar of St James's in James's Street from 1826 to 1867. He owned the fee farm grant of Ashfield House, near Mount

Tallant Avenue at the upper end of Harold's Cross, and leased the property to Henry Laurence Fry for 500 years from 1862. Over the following decades, many red-brick houses were built on the land, including Ashfield Park and Ashfield Terrace, in addition to Liscombe House. The original house is now called Ashfield Park House. The ground rent from this property was partly used to fund the running costs of the Harold's Cross Episcopal church. The annual accounts for 1864 show the general heads of receipts: pew rents (£467), Sunday collections (£190) and Ashfield ground rents (£67). Expenditure was listed as incumbents salary (£350), organist (£25), organ blower (£5), sexton (£35), caretaker (£11), collector of pew rents (£23), coals (£5), gas (£11) and so on. Thomas Kingston was very involved in the initial establishment of the Harold's Cross Episcopal Church, and after his death in 1867 a stained-glass window was provided in memory of him. He is buried in the abandoned and dilapidated (but historic) graveyard behind St James's church, which was recently 'taken in charge' by Dublin City Council.

In the 1869 vestry minute book, the congregation refers to themselves as the Reformed Church, and not to be confused with ordinary Protestants!

By 1903, the Episcopal church decided to surrender its independent status and go back into the fold of the main Church of Ireland parish system, and thereby benefit from central-funding arrangements. At that stage, the trustees were J.F. Dublin, Maurice Day, William Hayes (of HCR Chemists fame), H. Courtenay and William S.B. Homan. Maurice Day was in fact rector of St Matthias' church in Adelaide Road, another famous proprietary chapel, from 1894 to 1905. Thereafter, the Representative Church Body was responsible for Harold's Cross. However, even prior to 1903, parishioners of Harold's Cross had to be married in St Catherine's church in Thomas Street. The new parish of Harold's Cross comprised parts of Rathmines, Rathfarnham and St Catherine's, but the boundaries were redrawn to ensure that prosperous areas were included, so that the parish would be viable.

The Church of Ireland in general is a very democratic organisation (since the 1869 Act), and every year the congregation of each parish selects a group within themselves as a committee to organise and run the parish for the next year – the Select Vestry. They even interview and appoint the clergy. One undesirable feature of the Harold's Cross church accounts in the twentieth century was the listing in the year book of the amount subscribed by each parishioner, which was obviously a form of blackmail. On the other hand, the church set up a fellowship in 1941 to help the poor Protestants of Harold's Cross. For example, the 1946 year book records that five households got regular weekly cash sums (of varying amounts); seventy-three other cash grants were made for medicine, comforts, dental care, rent, bedding, maintenance and liquidation of debts, and 131 food vouchers were issued. £20 16*s* 3*d* was expended on new boots, shoes, clothes and other items, and Christmas parcels were donated to the needy. Part of the profit from the opening of the Kenilworth Cinema (later called The Classic) in 1953 was donated to the fellowship. The early years of this charity comprised the Second World War, or the Emergency as neutral Ireland called it, when jobs were scarce, and everything, especially food, was rationed in Ireland.

The church never lost sight of its original goal of gaining converts to Protestantism. In 1945, the rector of Harold's Cross, W.C.G. Proctor, recommends in the year book 'evangelising non church goers or agnostics by befriending such people, and invite them to a special Service in church, arranged for the purpose of interesting and instructing such people in the things of Christ'. Over the years, various people were converted or 'turned', but nowadays many Christians are striving for unification of the Catholic and Protestant religions, so 'poaching' may soon become a custom of the past.

The Garrison Church in nearby Cathal Brugha Barracks is very small, and for special services the relevant troops marched, in formation, to the Church of Ireland building in Harold's Cross.

The front façade of the Harold's Cross church is granite-faced, but all other elevations are plastered. The slated double-pitched roof is concealed behind battlemented parapets, including cleverly integrated chimney flues. Internally, there is a sloping/stepped gallery to the sides and rear, which provides a capacity of about 1,100. The original building was rectangular, but a new sanctuary and shallow transepts had been added by the early 1860s. Around £526 was spent in 1899 in narrowing the galleries in the transepts, re-siting the pulpit to the side, and general decorations and improvements. The south-west bell tower was added in 1914, but for safety reasons the top of the tower was demolished in 1985, and the half-ton bronze bell (cast by Taylor of Loughborough in England, and donated by the Spence family) now sits in the rear yard, mounted in its original Mathew O'Byrne patent frame. Various other small side porches were added over the years, and a sexton's cottage provided, although the latter had to be substantially rebuilt in 1941.

A special feature of the interior of the church is the ribbed and vaulted ceiling (painted blue), supported on slender clustered columns. There is a large number of lovely stained-glass windows dedicated to such people as Henry Vanston, Revd Thomas Kingston (d. 1867), Revd Margin A. Keana (d. 1868), Canon John Andrew Jennings (incumbent 1901–1923), and Mary Courtenay. However, the largest and most attractive stained glass is in the three-light west window behind the altar, in memory of William Booker Askin, rector from 1857 to 1901, who died in 1907 – the window cost £300 in that year. The east coloured window is in memory of Thomas Dunnill. Mayer of Munich made the upper window in the south transept, depicting faith, hope and charity, and they are thought to be responsible for most of the other windows. Some say that Early of Camden Street made the colourful low-level window near the west end of the south aisle.

The stained-glass window in the east porch is entitled 'The Good Samaritan' in memory of Stuart Nassau Lane, who died in 1958. This was made in 1960 by well-known Irish stained-glass artist Catherine Amelia O'Brien, who was associated with the famous studios An Tur Gloinne (the tower of glass), as were Evie Hone, Sarah Purser, and Michael Healy. Catherine O'Brien died in 1963 and is buried in Whitechurch Cemetery in Rathfarnham – another link with Harold country. Catherine, who signed herself as K. O'Brien, was also responsible for a beautiful stained-glass window in Delgany church, also depicting the good samaritan, although executed much earlier in her career, and of a more traditional design.

Wall-mounted marble memorial tablets are in abundance throughout the church, including ones to Mary Manifold (d. 1864, aged 12), and Richard Manifold (d. 1865 in India, aged 3), John Hawker Evans (superintendent of the Sunday school, who died in 1881), Revd Martin Keene (accidentally drowned in Bray in 1868, aged 28), Colonel Meadows Taylor, of Old Court (d. 1876), William Mallins (d. 1882), Revd Charles Coote Whittaker Duggan (rector 1923–1936), and Mary Palmer (d. 1891 – erected by nephew Sir Howard Grubb, the famous telescope maker). There is a large tablet and plaque to the dead Protestants of the two world wars (a particular feature of the Church of Ireland), in addition to a roll of honour for those who served (and survived) in the Great War (1914–1918). The oldest tablet in the church remembers Captain Holland Lecky McGhee (presumably related to the rector, Robert McGhee), who died in 1841, and this is positioned very high up on the south side of the sanctuary.

The organ on the rear gallery, so much a part of Church of Ireland services, was apparently built in 1855 by William Browne of Camden Street, although it was replaced in 1870 by Forster and Andrews of Hull, in England, at a cost of £500, and then rebuilt in the late 1930s.

Most of the original fireplaces can still be seen in the main church and on the galleries, with their raised hearths to better radiate the heat, although oil-fired central heating was installed later.

Protestant churches can be differentiated from Catholic churches by the absence of statues, stations of the cross and confession boxes, and by the abundance of large marble tablets and brass plaques commemorating deceased members.

The large basement is in fact at ground level, since the site is sloping, and the church proper is accessed by external granite steps. However, due to the proximity of the River Poddle, the basement was frequently flooded over the years, especially after hurricane Charley in 1986. Sunday school for religious education was held in the basement over most of the life span of the church, in addition to a national school and a youth club.

The rectory was built around 1875/80 at the corner of Leinster Road West and Harold's Cross Road, and was officially known as 'The Glebe House', but also as 'The Parsonage'. It was recently called Marleigh House and used as offices, but is now back in private residential use. However, over the years, the various rectors and curates resided in a variety of different big houses, generally in the Grosvenor Road and Kenilworth Road area.

Harold's Cross Anglican church, as it became known after 1903, amalgamated with Rathmines Parish in 1977. However, the congregation continued to dwindle, partly because of parishioners moving to suburbs such as Taney near Dundrum, and partly because of the current trend amongst all Christians towards secularisation. The church closed and was deconsecrated at a special Thanksgiving service on 27 June 2001, conducted by the popular Archbishop of Dublin, Dr Walton Empey. The remaining parishioners now attend services in Holy Trinity, Rathmines.

Incumbents in Harold's Cross were: Robert McGhee (1838–1846), John Griffin (1847–1856), William Askin (1857–1901), John Jennings (1902–1923), Charles Duggan (1924–1936), William Proctor (1937–1963), Herbert Packham (1964–1973), Thomas Mack (1974–1976), Erberto Neill (1977–1981, father of John Neill, the recent Archbishop of Dublin), and Neil McEndoo (1982–2001).

The Church of Ireland parochial hall was built in 1882 opposite the rectory to a design by Alfred G. Jones, at a cost of £550. This attractive granite building of about 2,000 square feet had a stage at the south end and a balcony at the north end, in addition to a small apartment. The hall was used by the rangers, the boys brigade, the girl guides, the brownies, the amateur dramatic society, and also for badminton. Variety concerts were frequently organised by the Young Men's Christian Association (YMCA), and Mount Jerome National School performed its annual concert here. The hall was sold to a firm of accountants in 1982, and nicely converted into offices, appropriately called Century House.

The Alexandra Guild House was a Protestant retirement home set up in 1954 for elderly ladies in need, and was located at 30 Leinster Road West. The guild is associated with Alexandra College, a girls' school that was then in Earlsfort Terrace, but moved to Milltown. The main part of the present house was originally called Linden and built in 1860. The house has obviously been extended over the years, and with the building of a rear extension in 1993 could accommodate twenty-seven ladies. A new purpose-built home at Kilternan was provided in 2007, and the old home awaits redevelopment.

RUSSIAN ORTHODOX CHURCH

Around 1054, the Christian religion split in two, the West being governed by popes in Rome, and the East by patriarchs in Constantinople (now called Istanbul) – the latter came to be known as the Orthodox Church. During the Reformation in the early part of the sixteenth century, the Western Church split into Roman Catholics and Protestants ('Protesters').

Over the past fifteen years, many Russians and eastern Europeans have emigrated to Ireland, no doubt attracted by the Celtic Tiger – a boom that lasted from about 1995 to 2007. Many of these people belong to the Russian Orthodox Church, and initially shared facilities with the Greek Orthodox Church, which was already established in Arbour Hill (near Collins Barracks).

With the closure in 2001 of the Anglican church in Harold's Cross, the Russian Orthodox clergy sought and obtained a lease of the building, renaming it St Peter and St Paul. They immediately set about altering the church to meet their specific requirements. Their service normally lasts about two hours, with everyone standing, so the seats were removed, and the timber floor sanded and varnished. The timber pulpit has been set aside, and the Communion table (altar) removed. The sanctuary is now separated from the nave by means of an iconostasis, a half-height timber screen, adorned with beautiful icons brought from Russia – icons are pictures of saints painted directly onto timber, and these are venerated by the congregation. The organ remains on the rear gallery but is not used, since the choir sings unaccompanied. The altered church was ready for their Easter ceremonies in 2002.

The official consecration and pontifical liturgy took place on 9 February 2003, starting at 9 a.m. and ending at 1.30 p.m., after which all participated in a well-earned cold buffet in the hall under the church. The chief celebrant was Bishop Theopan of Magadan (Russia), assisted by a host of other clergy including the new rector, Revd Fr Michael Gogoleff, and the new curate, Revd Fr George Zavershinsky (the latter now lives in the refurbished sexton's house). Invited guests included Most Revd John Neill (Anglican Archbishop of Dublin), and Dermot Lacey, lord mayor of Dublin City Council. As is usual with the Orthodox Church, the ceremony was very elaborate and moving, incorporating many centuries-old traditions, accompanied by plain chant and choir, and interspersed with various changes of ornate and colourful vestments. Much activity took place behind the iconostasis, where a new square timber-framed altar to be used as a repository for holy relics of Russian saints was carefully assembled, ritually sealed at each stage and covered with gold-embroidered cloth. The sanctuary behind the screen is sacred, and only clergy are permitted to enter the centre swing doors – akin to entering the gates of Heaven. Then the church was blessed with holy water all around the

The former Harold's Cross Anglican church was re-dedicated on 9 February 2003, as the Russian Orthodox Church of St Peter and St Paul, where priceless vestments were used throughout the long and elaborate ceremony.

inside. The Eucharist (Holy Communion) was prepared behind the screen by cutting up ordinary bread and mixing it into the chalice of wine, with some hot water added. The Holy Communion was then brought into the nave, and each person received a small spoonful of the mixture. In the Orthodox religion, babies are baptised and immediately confirmed, and can then receive Holy Communion.

It is interesting to note that the Orthodox Church celebrates Christmas on 6 January. Throughout the year, the original Protestant bell, which sits in a frame in the side yard, is rung for Sunday services.

A primary school has now been opened in the basement, catering for seventy children.

METHODIST CHURCH

Many people associate the term Protestant with the Church of Ireland (also called Anglicans or the Established Church). However, the term also includes Methodists, Presbyterians, Baptists, Quakers and even Brethren.

The founder of the worldwide Methodist Church, John Wesley, was born in Epworth, Lincolnshire, England in 1703. One of the most famous

The Methodist church at the corner of Brighton Square, 2002. The transepts were built as a memorial to the First World War.

Methodist establishments in Ireland is probably Wesley College in Ballinteer (a secondary school).

The Methodists built a lovely church at the south-east corner of Brighton Square in 1874, and its first minister was William Crawford. The builder was Beckett Bros, and the architect was Thomas Holbrook. The manse, lecture hall, two rooms off the hall used as a national school and the sexton's flat followed in 1879; then came the organ, church spire and railings in 1893, and finally the transepts and war-memorial window were added in 1924. The national school moved to a new building on Rathgar Avenue in 1896. In common with other Protestant religions, the Methodists have various clubs and societies, including Sunday school, women's work for overseas missions, boys' brigade, girl guides, band of hope (total abstinence from alcohol), men's fireside group, indoor bowls club and so on, all operating from the hall. Special Evangelistic services were held in 1921, 1939, 1947, 1952, and 1959 in the hope of attracting new churchgoers.

PRESBYTERIANS (CALVINISTS)

The Presbyterians in the locality have the option of going to Adelaide Road (newly rebuilt), or Christ Church at the top of Rathgar Road.

BAPTISTS

The Baptists are very much thriving in Grosvenor Road, at the corner of Grosvenor Place, in a church built in 1859 and generally known as Grosvenor Hall. The present Baptists acquired this hall in 1942, after they sold their 1887 church in Harcourt Street (backing onto Charlotte Street). However, even before they purchased Grosvenor Hall, the Baptists operated an out-station in Wharton Hall, near Harold's Cross Bridge, renting the hall from a Jewish charity for three evenings each week, calling it Mission Hall. Prior to 1942, Grosvenor Hall was owned by Brethren (Plymouth), although, ironically, the building was built by the Baptists in 1859, and then sold to the Brethren five years later. Grosvenor Hall is not a sacred building in the usual Christian sense, being more of a gathering place for Bible readings, and featuring music

This was the Baptist church in Harcourt Street (the site was re-developed as a dance hall called the TV Club, and is now a complex of office blocks used as Garda Headquarters) before the congregation moved in 1942 to Grosvenor Hall. (Courtesy of Grosvenor Baptist church)

and singing. The rock-faced granite exterior, with some sandstone dressings, belies the large size of the interior, which once had a gallery on three sides, but now only has a rear sloping gallery. Baptists are so named because members are only baptised when they reach adulthood, and babies/children cannot become full members. The sunken and tiled immersion pool is located in the centre of the stage, although normally covered over with trapdoors, and here members proclaim their faith by total immersion of the body (still wearing their clothes, but drying out afterwards in the room behind the stage).

BRETHREN

Nowadays, Brethren have the option of attending the Gospel Hall at 178 Upper Rathmines Road (since 1968), or Irishtown Gospel Hall, near Ringsend.

QUAKERS

In the nineteenth century, Harold's Cross had many Quakers (Religious Society of Friends), because of the presence of Greenmount Spinning Manufactory and Perry's Brewery, to name but two enterprises. Since 1957, the nearest meeting house for Quakers is at 62 Crannagh Road, between Terenure and Rathfarnham. Crannagh Road comprises a large modern sports hall with a small meeting room and adjoining open-air tennis courts. Churchtown Meeting House is much bigger and more frequented. Quakers were founded in 1652 by George Fox in the north-west of England, and spread to Ireland a few years later. Their new Bloomfield Hospital in Stocking Lane, Rathfarnham, is well known.

MUSLIMS

The local Islamic community has the Dublin Mosque on the South Circular Road, beside the National Stadium, which they bought from the Donore Presbyterian Church in 1983. They removed the seats and organ, carpeted the entire floor, built a woman's gallery along the west

Recent view of South Circular Road, with former Greenville synagogue on the left, and the former Presbyterian church on the right (the latter is now the Dublin Mosque).

side, and erected a *mihrab* (niche to indicate the direction of Mecca) in the centre of the east side wall, in addition to modifying the north rose window. During prayers, all Muslims face in an easterly direction, towards Mecca (Saudi Arabia), their spiritual home. Initially, the Muslims unsuccessfully

Interior of Dublin Mosque, with *mihrab* on the right.

tried to buy the vacant Greenville Synagogue across the road, which is now in business use (Mason Technology), although the wonderful stained-glass dome and many other features are still intact. Nowadays there are about 50,000 Muslims in Ireland.

JEWS

Harold's Cross is literally surrounded by Jewish establishments, and even today some Jewish people reside in the area and one or two businesses remain, although most Jews live in nearby Terenure. Over the past few centuries, there has been a Jewish presence in Ireland, generally businessmen from central Europe and Portugal who became prominent in the Dublin jewellery business, but those families have now died out. The current dwindling population owes its origins to Lithuanian refugees in the 1880–1910 period, mostly from the town of Akmenė in the north-west. Akmenė was a Jewish town, having been settled in the mid-nineteenth century, but following an accidental fire in 1893, which destroyed many businesses and homes, large numbers of Jews emigrated in search of fame and fortune. During the recent Celtic Tiger property boom in Ireland, thousands of Lithuanian Catholics came to Ireland for similar reasons, although the two religious groups do not mix or socialise. Between 1880 and 1940, the Jewish population in Ireland increased from a few hundred to over 5,000. The South Circular Road area between Donore Avenue and Portobello was the main residential area, with synagogues at Greenville (almost opposite the National Stadium), 46 Lombard Street West, 7 St Kevin's Parade, 3-4 Walworth Road, and 36 Adelaide Road. Greenville and Adelaide were big purpose-built establishments, whereas the others were small converted houses. Greenville Synagogue included a hall for wedding receptions. As their businesses prospered, many took up residence in Westfield Road, Kenilworth Square and Park, Leinster Road and so on.

Clanbrassil Street Lower was filled with Jewish shops selling kosher food, including Erlich, Goldberg, Rubinstein, Freedman, Newman, Citron, Ordman, Leopold, Goldwater and others. The Jews had a special poultry abattoir at 34 Lower Clanbrassil Street (the building was demolished in 2016) run by the Dublin Board of Sechita. Their cows were slaughtered under the control of the 'Shochet' in a special part of the city marts on the North Circular Road (now a housing estate). Kosher Meat Products operated from 5/6 Aideen Place at the top of Mount Tallant Avenue. The Bretzel Bakery in Portobello is a famous Jewish landmark, and still going strong. All of the Clanbrassil Street shops have been disappearing since the 1980s, replaced by Asian and Arab shops selling Halal meat and other products. During the 1980s, Fine operated a kosher shop in Terenure at the corner of Rathmore Villas, but nowadays Supervalu in Churchtown is the only shop selling Jewish food.

Not far from Upper Clanbrassil Street is 33 Bloomfield Avenue, where Chaim Herzog lived. Chaim was born in Belfast in 1918, but his father, Isaac, moved to Dublin in 1919, to become chief rabbi of Dublin (later of the Irish Free State). The family left Ireland in 1937 in order for Isaac to become chief rabbi of the rapidly expanding Jewish minority in Palestine, although Chaim had gone to Palestine two years previously, following his secondary education at Wesley College (Methodists). Chaim spent much of his career in the defence forces, followed by stints in business, broadcasting and the diplomatic service, and finally was elected President of Israel from 1983 to 1993. President Herzog visited Ireland in 1985 to officially open the Irish-Jewish Museum in the old synagogue, Walworth Road, Portobello.

The Jews built an impressive two-storey national school in Bloomfield Avenue in 1934, with one third State funding, although there was also a national school under the Adelaide Road Synagogue up until 1921. However, nowadays Stratford College in Rathgar is the only Jewish centre for primary and secondary education. Herzog House, the main administrative centre for Jews in Ireland, is incorporated into Stratford College. The original Bloomfield School closed in 1980, and was sold as offices.

The early Jewish community in Dublin had their cemetery at 67 Fairview Strand, which they acquired in 1718. A new spacious cemetery (called Beth Olam) was bought in 1898 at Aughavanagh Road near Harold's Cross, where there are hundreds of headstones and more than enough space to accommodate the present small community. Louis and Maurice Elliman (of cinema/theatre fame) are buried here, as is Robert Briscoe, former lord mayor of Dublin in 1956 and 1961. Sam Noyek (famous for timber supplies, including 'Wareite') choose to be interred on the Mount of Olives in Jerusalem. All of the headstones face west, so that the mourners face east.

Age-old customs include handwashing after each visit to a grave, and the bereaved family themselves backfill the grave after burial. Custom dictates that the bereaved does not visit the grave during the first year after death. Flowers are not permitted on the graves, although a pebble is usually left after each visit. Anyone trying to read the headstone inscriptions should remember that the Jewish calendar starts 3,760 years before Christ (BC), and their religious year starts in September.

Another grave in Aughavanagh Road is that of the famous painter Harry Kernoff. He was born in London in 1900, his father being a Russian Jew and his mother Spanish. The family moved to Dublin in 1914, and Harry spent most of his life at 13 Stamer Street in Portobello. From 1926 until his death in the Meath Hospital in 1974, he exhibited an average of six paintings every year at the Royal Hibernian Academy. Of particular interest to Haroldians would be his painting in 1926 of Larkfield House in Kimmage, home of Joseph Mary Plunkett from 1912 to 1916, and the headquarters from 1913 of the 4th Battalion, Dublin Brigade, of the Irish Volunteers. In 1955 Kernoff also painted a watercolour of Emmet House, Harold's Cross. All of his paintings are extremely colourful and lively, and many people regard him as one of Ireland's best painters in the twentieth century.

Paul Golden, the famous hypnotist, was Jewish, but choose to be cremated in Mount Jerome Cemetery.

Denmark Hill in Leinster Road West was a Retirement Home for Jews, the brainchild of Mrs Rebecca Solomon (née Potashnik), and started in 1950, when Mr Louis Wine sold the family residence. The Wines were prominent Jewish Irish citizens in Dublin, being involved in the antiques business in Grafton Street and in the legal profession (Mr Justice Hubert Wine of the Dublin District Court). The home was extended in 1972 and 1992, the latter being officially opened by Mary Robinson, the first female President of Ireland, bringing the capacity of the home to forty-one residents. This extension necessitated fundraising in America to the tune of $500,000. The extension included a small homely octagonal synagogue, with nice stained-glass windows, which together with the glazing at the top of the pyramidal roof created a bright atmosphere. The synagogue was open to non-residents in order to secure a quorum of ten men for a service, since most of the residents were female. Inside the home, the walls of the inner hall were completely covered with small brass plaques commemorating former residents. The home closed in 2005 and the patients transferred to Stocking Lane in Rathfarnham, where the Quakers have built a new mixed-use complex. The former home in Leinster Road West/Effra Road was redeveloped as townhouses in 2015.

Denmark Hill was built and occupied around 1855 by Frederick Stokes, one of the first and most influential Rathmines Commissioners. Stokes leased part of his original garden to Samuel Le Bas for 800 years from 1874, and the latter built a small terrace of houses bearing his name. All but one of these houses were acquired by the adjoining Jewish home.

An interesting Jewish premises from 1920 to 1970 was Wharton Hall, a small two-storey building which is still behind Daybreak newsagents near Emmet Bridge, but has recently been converted into apartments, and an extra storey has been added. This was owned by the Ancient Order of Maccabeans, a friendly society whose members (Brothers) paid a small weekly subscription in return for financial assistance in sickness and death. The Brothers also had to support the Zionist cause. The hall was rented out for Jewish wedding receptions, and the Grand Order of Israel and Shield of David Friendly Society also used it for their own meetings. On three evenings a week, Grosvenor Road Baptist Church rented the hall for gospel meetings. In the 1970s, Doggett printers were based here.

Just past the upper end of Harold's Cross Road, tucked away behind 77 Terenure Road North, in Rathmore Villas, is a small active synagogue called Machzikei Hadass, which has the outward appearance of a garage but a very homely inside. This was set up when the small synagogue at 7 St Kevin's Parade (off Lower Clanbrassil Street) closed down in the 1960s. The new synagogue was officially opened in April 1968 by Aaron Steinberg, but long before this, the hall was used as a Jewish social club for dances and other forms of entertainment. The synagogue can accommodate about fifty people, but attendances nowadays are usually much smaller. There is no gallery, but as usual the women sit behind a rear lace-curtained screen. The service starts at 9.30 a.m. on Saturday mornings and usually lasts for about two hours. The atmosphere is very relaxed during the service, akin to a family get-together. There is the usual central Bima (platform) from which the prayers are led, and the Torah scrolls are removed from the north-east ark. After the prayers, the group socialises at tables in the synagogue, drinking neat whiskey and nibbling herring slices, cream crackers and sweet cake. The Jews jokingly refer to this synagogue as the earliest-opening pub in Dublin. The current vice-president here is Joe Katz, who also runs a very interesting business from the old workhouse in Celbridge, County Kildare, making parchments and drum coverings from calf skins, using centuries-old skills.

Further up the road, just past Terenure crossroads, at 32a Rathfarnham Road, is the main synagogue for Dublin Jews. This had its origins at 6 Grosvenor Place in 1936, followed in 1940 by 52 Grosvenor Road (now the Rathgar Catholic Parish Centre), and finally moving to Terenure around 1948, initially occupying a Nissen army hut until the new premises was completed in 1953. The two foundation stones are dedicated to Samuel Noyek and Simon Fine. This spacious building has a long lean-to roof covered with corrugated asbestos-cement sheeting. The women and children are segregated from the men and occupy the rear sloping gallery/balcony. Following a small fire in 1965, the premises was substantially rebuilt and refurbished in 1967, and the opportunity was taken to install large stained-glass windows in the north and south elevations. The north window, depicting a walled city, was presented by Noyek Bros to commemorate the occupation of the Old City of Jerusalem (Palestinian section) after the Six-Day War with Egypt in 1967. The south window depicts ten religious festivals in vivid colours. The Samuel Taca Hall is beside the synagogue, and likewise the Millennium Mikvah Ritual Baths (used by women on a monthly basis). Prior to 2000, the Mikvah Baths were in Adelaide Road Synagogue, and before that, a portion of Tara Street Public Baths was set aside for the Jews. Using cars and buses on the Sabbath (Saturday) is no longer prohibited, although some Jews still walk to the synagogue, recognisable by either wide-brimmed black-top hats or tiny colourful 'skull caps'.

For many decades, the Adelaide Road Synagogue was the most important in Dublin, having been built in 1892 for £5,000, with the aid of subscriptions from other religions, following public advertisements in the press. The synagogue was sold in 1999, realising £6 million for the site (now a block of apartments behind the original façade), and its former members joined the Terenure Synagogue.

Near the south-east corner of Kenilworth Square, at 7 Leicester Avenue, is located the synagogue of the Dublin Jewish Progressive Congregation, so named because they are not so strict as the Orthodox Jews, allow women rabbis, and have no segregation of males and females in the synagogue (hence no gallery). It is said that most members are opposed to Zionism. Mixed marriages and converts are especially welcome. Rabbi Rudolph Brasch was sent from the liberal Jews in London in 1946 to pioneer a similar community in Dublin, and the initial services were held in the Friends Meeting House (Quakers) at Eustace Street, which building is now the Irish Film Theatre. After a year, he returned to London, and the new congregation acquired a house in Leicester Avenue, and soon after built their present synagogue alongside. Their first president was Bethel Solomons, the first Jewish master of the Rotunda Maternity Hospital (1926), and brother of the famous artist Estella Solomons. There is a lovely brass sculpture in the synagogue called 'The Tree of Life', the fruit represented by little brass plaques in memory of different births, marriages and deaths in the congregation, all the handiwork of Fergus O'Farrell in 1988 (Dublin Millennium Year). The synagogue was extended to the front in 1992, providing a large vestibule with three rooms at first-floor level. The progressive Jews have their own cemetery in Oldcourt Road, in the foothills of the Dublin Mountains, which was established by Bernard Spiro, and now contains more than 100 headstones facing various directions. The small plain prayer house was donated by the Gillinson family and contains a plaque in memory of Bethel Solomons and his wife Gertrude. Burials are much less formal than Orthodox funerals, and no handwashing is involved. Estella Starkey (*née* Solomons) was buried here in 1968 – the artist was married to Dr James Starkey, who used the pen name of Seamus O'Sullivan. Each grave contains only one body, so that a husband and wife are sometimes buried in different parts of the cemetery.

For many Jewish people, their religion dominates their way of life, with customs (especially dietary) going back thousands of years, and so they created their own micro-culture within Irish society. Besides their own special shops, schools, synagogues, and cemeteries, they organised their own golf club at Edmondstown in Rathfarnham (1944), and the Maccabi sports ground in Kimmage Road West (1954), where the Carlisle Cricket Club was based. The cricket club was started in 1908 by four lads from Carlisle Street, off the South Circular Road: R. Green, H. Levison, H. Hesselberg, and W. Weiner. The 8½ acre site in Kimmage was leased from Dublin Corporation for 150 years from 1954, at a nominal low rent

2003 view of the Maccabi Sports Pavilion on Kimmage Road West, before it was demolished to make way for an art gallery beside the Carlisle Fitness Club.

of £124 per annum, and a grand clubhouse was built in the same year. Names on the building committee included Alki, Barling, Black, Citron, Cornick, Davis, Esses, Jacobson, Jameson, Jackson, Keye, Mirrelson, Roberts, Samuels, Solomons, Spain, and Wine. The Maccabi Sports Club was part of the Maccabi World Union, which Jewish umbrella organisation was started in Hungary in the 1880s. The Maccabiah Games (mini-Olympics) started in Palestine in 1932, and are now held every four years in Israel. The property was sold to Ben Dunne (of supermarket fame) in 1999 for £4.13 million. Following a High Court action in 1999, the judge ordered the Dublin Maccabi Association to use the £4.13 million only for fostering education, art, sport, and intellectual activities amongst Jewish Irish citizens. Ben Dunne built the Carlisle Fitness Club and Pool on part of the site, and then demolished the old pavilion to make way for an art gallery (now closed).

The Jewish population in Dublin is currently estimated at about 850 and declining, although there are reports of some Israeli and South African Jews now settling in Ireland. Increased prosperity and education resulted in many Irish Jews emigrating to England, America and Palestine/Israel. The Orthodox absolute ban on mixed marriages also drove many young people to seek suitable partners in more populous countries.

7

EDUCATION

BACKGROUND

At the beginning of the nineteenth century, there was no formal education system in Ireland, and 'hedge schools' were operated privately on a fee-paying basis from houses, cottages, and outbuildings. By 1831, the government had introduced a national education system, although the school site and one third of the building costs had to be provided by local sources, and in addition, local funds had to be forthcoming to supplement the teachers' salaries, which were paid for by the Board of Education. The Lancastrian Monitorial Teaching Method was used in the new schools, allowing large numbers of children to be taught basic reading and writing with a small teaching force, and using the older children as monitors or teaching aides. Joseph Lancaster, a Quaker, started the teaching method in 1797 in London.

In 1838, the board opened a model school and training school for men beside their headquarters in Marlborough Street, which provided a two-year training period.

A Royal Commission of Inquiry in 1868 found that only about a third of teachers were formally trained. As a result of this, a payments-by-results scheme was introduced to supplement teachers' salaries, and lasted from 1872 to 1900. Each year, inspectors examined the pupils on the three Rs – reading, writing and arithmetic, and depending on the number of passes and fails, extra funds were allocated to the teachers.

In 1875 St Patrick's Training College in Drumcondra was opened by the Vincentian priests, and is still going strong.

In 1878, the Intermediate Education Act was introduced in an effort to create more widespread secondary education in Ireland. Under this act, public examinations were held, and winning students were allocated prizes and certificates, and their school fees paid directly to the school managers. The winning students were listed in the daily newspapers.

In most national schools of the day, children of all ages and ability were educated in one room, and generally the older children supervised and taught the younger children. Schools were supposed to be non-denominational, and applications for grants had to be signed by both Catholic and Protestant sponsors, although in practice separate denominational schools were established.

The earliest recorded schools in Harold's Cross date from the early 1820s, and both revolved around St Clare's Convent and Fr Henry Young. Fr Young started St Peter's School opposite St Clare's, and was probably instrumental in starting a school in St Clare's Convent, where he was chaplain. His sister, Catherine, was a nun there (later Abbess Mother Mary John the Evangelist, who died in 1858). The Loreto nuns started their first school in Ireland immediately beside St Clare's Convent, while awaiting alterations to their new venture in Rathfarnham.

FRIARY OF DISCALCED CARMELITES
(ST PETER'S FREE SCHOOL)

Fr Henry Young was transferred to Harold's Cross in 1818, having previously served in Francis Street, the main church of the Parish of St Nicholas Without. He said mass in the tiny church beside the entrance to Mount Jerome, and lived in 126 Harold's Cross Road (now No. 82), opposite St Clare's Convent. He also acted as chaplain to the convent. He gathered a few young working men to form a religious community of Brothers, loosely linked to the Carmelites in Clarendon Street and therefore called the Friary of Discalced Carmelites, and he lived with them in No. 126. In January 1819, he opened a general free school, St Peters, for 140 boys, in addition to an evening school for the factory workers. St Peter's School was run by a committee, with Fr Henry Young as guardian, Joseph Murphy of Harold's Cross Mills (later Harold's Cross Laundry) as president,

Mr Henry Russell of 24 Eustace Street as vice-president, and Peter Dowdall of Harold's Cross as treasurer. Fr Henry Young was transferred to Milltown in 1827, and in that year the Brothers linked with the Carmelite Brothers at St Joseph's in Monastery Road, Clondalkin.

A parliamentary report of 1826–1827 listed a Roman-Catholic day school in Harold's Cross run by Peter Byrne and Michael Crosbie. The schoolhouse was rented at £22 per annum (and cost £350), while Byrne had an annual income of £23 8s, and Crosbie of £23 16s, all supported by an annual charity sermon and local subscriptions. Furthermore, about thirty of the 240 boys paid 2d per week. When Catholic emancipation was achieved in 1829, the government recorded eleven Brothers residing in Harold's Cross (by now called St Teresa's), ranging in age from 25 to 40 years. In 1830, the teachers were Michael Crosbie and J. Leonard, and the former became the principal of the Harold's Cross National School, which opened beside Mount Jerome in 1833, at which stage St Peter's Free School closed.

In 1833, the Brothers in Harold's Cross started a mercantile academy in the house, a type of secondary/technical school. A parliamentary report of 1835 refers to the Harold's Cross Boarding and Day School, run by Mr Murphy, which catered for thirty-five males, with fees of 10s–15s a quarter, and £20 per annum for boarders. There were a prior and nine Brethren in the friary in Harold's Cross in 1837. Revd N. Donnelly spent a few months here in 1850 learning Latin. In later years, the house became known as St Joseph's Seminary. The seminary continued in operation until about 1878, when the house was returned to the parish of Rathmines. The large old house was demolished, and a new similar-sized house built in 1887, two-storey red-bricked at the front, and three-storey plastered at the rear. Coincidentally, No. 127 Harolds Cross Road was demolished around the same time, and three red-bricked houses were built in 1885, the present Nos 76, 78 and 80. Curates of Rathmines Parish, and later the Holy Rosary Parish, resided in No. 126 (now No. 82) until the 1970s, when it was sold and converted into flats/bedsits.

St Joseph's Monastery in Clondalkin started in 1795 as the Purgatorian Society, becoming a monastery in 1807. The boarding school dates from 1813. They had branches in Harold's Cross, Glasnevin, Clontarf and even Erris (County Mayo). Clondalkin closed in 1939.

ST CLARE'S CONVENT

The primary school was started around 1820. Fr Henry Young, in the first edition of the Catholic Directory in 1821, refers to 'a female day school, lately opened, where eighty children receive a literary and moral education, and are taught industry'. An advertisement for the annual sermon in 1821 in aid of the orphanage refers to a 'day school, wherein the poor children of Harold's Cross and its neighbourhood receive instruction'. Revd Donnelly in his *History of Dublin Parishes* also refers to a girls' school operated by the nuns in 1830.

A parliamentary report in 1835 refers to St Clare's Female Orphan School, with annual funding of £450 from a charity sermon and subscriptions, catering for eighty to ninety average daily attendance, and teaching reading, writing, arithmetic, needlework, and household work.

However, the primary school was officially established on 22 July 1839, and received approval from the Board of Education the following year, at the same time that the girls' section of Harold's Cross National School was transferred from the school beside Mount Jerome to St Clare's. The school had three large rooms, 59ft by 16ft, 34ft by 16ft, and 30ft by 16ft, with the upper storey of the building occupied as a dormitory for the female orphans. The rooms had a capacity to hold 200 children, but only about sixty to seventy were present in 1840. The school operated from 10 a.m. to 2 p.m Monday to Friday, and some of the pupils paid a penny a week.

When the board inspected the building in 1881, there were 166 children on the rolls, ninety-eight present, and an average attendance of ninety (thirty-two boys and fifty-eight girls). An application to the board for the salary for a second assistant teacher was refused, because the average attendance did not warrant it (an average of 105–120 allowed for a principal, two assistants, and two monitors). However, a year later, the situation had changed, and although there were only ninety children present on the date of the inspection, there were 183 on the rolls, with an average attendance of 110 (thirty-eight boys and seventy-two girls), and therefore the board allowed the salary of a second assistant. It should be borne in mind that St Clare's was in direct competition with Marymount School across the road, and also with the national school beside Mount Jerome.

In 1884, the situation had further improved, with 143 children present, 279 on the rolls, and an average attendance of 157 (51 boys and 106 girls), and this warranted a third assistant teacher.

Despite a dramatic increase in its fortunes, the school for some inexplicable reason closed on 16 August 1886, the nuns reporting that the schoolroom was required for some other purpose, although one possibility is that the nuns had reached an agreement with the Sisters of Charity in Marymount. Certainly most of the girls were transferred to Marymount, although the monitor, Kate Healy, was sent to Rathmines National School. However, it would appear that over the years, the school mainly catered for the orphans in the convent, and only a few local girls used it, others presumably opting for nearby Marymount. The following is a list of some of the principals and assistants throughout the school's forty-seven-year existence:

1840

Margaret Leahy (born 1810) – principal – £16 per annum (£20 in 1841)
Mary Leahy (born 1812) – assistant – £8 per annum

1853

Jane Gasson – principal – £22 per annum
Mary Fullem – assistant – £10 per annum
Mary Mulligan – monitor – £4 per annum

1881

Mary Sheridan – principal
Mary Prendergast – assistant
Bessie Dunne (born 1860) – assistant
Mary Forde – monitor.

1882

Mary Sheridan – principal
Mary Prendergast – assistant
Annie Leonard (aged 17½ years) – assistant – £27 per annum

1884

Kate Keogh – principal

Mary Prendergast – assistant – £27 per annum

Annie Leonard – assistant – £27 per annum

Kate Boyle (aged 27) – assistant – £27 per annum

Mary Dillon – monitor

Kate Shortt – monitor

Kate Healy – monitor

1886

Kate Keogh – principal (left 30 June 1886)

Mary Prendergast – assistant (appointed principal on 1 July 1886)

Annie Leonard – assistant

Mary O'Connor – assistant

The Board of Education files show that a total grant of £46 18s 4d was made to the school in 1853, and the amount of the grant in 1857 was £59 3s 4d. Although the salaries were approved by the board, it is possible that the teachers themselves were paid less. Many of the teachers were very young and had no formal training, and this applied to all primary schools. The monitors were in fact the best of the older students, who looked after and taught the younger pupils, although it is doubtful if they ever received payment, and interestingly enough, this practice still continues to the present day in many rural areas. In the case of St Clare's, it should be remembered that the nuns were an enclosed order, and unlike the Sisters of Charity in Marymount did very little teaching, relying instead on lay teachers. Some of the Board of Education archives make very interesting reading, for instance a report in 1872 concerning a very poor teacher, and another in 1874, in connection with a teacher who was dismissed without notice for 'insubordination'. In 1885, there was a complaint that the nuns had retained fees paid by the pupils (local aid was intended to supplement the teachers' salaries), and that for many years, teachers had only received a few pounds as local aid, and had regularly lost a large part of their results fees. The nuns were retaining the money for fuel and school repairs, but agreed with the board to refund £14 13s 8d.

Although the public primary school closed in 1886, presumably the female orphans continued to receive an education. A Department of Education list of approved schools in 1927 includes St Clare's Convent, which received payment under the capitation scheme.

Around 1951, the primary school again opened its doors to the public, and in the mid-1970s, the nuns built a new mixed primary school in the field running alongside Mount Drummond Avenue. The single-storey building currently has 330 children on the rolls.

LORETO NUNS

The Institute of the Blessed Virgin Mary was founded by Mary Ward (from Yorkshire in England) in 1609, in St Omer, France. She also started the Bar Convent in York, England, in 1686. The Irish branch of the IBVM is known as the Loreto nuns, and was started in 1822 by Mother Teresa Ball, also known as Frances (Fanny) Ball. Fanny was born in 1794 in 43 Eccles Street (now No. 63), to a wealthy Dublin Catholic family, and her father John Ball (a convert to Catholicism) was a silk manufacturer. Fanny was sent to school at the age of 9 to St Mary's Convent, Mickelgate Bar, York, as was the practice with many wealthy Catholic families of the day.

Dr Daniel Murray (later archbishop) bought Rathfarnham House with 40 acres in 1821 for £2,300 (paid by Anna Maria O'Brien *née* Ball), in preparation for the founding of the Loreto nuns in Ireland. On 8 August 1821, Mother Teresa arrived in Ireland from York in the company of Sr Baptist (Anne Therry of Cork) and Sr Ignatia (Eleanor Arthur of Limerick), and took up temporary residence for eight months with the newly-founded Sisters of Charity in Stanhope Street, while Rathfarnham House was being prepared. However, the three nuns were anxious to embark on educating young girls, and so they rented a small house adjoining the Poor Clares Convent in Harold's Cross for six months, from 5 May 1822 to 3 November 1822, and here they opened the first school of the Loreto nuns in Ireland. There is no information on the exact house which was acquired, but it was probably the present No. 87 Harold's Cross Road, which had been the Poor Clares Convent when they first arrived in 1804. In the first few days, the nuns received two pupils, but in a short time they had about twelve boarders in the house, including three Skerett girls, two Sherlocks, Ellen Sweetman, Maria Loghlin, Catherine Cashin, Eliza Waldron, Mary Burke, Mary Fottrell, Bidelia Jones, and Mary Fitzgerald. It was here that the three nuns prepared their prospectus for the new boarding school in Rathfarnham, and the fees were to be 35 guineas a year for under-12s, and 40 guineas a year for over-12s. When the nuns and their pupils departed in November 1822, the Poor Clares donated a gold monstrance to them, which the Loreto nuns used until recently in the Loreto Hall, 77 St Stephens Green (a girls university hostel). This monstrance was made in 1720 by Mother Margaret French, one of the first Poor Clares in Nun's Island, Galway, and is inscribed and dated under the base. Loreto Hall closed last year, and the Loreto nuns gifted the monstrance back to the Poor Clares in Harold's Cross.

The magnificent red-brick Rathfarnham House, built around 1725, is three storeys over a semi-basement, and is seven-bays wide. It had been vacant for a few years before the nuns arrived, and required some repairs and alterations (including an extra storey) to make it suitable as a convent, novitiate, and girls' boarding school, all renamed Loreto Abbey. In the next century, many granite extensions were built, including a fabulous chapel around 1840. Loreto Abbey closed in 1999, and reopened in 2015 as a public Gael-Scoil, but the nuns are still involved in Beaufort High School across the road and a girls' Primary School behind the former abbey. The nuns recently built a new convent beside the old abbey, adjoining their old walled cemetery, which contains a high cross in memory of Mother Teresa Ball, who died in 1861.

One of Fanny Ball's older sisters, Anna Maria, married the very wealthy John O'Brien, and became noted for her generosity in assisting a variety of convents. In particular, she became a great friend of Mary Aikenhead, the foundress of the Irish Sisters of Charity. In fact, Mrs O'Brien purchased Stanhope Street Convent for Mary Aikenhead in 1819. Mary Aikenhead served her novitiate in the Bar Convent in York, England, at the same time that Fanny Ball was receiving her education there.

Fanny Ball went on to found a large number of Loreto schools throughout Ireland, and indeed around the world, most of them aimed at middle- and upper-class ladies. However, after her death in 1861, no more schools were founded in Ireland until 1882, when the nuns decided to open a school

1720 gold monstrance presented in 1822 by the Poor Clare nuns to the Loreto Sisters when they left Harold's Cross to open a school in Grange Road, Rathfarnham.

at No. 4, Kenilworth Square in Harold's Cross, and later acquired No. 5. It appears that the school was set up in response to the Intermediate Education Act of 1878. However, the school only stayed here until 1889, after which it moved to Charleville House in Rathmines. The latter was sold to the Louis Nuns in 1912, who now have a large educational complex there.

Archbishop Daniel Murray was instrumental in founding numerous religious orders, including the Sisters of Charity, the Loreto Nuns and so on, and when he died in 1852, his heart was preserved in an urn in Loreto, Rathfarnham, while his mitre and slippers are in the heritage centre in the hospice, Harold's Cross. The archbishop's coffin is on open display, amongst those of the other archbishops, in the private basement of the pro-cathedral. When Loreto Abbey closed in 1999, the archbishop's heart was transferred to the nuns' adjoining cemetery.

Harold's Cross played a small helping role after the Loreto Nuns suffered a tragedy on 2 June 1986. That night the Loreto Convent on St Stephen's Green caught fire, and six nuns died. Their bodies were held in the recently extended mortuary chapel in the hospice until the funeral mass next day in Westland Row church.

HAROLD'S CROSS NATIONAL SCHOOL

Adjacent to the right-hand side of the entrance to Mount Jerome is a single-storey building, used in recent years as a lighting showroom. Around 1833 a small chapel here was converted into a national school.

The first boys and their teacher, Michael Crosbie, transferred from St Peter's Free School (opposite St Clare's Convent), and the latter became a Mercantile Academy.

The Board of Education was actively involved in the school from the very beginning, and they made an initial grant in 1834 of £94 to convert the old chapel into a national school, and a further grant of £20 in 1835 for requisites such as desks, books, and so on. The original T-shaped school was at right angles to the public road, occupying the rear of the site. The main part of the building was 45ft by 19ft 6in, and each of the north-west and south-west wings was about 20ft by 14ft 6in. A photograph taken in the 1860s clearly shows a church-like lancet window in the east elevation of the converted school. One of Lord Meath's maps, drawn at the beginning of the nineteenth century, shows a chapel with a definite T-shaped appearance and what seems to be a porch at the east end. The school operated from Monday to Friday, 9.30 a.m. to 3.30 p.m. In 1834, about a quarter of the boys paid a penny a week, and the school was assisted by an annual charity sermon. At this stage there were 150 boys on the rolls, with an average attendance of 100.

At the time of the initial conversion, the parish priest, Revd William Stafford, converted an upper part of it into lodgings which were rented to the Lenehan family for £5 per annum. When the father died in 1867, the son stayed on for ten years, and had to be paid £10 to leave. The school temporarily closed down in 1876, and the boys were sent to Rathmines National School. A report in the Board of Education files, dated 3 August 1877, stated that 'the 20-inches thick walls were of rubble stonework, with brick dressings around the windows' (no external plaster), and that the slated roof, including the timbers, was in poor condition, and likewise the timber floor. The school had 18ft-high rooms, two wings, and incorporated three old galleries.

In 1878, the school building was demolished and rebuilt by Meade & Sons, utilising the stones from the old school/chapel. The new building was much smaller than the original, being 33ft by 18ft, and 14ft 6in high at the sides, and 17 ft in the centre, occupying the centre of the site, parallel to the road. It had six windows, a fireplace, a front porch that also held the fuel, and two outside toilets, one for the boys, and one with a latch key for the master. However, this school could only hold seventy-four pupils, despite the fact that the average attendance in 1876 was 133, and naturally a dispute arose between the parish priest and the Board of Education regarding the total inadequacy of the new building and its poor finishing. Despite this, the board contributed two-thirds of the final cost of £336.

Not surprisingly, the school had to be extended to the rear in 1886, and the board paid two-thirds of the cost of £273.

A parliamentary report of 1892 recorded that at the end of 1890, there were 224 pupils on the rolls, with an average daily attendance of ninety-two, being taught by two teachers. The government paid £123 15s in salaries, and £37 3s 6d in results fees. The school also received local aid of £7 10s in subscriptions, and £20 11s 7d in school fees.

In order to supplement the teachers' salaries, results exams were held every year, and one exam in 1897 recorded tests in reading, writing, arithmetic, spelling, grammar, geography, music, drawing, algebra, geometry and measurement, although the infants were only examined in reading.

In 1900 there was an interesting enquiry into an assistant who was reprimanded and fined because he was seen in a jeering crowd in Bolton Street on St Patrick's Day 1900, at the lord mayor's procession, in particular jeering at the carriage which held the Lord Mayor of Belfast, and the High Sheriff of Belfast.

By 1906, there were 100 boys on the rolls, with an average attendance of 164, and therefore a new extension to hold ninety-two boys was proposed. It was decided to build a front extension to take up the whole of the playing yard, although it would only accommodate fifty-six boys. The extra classroom and three toilets were built in 1907 at a cost of £431, with the board contributing £287. Thereafter, the schoolboys had to play in Harold's Cross Park, and problems of overcrowding persisted. The following are some of the staff in the early days:

1834

Michael Crosbie (born 1798) – £10 per annum (increased to £12 per annum in 1840, and £15 per annum in 1842)
Jeremiah Ryan – assistant – educated at Central Model School in Marlborough Street

1844

James Murphy – principal

1849

James Murphy – principal – £20 per annum

1853

James Murphy – principal
William Corbally (born 1805) – assistant – £11 per annum

1859

Myles O'Reilly (born 1830)
Thomas O'Callaghan (born 1840) – assistant – £17 per annum

1863

Myles O'Reilly – principal – £38 per annum
James McArdle – assistant – £18 per annum
Two monitors at £4 per annum each

1885–1887

James Devine – principal
Thomas O'Dea – assistant – £35 per annum
Michael Fitzgerald – assistant – £35 per annum

1887

Thomas Macuana – principal (left 1891)
John Gallagher – assistant (left 1892)

1892

Denis Sheerin – principal (born 1870, left 1909)
Pat McDonnell – assistant
John Quinn – assistant
Eugene Byrne – assistant – £56 per annum

1895

Denis Sheerin – principal
Two assistants and two monitors
Tim Sexton was assistant in 1893–95. He trained in 1891–92 in St Patrick's
College, Drumcondra (he was born in 1866 in Clare)

1904

Denis Sheerin – principal
Three assistants and two monitors
Mr Quinn resigned as assistant, and was replaced by Tom Kennelly

1907

Denis Sheerin – principal

Patrick Stack from Kerry, assistant from October to December at £56 per annum, in addition to a residual capitation grant of 5 shillings per head per annum

1910–1930

W. Cooke – principal

1931–1937

Patrick Sheerin – principal

Harold's Cross National School had a girls' section from the very start, which lasted up until 1840, at which stage it transferred to St Clare's Convent. The Board of Education files for 1834 record that the girls' section was previously a chapel built of limestone and brick, with a slated roof and two rooms, 25ft by 25ft, and 25ft by 17ft. There were 120 girls in that year, although the average attendance was 148. The school operated Monday to Friday from 10. a.m. to 3 p.m., and religious classes were held on Wednesdays from 3.30 to 4.30. Some of the pupils paid a penny a week.

The first mistress in 1834 was Mary McMahon, who received £10 per annum. She was replaced by Anne Tobin in 1836 and Mary Anne Coote in 1837, all at £10 per annum, which was increased to £12 in 1840. The mistress in the girls' school was earning the same salary as the master (principal) in the boys' school, although it should be noted that there were no assistants in the girls' school.

When Harold's Cross became a separate Catholic parish in 1935, the decision was made to build a new national school in Clareville Road, on land bought from the Carmelite nuns in Mount Tallant Monastery. The old national school only catered for boys, but the new school, which opened in 1937, had separate boys and girls' sections, sharing a large hall. In 1973, the hall was extended, and an art room was also built. The hall is nowadays hired out during evenings and weekends for local sports and social clubs.

By 1988, the boys and girls had amalgamated into the boys' section, leaving the girls' section empty for many years.

Patrick Sheerin continued on as master from the old national school, followed by Tom Forde, Paddy Allen, Sean McManamon, and now Bernadette Kehoe from 2002 (the first female principal). Famous teachers along the way included Michael Noonan, TD (1963–1965), Tony McMahon (accordion player) and Sean O'Siochain (associated with the GAA and Gael Linn).

Following a recent first-floor extension, the school has about 296 pupils on its rolls, with boys generally outnumbering girls. The school roll books (registers) are kept in the principal's office, and go back as far as 1865. There is also an exam roll book of 1878.

The empty girls' section of the school was acquired in 1993 by Scoil Mológa as a mixed all-Irish primary school (Gael Scoil), and they have about 230 pupils on their rolls. Some of their pupils go on to Scoil Íosagáin and Scoil Eoin, two linked all-Irish secondary schools on the Stillorgan Road in Booterstown.

After 1937, the old school building beside Mount Jerome was used by the Catholic Church as a youth club for about twenty years (nicknamed the 'Old Stew House'), and later on, the Passionist Fathers ran another youth club called Aquarius. For the past few decades, the building has been used as a lighting/electrical showroom.

ANGLICAN NATIONAL SCHOOL

Just to confuse matters, the Anglican Church also ran a national school from the basement of their church, on the left-hand side of the entrance to Mount Jerome Cemetery. This was established as a private school around 1840, closing probably in the early 1890s. On 13 August 1895, the school reopened as the Mount Jerome National School under the control of the Board of Education, with Revd Askin as manager. It operated from Monday to Friday, 10 a.m. to 2.30 p.m., with religion every day from 2.30 to 3 p.m. During an inspection on 21 January 1896, it was recorded that there were twenty-one boys and eighteen girls present, with an average of twenty-five boys and thirty girls on the rolls, the majority being Anglican, but including five Presbyterians and one Methodist. A plan of the basement at that stage showed that there was a kindergarten under the chancel and four rooms under the nave, although the north-east one was reserved for an engine for the church heating. The boys had a separate playing yard and an outside toilet adjoining Mount Jerome Cemetery, whereas the girls' yard was on the side adjoining Mount Argus Road. An internal staircase linked the kindergarten area to the vestry behind the altar in the church above. It was also reported that there was a three-month epidemic of German measles and whooping cough among children in Harold's Cross, Kimmage and Terenure. The following were some of the teachers:

1865

Alex Shepperd – master
Miss Beatty – mistress

1881

Miss Suzanne Beatty (born 1852) – mistress

1895

Ed Foxe (aged 27 years) – principal at £44 per annum plus percentage of results fees. He had three years' training in the Church of Ireland Training College, Kildare Place

1896

Ed Foxe – principal
Frances Warren – assistant
Isabella Henchy – work mistress
Frances and Isabella were not paid by the board because there were not enough pupils

1900

Alice Burge – assistant at £39 per annum

1904

Elizabeth M.P. Ribton – assistant

1915

Thomas Brady – principal

1919

Mary Tyner – retired as second assistant

1925–1930

Ed Johnston – principal

Because the records were lost, nothing further is known about the school until about 1970, when Miss Ina Rogers is listed as the principal, assisted by Margaret Kingston, looking after forty pupils. Around this time, Rathgar National Schools, which had separate boys and girls' sections, had lost their two principals. A decision was taken to close the Mount Jerome School, and thirty children (nineteen boys and eleven girls) transferred to Rathgar in 1971, where the boys' and girls' schools amalgamated, all under the new principal, Ina Rogers, and the assistant principal, Margaret Kingston.

Rathgar National Schools were built by the Methodists in 1896 at the corner of Rathgar Avenue and Winton Avenue, although they had actually started in two rooms attached to the hall of Rathgar Methodist church in Brighton Square in 1879. Over the past century the schools have catered predominantly for Anglicans, Presbyterians, Methodists, a few Catholics, and a sizable number of Jews, until the latter opened Stratford College in Zion Road in the mid-1950s. Even in the early days of the schools, many of the pupils came from the Harold's Cross area, despite the presence of the Mount Jerome School. Today the school is the only Methodist primary school in the Republic.

After 1971, the basement of the Mount Jerome School continued to be used as a Sunday school for religious education, and also as a youth club, including ten-pin bowling.

In Harold's Cross, we have a perfect example of how the government failed to integrate Catholic and Protestant children in the primary education system. On the one hand, you had a spacious basement under a Protestant church that always had a low attendance, while on the other hand, the Catholic school about 50 yards away was cramped and overcrowded, and constantly building extensions.

MARYMOUNT (OUR LADY'S MOUNT)

The main three-storey school building was built in 1851, shortly after the Famine, at a cost of £1,900, partly offset by a donation of £500, and was topped off at roof level with a very large statue of Our Lady. The school was obviously much too large for a semi-rural locality, and it was in direct competition with the national school at Mount Jerome and the national school in St Clare's Convent. In the early days, the school was financed by donations, and also by charging the pupils a penny a week. By 1882, the nuns had decided to avail of the scheme operated by the Board of Education whereby the government paid the salaries of teachers and provided grants for building works, repairs, desks, in addition to providing free school books. The nuns agreed to abide by the rules and regulations of the board, and in theory were supposed to be non-denominational. In that year, it is recorded that the school had seven rooms but only two were used, one 39ft by 29ft by 14ft high for mixed infants, and the other 50ft by 30ft by 14ft high for junior girls. On the date of inspection of the school by the board in 1882, there were twenty-nine males (infants) present, and 114 females, although there were 228 children on the roll books. Up to then, the school was operating on donations of £87 per year, and school fees of £26 per year (a total of £113), and eighteen children were educated for free. Twenty-five of the children had formally been in St Clare's Convent School. School hours were from 10 a.m. to 12 noon, and from 1 p.m. to 3 p.m.

In 1884, only two of the seven rooms were occupied, and the board requested the nuns not to display 'holy pictures' and crucifixes during secular education. By 1885, the nuns had negotiated with the Board of Education for a generous capitation grant of 12 shillings per head per annum.

A parliamentary report of 1892 records 646 pupils on the rolls, with an average daily attendance of 291, under the control of eight teachers. In the previous year, £354 14s 1d had been received from the government, including £177 in capitation grants, and £101 19s in results fees. Our Lady's Mount also received £28 in local subscriptions, and £56 14s 4d in school fees.

In 1895 two extra classrooms were built, and in 1898 the Board of Education granted £1,000 for bringing these classrooms into use and improving toilet facilities. The rear external fire-escape staircase was added in 1928, but was used as a regular staircase.

Marymount, 1st Class, 1950. (Courtesy of Sisters of Charity)

Marymount School, *c.* 1950s. (Courtesy of Sisters of Charity)

The 1916 Easter Rising did not go unnoticed by the nuns in the hospice, as recorded in their annals:

> Easter 1916, the rebellion of Dublin, the school was closed for a week extra. A bullet was shot through library window, through partition into the hall. 800 loaves of bread were distributed by the school sisters to those suffering from the effects of the rebellion. Miss Rose Timmons, senior teacher, was arrested as suspect and imprisoned in Richmond Barracks for 12 days; nearly all the children were ardent admirers and earnest followers of the martyred leaders of the rebellion. Mr Pearse (shot 3rd May) had been a kind friend to our school and gave the children a day's outing at his place 'St Enda's College' in summer 1914–1915. R.I.P..

A later annual reported that the bullet had in fact hit the picture of Mother Mary Aikenhead which was hanging in the hall, and this was never repaired. Richmond Barracks was in Inchicore, but was later demolished and replaced by St Michael's Estate.

On 12 November 1920, there was heavy rainfall all day, and that night the Bohernabreena dam burst, with the waters rushing down into Dublin, resulting in severe flooding and damage in Marymount School and Greenmount Lane. On 4 September 1931, the school was flooded again, with up to 7ft of water in the basement classrooms. The floodwaters continued across the field in front of the school, and then flooded the new houses on Greenmount Avenue. The original line of the River Poddle was in fact under the school, and no doubt this was the route of the flood waters.

In 1929 the primary school certificate was introduced by the new government of the Irish Free State, putting primary school (national schools) education on a more structured footing. In 1932, the first government-sponsored medical inspection took place in Marymount, lasting three weeks, when cards for free dental treatment were given to deserving pupils (probably for the Children's Dental Hospital in Cornmarket, beside John's Lane Church), in addition to free spectacles (probably available in the Eye and Ear Hospital on Adelaide Road).

In 1935, a separate single-storey, over-hall infants' school was built, and this was recognisable by the lantern lights on top of the flat roof.

Marymount pupils, at hospice gates, c. 1950s. (Courtesy of Sisters of Charity)

This time the basement was built of thick reinforced concrete, strong enough for any future flooding.

A 'secondary top' was started in 1962, using four new 'prefabs' (prefabricated timber buildings) in the empty field behind the school, and the first batch of girls sat the intermediate certificate in 1965. The 'secondary top' was still officially part of the primary school, with girls receiving an extra three years' education on top of the primary certificate.

With the introduction by the government of free secondary education in 1967, the nuns decided in 1968 to convert the old primary school into a secondary school, and then provided an additional six prefabs in the rear field for use as a primary school. The previous year saw the retirement of Sister Magdalen Azevedo.

The archives of the Board of Education record that the nuns themselves engaged in all the teaching in the early years, and never employed lay teachers, although in later years a variety of lay women assisted in the school.

The year 1977 was very distressing for the pupils, as the secondary school closed without warning (this school having been in existence for only ten years), and 132 girls had to search far and wide for any school which might have a vacancy. The primary school was now based in the flat-roofed infants' school building, and closed in 1980, with the space then leased for fifteen years to St Michael's House (a voluntary organisation providing support for people with intellectual difficulties) at a rent of £15,000 per year. The secondary school building was demolished in 1981, and the only memento is the huge statue of Our Lady, which in July 2001 was positioned on the ground as a permanent fixture in front of the old convent building. In 1994, Dublin City Council culverted (piped) the original line of the River Poddle, which used to flow under Marymount School, years after the school was demolished. The oratory was demolished in the year 2000, and the infants' school in recent years. Part of the old school site is now occupied by a new hospice building, following the closure of the original building from 1888, and the rest of the site is now a large car park for hospice staff.

SCOIL ÍOSAGÁIN

The Christian Brothers started a primary school in 1949 at Aughavanagh Road, off Parnell Road (beside the Jewish cemetery), and it is still in use today, having changed very little. The Brothers, who always wore a long black soutane (dress) and carried a thick leather strap to punish the boys, are all gone. Many musicals were performed by the children in the hall, especially in the 1960s. The teaching of the accordion was a speciality of the Brothers. Sundrive Park (Eamon Ceannt Park) was used for playing Gaelic football.

When free secondary education was introduced in 1967, the Brothers built a three-storey monastery in their adjoining derelict field, and then commenced building a single-storey school (Colaiste Caoimhin) on a phased basis over the next five to ten years, which means that when the first batch left after five years, the building was only half finished. Woodwork and metalwork classrooms were incorporated in the first few years. The residents of Harold's Cross and Crumlin funded the school through bingo and a 'buy a brick' scheme, although presumably the government part-funded the project. The bingo was held every night in the primary school hall and in most classrooms throughout the school via a public-address system, the brainchild of the principal, Brother Kenny. The first principal of the secondary school was Brother Kelly.

Scoil Íosagáin tin-whistle and mouth-organ band in 1957. (Courtesy of Scoil Íosagáin)

Colaiste Caoimhin closed in June 1994, and was sold to a property developer in December 1995 for IR£1.26 million (a high price at the time), after which the school was demolished and the site covered with blocks of medium-rise apartments called Swanward Court (eighty-nine units). A swimming pool was built at the end of the 1970s, but this was sold and a block of apartments built in 2005, including a car lift to the basement. The monastery was sold in 1995 to the St John of God Brothers, who operated a mental-health facility for some years, but they recently sold the property, which now awaits redevelopment.

SMALLER SCHOOLS

Mrs O'Reilly operated a French and English School from Longford Row (near St Clare's Convent) in the early part of the nineteenth century. Around this period, Mrs Taylor operated a Protestant school for sixteen pupils, while Ms Monks had a school with seventeen pupils, and Mrs Ebbs had another school for twenty pupils, all in different houses around Harold's Cross.

Mrs Wood operated a 'seminary for young ladies' at 7 Upper Clanbrassil Street in the 1870s, in the same house where James Joyce's mother, Mary Jane Murray, lived for a period.

8

OUR LADY'S HOSPICE

Mary Aikenhead was born in Cork in 1787, her mother being a Catholic (Mary Stacpole) and her father a Protestant (Dr David Aikenhead). Her father at one stage was a member of the United Irishmen, and concealed Lord Edward Fitzgerald as a fugitive for a short time in his house. He converted to Catholicism in 1801, shortly before he died, and Mary Aikenhead followed suit in 1802, making her First Holy Communion and Confirmation in that year.

Mary trained as a nun in the Institute of the Blessed Virgin Mary in York, England (known as the Bar Convent), from 1812 to 1815. Meanwhile Dr Daniel Murray (later Archbishop of Dublin) had acquired an orphanage in North William Street, Dublin, and he put Sister Mary Augustine (the religious name Mary Aikenhead took) in charge. There was also a day school there, and in addition the nuns started to visit the poor in their homes. Prior to this, because of the Penal Laws, most nuns joined enclosed orders, and there was no such thing as 'walking nuns', that is, nuns walking around in public dressed in their habits. Thus, the Sisters of Charity started in 1815. Mary's sister, Anne, joined the order in 1823, but died in 1828.

In 1834, the nuns purchased the Earl of Meath's mansion in St Stephen's Green, and extended the house to create St Vincent's Hospital, which opened in early 1835, and was the first hospital in Ireland to be owned and run by nuns, with the assistance of Dr Joseph O'Ferrall. Now a modern office block housing the Permanent TSB Building Society headquarters occupies the site, following the transfer of the hospital to Elm Park, Merrion, in 1970.

The nuns continued to expand and open schools and hospitals in different parts of Ireland, but by 1845 Mary Aikenhead's health was declining, and she decided to move the motherhouse and novitiate from

Stanhope Street in Stoneybatter to a healthier location in Harold's Cross. She purchased Greenmount House in that same year and changed the name to Our Lady's Mount. The names on the title deed were Mary Aikenhead, Helena McCarthy, Isabella Tallenave and Mary Clifford. This was Mary Aikenhead's ninth foundation, and comprised nine nuns and twenty novices. The property in Harold's Cross was once known as Blackberry Parks, and the three-storey-over-basement residence was possibly erected around 1815/20, since it appears to be marked on Duncan's map of 1821, but not on Taylor's map of 1816. It seems that Joseph Robinson Pim bought the house in 1831, and he probably named it Greenmount because of his ownership of the adjoining Greenmount Spinning Manufactory. James Henry Webb, another Quaker, purchased the property from a Thomas Pim in 1845, but only retained it for a few months. At that stage, the property comprised just over 6 acres, and included the Mill Race (fed off the River Poddle), but there was no gate lodge.

Interestingly enough, Mary Aikenhead's friend from Cork, Cecilia Lynch, had entered the Poor Clares in Harold's Cross, so Mary was no stranger to the locality. Cecilia's religious name was Sr Mary Ignatius, and she died in 1846.

By spring 1846, Mary Aikenhead had built a three-storey rear extension, 60ft long by 24ft wide, comprising a chapel, refectory (dining room), and twelve rooms for novices (the misnomer 'cells' was used), for use as the novitiate. The original parlour had been turned into a temporary chapel when the nuns had bought the house, and this was now set aside as a night classroom for the factory girls in the locality. The classroom soon proved to be too small, and so the new refectory was set aside as the classroom, and the original parlour became the refectory. The completed accommodation comprised Mary Aikenhead and a small community of nuns, in addition to twenty novices.

The year 1859 saw the completion of the big chapel near the rear of the convent, although Mary Aikenhead died the year before. James Beardwood was both the architect and the builder. The south cloister, St Anthony, was added to the chapel in 1907. The church is a fine granite building, with polygonal stonework pattern, and features a lovely stained-glass rose window over the altar. Many of the other windows consist of hundreds of pieces of circular glass panes (bullion), each about 75mm in diameter and set in lead cames. The marble altar was purchased with the 100 guineas that Archbishop Daniel Murray left as a special bequest to Mary Aikenhead when he died in 1852. Above the altar there are a variety of statues carved by the Farrell brothers, including Christ washing St Peter's feet, St Stanislaus, and St Joseph. Up until 24 April 1970, five years after the Second Vatican Council, the priest had his back to the congregation and stood on a podium, but the steps are now gone, and the altar has been moved out into the middle of the sanctuary. The ornate cornices around the altar are noteworthy, including figures of different birds. The nuns had their individual wooden kneelers and separate wooden seats on both sides of the nave, on a slightly raised floor.

It would appear that the Sisters of Charity, who ran a blind asylum in Portobello House, originally intended to build a home for blind females in Harold's Cross, because the architect, Charles Geoghegan, designed a large building for the Harold's Cross site in 1861, but this scheme obviously never proceeded. However, within a few years, the same architect designed the Merrion Asylum for Blind Females, which opened in 1865 and is still going strong.

In 1879, one of the novice nuns working in St Vincent's Hospital on St Stephen's Green was infected with smallpox, which she passed on to fifteen other novices in Harold's Cross. Luckily they all survived, but this prompted the nuns to move the novitiate to Mount Saint Anne's in Milltown. The resultant vacant space in Harold's Cross was converted by Mother Mary John (Anna Gaynor) into a small hospice with nine beds, in order to provide comfort and care for dying patients. Up until recent decades, most people usually referred to it as 'the hospice for the dying', in the knowledge that anyone who entered was never discharged.

The nuns were also engaged in visiting sick people in their homes, and took pride in gaining converts to the Catholic religion – this part of Dublin had many Protestant churches. Converts were sometimes gained inside the hospice wards, when people were on their death beds.

It wasn't until August 1888 that a new purpose-built hospice was completed at a cost of over £11,000 (including a very generous donation of £8,000 from Charles and Catherine Mary Hamill). The architect was William R. Byrne, and the building contractor was Richard Toole. The front is ashlar-granite faced, with limestone dressings around the windows and porch. The rear elevation has a facing of less-expensive yellow-clay bricks.

Large wards were provided on the ground and first floor, and dormer-window-style accommodation for domestic staff and nurses at attic level. The projecting west wing was called the Hospital of St Charles Borromeo, in memory of the Hamill benefactors.

The 1881 Census recorded thirty-one nuns and thirty-three patients (twelve of them men). The 1901 Census records that there were ninety-nine patients in the hospice (thirty-nine men and sixty women), all Catholics, with a wide variety of ages, minded by thirty women. By 1911 the census recorded fifty-two nuns and eighty-eight patients (thirty-three men and fifty-five women). The figures for nuns probably includes lay nurses and domestic staff.

In the year 1910, another 13 acres of land was acquired from the Greenmount Spinning Manufactory as additional pasture land for the cows (the fields to the rear of the present St Joseph's). The hospice was run as a farm from the start, and even fowl and incubators were mentioned in the annals for 1922, while in 1928 a small electric motor was installed in the dairy for the churn and separator. The gate lodge was also built in 1910.

The small mill pond was bought in 1914 and is now the site of the grotto. The brick façade of the convent was plastered over in 1915. Electricity was introduced to the hospice in 1909 and central heating and a lift followed in 1933 (central heating in the attic dormitories was installed in the mid-1950s).

In 1935, the rose garden was laid out near the chapel. The farm got a major investment, with the building of deep-litter timber hen houses and a cow parlour for the milking cows – a 'byre for kine' is the quaint description in the annals. New pigsties were built beside the latter. No doubt the pony's accommodation was not neglected. That year also saw the building of a new laundry and equipment, and a new boiler and yellow-brick chimney stack, all for £8,000. The chapel saw a variety of alterations, with mosaic floor tiling laid in the sanctuary (complete with the shield of the congregation), and the Communion rails moved and curved, after removal of the wrought-brass infill. The organ gallery was extended forward, so that patients' wheelchairs could be accommodated, and the front balustrade replaced with the former Communion rail brasswork. New stations of the cross had been provided in 1932 by Earley of Upper Camden Street.

During the Second World War, the nuns built air-raid shelters and put wire mesh and cellophane on the windows. In fact, in January 1941, German bombs fell (accidentally?) in Terenure and on the South Circular Road, resulting in about twenty broken windows in the hospice, but no casualties.

During the war years, the Sisters of Charity took charge of St Patrick's Infant Hospital, in Temple Crescent, Blackrock, which was founded by Miss Mary Cruice in 1910 at 50 Middle Abbey Street, and then called St Patrick's Guild. Much of the work involved adoption of illegitimate babies. The nuns in Harold's Cross, in particular Sister Mary Gaulbert and Sister Mary Collette, were heavily involved and recorded the adoption of eighteen babies in 1945. The new parents were given a 'dowry' of £20 for their kindness.

During the centenary celebrations of 1945, it was recorded that 19,000 people had died in the hospice in the period 1883–1945, and this gives some idea of the huge turnover of patients, many only staying for a few days or a few weeks.

The main hedge-lined hospice avenue was widened in 1947 so as to accommodate more funerals. Up until then, only the hearses of private patients were allowed to exit from the avenue on to the main Harold's Cross Road. The majority of patients had to exit via the back entrance alongside Greenmount Court, on to Greenmount Lane/Avenue, and then on to Harold's Cross Road. Originally Greenmount Lane cut through the hospice grounds, possibly as a back entrance to Mount Jerome House in bygone times, but it seems that the nuns never brought coffins directly from the hospice into Mount Jerome Cemetery, even though the big green gates are still in the boundary wall, to the south-west of the main building.

St Michael's Nurses Home was opened in May 1948, including the enclosed arched bridge linking it to the main hospice building (originally Greenmount Lane ran under this bridge), thus releasing more accommodation for domestics in the attic dormitories.

St Joseph's Geriatric Centre, including sixteen private rooms, was designed by Mr Griffiths and built by W. & J. Bolger at a cost of £150,000. It was officially opened in 1961 by Mr McEntee, minister for health, and catered for short-stay elderly patients, thus partially ending the stigma of the 'hospice for the dying'.

In the 1960s, the hospice had a soup kitchen for homeless men in a small detached prefab to the east of the convent. At certain times of the day, a stream of men tramped up the hill for a simple but very welcome meal. There was also a hospitality suite to the left of the main convent, where parcelled loaves of bread were discretely given to needy people in the locality. Sr Joseph Declan, who came to the hospice in 1953 as a social worker, was in charge of the foregoing – she died in 1969.

In the late 1960s, various small extensions (usually sitting rooms) were added to the front of the old hospital, and in later decades a variety of rear extensions were also provided. In the 1990s, new buildings were constructed nearby, with the single-storey Caritas Palliative Care Centre on a very large scale being opened in 1993. This centre has its own small chapel, including a few lovely boxed panels of stained glass. A special exercise pool was opened behind St Joseph's in 1997. A large modern restaurant was opened for the benefit of visitors and relatives of the patients. 'Cashel', the pet Labrador, roams freely amongst the patients for therapeutic purposes.

At the rear of the hospice, the original sombre mortuary has been modernised and extended, and now has two distinct rooms, St Bridget and St Columba. Gone are the original wheeled beds with their marble mattresses and pillows. Carpeting, comfortable seating and soft music are now provided, and two boxed stained-glass panels enhance the new wing.

St Vincent's Hospital in Nutley Lane has now been handed over by the Sisters of Charity to the government, and the provincialate moved in 2002 to a new single-storey building at the rear of the hospice. Nearby is the two-storey education centre, built in 2007, which includes a fine lecture theatre.

Building work started in May 2004 on phase one of a new 100-bed extended-care unit directly in front of the old hospice. The flat-roofed former infants' school was demolished in 2008, and phase two built on the site. This new facility is called Anne Gaynor House in memory of a former nun. The old hospice building now lies substantially empty, but hopefully it can be remodelled for some useful purpose.

Work has recently commenced on a rear thirty-six-room palliative care unit with a budget of €20 million, to replace the old arrangement of shared accommodation. Also, in the front field, Focus Ireland, founded by Sister Stanislaus Kennedy of the Sisters of Charity, is currently building a small estate of thirty-one houses and apartments for the homeless.

Nowadays, the hospice has reverted to its core activities of hospice and hospital care. Farming activities were phased out in the 1970s and 1980s, and likewise the girls' primary and secondary schools, releasing more land for healthcare. There are still a few fields left, which no doubt will be utilised for more buildings in the next few decades. The River Poddle, which flowed along the west side of Marymount Infant School, under the bridge at the top of the avenue, into a small mill pond and then into the Greenmount and Boyne Co., was culverted in the 1970s to facilitate new buildings and alterations.

One might wonder how such a large organisation as the hospice survives financially, and in fact, the Health Services Executive (HSE) pays most of the bills, with additional funds being provided by the Voluntary Health Insurance (Vhi), donations and bequests. In recent years, a small amount of additional revenue was generated by the provision of a giant Christmas tree in front of the hospice in December, and the hundreds of electric candles are sponsored by individuals.

In the early years, various wealthy women financed Mary Aikenhead's developments. Miss Matilda Denis funded works to the North William Street Orphanage and Stanhope Street Convent. Mrs Barbara Verschoyle funded the acquisition of Sandymount Convent. Sister Francis Teresa O'Ferrall provided the £3,000 necessary to purchase the Earl of Meath's mansion in St Stephen's Green. In 1840, £3,000 was donated by the family of Mother Lucy Clifford. Mrs Elizabeth Redington paid for Clarinbridge, County Galway. Mrs Anna Maria O'Brien (*née* Ball) of Mountjoy Square and Rahan Lodge, Tullabeg, County Offaly, was a lifelong friend of Mary Aikenhead, and provided an income of £100 per annum. Anna Maria's younger sister, Fanny Ball, founded the Loreto Sisters in Rathfarnham in 1822. Fanny also opened a school in St Stephen's Green, a few doors away from Mary Aikenhead's Hospital (St Vincent's). However, it appears that some day-to-day funding in the early years was provided by the general public, spurred on by thousands of 'begging letters', personally handwritten by Mary Aikenhead, even after she became an invalid at the age of 44 years. One of the biggest sources of funding in the past was the 'dowry' that each novice provided on joining the order. Girls from poor families, without a dowry, would not be given the 'plum jobs' in the congregation, or would become lay sisters (not professed nuns).

In bygone days, the hospice also had voluntary collectors travelling around the country every Sunday collecting money – in 1915 it was recorded that there were forty-eight such volunteers, and they collected £2,200 the previous year. 'Mite boxes' would have been a feature on shop counters for many decades. Garden fetes, carnivals, sports days and annual sales of work were great sources of income.

The fete in 1920, which ran from 8 to 18 July and was organised by some of the school teachers and some parents, realised a profit of £4,000, which was a lot of money in those days. Some of the classrooms were central to the fete: the senior room was used for the 'café chateaux' (seemingly variety artists performed), St Mary's as artists' tea room and dressing room, kindergarten as tea rooms, the second room as ballroom, and the military hut (used by the school) served for the jumble sale. Irish dancing was carried on in the rear playground. The field opposite the school accommodated stalls and amusements, while the bandstand was placed beside the bridge (over the River Poddle). Amusements included hobby horses, mountain slides, swinging boats and so on, and there were also pony and donkey races. 'Mrs P. Gordon of Harold's Cross Bridge plied a motor boat from the bridge to James's Street harbour several times, which was a great success.' Palmistry and roulette were specifically excluded on a point of principle. On 11 July, sodalities from all over Dublin travelled in processions to Mount Argus for devotions to Blessed Oliver Plunkett, and by kind courtesy of the leader and the Fathers of Mount Argus they were allowed to disband outside the gates of the hospice, thus greatly swelling the crowds at the fete. On the second-last evening, there was a grand display of fireworks.

The 1948 Toft Carnival was a huge event, bringing an end to the austerity and gloom of the war years. It ran from 22 May to 22 June and raised £7,000 in aid of the new nurses' home building fund. The annals refer to the various attractions, such as the wall of death, roulette tables, whist drives, Kadir the Indian prince's tent, hobby horses, gliders, bumpers, mountain slides, the ballroom (held 500) with Jim Bacon and his band, the Ceilidhe Hall, jumble sales and golf competitions. There was even an illuminated windmill. For years afterwards, the school hall was called the 'Carnival Theatre', where Myles Breslin ran variety concerts every Sunday night with the artists performing for free, enabling all the profits to go towards the hospice. In the 1950s, Marymount Hall was used for weekly whist drives as a way of fundraising.

In recent years, the Sisters of Charity decided to build a major memorial to their foundress, Mary Aikenhead. This project entailed vacating the original convent building in Harold's Cross, building a modern convent in the hospice grounds, and locating the Mary Aikenhead Heritage Centre in the refurbished old convent, supplemented by a large modern extension. The new convent comprises two detached two-storey buildings called Maranatha and Ard Muire respectively, and some other nuns are housed in parts of the old St Michael's Nurses Home. The museum is devoted almost entirely to the life of Mary Aikenhead, using state-of-the-art audio and visual displays. The ground floor comprises a lounge area, a large display area showing the work of the Sisters of Charity in different parts of the world today, a small cinema, an internal courtyard with a water fountain, a simple oratory, and an art gallery. The latter contains a floor-to-ceiling oil painting entitled 'Taking the Veil', depicting Mary Aikenhead, Bishop Daniel Murray and Jane Bellew, painted by Nicholas Joseph Crowley RHA. This painting was first exhibited at the Royal Hibernian Academy in 1846. Jane Bellew, reputedly related to Henry Grattan, is shown as a beautiful young lady in a very fashionable outfit being received as a novice. Mary Aikenhead commissioned a few other portraits by Crowley. The National Galley has three other valuable Crowley paintings, which are displayed from time to time, the current one depicting a charming group of young ladies. Crowley was a child prodigy, specialising in portraits, especially of the clergy. He died in 1857 at the young age of 38 years, having spent the second half of his life in London. Another interesting and very valuable painting in the art gallery in the heritage centre is entitled 'The Adoration of the Magi', reputedly painted by Crowley.

On the first floor there are modern audiovisual display cases in the form of twelve shop windows, each with specially commissioned miniature wax models of people and artefacts, illustrating the life and times of Mary Aikenhead. A favourite must be the scene of a classroom with children running riot, in the midst of which is the teaching nun, in familiar black habit, with her eyes cast up to heaven! The north-west corner of the old convent at first-floor level comprises the bedroom where Mary Aikenhead died in 1858, aged 71. Among the articles on display in the bedroom and the adjoining room is her iron bed, a revolving round rent table with opening drawers every second space, a large oil painting of St Jerome translating the gospels from Aramaic and Greek into Latin and a fabulous portrait of Mary's benefactor and friend, Anna Maria O'Brien. There is also a cheque for £226 made out on 12 March 1845 to Mr Beardwood, who was an architect/ builder for the Sisters of Charity. The rest of the first floor of the old convent is a small museum containing Mary's bath chair (early wheelchair), an oil painting by Crowley of Mary Aikenhead, a small painting of Mary with her sister Anne, Mary Aikenhead's black trailing choir robe, and Archbishop Murray's lavishly embroidered and embellished mitre and silk slippers. There are marble busts of Mary Aikenhead, Anna Maria O'Brien and Archbishop Murray scattered throughout the centre. The top floor of the development is laid out as two apartments for five nuns, and called Shandon, with lift access. This ambitious project, costing millions of euro, was entirely funded by the nuns' private resources.

Mary Aikenhead is buried in the convent graveyard attached to the former St Mary Magdalen Asylum in Donnybrook, with a tall stone high cross over her grave and public vault. The stained-glass windows over the side altars in the hospice were donated in memory of her. Aikenhead Terrace in the Ringsend area of Dublin also commemorates this remarkable woman. However, we must always remember that the Irish Sisters of Charity was a vast organisation, comprising thousands of brave and dedicated women, all deserving recognition for their own unique contribution to Irish life. Mother superiors who carried on after 1858 deserve special mention, namely Helena McCarthy (1858–76), Anne Margison (1876–1905), Margaret Cullen (1905–09), Agnes Chamberlaine (1909–29), M. de Ricci O'Connor (1929–35), Mary Carew (1935–53), Theresa Heskin (1953–71), Francis Rose O'Flynn (1971–83), Ignatius Fahy (1983–95), and Una O'Neill (current).

The Sisters of Charity also have a large plot in Kilbarrack Cemetery, near Sutton.

On 21 January 2002, the hospice was incorporated as a limited liability company, and now has fixed assets of €80 million and paid-up share capital of €2, with two nuns owning a share each. The assets comprise the buildings but exclude the chapel, heritage centre, new convent, provincialate and fields. There is a varied panel of lay and religious directors, but no representative from the HSE, who provide most of the annual funding. The hospice is now the biggest employer in the area (around 508 workers in total and 300 volunteers), with an annual wage bill of €28 million, nearly 80 per cent of its income. There are now 218 beds in the complex.

The Sisters of Charity received a donation of part of the former Carmelite Convent in Sweetmount Avenue, Blackrock, including a spacious newly built twelve-bed hospice, which took in its first patients in December 2003 and is known as the Blackrock Hospice.

CHILDREN OF MARY SODALITY

The Children of Mary Sodality was started in Marymount School in 1860 by the superior of the hospice, Mother Mary Camillus Sallinave (of Spanish descent), although it was run by Sister Patrick Mooney (known as Mrs Mooney). They held their meetings every Sunday morning in the oratory on the top floor (second floor) of the school, and generally catered for the working women of the locality and further afield. Spring and autumn retreats were held every year, each attracting about 400 women and lasting for seven days. On the final day of each retreat, mass and benediction were held, followed by breakfast in the school classrooms. Each year, at least a dozen young girls were sent from the Dublin Docks to faraway missions, to train or work with various orders or convents usually as lay sisters or domestic staff, never to return again. The sodality was also a recruiting ground for novice nuns.

A marvellous photograph was taken in 1885 in the field in front of the original convent, showing hundreds of Children of Mary wearing their best clothes, with Archbishop William Walsh and a few priests in their midst. Coincidentally, in Feburary of that year Cardinal McCabe had died, and was succeeded by Archbishop Walsh in August.

Sister Mary Spinola Dunphy was in charge from 1906 to 1926, and during her tenure the oratory was built (1910) alongside the school, in addition to the concert hall (around 1920) behind the school, all paid for by the Children of Mary. The hall was extended in the 1950s to provide a proper stage, changing rooms, and so on. Sister Dunphy also started the boys and girls' sodalities, in addition to St Anne's sewing class, which produced many garments for poor people. St Mary Colman Craig was directress from 1926 to 1944, followed by St Mary Bernard Powell from 1944 to 1963. The semi-basement under the infants' school was converted in 1949 into a hall (nicknamed the 'Albert Hall') for sales of work, partly paid for by the Children of Mary because they used the hall for their annual party. Sr Agnes John was in charge from 1964, followed by Sr Elizabeth.

The rectangular oratory was in fact a small church with a capacity of a few hundred, but the tabernacle was empty, except when the monstrance was brought down from the main chapel in the hospice. The entrance and sacristy were at the west end of the building, whereas the altar was at the east end. The stations of the cross were originally white carved plaster, all the work of the artist Gabrielle Hayes in the 1930s, and were donated by Miss Keogh. At a later stage, the stations were painted by the nuns. Ms Hayes was responsible for the plaster carvings on the front of the altar and the unusual life-sized painting of St Bridget which hung in the oratory. She made the carved-marble stations of the cross in Galway Cathedral in the 1960s. Up to the 1950s and '60s, the sodality organised two torchlight processions annually around the hospice grounds, and four daylight processions during which the pale-blue cloaks and white veils were worn.

Because the nuns wanted the land that was occupied by the oratory, the children had their last meeting in the oratory on 29 September 1997, when a group photograph was taken, including Sister Colombiere McCarthy, and their final gathering was at a mass and party afterwards in the hospice chapel on 6 October 1997. It is sad to think that an organisation set up for the benefit of the factory girls in the district, which started off in a small classroom in 1860, and which was the source of many vocations to the Sisters of Charity and other convents, is now nothing but a happy memory. The stations of the cross from the oratory are now hanging in St Jude's church, Willington (near Templeogue), and the other church possessions, such as statues, tabernacle, monstrance, thurible, cruet and other plate were donated elsewhere. It seems that the granite cross and memorial plaque to Father Michael Browne, SJ (died 1933) ended up in rubble when the oratory was demolished in the year 2000. The site of the oratory, together with that of the old school, is now a landscaped staff car park.

1914 postcard of the chapel in Our Lady's Hospice. Note the steps up to the altar and the brass communion railings. (Courtesy of Sisters of Charity)

Ambulance delivering a new patient to the hospice, probably in the 1940s. (Courtesy of Sisters of Charity)

Bread being handed-out to poor people at the side of the hospice convent in the 1940s. (Courtesy of Sisters of Charity)

The hospice with cows grazing in front, c. 1950s. (Courtesy of Sisters of Charity)

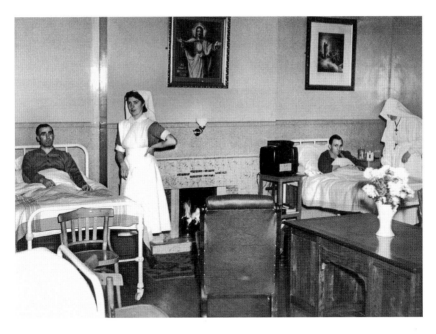

St Anthony's Ward in the hospice, c. 1950s. Note the roaring fire under the picture of the Sacred Heart of Jesus. There were no privacy screens in the wards in those days. (Courtesy of Sisters of Charity)

The official opening of the Caritas wing of the hospice in 1993 by President Mary Robinson, which was blessed by Archbishop Desmond Connell. Ned Ryan, the hospice carpenter and foreman, looks on. (Courtesy of Sisters of Charity)

Valerie Daff, chief physiotherapist, chats to Lord Mayor, John Stafford, at the opening of the new Hydrotherapy Pool in 1997. (Courtesy of Sisters of Charity)

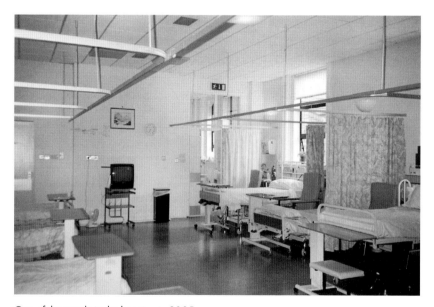

One of the wards in the hospice in 2005.

This beautiful stained-glass window by the Harry Clarke studios adorns the staircase behind the lifts in the old hospice building, and was a gift from the Jesuits when they sold Rathfarnham Castle to a developer in 1985 (the OPW then bought the castle in 1987).

This carved marble altar front sits in St Anthony's cloister beside the hospice chapel, and came from the old St Vincent's Hospital in St Stephens Green (the latter was owned by the Sisters of Charity).

Recent view of Mary Aikenhead's monument in the graveyard attached to the Sisters of Charity convent in Donnybrook.

Mother Mary Aikenhead's original bedroom and office in the Heritage Centre in the hospice. Note the round 'rent table' with actual drawers every second space! The old oil painting on the wall is of St Jerome. (Courtesy of Sisters of Charity)

Recent aerial photo of the hospice, with Mount Jerome cemetery in the background. (Courtesy of Sisters of Charity)

9

MOUNT ARGUS

The story of Mount Argus begins at Longford House, 10 Parnell Square, Dublin, with the birth in 1821 of Charles Reginald Pakenham, the son of the third Earl of Longford, whose country seat was in Tullynally House, Castlepollard, County Westmeath. Charles was an Anglican, and was in the Grenadier Guards in England. His uncle was the Duke of Wellington. He converted to Catholicism in 1850 and joined the Passionists in England in 1855, taking the name Father Paul Mary. The Passionists are an Italian order, and they founded the English Province in 1842, sending missionaries from Italy because of the low level of vocations amongst Englishmen. Revd Vincent Grotti was the superior of the English province in the 1850s, and in 1856 he sent Paul Mary to Dublin to become the rector of the first Irish branch. In August of that year, Paul Mary and a few other priests (including some Italians) moved into a farmhouse called Mount Argus, in Harold's Cross. The ordnance survey house books of 1845 described the house as being 51ft 6in long, 27ft 6in wide and 34ft high, with a basement of similar size but 8ft high, all of good quality. Paul Mary extended the farmhouse by adding on a small church with a capacity of about 600, although this was not recorded by the Landed Estates Court when the property was sold in 1858. Sadly, Paul Mary died in 1857 at the age of 36, but not before he had assisted in a month-long mission in Rathmines Church during the previous November.

The next project was the building of the novitiate, St Paul's College (recently called St Paul's Retreat), which was begun in 1859. Because of a disagreement, the builder, Meade (who built Harold's Cross Cottages) repudiated the contract shortly after commencing, and the priests had to organise and manage other contractors to build the three-storey L-shaped ashlar-granite structure, which was completed in 1863, including the belfry. In 1861, during the building works, the timber scaffold collapsed with twenty-five men on it, resulting in two fatalities – they died in the

Meath Hospital. The brick-vaulted ceilings in the enclosed cloisters are noteworthy, and so are the 16ft-high rooms on the ground floor. At the north-west corner of the monastery on the top floor, there was a lovely library, complete with a balcony around the four sides, with plenty of shelf space, all in pitch pine. Brother Mark Kangley is the artist responsible for the large oil painting of 'The Last Supper', which hung in the refectory on the ground floor below the library. The refectory also had a miniature high-level timber pulpit, where in bygone days the lives of the saints were recited while the priests and novices ate their meals in silence.

Soon the church proved to be too small for the increasing congregation, with Sunday masses on the hour from 6 a.m. to 12 noon, and so the bulk of the present church was built between 1873 and 1878 (although the foundation stone was laid in 1866). There are twin towers at the front, and St Michael the Archangel surmounts the pediment, while at a lower level there are statues of the twelve apostles. The year 1938 saw further improvements when the present sanctuary and transepts were added to the church, and the college was extended by a two-storey structure at the rear so as to form an internal lawned quadrangle or courtyard. In 1945, marble and mosaic tiles were added to the sanctuary. The interior of the church is massive, more in the nature of a cathedral, with accommodation for about 1,500 people, and features some lovely stained-glass windows in the nave (by Mayer of Munich in 1878) and five tall windows behind the altar (installed in 1962 by Earley of Camden Street, Dublin). There is an interesting collection of high-level paintings along both sides of the nave (twelve in total), eight of them the work of Brother Mark Kangley, which were hung in 1889 and depict the life of Christ. The former pulpit, by Pearse and Sharp of Dublin in 1883, includes a sculpture of St Paul of the Cross (the Passionist symbol), carved by James Pearse, the father of Padraig and Willie Pearse. The marble altar rail dates from 1956, and was donated by the men's sodality. Some people might have memories of the 'invisible choir': four high windows along the south end of the west side of the church adjoin the second floor of the monastery, behind which was a small chapel where the priests choir sang, and the music floated down into the church through the window openings. This room was known as the chapter house, opened in 1884, and features a large rose window, a large picture adjoining the chapel, carved-timber pews and wall panelling. On the floor below, the priests had an oratory.

The year 1893 was a sad year for many parishioners, when the original small church was demolished and some people carried away pieces of brick and stone as cherished souvenirs. The original church was situated just in front of the present private cemetery, and the original farmhouse was in front of the present church. The cemetery was laid out in 1893, and the central Celtic cross was erected by members of the Confraternity of the Cross and Passion in honour of Revd Sebastian Keens, who founded the confraternity in 1872 and died in 1890. The cross also commemorates the deaths of Revd Paul Mary Pakenham in 1857 and of Saint Charles in 1893. Attached to the back of the cross is the limestone holy-water font from the first chapel. The confraternity had different branches for men, women, boys and girls, each with a spiritual director, and a number of prefects. The senior men wore habits similar to the black soutane worn by the priests.

The Passionists will always be associated with St Charles (Houban), born in Munster-Geleen, Holland, who had a reputation for piety and healing the sick. He died in 1893 and was originally buried in the adjoining cemetery, although his body was transferred into a lead coffin in 1937 and then moved inside the church in 1949, where his altar in the east transept is now a shrine. There is also a private museum dedicated to his life in the ambulatory around the altar. He was canonised a saint in 2007.

Another priest here in the middle of the nineteenth century, Fr Ignatius Spencer, was related to Lady Diana, Princess of Wales, who died in September 1997. Originally a Protestant, Fr Ignatius became a Catholic in 1830 and a Passionist in 1847.

In 1913, the Passionists organised a monster Ovada bazaar in the RDS (their founder, Fr Paul, was born in Ovada in Italy), which had an Italian theme throughout. This was probably the forerunner of the sale of work, commonly employed by religious orders later in the century as a means of fundraising. The bazaar was so successful that the profits were almost sufficient to clear the entire debt on Mount Argus at that time.

Mount Argus has strong associations with the Garda Síochána (and the previous Dublin Metropolitan Police) ever since their first fortnight's retreat in 1893. The DMP had started an obsequies association in 1897 to provide funds for a proper burial for poor policemen, and this grew into a large fund, which was used to help the Passionists by paying for the front gates from Kimmage Road Lower in 1909 (and widening in 1963), a monstrance in the same year, a marble altar canopy in 1928, St Patrick's Chapel behind the altar in 1938, a lift in 1978, a granite baptismal font in 1979, a new Allen organ in 1993, new rear gates in 1997, in addition to mass vestments and other expenses over the years. Even in the 1960s, the Gardaí marched up Harold's Cross Road to Mount Argus, accompanied by their band, on their way to the annual retreat. On 13 December 1997, the Gardaí celebrated their seventy-fifth anniversary with a mass in Mount Argus. The Garda chaplain is currently Fr Joe Kennedy, a Passionist who is paid directly by Garda subscriptions, and receives a car to assist him in his duties. However, it should also be pointed out that the annual mass for deceased Gardaí is held in Aughrim Street church, Stoneybatter, not far from the Garda Depot in the Phoenix Park. This depot was the former Royal Irish Constabulary (RIC) Training School, and the Catholic constables attended Sunday morning mass at 10 a.m. in Aughrim Street church from the time it was built in 1876. The RIC paid for the original organ (£700 in 1895), and made other generous contributions over the years.

However, the bulk of donations and funding for the Mount Argus church came from the general public of Dublin, who paid for the statues on the front façade, interior statutes, stations of the cross, various lamps, the bells (in the bell tower), the twelve clerestory oil paintings, and even the internal polished-granite pillars holding up the church. So in many ways, the church belongs to the citizens of Dublin, and will always stand as a memorial to their generosity.

In 1920, about 50,000 people walked in procession through the streets of Dublin in commemoration of the martyrdom of Blessed Oliver Plunkett, which ended in front of Mount Argus where sermons were preached, including one in Irish.

Another activity associated with Mount Argus, and famous throughout Dublin, was the saying of the Seven Last Words every Good Friday night. May processions, accompanied by the Artane Boys Band, were also a big attraction.

Patrick Pearse is reputed to have received the sacraments in Mount Argus a few days before the Easter Rising in April 1916.

Opposite the church, up to the 1980s, was a lovely mill pond with a central island inhabited only by ducks, where there was a statue of Our Lady Queen of Heaven carved by John A. Deghini and Sons in 1927. This firm was responsible for a number of other statues inside the church. One of the family members lived in Westfield Road, and another at 20 Parnell Road, where even to this day pieces of marble are unearthed during gardening. Their business was located at 1–3 Lower Exchange Street, having been established in the 1860s. Also opposite the church is the Lourdes Grotto, which was built in 1930 and was once an integral part of outdoor processions. The grotto was recently restored, including a new altar. Likewise, the Calvary is still opposite the church, although in bygone days it was semi-housed in a large structure complete with pyramidal-shaped slated roof.

The Little Sisters of the Assumption acquired some land from the Passionists in 1975, just inside the back gate, and built a new two-storey convent. These nuns started an Irish branch in 1891, at 116 James's Street, moving to 49 Lower Camden Street in 1896. In 1902, they acquired the adjoining house, 1 Upper Camden Street. Their old premises was opposite the famous Bleeding Horse pub, and is due for redevelopment soon.

Originally Mount Argus was a private Catholic church, but in 1974 it acquired parish status, resulting in some confusion since many parishioners of the Holy Rosary church in Harold's Cross now found themselves as parishioners of St Paul's, Mount Argus. However, many people in the locality attended both churches for different events, especially for the men's sodality and retreats in Mount Argus, so perhaps the transition was not so difficult.

In the 1980s, Mount Argus was constantly in the public eye because of problems of dry rot, which started in the roof of the retreat house and then spread into the church roof. The Passionists mounted a major fundraising exercise, and were probably the first in Ireland to use the media to its full extent, netting about £2.5 million for the repairs. These were completed in 1986 and the church was re-dedicated.

Next, the priests applied for planning permission to build an estate of houses on a major part of their farm, in order to enhance its value, and when permission was obtained they sold 18 acres to a house builder for £3.605 million in 1989. Up until this time, the priests had a fine herd of cows, which could be seen grazing in the fields, and the farm buildings were located at the rear of the retreat house. Incidentally, the sport of handball was very popular in the past, and the priests had a big alley beside the farmyard, consisting of three high walls, with no roof. This sport was probably the forerunner of modern-day squash, except that human hands were used instead of rackets. All of the farm buildings were demolished, and 236 houses built in the early 1990s, which now surround the church on three sides. Part of one of the front fields was converted by the builder into a small public park, complete with fountain and storm pond, including a short section of the River Poddle, with the famous 'stoneboat' or 'tongue'.

For many years, the church belfry had a peal of eight bells, which were cast in 1890 by Matthew Byrne Fountain Head Bell Foundry. However, the bells were taken down, probably at the same time as the treatment for the dry rot was performed on the premises, and they now sit forlornly in a rear outbuilding. It would be nice to think that the bells could be hung in some other church, either in Ireland or overseas. The priests also had a carillon of small bells for playing hymns mounted in the belfry over the retreat house, but these were also taken down. Two of these are held in the archives, and were designed to swing (no hammers on outside).

Nowadays religious communities all over Ireland are dwindling, and Mount Argus is no exception, with recruitment at a standstill, the last single ordination having taken place in 1993. The priests still wear the black soutane (dress), including the famous heart-shaped logo.

In 2008, the priests sold the monastery for €2 million and the large front field for €17 million, to a property developer. The field included the land formerly occupied by the Loader Park mill and cottages, which were partly owned by Dublin City Council (see next chapter), so the priests paid the council €1.6 million for their share. The Charitable Commissioners approved the sale of the land on the basis that the priests were going to spend €8.2 million on a new monastery (opened in March 2010), €2 million on separating the church from the old monastery (completed), €2 million on a new monastery in Belfast, and €5 million on projects in Africa. The contents of the monastery were auctioned off in June 2010, including some vestments, priests' missals, brass candlesticks, crucifixes, pictures, furniture and other items. Now the monastery awaits conversion into apartments, and 200 apartments are currently being built in the large front field.

The Landed Estates Court (LEC) sold the property (called Rathland and Flaggerfield) for £2,300 in 1858, presumably to the Passionists, at which stage Revd Vincent Grotti and others (the priests) were yearly tenants of Joseph Byrne at a rent of £143 18s per annum. The court particulars refer to an excellent dwelling house but there is no mention of a new church, which was built in 1856.

Vincent Grotti and others obtained the fee farm grant from the Earl of Meath in 1863, and the freehold was sold to the Monte Argentario Trust in 1980 for £1,000. Revd Vincent Grotti was the superior of the English and Irish province of the Passionists.

The west portion of Mount Argus (called Rathland) was on the Earl of Meath's land, and its eastern boundary was the millpond and the old line of the River Poddle. Most of the present big field, where blocks of apartments are currently being built, was owned by the Protestant Archbishop of Dublin and was called Flaggerfield. Once it had been part of Madgins Farm. Flaggerfield was leased by Goodwin to Anderson for fifty-five years from 1719. When the property was sold by the Landed Estates Court in 1858, James Geraghty had leased it to Joseph Byrne for twenty years from 1842, and there were two subleases, one to Mrs Murphy of a mill pond for fourteen years eleven months from 1847, and another to Robert Stephens, Andrew Walton and William Courtenay for twelve years eleven months from 1850, of a reservoir (supplying water to an adjoining paper mill: Loader Park).

The large field to the south of the driveway, bordering Lower Kimmage Road, was acquired by the Passionists at a later stage. Loader Park was acquired by the Passionists much later – see next chapter.

Postcard of Mount Argus from the beginning of the twentieth century, before the new sanctuary and transepts were built in 1938. (Courtesy of Passionist Fathers)

The famous Hogan sculpture depicting the Ascension, in the former library of Mount Argus.
(Courtesy of Passionist Fathers)

Novices attended lectures on theology and other religious subjects in St Paul's Retreat. (Courtesy of Passionist Fathers)

A special Mass in Mount Argus to celebrate Blessed Charles being canonised a saint, 3 June 2007.

10

MILLS

Archer, in his *Statistical Survey of County Dublin* in 1801, records eight mills in Harold's Cross – one corn mill owned by Mr Hyland, one calendar mill owned by Mr Armstrong (rollers used for flattening linens), two paper mills and one wire mill owned by Mr Cuppaidge, one skin mill owned by Wall Cogan Murphy (possibly rabbit skins), and two corn mills owned by Bermingham Murphy and Co.

The mill books prepared by the Valuation Office in the 1850s record Jonathan Pim as owning Greenmount Cotton Manufactory, comprising 4 acres, 3 roods and 32 perches, with a valuation of £293 (£270 for the mill and £23 for the land). Peter Murphy's flour mill (later the Harold's Cross Laundry) comprised 1 acre, 3 roods and 12 perches, with a valuation of £98. Samuel Figgis had a paper mill at Loader Park, with a valuation of £114.

LOADER PARK

Up until the 1980s, Loader Park (in earlier times called Lowther Park), was a cul-de-sac leading to a courtyard, surrounded by fourteen two-storey terraced cottages, all on the left-hand side of the rear entrance to Mount Argus. In one corner of the courtyard was a four-storey hall with slated roof. This hall was once part of a large paper mill, probably built at least in the early part of the eighteenth century and powered by the River Poddle. This continued as a paper mill until 1870, after which it was converted into a flour mill for Ryan of Kilkenny.

Loader Park Flour Mills were put up for sale on a few occasions in 1874–76. The different auctioneers described the four-storey premises as having been refurbished within the last few years at a cost of £1,000, and having eight pairs of French burr millstones, capable of handling 800–1,000 barrels of wheat a week. The River Poddle fed a turbine with a fall of 18 feet, and there was also a 30hp steam engine. The premises included a house, a gate lodge, three workers' cottages, a mill pond and a chimney shaft. The premises burnt down in 1879.

Fanagans Undertakers bought the former mill and dwellings around 1895, and used the mill buildings as stables for their horses. The Passionist priests bought the mill from Fanagans in 1937, and set up St Gabriel's Boys' Club in the building. Amateur concerts were also held in the hall, and in fact the stage was positioned directly above the River Poddle, which no doubt helped to keep the feet of the dancers cool! The boys' club originated in 1944 from the boys' confraternity (sodality) in Mount Argus church, under the praesidium of the Legion of Mary, and its activities included basketball, football, boxing, leatherwork, boot repairing, library, choir, drama, and an annual holiday (from 1950). The drama section was organised by May Spinks (musicals), Andy O'Loughlin (light opera), and Michael O'Connor (plays), and its first show in 1953 was *The Pirates of Penzance*. When the boys tired of dressing up for the female roles, girls were admitted to the club, thereafter to be called a youth club. Later the club became the Harold's Cross Musical Society, under the control of May Spinks (see section on the Holy Rosary church, p. 49).

In the 1960s, the priests ran the Mount Argus Pools from a house beside the mill building, No. 13, which they bought from Fanagans in 1958. In those days, many charities collected money in this way, which involved placing bets on English soccer matches. Every week hundreds of people paid 1 shilling each, and the results were printed the following week on a leaflet that was distributed to each person by the collectors, who retained a 25–33 per cent commission.

By 1981, planning permission had been obtained to refurbish the dwellings and to build three new houses. However, Dublin Corporation had plans to build a road from Lower Kimmage Road across to the Mount Argus Road via Loader Park, and in 1984 the corporation compulsorily purchased the dwellings from Fanagans for £51,000 and re-housed the remaining weekly tenants in Crumlin. Without any good reason, the houses were demolished in 1984, the land given to the Passionists,

Former Loader Park mill building off Mount Argus Road (beside the Scout Hall), being used by the Passionists. (Courtesy of National Library of Ireland)

and the road plans dropped. Around this time, the mill building caught fire and was then demolished, and a new sports hall of basic architectural quality was built in its place. Nearby is a small granite building called St Paul's Hall, which is still used by the boy scouts.

In 2008, the former Loader Park land and the adjoining large field were sold by the Passionists to a developer, and part of the money was given to Dublin City Council, who had originally purchased part of the site in 1984. A developer is currently building 200 apartments on the site, and recently excavated the stone foundations of the historic Loader Park Mill and workers' cottages.

Loader Park was sold in two lots in 1857 by the Landed Estates Court (LEC), and the court particulars provided very interesting information. Lot 1 was described as the upper mills of Loader Park, originally in the possession of John Anderson, a millwright. A deed in the Registry of Deeds records a lease for fifty-five years from 1719, from Goodwin to Anderson, at £60 per annum, noting that the previous occupier was Maurice Coffey. Roque's map of 1760 shows a corn mill here.

The LEC particulars go on to say that Hugh Kerr was the next occupier after John Anderson, followed by George Cuppaidge, Laurence McDonnell, John Cahill and Daniel Laffan (paper manufacturers), Daniel Laffan (paper

manufacturer), and lately Charles Lett. These people were obviously
subtenants, since Griffith's Valuation in 1850 records Samuel Figgis as
the tenant of Richard John Hicks.

The property was bought from the LEC by Walton Stephens and Co. and
it is interesting to note that Robert Stephens, Andrew Walton and William
Courtenay held a sublease of a reservoir on the adjoining Mount Argus
property for twelve years and eleven months from 1850.

The LEC was selling the property with title commencing at a lease for 999
years from 1836, from Percy Lorenzo Harvey to Joseph Martin, at a rent
of £160 per annum. The lease required the tenant to insure the property
against fire for £1,000 and also to spend at least £500 within two years
on repairing the building, machinery and fixtures. The list of machinery in
the mill was very extensive, including a newish 30hp high-pressure steam
engine, a newish 40hp high-pressure steam boiler, a 60in Fourdrinier
paper machine, a breast-shot waterwheel (16ft in diameter, 2ft 10in wide),
and another breast-shot waterwheel (22ft in diameter and 10ft wide).
The breast-shot waterwheel would have received water from the River Poddle
at mid-height, unlike the more efficient later models, which were overshot
(water came in from the top). The combination of water and steam power
meant that the mill was self-sufficient, even if the River Poddle ran low in the
summer. The mill was capable of producing 1 ton of paper a day, suitable for
newspapers and printing. There were two large ponds, one to supply water to
the waterwheel, and the other used as a settling pond for the sludge arising
from paper making, in addition to a much smaller filtering pond.

Lot 2 was a few hundred yards away, comprising a 3-acre field, bounded
by the present Sundrive Road on the south and on the east by the
River Poddle. This field was called Loader Park (in the past, fields were
called parks) or Tongue Field, because of the presence of a thirteenth-
century 'tongue' dividing the River Poddle in two at one corner of the
field. Sundrive Road was called Park Lane in those days, although in the
eighteenth century it was called Dark Lane. This field was described as once
having a windmill. It was let in 1857 to James Carroll, market gardener,
on a yearly tenancy at £18 per annum, and title derived from the same
lease as Lot 1, of 999 years from 1836. Carroll in fact bought the field from
the LEC for £280, although Dublin Corporation retained a right of way to
the city watercourse (drawing water from the River Poddle at the 'tongue').

Both lots 1 and 2 were never part of the Earl of Meath's estate, although one of the mill ponds was on the Mount Argus land without any formal lease or title. Tongue Field is now covered with the houses around Sundrive Park, including the old Apollo Cinema, which was demolished in 2003.

Note:

After the Famine, the Encumbered Estates Act 1849 was enacted to sell off estates (small and large) with heavy debts or bankrupt. Further acts of 1858 and 1859 created the Landed Estates Court, which operated until about 1879.

The Representative Church Body Library is in possession of a rough map dated 1714, drawn by 'Gab Stoakes', showing a plot of land 4 acres in size owned by St Patrick's Cathedral. This stretched from the present Mount Jerome entrance to the recent Loader Park, between existing old mills, and corresponds with the wedge of land between the present Mount Argus Road and Lower Kimmage Road. The map has a little sketch of a two-storey mill at Loader Park, called Mrs Carr's Mill (Kerr's?), and a larger two-storey L-shaped mill near Mount Jerome with no name, both with waterwheels.

THE GREENMOUNT AND BOYNE LINEN COMPANY

The biggest employer in the locality in the nineteenth and twentieth century was the Greenmount and Boyne Linen Co., near the canal end of Harold's Cross, but set back a few hundred yards from the main road. There was a corn mill on this site, called the Wood Mills, being leased by the Earl of Meath, firstly to George Spence from 1691 and later by Frederick Falkiner of Abbotstown from 1760. In 1807, Joshua Fayle leased the property to James Greenham, who built a cotton mill that later became known as the Greenmount Spinning Manufactory. Greenham did a lot of business with Thomas, Joseph and Jonathan Pim of 22 South William Street, cotton merchants, and obtained a mortgage from them. Greenham got into financial difficulties in 1814 and the Pims foreclosed on the mortgage, taking over the mill.

It is interesting to note that the Pims also purchased corduroy from the Richmond Bridewell, on the opposite bank of the Grand Canal, from as early as 1820. This was the output of some of the prisoners who operated handlooms.

Joseph Robinson Pim became involved in the company in the 1830s and installed power looms, thereby reducing the workforce from 300 to 150. A large proportion of the workforce comprised girls in the 13–18 age bracket. The River Poddle drove the huge 22½ft in diameter and 11ft wide waterwheel, which revolved 4½ times a minute and had a fall of 19ft, while providing 25hp for nine months of the year, and 12hp for three months of the year. By the late 1830s, there were steam and water power in the mill capable of driving 100 power looms and 6,000 spindles. A boiler house with tall brick chimney provided the necessary steam, utilising the plentiful supply of water from the ponds.

Additional land was acquired and various extensions were added over the coming decades, including a four-storey brick building built around 1860/1865. By virtue of a lease dated 1861, Jonathan Pim, William Harvey Pim and Thomas Pim were leasing all of the mill land from Elizabeth Fayle of Leinster Road (widow of Joshua Fayle).

An 1876 trade directory has an entry for the Greenmount Spinning Co. – cotton spinners and cotton-and-linen manufacturers of damasks, drills, ducks, towellings, plain linens, and so forth. Their products over the years included bedsheets, tablecloths, white linen suits (for the British in hot climates) and chauffeurs' liveries (uniforms).

In September 1890, the women went on strike, with the weavers demanding 4 pence (4d) per cut, the right to join a trade union, and the abolition of the system of fines (a week's pay kept by the company). There was another strike over pay in December 1936. The average weekly wage then was 25s for a forty-eight-hour week, but it was still based on output. For example, the company paid the women 4s 11d for weaving 50 yards of waste twill sheeting, which usually took 1½ days.

In June 1899, there was a big fire in Greenmount, causing £2,000 worth of damage. Luckily for the 400 workers, both the Dublin city and Rathmines fire brigades were able to put out the fire, using water from the millpond. In 1946, there was another fire in the weaving shed. At that time, Mr Chambers was the manager.

In March 1916 (during the First World War), Pims converted the staff football pitch into twenty allotments for growing food, charging the workers a penny per week. Each plot was 30ft wide and 30 yards long.

In 1922, the Greenmount Spinning Co. was put into liquidation and closed with the loss of 600 jobs (mostly women). An attempt to sell off the machinery by auction was stopped by the workers, who occupied the buildings and erected fortifications and sandbags. The *Freeman's Journal* of June 1922 contains two very interesting photos of the striking workers.

In December 1922, the Greenmount Spinning Co. was acquired for £25,000 by the Boyne Weaving Co. of Drogheda to create the Greenmount and Boyne Linen Co., although at this stage there was no Pim involvement. However, the Quakers maintained an interest in the business, since Senator James G. Douglas was a director from 1931, and then chairman, before he died in 1954. Many people will be familiar with his family business, Douglas of 17–19 Wexford Street, which started in 1925 and specialised in bedsheets, tablecloths and so on. The Greenmount & Boyne Co. continued in business up until 22 October 1965, when the Dublin operation closed down with the loss of 120 jobs, and the property was bought by Cross Properties Ltd in 1968 for £80,000. However, the linen company continued its operations in Drogheda until 1976, and even retained a showroom in Harold's Cross. In Drogheda, the different departments were: spinning, making-up, weaving, bleaching/dyeing/finishing, H-department, wareroom, sizing and drawing-in. The shifts were now 7 a.m.–3 p.m., and 3 p.m.–11 p.m.

The Harold's Cross buildings were converted into the Greenmount Industrial Estate, nowadays housing a variety of small businesses. Today, the four-storey brick building is a noted landmark. The internal upper floors consist of very thick planks, supported on widely spaced timber beams, in turn supported on slender cast-iron columns. Both edges of the flooring planks are grooved to allow insertion of steel strips between adjoining planks. Original parts of the other single-storey factory buildings are still visible to this day, especially the cast-iron columns supporting timber roof beams, lath and plaster ceilings, stone-flagged floors, and so forth. The factory immediately to the west of the four-storey building has a usable basement, with slender cast-iron columns/beams supporting segmental brick arching. However, pride of place goes to the original mill building at the centre-south side of the site, where many of the old thick stone walls and thick timber-plank floors are still to be seen, although the building is clad externally with modern metal sheeting. The 16ft-high, cast-iron, water-driven turbine that took over from the original timber waterwheel in 1901 to drive the various weaving and spinning machines is still in the basement. This is a double-vortex turbine supplied by Gilbert Gilkes & Co. Ltd, Kendal, England, for £236. The 30hp machine is numbered 1471, weighs 7½ tons, has a 36in horizontal shaft, a fall of 14ft, and a flow rate of 1,512 cubic feet per minute. This building originally had a double-A roof profile, but is now a single A as a result of an attic conversion.

In its heyday, water from the River Poddle played a big part in the operations of the mill, both for providing machine power and for bleaching the brown linens to a white colour. There were two large mill ponds, one on the hospice side and the other on the west side of the factory. The Sisters of Charity bought the former in 1914, and the ESB acquired the other pond in the 1960s, filled it in, and built a three-storey office block and a single-storey archive store.

Even in the 1950s, at least 75 per cent of the workforce comprised women from the age of 14 upwards, operating on a 'piece-work' system – their wages dependent on their output. Generally, men called 'tenters' were employed to repair the looms, although a 'tenter' was actually a cloth-stretching machine using hooks (hence the expression – 'on tenterhooks'). Other interesting job titles were card cutter, mounter, winding master, yarn dresser, yarn slasher, yarn bleacher, yarn winder, warper, cloth picker, drawer-in, cropper, damask mounter, cloth passer, and of course weaver and spinner. The big factory 'hooter' could be heard throughout the neighbourhood, signalling start and finish of shifts and dinner break. In the 1960s the shifts were 7 a.m.–5 p.m. and 5 p.m.–11 p.m., with an extra shift of 8 a.m.–12 noon on Saturday.

The Greenmount Spinning Co. had a staff band called Lord Edward's Fife and Drum Band, and a newspaper report in 1896 refers to the band accompanying the staff (300) outing to Poulaphouca. There was also a girls' gymnastic club.

The Pim family seat was in Mountmellick in County Laois, although they were originally from Leicestershire (England). Thomas and Jonathan Pim came to Dublin around 1785 to serve their apprenticeship in the cotton industry, and by 1800 they had started their own merchant business importing cotton from America and goods from Manchester, which included owning and operating a number of merchant ships. Around 1804, they bought a big house at 22 South William Street in which to reside, and later also acquired No. 23 for warehousing purposes. Even today, this street is still the centre of the 'rag trade' in Dublin.

Another member of the Pim family, Thomas, was involved in the tobacco industry in Tullamore, County Offaly, in partnership with Robert Goodbody, in a firm called T.P.&R. Goodbody, in the second half of the nineteenth century. Following a disastrous fire in 1886, the company moved to Greenville, off Donore Avenue in Dublin, near Harold's Cross. Two of their popular cigarettes were Golden Flake and Navy Cut. The Greenville mill was on the site of Donore Castle and Roper's Rest, and later became the White Swan Laundry – it is now the White Swan Business Centre.

In 1841 Jonathan (Junior) Pim and William Harvey Pim started the famous Pim's Department Store in 75 South Great George's Street in Dublin, on the site of an old army barracks. The store continued in business up until the 1960s. In the early days, some departments of the shop were in nearby Exchequer Street. A bland office block called Castle House was built on the site in 1975.

The Pims were members of the Religious Society of Friends, commonly known as Quakers, and Jonathan (Junior) Pim was the first Irish Quaker to become a member of parliament, serving from 1868 to 1874. Other noted Quakers in Irish life included the Jacobs, famous for biscuits, and the Bewleys, famous for coffee. The Quakers' charitable works included Famine relief in the mid-nineteenth century. Many Pims are buried in the leafy and peaceful Quaker burial ground at Temple Hill, Blackrock, County Dublin, where there is also a small meeting hall. All of the simple limestone headstones are identical, regardless of rank or wealth in life. Despite their small numbers, Quakers were to the forefront of the Industrial Revolution in Ireland.

GREENMOUNT OIL COMPANY

A large part of the site between the Greenmount Spinning Manufactory and Harold's Cross Road comprised a brewery, started around 1867 by Alexander, Perry and Co., brewers of mild and pale ale. The two partners in this venture were Robinson Gale Perry and his cousin William James Perry. Bitter beer could be purchased in 1868 for 1 shilling a gallon! The Perry family were important Quakers from Laois, and their main seat in Dublin was Obelisk Park in Blackrock, in addition to nearby Ardlui House. The Perrys were shareholders in the new Kingstown railway (to Dún Laoghaire), as were the Pims. Some might think it unusual for Quakers to be involved in the brewing industry, bearing in mind their strong support of the temperance movement. The Perry family vault was built in 1844 in Mount Jerome Cemetery, and is reputed to have been designed by the famous architect John Skipton Mulvany because of its similarity (in miniature) to Broadstone Railway Station in Dublin – this contrasts sharply with the standard simple Quaker headstone in Temple Hill, Blackrock.

The brewery changed to the Irish Whiskey Distillery around 1873 and lasted for about twenty years. The *Irish Builder* magazine recorded in 1873 that the conversion of the brewery into a distillery was almost finished. At that stage, the main five-storey building was about 6 years old, built of limestone with chiselled granite dressings around the windows, and was 100ft long and 243ft deep (on average). The floors were supported by wrought-iron box girders. The brick chimney stack was 140ft high. The output was expected to be 270,000 gallons of whiskey per annum. The conversion work was carried out at a cost of about £10,000 by builder S.H. Bolton to a design by E.H. Carson. The main building received new floors for grain lofts, a kiln was provided on the third storey, and millstones were installed on the second storey, driven by engines on the first storey. Copper stills were built at the rear of the main building. There were two stores, each about 100ft long with an average depth of 35ft, one to be used as a bonded store and the other for wash-backs, mash tuns, and so forth.

In 1877, a newspaper reported the death of two men while repairing a vat, because of stale air.

A Belgian by the name of Louis le Brocquy (the famous artistic family) then started an oil-blending business on the site, which operated up until about the 1960s. Louis was born in 1861 in Brussels but worked from 1884 to 1886 in his uncle's business (Schaaff and Maurer in Dusseldorf, Germany), which produced lubricating oils and greases. While on holiday with relatives in Ireland in 1886, he decided to stay here. He set up a similar oil business on Ringsend Road that same year, entering into a ten-year lease, and called the company the Dublin Oil and Grease Works, with home and office at 3 Clanwilliam Place. The business prospered, and Louis needed to expand. He bought the former distillery in Harold's Cross in January 1896, and set about removing the old machinery and equipment, renaming the firm as the Greenmount Oil Co. However, a few months before the Ringsend lease expired, the Ringsend premises caught fire on the night of 3 July 1896 and was burnt to the ground, but not before the safe was rescued. Norwich Union Insurance Co. paid for the damage, though not for the extra stock of oil that had been built up in preparation for the move to Harold's Cross. In the following years, a good-export business was built up, and an office in Liverpool flourished for a few years.

On 1 September 1905, the company was formed into a limited liability company. The managing director was Louis le Brocquy, General Baumont was a director, and his young son, T.R. Baumont, was secretary. The shareholders were Louis le Brocquy, General Baumont, Madame Josephine le Brocquy (*née* Van den Ende), Frau Melanie Maurer, W. A. Dinamore, Francis P. Long, Michael Crowley, Augustine O'Callaghan, Edward Lutman, Robert Dobbyn, T.R. Baumont and J.C. Haselhurst.

The le Brocquys were very fair minded, giving their key staff shares in the company. For instance, Edward Lutman was the esteemed foreman, and he lived in the house beside the oil company at the corner of Greenmount Avenue and the main road. Augustine O'Callaghan was a commercial traveller for the Munster and Connaught regions. Robert Dobbyn was one of the main directors from 1917 to 1944, having worked in the firm for fifty years.

Albert le Brocquy (the father of Louis the artist) became secretary in 1910, at the age of 22, and later became a director. However, the founder, Louis, remained managing director until his death in 1950.

The company had a large export business, including supplying the ships of the British admiralty and the Whitehead Torpedo Works. During the First World War, they also supplied the Russian Baltic fleet with torpedo oils.

Around 1900, the company installed a plant for refining mineral oils known as white and half-white oils, for medicinal liquid paraffin, transformer oils, edible mineral oils for the confectionary and bakery trades, cosmetic oils, stainless oils for the textile industry, turbine oils, and other types of oil.

In 1950, the company had an output of 946 tons, comprising 162 tons of lubricating grease, 373 tons of white oil, 297 tons of lubricating oil and 114 tons of by-products.

In the mid-1950s, the managing director, Noel le Brocquy, was very interested in the recycling business, such as recovery of used lubricating oil (engine oil and others).

Around 1953, Ken O'Reilly Hyland became a director and a small shareholder, but by the late 1960s all the shareholdings had been acquired by his company, Burmah-Castrol. The buildings were demolished soon after this, including the big Jubilee Shed, which was built in 1911.

In the 1950s, a petrol filling station fronted onto Harold's Cross Road, and continued in operation during the 1960s and '70s, and for a while Co-Op Taxis operated from the site.

Boyne Court Apartments and Greenmount Office Park, built in the early 1980s, now occupy the major part of the original oil company site. The north end of the site, with frontages to Parnell Road and Harold's Cross Road, was known as Cherry Orchard as far back as 1837, and probably before, but was never built on until the 1980s, when the two-storey Harmsworth office block was built. The mid-1990s saw the building of duplex apartments in the centre of the site, Harold Bridge Court, finally completing the redevelopment of this area.

Aerial view in the 1950s, with Greenmount Oil Company in the foreground, and the Greenmount and Boyne Linen Company behind. Griffith Barracks is at rear right. (Courtesy of the National Library of Ireland)

View from the Hospice, with the former cow parlour on the right, the former Greenmount Mill in the centre (with doubled pitched roof), and the four-storey Greenmount and Boyne building on the left, 2001.

HAROLD'S CROSS LAUNDRY

A big site at the junction of Mount Argus Road and Lower Kimmage Road, opposite Mount Jerome Cemetery, was occupied by a flour mill for most of the nineteenth century. The Representative Church Body Library has a rough 1714 map, including a sketch of an L-shaped, two-storey mill, with the usual waterwheel. A Lord Meath map of 1787 also shows a mill and waterwheel. The 1850 Ordnance Survey house books contain an interesting description of Peter Murphy Flour Mill, stating that one building was 49ft long, 37ft wide, and 44ft high, while another was 19ft long, 16ft 6in wide, and 44ft high. The 14ft-diameter waterwheel revolved six times a minute, had a fall of 12ft, and powered two pairs of grinding stones, one 4ft 8in in diameter, and the other 4ft 2in in diameter. The mill operated eighteen hours a day for eight months, and ten hours a day for four months.

Sheridan Bell Foundry provided an estimate in 1843 of £175 for a new iron waterwheel being 15ft diameter, 8ft wide, with forty-two iron buckets (each 8ft long and 2ft wide, and No. 9 gauge iron), a cast-iron shaft and seven oak spokes in each side. John Jellicoe was the mill operator in 1861.

This flour mill lasted until 1894, when the four-storey building was converted into a laundry under the management of Mr Elliott, who left near the end of 1896 to start the Mirror Laundry at Dolphin's Barn. Ms Kelso was the next manageress, but went on to found her own famous laundry in Rathmines in 1914. A newspaper report in 1896 records that

George Bryers of Kenilworth Square was the chairman, Mr La Couse Murphy TC was the managing director, and both Mr F.S. Whitney and Mr Trevor N. Smith TC were directors. In the 1920s Nathaniel Smith was a director. The residence (Ashleigh House) was incorporated into the centre of the complex of buildings.

The River Poddle played an important role in providing power for the machines via a waterwheel. A feature article in the *Rathmines News and Dublin Lantern* in 1896 displayed a photo of the laundry, including the waterwheel. A major flood in Dublin in September 1931 caused the Poddle to burst its banks and flood the laundry, with the result that all the clothes had to be washed again. In April 1938, at which stage 150 workers were employed, there was a fire in the laundry, but the business was able to resume within a few weeks.

The laundry had receiving offices around the city, including one at Kelly's Corner (64 South Richmond Street); 50 Capel Street; 109 Great Brunswick Street (now Pearse Street) and 5 Elm Grove (Ranelagh). W.G. Mellon was the manager in 1954. In the 1960s, the laundry was known as Ever New Cleaners, but the four-storey building had been partly demolished by then, retaining only low-rise buildings. The laundry was sold in 1968 for £30,000. Heatovent Heating Suppliers occupied the complex for a period in the 1970s, and then Laurence Court Duplex Apartments were built in the 1990s.

Near the top of Harold's Cross Park there is a rare handkerchief tree, planted by Deputy Lord Mayor Mary Freehill on 20 October 1995 to commemorate the fiftieth anniversary of the laundry workers' strike organised by the Irish Women Workers' Union. This was a city-wide strike of 1,500 women that lasted for fourteen weeks and resulted in all workers (including men and women in other industries) getting a fortnight's paid annual holidays, instead of one week's holidays. Besides the women from the Harold's Cross Laundry, other laundries in the strike included Kelso, Swastika and White Heather. The union was founded in 1911 by Delia Larkin and her more famous brother, Jim Larkin. It will take about fifteen years for the tree to become established, after which it will grow into a very tall deciduous tree and will have most unusual but beautiful white flowers every May. The tree originated in China and is also known as a ghost tree or a dove tree, but its botanical name is *Davidia Involucrata*.

11

BUSINESS

HAROLD'S CROSS BUTTON FACTORY

One of the oldest recorded businesses in Harold's Cross dates from at least 1782, and was a button factory operated by John Lloyd in the vicinity of St Clare's Convent. The nuns' title deeds record that in 1782 John Lloyd, button manufacturer, sold part of his property in Harold's Cross, including Frawley's Field, to Wilmot, who in turn sold it to the nuns (Sister Elizabeth Byrne and Sister Agnes Tommins) in 1804 for £200. By 1794, Lloyd was in partnership with Ridley, operating both from Harold's Cross and 11 East Cole Alley. In the following year the city address was 36 Castle Street.

An apprenticeship indenture dated 1800 between Thomas Curtis of Harold's Cross and John Lloyd of Harold's Cross indicates that the button factory was still in operation, presumably on the remaining portion of the land adjoining the nuns.

Recently, two rare Lloyd & Ridley half-penny copper coins/tokens dated 1794 were sold in England. The edge inscription reads: 'Payable in Dublin or Harold's Cross Button Factory'. One side of the coin has the letters 'L' and 'R' interlaced, and the other has the figure of Justice.

TELECOM ÉIREANN DEPOT, GREENMOUNT LANE

This building, distinguished by its 'north-light' roof, is sandwiched between the Greenmount Industrial Estate and the Greenmount Office Park, and was built in 1951 for W.P. Poole and Co. (changed to Booth Poole in 1955) for their car-servicing department. The company assembled MG and Wolseley cars at their new premises in Islandbridge. In passing, it can be noted that Brittains assembled Morris Minor cars on nearby Grove Road near Portobello Bridge. The Department of Posts and Telegraphs bought the building in 1965, and Telecom Éireann continued to use the building after the Government Department was split into two semi-state bodies in 1984.

In the 1960s, Taylor Signs had some stores and workshops opposite this building on the edge of the Greenmount Industrial Estate, although their main premises was on Grove Road alongside the Grand Canal, where they had started in the 1930s. Recently Taylor Signs moved to modern premises in Dublin 10, and a block of apartments was built on the Grove Road site.

TAYTO LTD

In 1954, Joe 'Spud' Murphy from Dublin started this famous company, manufacturers of potato crisps, at O'Rahilly Parade, off Moore Street. Up until this, crisps were imported and had no flavour. Joe was the first in the world to introduce the cheese-and-onion flavour. In those days, the packet was light brown in colour, with some purple and white tinges, and included the familiar friendly little man, all for 4*d* (old pence).

Tayto moved to Mount Pleasant Industrial Estate in Rathmines in 1956, where they stayed until 1981. They also started a sister factory in 1961 at Tivoli Avenue, Harold's Cross (now PLM Heating & Plumbing Suppliers), staying until 1968, at which stage a modern factory in Coolock had been built. By 1979, extra space was required, so they obtained part of the former Clarnico Murray sweet factory in Mount Tallant Avenue, staying until 2003. From 1999, Tayto Ltd was part of the Cantrell and Cockrane Group, but in 2006 Largo Foods bought the company, and all operation are now based in Ashbourne, County Meath. Irish potatoes (Saturna variety) are still used to make cheese and onion, salt and vinegar and smokey bacon crisps, all for around 55 cents a packet.

In bygone days, the vans from the Tayto factories obtained all their petrol from the nearby Doherty's garage in Harold's Cross (opposite the present Maxol petrol station), and the plastic bags for the crisps were obtained from Bailey Gibson on the South Circular Road, beside Player Wills Cigarettes.

CLARNICO MURRAY SWEET FACTORY

Mount Tallant Cottage (a substantial house, with a gate lodge) was located at the Harold's Cross end of Mount Tallant Avenue as far back as 1837, and probably long before that. By 1882, the house was called St Pancras. Around 1926, Clarnico Murray demolished the house and built a factory called St Pancras Works for the manufacture of sweets, the most notable being iced caramels and macaroons. In 1938, a quarter of a pound of maple brazils could be purchased for 6*d* (six old pence).

The company moved to Deansgrange in 1973 and was taken over by Trebor Ltd in 1974. By 1978, the company was located in Walkinstown, and then moved to Tallaght.

Trebor Bassett is now part of the Cadbury Group, and you can still buy Clarnico iced caramels, mint creams and choc mint creams. Amongst their huge range of other sweets are Maynards Original Wine Gums and Bassetts Liquorice Allsorts.

St Pancras Works was recently occupied by Eurosnax (part of Tayto), and Capco (distributors of suspended ceilings and roof slates), but the building was sold in recent years and demolished in 2016, in preparation for redevelopment.

The detached building fronting onto Mount Tallant Avenue was built in the 1930s for Brown and Polson, manufacturers of cornflour, semolina, baking powder, and even cornflakes. The premises is now occupied by Woodworkers and Hobbies Supply Centre, owned by the Milofsky family who came to Ireland from Poland in 1923. L. Milofsky & Sons Ltd started making quality household furniture in Jervis Lane in 1948, moving to Mount Tallant Avenue in 1957. In 1970, they stopped furniture manufacture, and started supplying the cabinet-making and DIY sector, including a shop near Emmet Bridge (formerly Sweeney's grocery, and now Daybreak newsagent). The shop closed in 1985, and now all retail and storage activities are based in Mount Tallant Avenue.

KENILWORTH LAUNDRY

The Kenilworth Laundry was set up in competition to the Harold's Cross Laundry around 1895, but appears to have lasted for only about twenty-five years. It was located to the rear of the present Kenilworth Motors (on the site of the recently built Rosary Hall), and the lane alongside is still called Laundry Lane. They specialised in handwashing as opposed to machine washing in the Harold's Cross Laundry, and they also had a receiving office at 16 Lower George's Street, Dún Laoghaire. Roger Webb was the manager in 1918.

Kenilworth Motors started on the site of a house called Westfield Lodge around 1960, and was a Volkswagen Dealer for about twenty-five years before it became an Opel Dealer.

HAROLD'S CROSS GARAGE

Harold's Cross Garage was located beside the dog track entrance, and appears to have been the Harold's Cross Furniture Mart in 1900. The Zenith Garage started in 1935, to be superseded by Harold's Cross Garage in 1950, and included the usual petrol pumps near the edge of the road. Ned Murphy operated the business for the next thirty years or so, including an Austin car dealership. T.R. Motors, who service Mercedes-Benz cars, acquired the property in the 1980s, and after a serious fire in 1992 rebuilt the entire premises, squaring off the original L-shaped front. Petrol sales are no longer part of their business.

The garage achieved national fame in 1980, when it featured in the *Live Mike* on Raidió Teilifís Éireann (RTÉ). Mike Murphy was the programme host, and spent his time (disguised, of course) playing practical jokes on unsuspecting members of the public, while hidden cameras recorded the event for posterity. This particular episode was made more interesting, because the owner of the garage was Ned Murphy – Mike's father. Mike, disguised as a Traveller, wanted to test drive a car around the block, and Ned chased him off the premises, accompanied by the usual curses! Earlier, Mike tried a similar stunt in nearby Paddy Walsh Cycles, and Paddy also chased him away.

Murphy and Gunn have been located for many years at the corner of Kenilworth Square and Rathgar Avenue, now specialising in the sale of Hyundai cars and the servicing of BMW, Toyota and Lexus cars.

Petrol could be obtained at the Shell filling station on Parnell Road from the 1960s onwards. Following closure during the recent recession, Applegreen filling station now carry on this type of business.

CLASSIC CINEMA

Some of Elmville Cottages were demolished in 1952 to make way for the 1,110-seater Kenilworth Cinema in Harold's Cross, which opened in July 1953, with Mario Lanza in *Because You're Mine*. The cinema belonged to the Sundrive Cinema Co. Ltd, which owned the Sundrive (built 1935) and the Classic in Terenure (built 1938). When the Classic closed in 1976, the name was transferred to the Kenilworth Cinema in Harold's Cross, and in 1980 the building was converted into two screens by the new owner, Albert Kelly. In the 1950s–'70s, when you went to the 'pictures', you enjoyed two films, trailers of the following week's films and newsreel, lasting about three hours in total, compared with a modern evening out, where only one film is shown.

The Classic was famous for showing the cult film *The Rocky Horror Picture Show* at a late-night screening, every Friday night since 1980. The audience dressed up in fancy regalia, joined in the actors' words, and sometimes threw rice at each other and at the screen! After the show, some of the audience went to 'swingers' parties in different suburbs, which involves partner swapping and were referred to in trendy circles as 'The Lifestyle'.

After fifty years of entertaining the public, the cinema finally closed its doors on 30 August 2003, after screening *Veronica Guerin*, and the building was demolished a few years ago, leaving a vacant site.

In the 1970s, the remaining Elmville Cottages were demolished to make way for the Thorn Lighting warehouse in the rear field behind the cinema, and this is now used as the city 'pound' where abandoned cars are temporarily stored.

Sundrive Road with
a policeman helping
children to purchase
sweets from a vending
machine, c. 1950s.
(Courtesy of
The Stoneboat
public house)

The foyer of the Classic cinema before it closed in 2003. The cashier was on the left.

HAROLD ENGINEERING

Harold Engineering was started by local man, Seamus Whelan, in 1963, in Shamrock Villas, and was engaged in the distribution of garage equipment. In the 1970s–'80s, they started to acquire and amalgamate a terrace of houses on Harold's Cross Road, called Shamrock Terrace (built around 1875) at the corner of Mountain View Avenue, for use as showrooms. One of these houses was the local dispensary in the 1960s. The company was sold in 2007 and moved to Rathcoole, County Dublin.

O'CONNOR'S JEWELLERY

Backing onto the dog track, O'Connor's Jeweller started in Anne's Lane, off Grafton Street, in 1949, and moved to 133 Harold's Cross Road in 1964.

A map of 1853 shows Cannons Lane here, and it may also have been called Maher's Lane at one stage. Locals called it Hell's Lane, because of the poor people's tiny cabins which lined it in the latter half of the nineteenth century. Walsh Building Contractors acquired the property around 1915, although they had been established in 1879, and they remained here until 1960.

Following a major robbery in 1987, O'Connor's Jewellers were nearly ruined, but they carried on until 2010. The jewellers owned a few houses fronting onto the main road, where they had originally planned to build a showroom, but after the burglary they sold it to a developer who built the Park View Court apartments in 1991.

Recently, Dublin Hampers acquired the premises, and R & P Credit Ltd also operate from the building.

ABATTOIR

On the city side of the Grand Canal, adjacent to Emmet Bridge, behind the Harold House pub, there was a slaughter house for cows and sheep in the 1960s and '70s, operated by William Bowers & Sons Ltd. Even in the early 1960s, the animals were driven by stick along the main roads from the outlying farms, and the young lads in Harold's Cross joined in the herding operation. Sometimes the animals would cause chaos, since they had to share the road with cars and other vehicles. Cow dung dropped on the roads provided the local gardeners with free fertilizer, and helped to produce many a prize rose. Gradually big trucks took over animal transport, but you could still watch the unloading operation at the canal-side gates. In 2003, the site of the abattoir extending out to the canal and a plot along the south side of Harold House were redeveloped as a four-storey block of apartments, with a car showrooms on the ground floor (Ken Lawford Nissan cars).

Up near the Classic Cinema, Harpers Butchers slaughtered their cows and sheep on their premises, keeping the animals in the small field behind the shop.

SCRAP-METAL MERCHANT, 31A UPPER CLANBRASSIL STREET

Mullens, the scrap-metal merchant, started around 1950, and is still going strong. Even until recent times, horse-drawn carts from far and wide would trundle in this direction, laden with old cast-iron baths, lead pipes, copper wiring, and so forth. The scrap is accumulated in the large rear yard, and then shipped every few months to Europe. In the early days, Mullens also collected feathers and rags, and had a branch at 23/25 Garden Lane, off Francis Street.

GORDON'S FUEL DEPOT, UPPER CLANBRASSIL STREET

Gordon's has been trading in this location, adjacent to Emmet Bridge, since around 1910, selling all kinds of fuel for the domestic fireplace. In bygone days, coal and turf were delivered by barge, utilising the adjoining Grand Canal. Nowadays, home-heating oil and commercial diesel form a large part of their business.

BANKS

From 1935 to 1940, the National Bank Ltd had a small premises in the house immediately to the south of the present Peggy Kelly's public house (formerly The Greyhound). Otherwise there were never any banks in Harold's Cross, and only in the last few years has a 'hole in the wall' automatic teller machine appeared beside Rosie O'Grady's pub, near the upper end of Harold's Cross, in addition to an ATM inside the Spar shop at Kenilworth traffic lights. Cooneys/Centra Supermarket now has an ATM inside the shop.

BUILDERS

George P. Walsh and Sons Ltd were based at 133 Harold's Cross Road from 1915 to 1960, but were established in 1879 and carried out a lot of church work. Their premises was then occupied until 2010 by O'Connor's Jewellers.

James Clarke of 13 Upper Clanbrassil Street and Wesley Place, also went in for much church work.

BRICKWORKS

Towards the end of the nineteenth century, the Dublin Brick and Tile Co. operated from Sundrive Road at the rear of Mount Argus. At an annual general meeting in 1894, the company reported very good profits, generated by a workforce of around seventy-five.

A company letterhead signed by the company secretary, P. Deey, dated 1918, for the Dublin Brick Co. Ltd, lists brickworks at Mount Argus, Dolphin's Barn, and Rathnew in County Wicklow, and offices at Dolphin's Barn. The large Rathnew Brickworks closed the following year. The yellow colour of the Dublin brick is well known, with the modern St Mary's church (Anglican) in Crumlin being a good example, and likewise the former Player Wills cigarette factory on the South Circular Road, near Dolphin's Barn.

After the company ceased trading, the huge clay pits were the scene of many accidental drownings before being filled in with household refuse from the 1930s onwards, and Sundrive Park was created in the 1950s. In recent years, Sundrive Park was renamed in honour of Eamon Ceannt (Kent), a signatory of the 1916 Proclamation, who was based in the

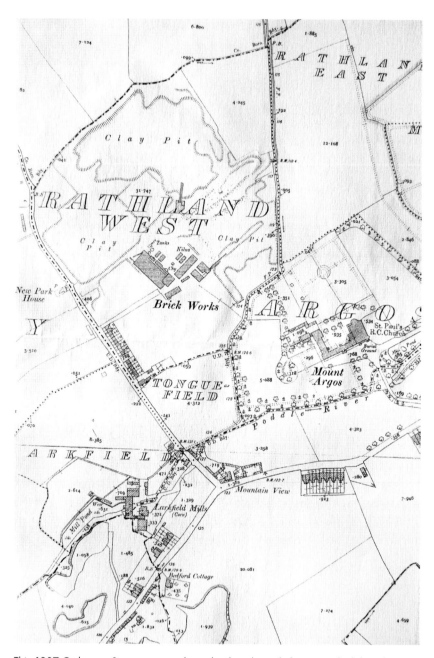

This 1907 Ordnance Survey extract shows brickworks and clay pits, which later became a household waste dump, and was then covered over to create Sundrive Park (now called Ceannt Park). Larkfield Mills was on the site presently occupied by SuperValu Shopping Centre. (Courtesy of Trinity College Map Library)

nearby Larkfield Garrison (a disused mill). The park extends to 42 acres, and includes an athletic track combined with a cycling track/velodrome.

A small patent brickworks operated in the 1870s where Harold's Cross Cottages were later built.

GREYHOUND TRACK

On Tuesday and Friday evenings (there were three meetings per week in the past), Harold's Cross is crammed with punters visiting the greyhound racing track, which was opened on 10 April 1928 on an 11-acre site known locally as Butterly's or Buckley's Orchard. Harold's Cross was the second track in Ireland, the first being Shelbourne Park, which opened the previous year, while the first track in England (Manchester) only opened in 1926.

There was much controversy in the beginning, and the local churches objected on moral and religious grounds. Sir Simon Maddock, the chairman of Rathmines Urban District Council, was involved in the initial sale of the site, although he died in 1927. Two houses were demolished to make way for the main entrance.

The Dublin Greyhound and Sports Association Ltd was behind this venture, and the initial subscribers were John J. Flood from Blackrock, Walter Butler from Percy Place, and Edward Teehan from Dalkey. A lease was entered into for ninety-nine years from 1931, and the company acquired the fee farm grant (nearly freehold) in 1969.

Bord na gCon, a semi-state company, purchased the stadium in 1970, and a new grand stand was completed in 1978.

The year 2000 brought major changes, with the sale of excess land for housing and the opening of an extended and modernised new grand stand in September 2001 by the taoiseach, Bertie Ahern. Now there are two bars, Dobbin's 126-seater restaurant, a café, and two corporate boxes, all spread over three floors and linked by lift, in addition to a new 150-space car park at the south end, and a separate indoor parade ring and dog kennels, all costing £6.6 million. Patrons can now operate handheld 'totalisers' and watch the race on individual computer screens while enjoying their meal in the restaurant.

A night out (admission charge is €7) comprises ten races at fifteen-minute intervals, each with six dogs running an average distance of 575 yards in

Recent photo of the greyhound track, with O'Connors wholesale jeweller's on the right.

an anti-clockwise direction. The dogs are so fast, reaching speeds of up to 60kph, that the average race is usually over in half a minute! Modern tracks are made of loose sand, and a mock hare travels along a metal rail.

The world's longest-running television chat show, the *Late Late Show*, had an interesting connection with the dog track. The show owned a greyhound, not surprisingly called Late Late Show, which ran and won on 2 February 2001, while at the same time setting a new course record.

The most famous dog associated with the track was probably Spanish Battleship, which won three successive Irish Derbies, two of them at Harold's Cross, between 1953 and 1955.

Harold's Cross track is destined to be sold and probably redeveloped as apartments and houses.

The greyhound racing industry in Ireland in 2014 attracted 644,000 people to 1,736 meetings, with prize money of €7.4 million. Most of the dogs are individually owned by part-time owners/trainers.

Shelbourne Football Club ('Shels'), which started in Shelbourne Road, Ringsend, in 1895, were based here for a few seasons in the 1970s and 1980s, utilising the large green area in the centre of the track, although their home ground is now Tolka Park in Drumcondra. Other soccer clubs also used the grounds in earlier decades.

The Leinster Motorcycle Dirt Track Races were held on the dog track in 1928, and the event was captured on British Pathé News. The video is available on their website, with views of the brand-new grandstand, the motorcycles and riders, and clouds of dust.

MISCELLANEOUS BUSINESSES

Burke Brothers occupied 119 Harold's Cross Road from the 1960s to 2003, specialising in artificial-flower wreaths, much needed in Mount Jerome Cemetery.

Bosonnet and Sons had a jam factory at the west end of St Clare's Avenue in the 1960s, producing beautiful aromas in the immediate neighbourhood. If you collected enough empty jam jars, you could return them to the factory for a free pot of jam.

D.D. O'Brien, floor-tiling specialists, set up in 1953, moved to Harold's Cross in 1965, where they continue to thrive.

W. Kavanagh & Son operated from 12 Dame Street prior to the 1920s as gun and rifle manufacturers, and their gun-fitting ranges were located at Larkfield, Kimmage, where there was plenty of open space in which to practise. They also held clay-pigeon shooting tournaments there.

Twinem Bros (who were Quakers) ran their business of druggists and mineral-water manufactures from the big house and rear factory at 121 Harold's Cross Road (now No. 92) at the corner of St Clare's Avenue, in the opening years of the twentieth century, but later operated from 31 Lower Clanbrassil Street and 66a South Circular Road. J.C. Kenna, manufacturers of vinegar, sauces and mineral waters, carried on a similar business from the Harold's Cross premises in later decades. The double-fronted house was converted into bedsits in the 1960s.

PUBLIC HOUSES

Up until the late 1960s, women rarely frequented public houses, and pubs were 'men only', being generally dingy, sometimes with sawdust on the floor. More often than not, pubs were only a corner of a much larger grocery shop, as is still the custom in some rural parts of Ireland. General economic improvements heralded the 'lounge bar society', as the clergy denounced it from the pulpits, and gradually pubs and lounges became more attractive and comfortable, and women are now well able to 'knock back the pints'.

Many of the pubs in Harold's Cross were listed as grocers originally, although it is probable that most of them also had a small drinking area. The main road through the village had (and still has) more public houses than many towns in Ireland.

The Grove Inn on Grove Road alongside the canal was called Union Tavern for many years as far back as 1875, when a row of houses along here was called Union Place. Now demolished, it has been replaced by a block of apartments.

The Irish House beside Emmet Bridge was called Lloyds in the 1930s, and O'Looney's in the 1940s, '50s and '60s, and was listed as grocers, tea, wine and spirit merchants from 1875 onwards. The pub derives its name from a very famous pub called the Irish House, once located at the bottom of Winetavern Street (the present free-standing corner column of the civic offices). A picture in the lounge in Harold's Cross showed the original Irish House with all its external ornamentation. In July 2003, the pub reopened as O'Looney's Irish House, but the property was demolished in 2005, and apartments/townhouses built on the site.

The three-storey public house opposite the hospice entrance was owned by the Walsh family from 1928 to 1948, and before that, the Mahers operated a pub/grocers from about 1899. In 1946, the Walshes changed the pitched roof to a flat roof, and plastered the original red-brick façade. The Carroll family bought the pub in 1948, changed its name to the Lantern Inn in 1969, and retired in 1993. The pub changed hands a few times after that, but is now closed and unused.

Peggy Kelly's, beside the dog track, was a grocer and spirit dealer in 1870. From about 1878 to 1895, it was called the Royal Oak Tavern, although that name was also referred to in eighteenth-century descriptions of the locality. From 1931 to 1953, the O'Dwyers operated the pub. The Flanagans bought the property in 1953, and changed the name to the Greyhound in 1960, and only in recent years have they changed the name to Peggy Kelly's (the owner's mother's name). The three-storey section was probably rebuilt about 1907 (as were the adjoining two private houses), and the opportunity was taken to extend the pub out beyond the original building line, and to absorb the tiny front garden.

McGowans was owned by Mahers for many years in the early days, except for a break from about 1900 to 1918, when McKennas owned it. An advertisement in 1938 refers to 'Mahers, Wine and Spirit Merchant'. Originally the pub occupied only the second building from the corner, but about 1946 the corner shop was acquired to make a larger public house. The year 1948 saw the emergence of Marrons pub, complete with sawdust on the floor, and well known for back-room poker sessions! From 1977 to 1985, it was called Kenny's Park Inn, and in the 1990s became the Inn in the Park, run by the Ramsbottoms from Stradbally in County Laois.

The single-storey McGarry's, opposite the top of Leinster Road, was rebuilt in 1997, and operated as Quinn's. In the 1830s, there was a large police station approximately on this site, but this was replaced around 1875 with a pub and a house called Abbey View, the latter set back from the road. Initially William Maher occupied the premises as a grocer's and pub. Longs then occupied the premises for many years, and they also owned Longs pub in Donnybrook village, the latter still going strong, although recently turned into a trendy 'watering hole'. Healys acquired both pub and house in 1929. Kierans changed the name to the Leinster in 1982, and for many years after the pub attracted a rugby football clientele. The adjoining house was demolished and apartments built in 1994.

Three-storied Rosie O'Grady's was called Park House, and was owned by William Cahill from about 1890 to 1929, after which Doherty's acquired it. The original premises was smaller, but was rebuilt three-storeys high in 1899. Even though Langan bought the premises in 1941, the name Doherty continued in use until 1985 (because of family connections). Rosie O'Grady was the name of a popular American song at the turn of the nineteenth century, and this name was used after 1985. Nowadays the pub is the favourite of people 'up from the country'. The Doherty family started the adjoining garage around 1940, and it operated for about forty-five years, after which it was converted into a few small shops, including a launderette.

The Harold House at 34–35 Upper Clanbrassil Street has a licence going back at least to 1840. Frank McKenna owned it from about 1887 to 1915, and then the Maher family until 1930. From 1900 to 1918, McKenna also owned the Inn in the Park, thus having the distinction of owning a pub in Dublin city and another in the Rathmines township, within a few hundred yards of each other! There must have been family connections, since the Mahers owned The Park Inn for a few generations.

Opposite the Harold House is the vacant Man of Achill, previously called The Poplars, which is reputed to be the oldest pub in the area, dating from about 1760, and it was once called Ye Olde Grinding Young. Flora Mitchell's painting of the front, including the landlord's two dogs, is owned by the National Gallery. When the property (listed as 30 Upper Clanbrassil Street) was sold in 1873, the auctioneer referred to recently erected malting stores, lofts, cistern, kiln, and so forth at the rear, capable of making sixty barrels of malt a week. The premises included six houses to the rear of No. 29, known as Doyle's Court.

Beside the Man of Achill was Cyril McDermot's pub, recently called McKenna's. Part of the film *The Quare Fellow*, bases on the play of the same name by Brendan Behan, was shot here in 1961. Nowadays, the premises operates under the name MVP (Minimal Viable Pub), a café during the day and a pub after 4 p.m.

The Cat and Bagpipes was leased in 1734 from Challoner (a brewer) to Middleton (a tallow chandler), and was situated in Barbers Land, possibly a predecessor of either the former Lantern Inn opposite the hospice entrance or Flanagan's/Peggy Kelly's beside the dog track.

The *Hibernian Journal* of 1772 reported: 'the Magistrates are requested to inspect the house known as "The Sign of the Dusty Miller" at Harold's Cross, where every Sunday is spent in dancing, drinking and rioting by a set of wretches of both sexes, who render the passing of the roads dangerous to the peaceful who pass that way'.

SHOPS

The heart of every town and village is its collection of shops, and in Harold's Cross, these lie between the top of the park and the Rosary church. Well-known names on the west side in the 1960s were Farren's butchers, Marguerite drapery (Lawlor's), Kilmartins turf accountants, Anne's newsagent, The Magnet sweet shop, Concannon's bakery, and Murdock's hardware (the latter was actually on Shamrock Terrace). On the east side, beside the former Protestant girls' orphanage, was Healy's grocers, until it closed only a few years ago. It had started here around 1948, although there was a shop in this location as far back as 1860, operated variously by Somers, Palmer, Winnifred Doyle, Moore, Matthews, and O'Connor, until Thomas Healy took over. Cooney's grocery and off-licence traded from 1935 (but was built as a shop in 1893), although it was recently modernised and now trades under the Centra banner. Gowran's grocery was on the east side of the road, but also operated a butcher's on the opposite side, famous for barbequed chickens on Sunday and homemade spicy hamburgers. Long before BSE (mad-cow disease) was ever heard of, Gowran's specialised as a pork butcher's only. Opposite the top of the Park in a very old three-storey building was Paddy Walsh Cycles, which started around 1960 (his brother, Kevin, was the local chimney sweep before the advent of central heating in the 1970s), but was demolished and rebuilt as a shop in 2006, with two floors of apartments overhead. In previous generations, Corrigan's was a famous grocery shop, located between the present T.R. Motors and Peggy Kelly pub.

Further up Harold's Cross Road, the single-storey Deveney's grocers and off-licence was demolished in 2004. A little further up, at Kenilworth traffic lights, partly on Rathgar Avenue, the 1908 corner building (Kenilworth Buildings) was once occupied by Lennon's confectionery, but is now a Spar supermarket.

An interesting sweet shop in the period 1925 to 1940 was 'Corners', where Flynn's florist is now, opposite Mount Jerome Cemetery, owned by the Corner family and appropriately sited at a corner! The Punnet florist occupied the shop in the 1940s, '50s and '60s. Just to confuse matters, in the 1950s there was a shop at the junction of Westfield Road and Lower Kimmage Road, called The Corner Shop, run by two sisters of the famous Eamon Ceannt (Kent), as a sweet shop and lending library, but nowadays Fanagans Undertakers have a funeral parlour here.

Near Mount Jerome, in the former Hall Electrical Wholesale, there was a shoemakers called Mooney's, where most people had their shoes 'soled and heeled'. Nowadays people throw away their worn-out shoes, but perhaps in the future 'recycling' might be an alternative, as is currently happening with bottles, cans, paper, clothes and other items. The adjoining forge for horseshoes was still busy in the 1950s, and was later replaced by a two-storey house.

Paddy Walsh Cycles was demolished a few years ago and replaced by much taller offices.

The shops at Emmet Bridge, including Galtee Dairy, Delaney's Cycles, O'Daly's tobacconist, Millington butchers, Salmon barbers, and Sweeneys grocery, 1967. (Courtesy of Dublin City Libraries and Archives)

At the corner of St Clare's Avenue, Broe Headstones had its workshop and front yard, although a new shop was recently built on the site. There was previously a house here called Peachmount. Adjoining is Siopa Linn, a small builders' providers, previously occupied by Balmer's Sweets. A long time ago, the house was called Hollymount.

McCauls Pharmacy (The Medical Hall), with its distinctive chromium plated-steel shop front, at the corner of Greenmount Avenue and Harold's Cross Road, traded from 1948 to 1995, taking over a previous pharmacy. Much business was conducted with the adjoining hospice, but nowadays there is an insurance broker in the building, and the hospice has its own in-house pharmacy. Nearby No. 48 was, for many years, the Beehive sweet shop, and before that, O'Loughlins. The four shops along here, and the eight semi-detached houses in Greenmount Avenue, were built in 1928–30 by the Rathmines Public Utility Society, allowing workers to buy their homes over a twenty-year period at moderate weekly rents – the yearly rent was £52, which included rates and outside repairs by the society.

Towards the upper end of Harold's Cross there were two pharmacies, Walsh's and O'Connell's, the latter being the first in Dublin to start late-night opening in the 1970s. Now only Hickeys Pharmacy remains.

Hayes Conyngham and Robinson (HCR) had a large chemist shop at Leonard's Corner, at the corner of the South Circular Road and Upper Clanbrassil Street, from the early 1960s until the mid-1980s. Before that, they had a branch on the other side of the traffic lights at 54 Lower Clanbrassil Street, which was opened in 1910. Leonard's shop was built around 1860, near the junction of the two roads, and was a general store, selling groceries and hardware. Misstears Medical Hall (chemist) was built on the corner in 1900, and therefore, in different periods, the road junction was known as Misstears Corner and Leonard's Corner, the latter title surviving to this day. Louis Mushatt trained in Misstears chemist, and then went on to establish his own famous chemist shop in 3 Francis Street – KK was the brand name for his concoctions, which Dublin wags interpreted as Kill or Kure! Citron was another Jew who operated as a chemist from about 1936–1944 at 81 Lower Clanbrassil Street.

No description of Lower Clanbrassil Street would be complete without mentioning 'three brass balls' – the symbol of the pawnbroker. Kilbrides, and before them Langans, had operated as pawnbrokers from No. 53 for over a century. Pat Carthy was the owner in 2001, but alas, this pawnshop is now gone. When someone wanted a small loan, the pawn shop provided the money, taking a valuable article as security – often a gold wedding ring, or a good watch, and even suits and good household items. The article could be redeemed when the loan (with interest) was repaid in one lump sum. If the loan was not repaid, then the article was sold at a city-centre auction room, and the pawnbroker made a good profit.

One shop in Upper Clanbrassil Street was called The Pixie, famous for its Russian slices, later called Tipsy Cake. In the 1960s most shops sold small packets of biscuits, each containing about four biscuits, for example Nice Biscuits. Mag Carroll's was a famous and popular shop opposite Isaac Mullens scrap merchants, and she seems to have sold just about anything. Matt Hackett, a little further down the road, was also very popular with locals.

The present Daybreak newsagents just on the south side of Emmet Bridge was a major grocery shop from 1910 to about 1970, owned by Sweeney's. The shop was 'choc-a-bloc' from floor to ceiling, with every conceivable item of groceries stacked on wall-mounted shelves. You handed the grocer your written list, and he climbed up and down step-ladders for your requirements, and then loaded them into your own shopping bag. The Sweeney family operated another smaller grocers from 71 Harold's Cross Road (opposite the hospice entrance – now Special Care drycleaners) during the same period. To this day, there is no big supermarket in Harold's Cross, and most families travel to surrounding districts for their weekly shopping.

A few doors away from Sweeney's, the three-storey Delaney's Cycles and Motorcycles is still in business, having started in 1919, with Jimmy Delaney's son still at the helm. The traditional retail practice of closing for a half-day on Wednesday is still carried on. At the other end of Harold's Cross, at No. 281, is a more recent shop, Capital Motorcycles.

In the past, most of the big shops employed messenger boys who delivered your groceries or meat on bicycles specially adapted with a big front carrier cage/wicker basket.

In the 1960s, electric-powered bread vans delivered fresh loaves on a daily basis to your house (there was no sliced bread). The Kelso Laundry van from Rathmines called every week with white sheets, tablecloths and shirt collars. Pint-sized glass bottles of milk, with red or orange metallic foil caps, jangled on the doorstep early every morning. Occasionally thirsty birds pecked at the foil caps to sample the cream at the top of the bottle. For many years, even in the '60s, bottled milk was delivered by horse and cart. Side-entry bin lorries, into which steel bins of rubbish were manually tipped, were a far cry from today's compactor lorries which automatically lift and tip over 'wheelie bins' full of household rubbish. Black-faced coal men, under bent backs, delivered heavy sacks of Polish coal to most houses, and even sacks of turf were doing the rounds. Smokeless coal was introduced in the 1990s, but its use is now rare, since most people prefer oil or gas-fired central heating.

POSTAL SERVICE

Prior to Ireland's independence in 1922, all postboxes displayed the royal insignia, depending on which king or queen was on the throne when the cast-iron boxes were made. Thus, VR represents Regina Victoria, who reigned from 1837 to 1901. ER VII represents Rex Edward VII (1901–1910), while GR represents Rex George V (1910–1936). Frequently the symbols were interwoven and included the letters P and O (post office), in addition to a separate crown, all projecting above the box surface. After independence, some postboxes displayed SE and a harp, representing Saorstát Éireann (Irish Free State), the official title for the country up until 1937, when Éire (twenty-six counties) adopted a constitution. The SE symbols were applied to new doors, or fitted to some older wall boxes, in the period 1922–1925, but these boxes are few and far between. P & T appears on postboxes after 1925, using Old Irish lettering and symbolising the Department of Posts and Telegraphs, until 1984, when the Government Department was split into two semi-state bodies, An Post and Telecom Éireann (the latter was recently a public company called Eircom plc, and changed to Eir in 2015).

Early postboxes were painted bronze-green, but changed to red around 1884. After independence, Ireland's boxes were painted a dark-green colour still used to this day.

The Irish postal service started in 1784, initially using expensive mail coaches (horse-drawn coach) traversing a handful of rough roads between selected towns. *The Pettigrew and Oulton Directory* for 1837 lists

Harold's Cross as a location for the Two Penny Post. By 1843, John Longford is listed as a receiving house (1844 as a post office keeper) at Longford Terrace beside St Clare's Convent (now No. 87). By 1860, this post office seems to have closed, to be replaced by the first postbox in Harold's Cross, one of the first in the country, outside Oldcourt at the top of the Green. Not until 1875 is a post office listed, this time in a shop (the recent Healy's). Thereafter the post office moved to different shops in the locality.

A small box (33in by 13in) is built into the boundary wall of St Clare's Convent, made by W.T. Allen of London, in the period 1886–93, with the plain letters V and R separated by a small crown. A much larger box is built into Mount Argus boundary wall (47in by 20in) by the same maker, but has no insignia and dates from 1879–1887. Cathal Brugha Barracks has its own medium-sized wall box, of the same vintage as St Clare's.

Postboxes on Mount Drummond Avenue, Grosvenor Square, Leinster Road West and Brighton Square were cast by Andrew Handyside of Derby in the period 1893–1901, with simple interwoven Victorian symbols. The same maker is responsible for a postbox near Mount Tallant Avenue, with no insignia, possibly made around 1883/1887. Handyside also made the large-diameter postbox (size A), at Leonard's Corner around 1879/1883, the oldest in the area. All other postboxes in Harold's Cross are smaller (size B).

The postbox at the junction of Kenilworth Park and Wilfrid Road was made by McDowall Steven of Glasgow in the period 1904–1910, with very ornate Edward VII symbols. A similar box is provided on Kenilworth Road. The box on Rathgar Avenue is slightly different and dates from 1901/1904, made by Handyside.

The postbox outside the Kenilworth Post Office is comparatively modern, probably dating from the 1950s, and cast by Carron Co. of Scotland for the Department of Posts and Telegraphs. Carron also made the one at the corner of Tivoli Avenue (1922), which has no insignia, and another on Parnell Avenue (1930s), with the words 'Post Office' inscribed. Some of the twentieth-century postboxes in Ireland were made in Enniscorthy, County Wexford, by Jessop Davis. Thomas Jessop Davis was a member of the distinguished Quaker milling family, and his St John's Foundry

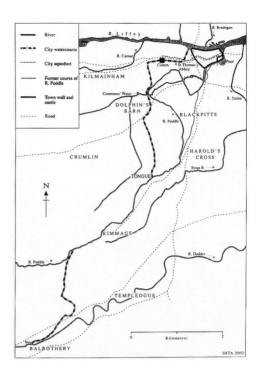

Sketch map of south Dublin, showing the River Poddle and River Swan flowing through Harold's Cross, and the 'tongue' dividing the Poddle in Mount Argus. (By permission of the Irish Historic Towns Atlas, Royal Irish Academy.© RIA)

operated from around the 1890s to the early 1960s. In recent decades, Tonge and Taggart of Dublin made some postboxes (Kenilworth Square South, 1986).

Until recent years, a postbox was located opposite the hospice entrance, outside the post office, made by Philip Pierce & Co. of Wexford, with P&T logo. The family business was set up in 1839 and sold in 1964. An Post has replaced it with a simple-sheet steel box mounted on a cruciform post, much favoured by An Post staff because of its easy emptying facilities (no bending!).

12

CANAL, RIVERS AND TRANSPORT

GRAND CANAL

The Grand Canal was built in slow stages during most of the second half of the eighteenth century, reaching Shannon Harbour on the River Shannon in County Offaly in 1803. The original terminus of the Grand Canal in Dublin was St James's Harbour near Suir Road, but a 3.8 mile-long circular line, started in 1790, extended it to Ringsend Basin, the latter officially opened with great celebrations in 1796. Passenger and cargo barges ran between Dublin and Shannon Harbour, with passengers often staying in Portobello Hotel, where there was a small harbour until recent years. The canal locks are still nearby, but the lockkeeper's lodge on the south bank is gone. In the early years, the barges were pulled by horses, which trundled along the tow path on the south bank of the canal. The path ran under each bridge, where the waters narrowed. Passenger boats were discontinued in 1852, but goods transport continued for another hundred years or so, during which time, steam power replaced the horses.

Clanbrassil Bridge was opened in 1791, named after the 2nd Earl of Clanbrassil (James Hamilton, 1729–1798). All of the canal bridges were named after directors of the Grand Canal Co. However, Clanbrassil Bridge was generally called Harold's Cross Bridge, especially in the twentieth century. It was rebuilt in reinforced concrete in 1936, with the width being increased from 32ft to 50ft, and the height underneath being reduced by 18in. It was renamed Robert Emmet Bridge, in honour of the patriot's associations with the area. The popular Lord Mayor of Dublin Alfie Byrne performed the official opening ceremony on 31 January 1937.

The Grand Canal Co. amalgamated with Córas Iompair Éireann (CIÉ) in 1950, and transport barges still operated until about 1960. The Office of Public Works took over responsibility for the canal in 1986. The original line of elm trees alongside the canal died out many years ago, but Dublin City Council has replanted them in recent years.

In the few decades prior to the 1880s, canal water was piped to many houses in the area, although some people considered the water unsafe to drink. This canal water was stored in a reservoir at Gallanstown, near Clondalkin.

Many people, both old and young, still spend hours on the canal banks, fishing for pinkeens and bigger fry, such as bream, roach, rudd, pike, perch, tench and carp. Large flocks of beautiful white swans still congregate on the canal waters, especially on the stretch between Emmet Bridge and Portobello Bridge.

The canal was frozen-over frequently in the past, when it was possible to skate on the ice, although occasionally people fell through. Over the decades, a few people accidentally drowned in the canal.

A major civil engineering project carried out in the early 1970s was called the Greater Dublin Drainage Scheme, and the Grand Canal Drainage Tunnel was a substantial portion of the project. Near the south side of

Watercolour of Clanbrassil Bridge (now called Emmet Bridge) painted in 1817 by Cecelia Margaret Campbell. (Courtesy of the National Library of Ireland)

the canal, at a depth of about 30ft underground, a 12ft-diameter drainage tunnel was bored, utilising temporary vertical shafts at widely spaced intervals for access and ventilation. The tunnel is lined with precast concrete segments, bolted together, and there are two compartments – one quadrant for foul sewerage, and the remainder for surface water; in other words, there is a smaller sewer inside the larger sewer. An English firm called Buchan had the contract for this tunnel, but most of the workers were Donegal men returned from England. A large site office, storage area and access shaft were located beside Emmet Bridge on the derelict Greenmount Oil Co. site.

In some locations, rock was encountered during the tunnel-boring operations, necessitating careful drilling and explosive blasting because of nearby houses, although vibrations were still felt in some properties. The contractor reactivated the loud factory hooter in the Greenmount Industrial Estate, and just like an air-raid siren used in the world wars, the hooter sounded throughout the neighbourhood before and at the finish of blasting operations, so as to forewarn householders of possible vibrations.

THE RIVER PODDLE

The River Poddle rises at Cookstown in Tallaght and empties into the River Liffey along Wellington Quay. This little river was once the water supply for the citizens of Dublin, and has played a major role in the development of the city, providing water and power to many mills and businesses. Around 1240, part of the original River Poddle was diverted by the monks of St Thomas Court, around the present entrance to Mount Jerome, in order for them to have a good water supply. This branch became known as the Abbey Stream, and later as the Earl of Meath's Watercourse. The original Poddle River carried straight on, running under Marymount Secondary School, although one of Lord Meath's maps, drawn around 1810, refers to this branch of the river as having been filled in. In 1245, a 'tongue' or 'stone-boat' was built in the present Mount Argus area to split the waters, so that one third of the river was diverted towards Dolphin's Barn and then to a large cistern at James's Street, to supply the city of Dublin. This simple stone structure is still in position, and is reputed to be the oldest manmade waterworks in the world; furthermore, it is now a national monument. The field in which it is situated was known as The Tonguefield, as can be seen on the 1837 Ordnance Survey map.

In the eighteenth and nineteenth centuries, the River Poddle was the driving force for machines in Loader Park Paper Mills, Harold's Cross Flour Mill (later Harold's Cross Laundry), and the Greenmount Spinning Manufactory. Mill ponds were often situated beside the larger mills, and these were, in effect, large cisterns or water tanks used to store water so as to regulate the water pressure (especially during winter floods) at the waterwheel or modern cast-iron turbine, and also to build up a reservoir of spare water to cater for dry spells in the summer.

In the 1960s, the River Poddle could be seen in the mill pond in front of Mount Argus church, alongside the road at the very bottom of Kimmage Road Lower (including the sluice valves), along the east side of Mount Jerome Cemetery, at the west end of St Clare's Avenue, along the west side of Marymount Infant School, including a small mill pond at the top of the Hospice Avenue, and along the east side of the Shell garage on Parnell Road, before it flowed under the Grand Canal and on into the city.

Nowadays the ponds have been filled in, and substantial parts of the river are culverted (enclosed in big pipes). In Mount Argus, the original pond with its wildlife island is now gone, replaced by a flood-storage pond in the nearby park serving the houses built in 1990–1991. However, the Poddle still winds its way alongside the Kimmage Road boundary wall. When front gardens at the bottom of Lower Kimmage Road collapsed into the Poddle in the late 1970s, the river along here was culverted, but it can still be seen at the back of the Russian Orthodox church and alongside the cemetery. All of the hospice and Greenmount sections are now concealed. The Poddle was connected into the Grand Canal drainage tunnel in the 1970s, but the section between the Grand Canal and the River Liffey still runs underground.

THE SWAN RIVER

In bygone days, the Swan River, which rose in Kimmage Manor, passed through Kimmage Road Lower, Westfield Road, Wilfred Road, Tivoli Avenue,

Leinster Road, and on through Rathmines towards Irishtown. Duncan's map of 1821 shows the Clandaube Bridge over the river on the main Harold's Cross Road beside McGarry's pub (at the top of Leinster Road), but by the 1860s, the river mostly ran underground and was used to drain the Rathmines township.

RESERVOIR

On the subject of water, mention must be made of the enclosed reservoir and pumping station, which were built in 1878 in the present Leinster Place (behind Centra/Cooney's grocery) to pump canal water to the Rathgar area. Around 1903/1905, Leinster Place houses were built on the site.

In the 1880s, the Rathmines Commissioners built the Glenasmole Water Works (near Bohernabreena), utilising the River Dodder in addition to a filtering plant some distance away at Ballyboden, which further improved the water-supply position in Harold's Cross and Rathmines.

Prior to the availability of a public water supply, many houses in the area had their own artesian water well in the back garden, operated by a hand pump.

TRANSPORT

Horse-drawn trams with open-topped upper decks, running on tracks, were introduced to Dublin in 1872, but it wasn't until 1879 that the Dublin Central Tramways Co. opened a line from College Green to Terenure via Harold's Cross. In 1883, the route was extended to Nelson's Pillar in O'Connell Street, and to Rathfarnham. The symbol for this route was a green Maltese cross. Because of the extra strain on the horses at hills, an additional horse was usually added in the pack. This was called a 'trip' or a 'trace' horse, and especially needed coming over Emmet Bridge. The entire tram network was electrified from 1896 onwards, but horse-drawn trams still operated through Harold's Cross for about another three years. Although buses started to appear on the streets of Dublin after 1925, the last tram to Rathfarnham was in 1939.

A recent view of the Grand Canal, with Gordons Fuel Depot alongside, and Griffith Barracks in the background.

In the 1960s, there was no shortage of public transport through Harold's Cross in the form of double-decker buses manned by a driver and a conductor, with the open doorway at the rear, where a late passenger could always grab onto the vertical chromium-plated bar. The buses that passed through were the 16, 49, 54, 55 and 65, and you had the option of going to the city centre, the Dublin Mountains, or the Blessington Lakes. Even with the modern one-man buses, these options are still available. The 19A also passes through now.

Prior to the advent of traffic lights in the 1960s, the Garda Síochána had to perform 'point duty' at the major junctions in the city centre. A garda would have been very useful in Harold's Cross, since there were many traffic accidents at the bottom of the Park. The traffic entering the city from the Terenure side had the right of way, and traffic approaching from Kimmage had to yield. The situation probably was not helped by the presence of a zebra crossing for pedestrians at the wide stretch of road between St Clare's Convent and the hospice. For a while, traffic islands were introduced to segregate the traffic, but these were frequently demolished in accidents. Over the years, there were various combinations and positions for the zebra crossing, traffic islands, and eventually traffic lights.

In the 1960s–70s, there were fewer cars and trucks on the road than in the present day, and the small number of people who owned cars in the Harold's Cross area were able to park freely on the side of the road. In the past twenty years, parking of cars has been severely restricted by the provision of double yellow lines in most places. In 2000, a bus corridor was introduced through Harold's Cross in both directions, and only a small

1878 painting of
the Waterworks in
Harold's Cross (now the
site of Leinster Place
houses), including the
boilerhouse, chimney,
pumphouse, and covered
cistern/reservoir. (Courtesy of
Seamas O'Maitiu)

In 1986, the River Poddle
could be seen flowing
alongside the west of
Marymount Infant School,
and then on into the
Greenmount Industrial
Estate. (Courtesy of
Dublin Corporation
Drainage Department)

number of cars are allowed to park in special bays inset into the footpath, but only if they have a parking permit or pay a parking charge, from 7 a.m. until 7 p.m., Monday to Saturday. Besides the main road, parking meters have been introduced at Mount Jerome Cemetery, Leinster Road, Leinster Road West, and other areas.

Other recent changes include traffic lights beside the entrance to Mount Jerome Cemetery and cycle lanes along Grove Road and Parnell Road. Now the Canal Road forms part of a Ring Road for Dublin, and Emmet Bridge is designated as Junction 57.

In the early part of the nineteenth century, a toll had to be paid by carriages passing through Harold's Cross, but around 1836, the toll was lifted for carriages travelling to funerals in Mount Jerome Cemetery. Some old maps show a turnpike (toll booth and gate) at Leonard's Corner.

In 1986, there was flooding in Harold's Cross associated with the River Poddle. Here, the back gardens of houses on Greenmount Avenue were flooded, and likewise the hospice field opposite the Oratory and Marymount Schools. (Courtesy of Dublin Corporation Drainage Department)

13

HOUSING

GREENMOUNT

Not surprisingly, the Greenmount Spinning Manufactory was the inspiration for the names of a variety of houses and streets in the area. The manufactory itself dates from around 1808. The convent building in the hospice was called Greenmount when the Sisters of Charity bought the house in 1845, and changed the name to Our Lady's Mount. The collection of two-storey cottages called Greenmount Court would appear to have been built in the 1820s or '30s, for renting to the mill workers. The single-storey cottages with segmental (slightly curved) timber roofs in Greenmount Lane and Limekiln Lane were probably built in the 1850/60s, by the Pims for their workers. Originally these roofs were most likely covered with tar and calico (plain white cotton cloth), and this roof design is a particular feature of other Quaker houses, such as in Portlaw, County Waterford. Most of the cottages were sold to the tenants around 1968. Factory Lane, with about eight cottages, was located off the west side of Greenmount Lane, roughly opposite the present redundant P & T depot, but these were demolished in the middle of the twentieth century, to make way for a modern extension to the mill, complete with north-light roof.

As far back as at least 1800, there was a kiln in the Cherry Orchard area (the present Harmsworth Offices) for the making of lime, which was used in mortar before the advent of cement, hence the name Limekiln Lane. Limestone was burnt to a powder, and the lime was then spread on fields as a fertiliser. Lime was extensively used as whitewash (considered a disinfectant) before the mass production of paint, and was also used for making bleaching powder. Landed Estate Court particulars referred to two extensive lime kilns built by Richard Bergin in 1800, but by 1856 Charles Henry had acquired the premises, and a house was let to eleven people at weekly rents ranging from 1s to 2s 4d. Griffith's Valuation in the 1850s lists Bergin Lane (probably the forerunner of Greenmount Lane), and amongst the many houses here, Michael Doyle occupied a big house and lime kilns, with rateable valuation of £21 7s and £18s respectively. *Thom's Directory* of 1844 lists the same occupant and use. During the nineteenth century, the Richmond Bridewell (now Griffith College) operated two large lime kilns.

The two-storey houses in Greenmount Avenue are comparatively modern, dating from 1928/30.

On the left-hand side of the entrance to the hospice there was previously a house called Greenmount Cottage, which probably dated from around the 1820s, but by 1920 it had been demolished to make way for the oratory in the hospice.

Opposite the hospice entrance, and slightly set back from the surrounding buildings, was a large house called Greenmount View, which was demolished around 1883, and two big semi-detached houses were built in its place, the present Nos 75 and 77.

Around the beginning of the 1850s, a group of houses was built opposite the west side of the Green, called Greenmount Terrace, and these were set well back from the road. They are single-storey over basement at the front, and three storeys at the rear. The very long back gardens (about 200ft) run downhill to the River Poddle, and at varying times the adjacent area was subject to flooding but also contained ornamental fountains. Some of these back gardens seem to be abandoned, and obviously have development potential. The houses stretching from here to Mount Jerome appear to be late-eighteenth century, and those with no back gardens are thought to have been built on the Commons of Harold's Cross, and are excluded from Lord Meath's estate.

DUBLIN ARTISAN DWELLINGS/HAROLD'S CROSS COTTAGES

The Dublin Artisan Dwelling Co. started in 1876, with the aim of providing reasonably priced rented accommodation for working men and their families. The directors of the company at that stage were Sir Arthur E. Guinness,

R. Martin, R. O. Armstrong, William Findlater, E.H. Kinahan, F. Stokes, and R. Warren. The trustees of the company were E.C. Guinness D.L., W.D. La Touche, D.L., Jonathan Pim and John E. Vernon. A large field near Clanbrassil Bridge was purchased, which in 1882 was the site of a patent brickworks. By 1885, they had completed the thirty two-storey red-bricked houses in Armstrong Street, and the 120 plastered single-storey cottages. Later the company purchased more adjoining land, and in the period 1897–1900 they built 168 two-storey yellow-brick houses, now called Fitzgerald Street, Darley Street, and so forth, including single-storey cottages in Emmet Street. Ashworth Place is named after the company architect, C.H. Ashworth. In the 1960s, the tenants were allowed to purchase the cottages, and nowadays they are fetching great prices on the open market.

LOCAL-AUTHORITY DWELLINGS

The largest Local Authority scheme of two-storey houses in the area is Mount Drummond Avenue and Square. Part of the land was compulsorily purchased from the Sisters of St Clare, and the houses were built in 1941. The present central line of trees was the original north boundary of the nuns' property. The name Mount Drummond Lane was used as far back as 1844, when there were only fields in this locality. Rocque's map of 1760 shows Chicken Lane, which later became Hen and Chicken Lane, and eventually Mount Drummond Avenue. There was a house called Mount Drummond, not far to the east of St Clare's Convent (around the present 49 Mount Drummond Square), with its driveway opposite the present Fitzgerald Street, and this was owned in the 1830–1850s by Ralph Laurenson. It was later rented by the Smith family, fruit and market gardeners, although the Poor Clares were landlords from 1907 to 1914. Laurenson, being a barrister, might have named the house in honour of Thomas Drummond, under secretary of Ireland in 1835, who was responsible for modernising the old police force in Dublin. The house and land were later called Grosvenor Gardens. At the bottom of Mount Drummond Avenue, senior citizens' apartments called Mount Drummond Court were built in the 1980s on the site of Emmet House (also known as Greenfield House) and Jassmine Cottage (also known as Plantation).

The group of three two-storey red-bricked houses called Zuma Terrace was built privately around 1905. The statue of Our Lady of the Rosary in the green area at the junction of the avenue and square was erected by the residents in 1954, the Marian Year, and some people still publicly recite the rosary here on one or two evenings a week.

The five-storey Grove Road Flats alongside the canal was built in the early 1960s, on the site called Holbrook Cottages in the early part of the nineteenth century, and Union Place in the latter part of the nineteenth century.

ST CLARE'S

St Clare's Convent was probably the inspiration for a number of houses in the neighbourhood. St Clare's Terrace at the top of Mount Drummond Avenue was built in 1900. At the end of the eighteenth century, a group of houses on Parnell Road near Clanbrassil Bridge was also called St Clare's Terrace. Even today, there is a group of three houses probably built around 1875 at right angles to Parnell Road, near the bridge, called Clare Villas.

St Clare's Avenue, opposite the bottom of the park, required the demolition of a house called Peachmount, and the houses along the south side of the avenue were built in the late 1930s, while the rest were erected in the late 1950s.

PARNELL

In the old days, the Parnell Road area was called the Double Mill Field, probably on account of the Wood Mills, which later became the Greenmount Mills. This stretch of the Grand Canal was constructed in the early 1790s, and the bridge at the top of Donore Avenue was named Parnell Bridge (although locals nowadays call it Sally's Bridge), after Sir John Parnell, MP for Queen's County (Laois), chancellor of the exchequer in 1787, and of course the grandfather of Charles Stewart Parnell. Most of the old houses on Parnell Road were probably built shortly after the opening of this stretch of the Grand Canal. However, in the early days, the houses were divided up into groups, with the three-storey houses near Clanbrassil Bridge called St Clare's

Terrace (at one stage Bergin Place); the two-storey houses up as far as the present Greenmount Lane were called Lower Parnell Place, with the houses beyond that called Middle Parnell Place, and a small group of three houses past the River Poddle was called Parnell Place Upper. By about 1907, all of the houses were listed as Parnell Place, and the name was probably changed to Parnell Road in the 1930s, after Dublin Corporation assumed responsibility for the area from the Rathmines and Rathgar Urban District Council.

The name Rope Walk is shown on maps in the 1870–1930 period, running parallel to the canal through the area now occupied by Parnell Avenue and Arbutus Avenue. The name probably derives from a rope maker's factory, since early maps show buildings or sheds around a long narrow yard, and certainly, ropes were in demand for horse-drawn barges along the canal, for ships' sails, and also for tying timber scaffold poles together on building sites. The nearby Greenmount Spinning Manufactory may have operated a subsidiary company. Space was required to lay out the long ropes on the ground during manufacture, with the individual threads or strands of hemp being wound up and intertwined. Roper's Rest was once a mill in Donore Avenue, beside Greenville Mill, and was named after Sir Thomas Roper, Baron of Bantry. This is now all part of the White Swan Industrial Estate. There is still a Rope Walk Place in Ringsend, beside the docks area.

In Rocque's *Environs of Dublin* 1773, the road from Dolphin's Barn to Harold's Cross is called Hangman's Lane – could this be another reference to ropes!

The Greenmount and Boyne Linen Co. leased 2 acres, 1 rood and 34 perches of land to Joseph Somers (builder) for 999 years from 1927, with a covenant to build thirty-three houses to the value of £600 each. These houses were built in the early 1930s, being called Parnell Avenue, Arbutus Avenue, and the adjoining section of Parnell Road up to No. 44. The last house is twice the size of the others, enjoying a 0.3 acre back garden, and was occupied by the builder. The Catholic boy scouts of Ireland built 'a den' in 1982 in part of the back garden of No. 44, with access off Arbutus Avenue.

The three big houses comprising Parnell Place Upper were demolished in the 1960s. Originally there were plans for a large office block on the site, but the only structure to be erected was a Shell petrol station. It was not until the late 1980s that Parnell Court was built, comprising back-to-back townhouses and some semi-detached houses.

HAROLD'S CROSS ROAD

Because of piecemeal development over two centuries, the numbering system has changed a few times, the last in 1932. For example, 126 Harold's Cross Road is now No. 82. In the past, houses were listed consecutively, starting at the shops at Harold's Cross Bridge, running up past the Kenilworth traffic lights, and returning back down Harold's Cross Road on the hospice side. Nowadays, odd numbers are on the east side of the road, and even numbers on the west side. At the moment, houses on the Harold's Cross Road are numbered up to 351 and 430, respectively. However, in the early development of Harold's Cross, houses were built in small groups and called terraces, unlike the modern trend for semi-detached houses. Over the years, the numbering system has always started at Harold's Cross Bridge, and the following brief description does likewise.

Wharton Terrace was a group of houses parallel to the canal, probably built around 1875, demolished around 1968, and now the site of a large ESB sub-station, built in the late 1980s. The terrace may have been named after the Duke of Wharton, whose family (Loftus) previously owned land in the neighbourhood.

The north side of Le Vere Terrace dates from around 1905, replacing a previous group of cottages called Liverrier Lane in the 1850s, owned by John Lavaria.

The group of houses with plastered finish to the north of St Clare's Convent was previously called Longford Row, and probably dates from the late-eighteenth century. *Thom's Directory* of 1844 lists one of the residents as John Longford, who had a post office near the convent (the present No. 87).

The yellow-bricked houses opposite Longford Row were built in the 1830s. Elizabeth Carruthers leased part of the land to Thomas Clarke for 999 years from 1836 at £40 per annum, and he built Clarke's Buildings (now Nos 66 to 74), and then let them as either monthly or yearly tenancies at around £24 per annum to respectable tenants. He also built a house for himself, with fine garden behind, and retained a large rear field. Following the death of Thomas Clarke, the Landed Estates Court sold Clarke's Buildings as lot 1 and lot 2 to James Bourke in 1861, for £1,130. The red-bricked Nos 76 to 80 were built around 1885, replacing Thomas Clarke's own house. The large rear field later came into the possession of the hospice, and was the site of the prefabs for their primary school in the 1960–'70s. The house to the immediate south of Clarke's own house was St Joseph's Seminary – it was rebuilt around 1887 and used until the 1970s by some of the priests of the Holy Rosary Parish. The terrace of three-storey houses further south is probably early-nineteenth century, provided with flat roofs at a later date, and new pitched roofs in 2016.

Just past St Clare's Convent was a pair of old houses called Rose Villa, which were demolished in the 1960s to make way for Park View Mansions, one of the earliest blocks of apartments to be built in Harold's Cross in 1973.

There is an interesting selection of houses between St Clare's Convent and the dog track. The terrace of double-fronted houses with steeply pitched slated roofs, which is set back from the road, appears to date from the second half of the eighteenth century. When No. 129 was renovated in 2002, the builder found thick rubble-limestone front and back walls, thin brick party walls, a light roof structure, and evidence of an unusual arrangement of previous window and door openings, all suggesting that an original building may have been converted into a terrace of houses. Further along, No. 139 is part of a more 'modern' terrace, having being built only in 1833, although the apartment block, Parkview Court, dates from 1991. No. 147 is an eighteenth century double-fronted house that features beautiful geraniums in the ground-floor front windows all year round. The panelled hall door is a reminder of a bygone age, since it is still 'grained and varnished' the traditional way, and even a coloured striped canvas is used to protect the door paint in summertime.

In May 1999, excess land of 4.86 acres at the Greyhound Stadium was sold to Garland Homes Ltd for a record £10.6 million, which represents about £131,000 for each of the eighty-one sites. The private gated estate of three-storey townhouses was completed in 2002, and is called Leinster Park.

Old Court, near the corner of Park View Avenue, was possibly built at the beginning of the nineteenth century. Being very large and rambling, it appears to have been subdivided around 1907 to form Old Court, New Court and Eyre Court. The latter was occupied in the opening decades of the twentieth century by Samuel Samuels, whose jewellery shop was in 6 Henry Street. Sam's real name was Joshua Honigbaum. He came to Ireland from Hull in England in 1897. The shop in Henry Street included a variety show and a waxworks on the first floor. Before that, James Ellis, TC, occupied the house around 1900 – he had a big drapery store at 64–65 South Great George's Street. Eyre Court was allowed to fall into disrepair in the 1970s, then was demolished, and modern apartments built in the mid-1990s, retaining the old name. Local people speak of a small ballroom for entertaining guests in the original Old Court House. The red-bricked houses in the adjoining Park View Avenue were built in the period 1903–1906.

At the top of the Green, a small group of three-storey houses was known as Harold's Cross Terrace and was apparently built before 1806. These houses and the former Paddy Walsh Cycles were on the archbishop's land, and originally leased by James Geraghty, but converted to free farm grant in 1863. The two-storey red-bricked houses at the west of this terrace were probably built in the 1880s. The present McGowan's public house was previously in Victoria Terrace. At the corner of Mount Argus Road and Lower Kimmage Road is a deceptive group of houses, being single storey at the front and two storey at the rear, and these were known as Metcalfe Terrace when built in the 1870s.

The red-bricked houses from the corner of Park View Avenue up to Centra/ Cooney's grocery were built in 1893, and known as Claremount Terrace.

The houses where Harold Engineering was located were built in 1875, and known as Shamrock Terrace; the group of houses to the south towards McGarry's public house was known as Mountain View Terrace, and probably date from at least the 1830s.

Almost opposite the Holy Rosary church is Tivoli Terrace, probably built around 1860, although only three of the houses now remain, since two new shops/houses were built in the early 1960s. Around the corner in Tivoli Avenue there was previously a group of old houses, which were demolished to make way for new houses about sixty years ago.

Two-storey Fitzpatrick Cottages are still hidden behind Deveney's shop/ Cruz del Campo, although the shop and old house were demolished in 2004 to make way for the present shop and apartments overhead. Most of the nineteen two-storey Ryan's Cottages are gone (immediately to the north of the cinema site).

On the west side of Harold's Cross Road on both sides of Kenilworth traffic lights are nice groups of red-bricked houses with red-tiled roofs, previously called Elmville, and these were built around 1907. Waverley Terrace, on the opposite side of the traffic lights, dates from about 1882.

The group of shops at the corner of Rathgar Avenue was known as Kenilworth Buildings, built in 1908.

Between Kenilworth Motors and Mount Tallant Avenue is a group of red-bricked three-storey houses which has its own slip road: these were built in the late 1850s and were known as Mount Tallant Terrace.

The first few houses past Mount Tallant Avenue were built around 1905 and called Pretoria Terrace, while the houses beyond that were called Ashfield Terrace and were built in the 1860s–'70s. Opposite Mount Tallant Avenue, the lower group of houses was called Abercorn Terrace, whereas the upper group was called Avondale Terrace – both were built in the 1860s–'70s, and all were red-bricked.

The houses at the top of Leinster Road were built in the 1850s on part of what was previously known as Mowld's Farm (also known as Cullen's Farm), although by this stage the Evans family from Mount Harold House owned the land. The Evans estate included all the land in Leinster Road West and some on the north side of Leinster Road from the present Park View Avenue to No. 73, where John Hawker Evans lived (sometime secretary of Rathmines township). The red-bricked houses called Mount Harold Terrace, backing onto the Holy Rosary church, were not built until around 1890. Many people will be interested to hear that Leinster Road was formed in the 1830s, and was a private road up until about 1905, with a set of gates opposite the present McGarry's pub, despite the fact that the road was in the Rathmines township. Many of the villa-style houses in Leinster Road West date from the 1860s.

Only about twenty houses had been built in Grosvenor Square by 1865, and the rest were completed in the following decades. This particular square is surrounded by a labyrinth of lanes which provided rear access to the big houses, but over the years a lot of garages (for car parking) and small workshops have been built alongside these narrow routes. Nowadays, the park is home to the Stratford Lawn Tennis Club (previously called the Leinster Tennis Club), and the Kenilworth Bowling Club. The latter was founded in 1892 in Kenilworth Square, but moved to a new clubhouse in Grosvenor Square in 1905, and admitted ladies in 1930. They have one grass pitch and another all-weather, in addition to indoor space for winter play. There is keen competition annually for the beautiful silver Minnis Perpetual Trophy.

The fine houses in Kenilworth Square were built in the early 1860s, and display a wonderful variety of designs, mostly having red-brick facades. This square was probably the most prestigious address in the neighbourhood. Kenilworth Lane nowadays has quite a number of modern mews houses. The park is now used as training grounds for St Mary's College Rugby Club in Rathmines.

The east side of Brighton Square was built in the late 1860s, but it was not until 1876 that the west side was built. The triangular-shaped park is used by the Tara Tennis Club, and owned by the surrounding residents, but seems little used.

The lovely red-bricked houses in Kenilworth Park, Casimir Road and Westfield Road were built in phases from about 1900/1915, with the nearby section of Lower Kimmage Road following in the 1920s and 1930s. Casimir Road was probably named in memory of Countess Markievicz's Polish husband. The first eleven houses on Kimmage Road Lower to the north of Casimir Road were known as Zion Hill Terrace.

Most of the houses on Mount Argus Road were built in the late 1930s, although some date from recent decades. Up until the late 1960s, there was a farm and house called Rathlands House, just on the right-hand side of the rear entrance to Mount Argus, which was a market garden in the post-war years. Three blocks of flats (Manor Villas) were built here in 1971, followed by a small estate of houses called Mount Argus Grove, and at a later date, a larger estate of local-authority houses was built backing onto the huge Ceannt Park, with its athletic and cycling track. Even up until about 1900, Mount Argus Road was called Papermill Lane because it led to Loader Park Paper Mill.

CLANBRASSIL STREET UPPER

Both sides of this road are lined with old terraces of houses, varying from single storey to three storey, mostly dating from the early-nineteenth century.

The area around the Harold House public house was a warren of lanes with small cottages, including Garden Terrace, Orr's Terrace, Costello's Cottages and Reilly's Cottages, most of which are now gone.

The Marian Shrine in Mount Drummond Square was built in 1954. Note Cathal Brugha Barracks in the background.

Kenilworth Bowling Club is still going strong, with its 1905 clubhouse extended over the years.

BARRACKS

POLICE STATION

In the 1830s, there was a large police station in Harold's Cross, roughly on the site of the present McGarry's public house opposite the top of Leinster Road. In the 1850s, the station was relocated nearby to a smaller house, 12 Tivoli Terrace, but this police station closed around 1875/1880, and Rathmines became the hub of the E Division.

THE 'BUGGY' BARRACKS

The Irish Volunteers were a voluntary local defence force, with Freemasonry involvement, comprising both Catholics and Protestants, set up during the American War of Independence (1775–1783), because English soldiers were sent from Ireland to fight the Americans, and it was feared that France and Spain (who supported the Americans) might attack England via Ireland. The Volunteers supported Grattan's Patriot Party, which was pressing for the Irish Parliament to be independent of English control. The Volunteers wore colourful uniforms with top coats of sparkling red or navy blue, and cream-coloured breeches, as can be seen from a large painting by Francis Wheatley in the National Gallery, depicting the Dublin Volunteers assembled in College Green to celebrate the birthday of King William III on 4 November 1779. During this period, the Uppercross Fusiliers (Volunteers) practised on Harold's Cross Green, and were jokingly called the Uppercrust Fusiliers by the local wags.

Wolfe Tone was a Protestant Dublin barrister, and he founded the United Irishmen in Belfast in 1791, initially as a peaceful Protestant pressure group, but then the ranks were swelled by Catholics who were in favour of armed action, and French military assistance was sought in 1796. The British Government responded by increasing the strength of their militia (army), and recruiting a part-time auxiliary defence force called the Yeomanry, made up of affluent Protestants. In Harold's Cross, the previous name of the Uppercross Fusiliers was adopted for the Yeomanry, and previous Volunteers were recruited again.

Local folklore refers to a small Yeomanry barracks a long time ago beside the present Mount Jerome Cemetery, in the two buildings (Nos 148–152), recently occupied by a lighting showroom and wholesale electrical shop. The three-storey building was nicknamed the Little Buggy, and the four storey was called the Big Buggy (at some stage, the top two storeys were removed, so the building is presently two storey with a flat roof). It seems that 'bug' was old slang for a detective or policeman, although the nickname 'buggy' could also imply that the barracks was filthy and full of bugs.

CATHAL BRUGHA BARRACKS

The Portobello Army Barracks was built in stages in the period 1810–1815, to a design by Benell, Brownrigg and Behan. The barracks is shown on the 1816 Taylor's map as the Horse Barracks (for cavalry), and in fact it was designed for '6 Troops of Cavalry'. The riding school was in the south centre of the barrack buildings – to the west of that was a cluster of detached buildings, including smithies (for shoeing horses), handball court, prison and canteen. There were small magazines (for storing gunpowder) in both the south-west and north-east of the barrack campus. Shortly afterwards, the name Portobello was chosen for the barracks, being Spanish for 'beautiful harbour', although on Rocque's map of 1760 Portobello is marked as the area to the south-west of the present Kelly's Corner. The first occupiers in 1811 were the 6th Dragoon Guards. Various extra plots of land were gradually acquired in subsequent decades, bringing the barracks up to 42 acres.

In 1817 there was a famous balloon ascent from this barracks, when William Sadler crossed the Irish Sea to Holyhead in North Wales.

Bust of Cathal Brugha in the museum in the former Guardhouse of Cathal Brugha Barracks.

Lewis records that in 1837, there were twenty-seven officers, 520 soldiers, stabling for 540 horses, and a hospital for forty patients.

The cavalry remained in the barracks from 1815 to 1888, after which only the infantry used the barracks.

The 1881 Census records a population of 1,055 (835 men and 220 women), 724 of whom were soldiers. The situation was broadly similar in 1901. However, by 1911, the barracks had doubled the number of soldiers to 1,424, with an overall population of 1,756 (1,546 men and 210 women). For the purposes of the census, officers were not classified as soldiers. The women were probably soldiers' wives living in married quarters.

A masterplan dated 1911 provides a good idea of the layout of the barracks. Beside the original Grove Road entrance were the guardhouse (a small prison), the chapel and the infants' school. At the north-west corner were the quartermasters' quarters (a detached house with garden, originally called the Barrack Master Quarters, rebuilt in 1897, and now called Sarsfield House), and officers' quarters and mess (dining rooms). At the north-east corner were gun sheds, magazine (storage of gunpowder), two semi-detached houses for warrant officers and one house for a quartermaster, in addition to a range of buildings for officers and mess. Large drill grounds separated the north-east and north-west officers' quarters. The soldiers' barracks, comprising large dormitories, were grouped around the two central parade grounds, including a recreation building in the east ground. The south-west comprised workshops, tailor and shoemaker, canteen, laundry, stables, ballcourt, gymnasium and sundry accommodation. The south-east, accessed off the Military Road in Rathmines, comprised the new guard house and a walled enclosure for the hospital and the staff building. The extreme south part contained six two-storey blocks for married quarters, including another school, a large recreation grounds for football and other facilities. The single-storey school had accommodation for 108 children and 36 babies, spread over four classrooms, each 22ft by 18½ft, with toilets in the middle. The older schools near the Grove Road entrance also used the church, utilising the central folding partition. There was a Morris tube range both at the north-west and south-east corners of the barracks – these were rifle ranges. Two semi-detached bungalows were provided for barrack labourers. Toilets were in separate detached buildings. The official accommodation schedule catered for fifty-two officers, four warrant officers, 1,611 non-commissioned officers and men (including 105 married), and twenty-six horses (including eleven for transport purposes).

Many of the buildings were rebuilt in the period from 1894 to 1902, and a second entrance was provided off Military Road shortly before 1900. The gym opened on 28 January 1902, and cost £6,305. The former riding school was demolished and replaced by a recreation establishment (recently housing the military archives).

During Easter week 1916 (the Rising started on Monday 24 April), the barracks was occupied by the 3rd Reserve Battalion of the Royal Irish Rifles, under the temporary command of Major Rosborough. On Tuesday 25 April, the journalist and pacifist Francis Sheehy Skeffington while walking home to 11 Grosvenor Place, was arrested by British Army soldiers stationed in Davy's public house beside Portobello Bridge, on suspicion of being involved in the Easter Rising, and brought to Portobello Army Barracks. At 11.30 p.m. that night, Captain Bowen-Colthurst decided to bring a raiding party of forty soldiers to Alderman's Kelly's tobacco shop at nearby Kelly's Corner, and brought Francis Sheehy Skeffington along as a 'hostage'. On their way, they met a nineteen-year-old bicycle mechanic, James Joseph Coade, of 28 Upper Mountpleasant Avenue, and the captain shot him in the left thigh for no reason. Some of the soldiers brought him back to the barrack's hospital, where he died before midnight. Meanwhile, Alderman Kelly was not in his shop, but the captain arrested two innocent civilians on the premises, Thomas Dickson and Patrick James McIntyre, and the party returned to the barracks. Next morning, on 26 April, the captain ordered his soldiers to shoot the three prisoners in the small exercise yard behind the guard house, adjacent to the Rathmines Road entrance. The three bodies were wrapped in sheets and buried in the barrack square, with Father O'Loughlin performing the 'burial rites' on the spot – at a later date, the bodies were exhumed and buried in consecrated ground. Following a military trial on 7 June, Captain Bowen-Colthurst was found guilty of murdering the three men, but insane, and imprisoned for eighteen months in Broadmoor Criminal Lunatic Asylum, England. A subsequent royal inquiry in August 1916 found that Bowen-Colthurst and his colleagues had lied about events and tried to cover up the true facts. He then emigrated to Canada, where he lived to the age of 80. He was not tried for the cold-blooded murder of the youth, James

Joseph Coade. A bas-relief of Francis Sheehy Skeffington, erected in 1970 at the Rathmines entrance to the barracks, partly commemorates the event.

In 2011, a small museum was opened in the former guard house, with exhibits about Francis Sheehy Skeffington, Cathal Brugha, Richard Mulcahy and especially Michael Collins, including his death mask (by Albert Power RHA) and the tricolour national flag which was draped over his coffin during the funeral procession through the streets of Dublin. Four prison cells can be seen, and likewise the rear exercise yard where the three men were murdered on the instructions of Captain Bowen-Colthurst. A large room features exhibits about the role of the present army in peace-keeping missions.

During the First World War, the Rathmines Ambulance Division of the St John VAD (Voluntary Aid Detachment) was attached to the Royal Army Corps Depot at Portobello Barracks, dealing with injured soldiers arriving on hospital ships from the Continent. During the 1916 Easter Rising, they were also on duty during the firemen's strike in Rathmines.

The British Army moved out in 1922, but it was not until 1952 that it was renamed Cathal Brugha Barracks, in memory of the 1916 and anti-Treaty veteran. After 1922, Portobello became the army headquarters of the Irish Free State, with General Michael Collins as commander-in-chief, General Richard Mulcahy as chief of staff, and Major General Sean McMahon as quartermaster general. Michael Collins lived in Red House (a two-storey detached red-brick building that was formally the doctor's quarters opposite the old hospital) from May 1922 to 22 August of that year, before being shot in Cork during the Civil War.

During the Civil War, the barracks came under sniper attack from the anti-Treaty side on the night of 9 November 1922 and also on 8 February 1923, and returned fire, leaving many bullet holes in the brickwork of the cottages along its west side. The Dublin Artisan Dwelling Co., as owner, sought compensation from the new government for repairing the brickwork on a total of seventeen cottages on Greenfield Place, St Clare's Terrace, Fitzgerald Street, Ashworth Place and Harold's Cross Cottages, and was awarded £4 17s plus costs.

The famous Tailteann Games, an Irish sports event on similar lines to the Olympic Games, were first staged in Dublin in 1924, with the boxing events taking place in Portobello Barracks.

Since the 1960s, the barracks has been heavily involved in peace-keeping missions for the United Nations in the Congo, Cyprus, Sinai, Israel (the disputed Golan Heights between Israel and Syria), Lebanon, Egypt, Iran, Iraq, Afghanistan and Pakistan.

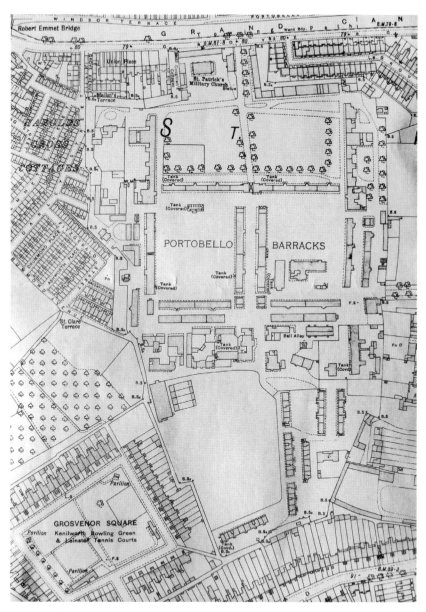

1938 Ordnance Survey extract, showing Portobello Barracks (renamed Cathal Brugha Barracks in 1952). (Courtesy of Trinity College Map Library)

Recent photo of the former Guardhouse off Military Road (now a Museum), where Captain Bowen Colthurst ordered the murder of three innocent civilians in 1916.

Michael Collins walking in Portobello Barracks in 1922. (Courtesy of Cathal Brugha Barracks)

The Army School of Music and the forty-five-piece Army No. 1 Band are based in this barracks. The Irish Army, in fact, has three bands, established in 1923, the No. 1 Army Band in Dublin, the Band of the First Southern Brigade in Cork, and the Band of the 4th Western Brigade in Athlone. The School of Music was started in 1923 when two German musicians were head-hunted and brought to Ireland – Colonel Wilhelm Fritz Brase and Colonel Christian Sauerzweig. They were directors until 1940 and 1947 respectively. In 2003, the bands acquired a brand-new uniform, navy blue in colour with red and gold trimmings. However, even prior to the Irish Free State taking over the barracks, the British Army also had its own bands, as evidenced by the band room/band block in the centre west of the barracks.

Nowadays, the barracks is the headquarters of the 2nd Eastern Brigade and the 2nd Eastern Brigade of the Reserve Defence Forces (previously known as the FCA). The 2nd Cavalry Squadron is also based here, with its fleet of powerful motorbikes for use in escorting the President of Ireland on official engagements.

Near the canal entrance is the Garrison church, now called St Patrick's, which was built in 1842. In 1925 a rear stepped-gallery was built, and a sacristy and altar boys' room were added at the east end, and then re-dedicated for Catholics – prior to this any Catholic soldiers used Rathmines church. In 1939, the world-famous Irish stained-glass artist, Evie Hone, made the three-light east window, depicting the Good Shepherd with St Patrick and St Joseph. It is interesting to note that the three original stained-glass windows, designed by A.E. Childs and installed in 1912, were removed by the British Army in 1922, and now grace St Barbara's Garrison church in Deepcut, Surrey, England. The roof structure features attractive cast-iron struts.

The building of the Garrison church in 1842 necessitated a new guard house (guarding the main-entrance gates) to the east of the church. The original guard house to the west of the church became a national school, and a new infants' school was built just to the south.

The 2nd Eastern Brigade Headquarters dates from 2007, yet its design blends very well with the older buildings.

Part of the land near Leinster Road, which was previously used as married quarters for soldiers, was sold off in the 1980s for private duplex

The former hospital in Cathal Brugha Barracks (the gabled stone building on left) in 2003. The hospital was recently partly demolished to make way for a new Military Archives building. The Red House is in the centre, where Michael Collins lived in 1922, and which was formerly the accommodation block for the hospital staff.

Rathmines Ambulance Division, St John's Voluntary Aid Detachment (VAD), County Dublin. These volunteers during the First World War were attached to Portobello Barracks. (Courtesy of Military Archives, Dept of Defence).

apartments called Grosvenor Lodge, and now the barracks has a reduced area of about 36 acres.

GRIFFITH COLLEGE, SOUTH CIRCULAR ROAD

The famous architect Francis Johnston, who was employed by the Board of Works (now called the Office of Public Works), designed this building for Dublin Corporation as the Richmond Bridewell (prison), to accommodate persons committed by the recorder and city magistrates for misdemeanours and petty offences. It cost £41,300 including acquisition of the site. The site was previously the property of Grimwoods Nurseries (flowers, plants and so on). The foundation stone was laid in 1813, and in December 1818 a batch of eighty-five prisoners from James's Street Bridewell was transferred here, bringing the furniture from that prison with them. They were supervised by a sergeant and six army privates. This prison should not be confused with the Richmond General Penitentiary in Grangegorman, which included the Richmond Lunatic Asylum.

An official report in 1819 gives a good description of the new prison. The three-storey range of buildings was shaped like a hollow square, surrounded by a 15ft-high wall, with a 27ft-wide gravelled path between the building and the wall, all of this occupying about 4 acres. At each angle of the boundary wall was a rampart with a parapet fitted as a post for a sentinel (guard). The main entrance was in the centre of the north boundary wall, having within the gateway, the turnkey's lodge on one side and the guardroom on the other, with sleeping quarters overhead. The governor's rooms were opposite the entrance, comprising offices at the front, and his apartments were at the rear. Prisoners (twenty-three males and thirty-eight females) were accommodated in separate wings, sleeping in dormitories that were not used during the day. The two dining rooms, each 72ft x 18ft, were on the ground floor, with workrooms above and dormitories on the second floor. The kitchen was in the centre of the complex, with a chapel above (subdivided into male and female sections), and there was a schoolroom on the top floor. The rear infirmary (hospital) comprised six rooms, each 24ft x 18ft. There was a single-storey building at the rear with four cells, each 8ft x 8ft, for solitary confinement, with only a slated roof overhead (no ceiling). There was also a rear laundry where sixteen prisoners could work, with a drying loft overhead. Four looms and a few spinning wheels were installed in the prison soon afterwards. The schoolroom was supplied by the Education Society (a voluntary body), and catered for about twelve young boys. Some of the girls did knitting. A quartern loaf of bread (weighing nearly 4½lbs) was issued to each prisoner four days a week.

Initially the prison was badly run by two governors in succession, with reports of escapes, some men and women sleeping together and other violations, until Thomas Purdon was appointed in December 1820.

By the 1824 report, the governor was in charge of 160 males and 122 females. The men slept in forty-seven cells, each 7ft by 8ft, while the women still slept in dormitories. The men were occupied by weaving (112), labouring (thirty) and tailoring (ten), while eight were sick. The women mostly did spinning and weaving, while 8 were sick. A schoolmaster was available to males only, three times a week. By now, a tread-wheel by Mallet had been installed, and acted as a water pump – this hard-labour sentence comprised two-minute stints on the wheel and one-minute rest, for many hours, with a labour force of thirty-two men.

Within two years, there were seventy looms in operation, with the inmates making corduroy for their own prison clothes and also for sale to commercial manufacturers. This resulted in a profit for the city authorities, and some money was paid to the prisoners involved. Pims of William Street had reached an agreement in 1820 with the prison authorities. The former would supply the materials to make cotton cord and pay 3 pence (3d) per yard of weaving (corduroy). More cells had been formed from the large rooms, for females as well as men. A second tread-wheel had been installed, pumping water from the Grand Canal up to a large cistern on the roof. This involved a payment of £25 per annum to the Grand Canal Co. A bakery staffed by some of the prisoners was now supplying all the bread needed for the prison. One room was set aside for women prisoners accompanied by young children. Total silence was required throughout the prison.

The official report for 1831/32 records seventy-six females, occupied in burling cloth (fifteen), needlework (twenty-four), laundry (thirteen), house (sixteen), sweepers (two), sick (one), unemployed (five). The 161 males were occupied in weaving (seventy-eight), gardening (ten), house (thirty-four), tread-wheel (sixteen), trades (twelve), approvers (two), sick (five), unemployed (four). 'Approvers' were presumably supervisors. The industrial employment made a net profit of £322, divided between Dublin Corporation and the workers concerned.

In 1836, stone-breaking was carried out by sixty-one males because weaving work was not required by commercial manufacturers.

All female prisoners were transferred to Grangegorman Female Penitentiary in 1837, and thereafter the Richmond Bridewell was for males only.

By 1839, the prison had been extended eastwards, outside the original boundary wall, comprising five radiating wings of three storeys, providing ninety-five cells, each 9ft by 7ft by 10ft in height. Short-term prisoners (less than one month) were kept here, wearing their own clothes, under a total silence regime (as in the older prison). They did not work and stayed in individual cells for twenty-two hours a day – the other two hours were used for breakfast, dinner and exercise in the yards. Meals were taken in the corridors outside the cells, and beds were replaced with a seat during the day. In the main original prison, the governor was still in the process of converting large rooms into ninety-six more cells. A basic form of heating was introduced into parts of the prison, comprising 1 inch-diameter gun-barrel pipes at high level in corridors, but no radiators.

The year 1841 marked some interesting changes. A juvenile fifty-cell section was opened in part of the north block to accommodate boys from Smithfield Penitentiary, with three or four boys crammed into each cell, size 7ft by 6ft. Three wide corridors were used by the boys as a dining room, schoolroom and workroom. A schoolmaster attended from 10 a.m. to 2 p.m. every day. In addition, lunatics were being admitted, occupying a lot of space in the hospital wards, and disrupting the governance of the prison. Also, more drunks were being held in the new radial wings. The population was swelling, and when the prison inspectors visited, sixty-nine prisoners were picking wool, fifty-four were engaged in whitewashing (painting cell walls with lime) and domestic duties, forty-four in trades, twenty-one on the tread-wheel, fourteen in the laundry, six on outdoor activities, forty-one unemployed in the radial wings; twenty-six were drunk and nineteen sick and lunatic. The twelve small cells for solitary-confinement punishment were deemed unfit for purpose, with the door of each opening into a yard. The hospital wards in the south and south-east had straw on the beds.

The report for 1842 records sixty-seven boys in the juvenile section, aged 9 to 16 years. Most of their crimes were petty, such as stealing handkerchiefs, robbing a till and so on. There were also four orphans who had been found abandoned in the street in the period from 1835 to 1838, one an infant then, two of 3 years, and the other 5 years' old. The juveniles spent their time picking oakum, wool picking, and burling. Many attended the schoolroom, where they used the *Dublin Spelling and Reading Books*, *4th Class Book*, *Goughs and Thompsons Arithmetic*, *Table Books*, *Butlers and the Established Church Catechism*, *Pinnock's Catechism of Geography*, and *Murray's Small Edition of the English Grammar*.

Meals in the prison by this time comprised a breakfast of 7oz of oatmeal and one pint of buttermilk, while on Sundays prisoners received half a pound of bread, 2oz of oatmeal, and a naggin of new milk. For dinner four days a week there was a quarter (two pints) of ox-head soup (real ox heads were used) mixed with 1oz of oatmeal, and 3lbs of potatoes. On the other three days, there were 3lbs of potatoes and 1lbs of buttermilk.

Prison salaries were quite high, amounting to £2,000 per annum, with the governor, Thomas Purdon, receiving £400, the deputy, Rose Cooper, £220, the Protestant schoolmaster, Robert Hamill, £52, the assistant Catholic teacher £30, while the fifteen turnkeys (warders), three watchmen and gate porter received amounts between £52 and £30. The Catholic and Church of Ireland chaplains each received £40. The governor had offices in the centre of the north block, and he and his family lived in the spacious apartments to the rear of the offices. Most staff also lived in the prison. Free coal, candles (for light) and soap were also supplied free of charge, together with uniforms.

During 1842 there was an average of 280 prisoners daily, while on the date of the prison inspectors' visit there were 268 present, including fifty-nine boys, twenty-one lunatics and eighteen drunks. The annual turnover of prisoners in the Richmond Bridewell tended to be high because all sentences were for very short periods, for example, in 1841, 6,118 prisoners were committed, comprising 3,557 drunks, 2,008 ordinary prisoners, and 553 boys under the age of 16 years. Many prisoners were repeat offenders, especially drunks who regarded the Richmond (the radial wings) as a free-boarding house. At this stage the prison had 291 cells, six large workrooms (usually the 12ft-wide corridors), four solitary cells, a large schoolroom, a chapel with four divisions, an infirmary with six wards of ten beds each, a laundry and a communal kitchen. The laundry did the washing for a number of army barracks on a contract basis, and the fifteen prisoners shared some of the net profits. A few prisoners did weaving in their cells, but contract work was in short supply.

The report for 1844 noted sixty-five lunatics in the infirmary, which was in a filthy condition, with some of the patients/prisoners half naked. Elsewhere in the prison, the prisoners slept in hammocks and washed themselves in the open yards at pumps. The old prison comprised 180 cells, average size of 10ft by 8ft, and all 11ft high, served by ten exercise yards with privies and water. The cells in the radial wings had lower ceilings.

The Famine throughout Ireland in 1845 and subsequent years resulted in many people trekking to Dublin seeking food and shelter, and some of these ended up in the Richmond Bridewell. For example, the report for 1849 recorded 538 prisoners when the inspectors visited, including eighty-nine tramps from all over Ireland. A special reception ward was set up to receive new prisoners. Here, baths were provided, and old clothes were dealt with in a fumigating room. Dominic Marques was appointed the new governor at £300 per annum (much less that Thomas Purdon, but still a fantastic salary in that era), and the Catholic curate was earning £100 per annum. The laundry had just been rebuilt by the prisoners. The prison bakery provided its own bread, and also that for the Grangegorman Female Penitentiary. The treadmill now had two wheels. The diet for lunatics and juveniles was supplemented by meat.

By 1850 Newgate was no longer a remand prison for untried prisoners (catering only for convicted prisoners (convicts) until it closed around 1860), and the former were transferred to the Richmond Bridewell. A 'capstan mill' for grinding corn was in the course of erection by the prisoners, to be used as an alternative form of hard labour to the tread-wheel. The three-storey building had two pairs of stones, worked by twenty men, with the granary on the top floor, the circular stones in the middle, and the machinery (by Perrott of Cork) on the ground floor. Adjoining was a covered space, 50ft x 50ft, for the men operating the capstan, which could grind thirty barrels of wheat a week. Originally, the schoolroom catered for adults and juveniles, but now only the latter are catered for – fifteen boys between the ages of 10 and 12, fifty-three of

12 to 15 years, and fifteen of 15 to 17 years. The eighty-three boys made up almost half of the prison population.

By 1852, all the privies were gone, and a small number of water closets and urinals were provided. A new water pipe had been laid from the canal, including three filtering chambers, and the treadwheel operated three pumps (water wells for drinking water). There were now twelve looms for weaving, kept in individual cells with the weavers. The effects of the Famine were still being felt in Dublin, with many orphans and young vagrants ending up in the Richmond Bridewell. Various punishments were part of the penal system, including solitary confinement for a few days, bread and water, half rations, dark rooms, and 'shot drill' with a 9lbs ball.

By 1856, there were no lunatics in the Richmond Bridewell (Dundrum was opened a few years previously), but between a third and half of prisoners were juveniles, including orphans. Vegetable soup (probably from the prison garden) was now given to the short-term prisoners. On 18 November, a fire broke out in the central chapel, whereby the chapel, schoolroom and stores of yarn were destroyed, and likewise the bakery roof.

The report for 1857 records that the number of lunatics was starting to rise again, with fourteen present when the inspectors visited. Juveniles were still too numerous, including a few boys under the age of 10 years. The prison also handled soldiers and sailors who had been tried by court martial, some for desertion. The number of punishments for breach of prison rules was extremely high, with 433 cases of confinement to dark cells (there were nine dark cells), 418 cases of 'other' (bread and water, half rations and so on), thirty-three cases of whipping and four cases of solitary confinement. The prison locked down for the night at 4.30 p.m. in winter and 6 p.m. in summer. Following the fire in 1856, a new Catholic chapel had been built, and also a new Protestant chapel.

Some of the prisoners made most of the clothes, which consisted of vests, shirts, trousers, jackets, caps, and also their shoes. Underpants, socks, jumpers and coats were not worn by prisoners. By now, hard labour on the treadwheel was reduced from seven hours a day to four and a half hours, and the treadwheel was partitioned to stop chat between prisoners. The whole ethos of the prison concentrated on keeping the prisoners apart and dividing them into different classes, to prevent the hardened criminals from contaminating the less experienced ones. Hence the constant drive to provide as many single cells as possible, where meals were taken. The governor divided prison occupations into punitive labour (treadmill, capstan mill, cleaning and so forth) and industrial labour (picking coir fibre, weaving, mat making and various trades), the latter yielding a net profit for the prison and the men involved. By now the bakery had ceased operations. The diet varied little over the years, but we learn now of a cheaper substitute – two days a week, 'gruel' was served instead of milk, and consisted of 1 ounce of oatmeal mixed with a pint of water.

By 1861, gas lighting had been introduced into most cells, operating from sunset until 8 p.m. for anyone who wanted to read. Heating consisted of a high-level hot-water pipe running across the cell, which was really useless. The capstan mill for grinding corn was discontinued due to a recent fire, after only ten years of operation, and soon the ground floor was allocated as a dayroom and dining room for the increasing number of lunatics (fifty in 1862). The latter worked in the governors' large garden outside the west side of the prison. Around this time, a railings had been erected in front of the north-east and north-west corners of the prison to enclose waste ground.

The photographing of prisons was introduced into the Richmond Bridewell in 1862, and became an important tool in the fight against crime.

On 10 August 1864, a soldier from the 9th Lancers who had been sentenced to hard labour in the Richmond Bridewell went into the machine room of the treadmill and deliberately crushed his hand in the cogs, so that he would be discharged, as unfit for service, from his regiment upon his release from prison (which he was). This year also saw an increase in the number of lunatics to forty-five, although nine died during the year – twelve had died the previous year. Fourteen juveniles were present when the inspectors visited, including three under the age of 10 years, although most juveniles were now just passing through on their way to reformatories in Glencree or Upton, or Rehoboth (the latter Protestant).

Normally prisoners did not escape from the Richmond, but the easy escape (with the aid of a ladder) of the political prisoner James Stephens in November 1865 resulted in an enquiry and the dismissal of the governor, Dominic Marques, by the Lord Lieutenant. The new governor, Richard Boyd, received a salary of £300 per annum, which increased to £350 two years later. New security measures included keeping the most important keys in the governor's bedroom.

Coming up to the end of the 1860s, various interesting facts are recorded. Most of the laundry work was now done in the Grangegorman Female Penitentiary, and in return some prisoners in the Richmond made linsey-woolsey for the females. Mat making was still the main profitable occupation in the Richmond. With the fall-off in the number of lunatics, the capstan mill (part of which had been converted into a dining room) was demolished. The punishment cells were under the Protestant church, and frequently the prisoners disturbed those worshiping above them. These particular cells had no glass in the windows, which made them very cold in the winter months. Cocoa fibre, made by some prisoners, was used as toilet paper, and sometimes clogged up the drains. Visits were allowed every three months, and visitors could only partly see the prisoners through a grating. All prisoners got a monthly bath, going to the reception ward for such purpose. The toilets were in open sheds, and the numerous exercise yards had now been asphalted. A new schoolroom had been fitted out, with forty-two separate compartments/stalls for the boys. A 9-year-old boy (who may have been younger) was under a sentence of one week for stealing a mat! In 1869, twenty-nine convicted soldiers and sailors were present on a particular day. Potatoes were creeping back into the diet, but only for a few months of the year.

The 1870s saw an increase in the prison population, so that many cells were frequently occupied by a few prisoners. For example, in September 1874, 429 prisoners were accommodated in 262 cells. However, the opening of the Grangegorman Male Prison around this time resulted in a gradual decline in the numbers in the Richmond, especially in the 1880s, enabling the Richmond Bridewell to close on 31 March 1888. On 21 June 1888, the Prisons Board transferred the premises to the War Department. A map of 1889 shows two lime kilns near the south-east corner of the site. The map also shows two Catholic chapels in the centre of the prison and an Episcopal chapel. The River Poddle is marked running alongside the west of the governors' large garden, in addition to another culverted branch running alongside the east boundary of the site.

The 'Liberator', Daniel O'Connell, was a prisoner in the Richmond Bridewell in 1844, although he was treated as a dignitary on the orders of Dublin Corporation. Daniel, as leader of the Repeal Association (Repeal of the Act of Union in 1800, and setting up again the Irish Parliament in College Green), held 'monster meetings' around the country, the biggest being at the Hill of Tara in County Meath. A proposed 'monster meeting' at Clontarf in October 1843 was banned, and reluctantly cancelled by O'Connell. While O'Connell was advocating political solutions to Ireland's quest for freedom, Young Ireland was set up with more forceful inclinations under the leadership of Thomas Davis, Charles Gavin Duffy, John Blake Dillon,and William Smith O'Brien, who also started *The Nation* newspaper. Daniel O'Connell and Charles Gavin Duffy were arrested in 1844 and 'imprisoned' for three months in the Richmond Penitentiary (as it was renamed for a few years), along with John O'Connell (son of Daniel), Dr John Gray, 'Honest' Tom Steele, Thomas Ray, Richard Barrett, Thomas Tierney and P.J. Tyrrell (collectively called 'The Repeal Martyrs' or 'Traversers'). However, to be more accurate, these men were given individual fully furnished luxury apartments. In fact, Tom Ray commissioned artist Henry O'Neill, RHA, to paint nineteen watercolour scenes of the apartments, which show carpeting, wallpaper, canopied four-poster beds, pianos, bookcases, fireplaces, curtains and other comforts. The various bedrooms and sitting rooms were very spacious (20ft by 17ft average), with 12ft-high ceilings, and the Liberator's bedroom was 25ft by 21ft. A small private Catholic chapel was included, showing mass in progress. The dining room (30ft × 21ft) shows a big oval table surrounded by ladies and gentlemen in fashionable outfits, and a decanter of whiskey in the corner, next to Daniel O'Connell wearing his green beret. The drawing room was well stocked with books. The paintings include the governor's (Thomas Purdon) and deputy governor's (Rose Cooper) separate gardens, each filled with flowers and shrubs, in addition to a mound and small watchtower, which was nicknamed the Hill of Tara. One of the paintings refers to the north block, including tower and clock, as the gaol, and the repeal state prisoners' apartments behind – in fact the O'Connell prisoners occupied the governor's own apartments, and presumably he and his family made temporary arrangements to live in the front offices or rent a nearby house. The governor's gardens were in the area now occupied by the National Stadium and a primary school. The nineteen paintings were later bought by Brother Allen of the O'Connell Schools in North Richmond Street, because it was Daniel O'Connell who laid the foundation stone for that famous Christian Brothers school and novitiate in 1828. In due course, the Brothers sold the paintings to the National Museum.

Not to be outdone by Tom Ray, Dr John Gray (later Sir) commissioned the famous artist Nicholas Crowley to paint an oil portrait of Daniel O'Connell while in the prison. Daniel O'Connell was released from prison after three months but died in 1847, and is buried in Glasnevin Cemetery. Thomas Davis of the Young Irelanders died in 1845, and is buried in Mount Jerome.

By the early 1890s, the British Army was in occupation, and renamed it Wellington Barracks. Its first soldiers were the Royal Munster Fusiliers. The original complex was square shaped, with a cruciform-shaped building occupying the central area, resulting in four internal courtyards. However, substantial parts of these internal structures were demolished, including the governor's apartment block behind the clock tower, and the central kitchen, chapel and so forth. Three of the radial wings to the east of the original prison were demolished to make way for blocks of married quarters. Likewise the central gatehouse opposite the clock tower disappeared, and also the four original 15ft-high boundary walls adjacent to the four main walls of the prison. A new low boundary wall was erected adjoining the public footpath, granite-faced externally and limestone-faced internally, with high railings on top, marking the front site boundary, corresponding with the north elevation of the original projecting gatehouse. A new guardhouse was completed at the north-west corner of the site on

1844 painting by Henry O'Neill, depicting the governor's garden on the west side of Richmond Bridewell, with the pavilion/marquee on the left (the latter was nicknamed Mullaghmast in memory of a Monster Meeting held there in 1843 by Daniel O'Connell). (Courtesy of Irish Christian Brothers)

1844 painting by Henry O'Neill, depicting part of the deputy governor's garden (Rose Cooper), including a mound nicknamed 'The Hill of Tara'. Note the outdoor gym right under the prison wall. (Courtesy of Irish Christian Brothers)

11 November 1893 at a cost of £2,389, including prisoners' cells in the central section and regimental offices in the west wing. Originally the prison land did not have frontage onto the canal, being separated from it by houses called Wellington Place, but these houses were acquired and demolished to make way for other army buildings, although the name Wellington was passed on to the new army barracks. A south-east entrance, off the canal wharf, was formed at that stage (the stone pillars and iron gates can still be seen today at the west end of Gordon's Fuel Depot) – in fact, a large coal bunker was provided just inside this gate.

In 1910, the accommodation schedule listed space for nineteen officers, fourteen sergeants, 561 non-commissioned officers and men, thirty-six married soldiers and twelve horses.

However, during the 1916 Easter Rising, Wellington Barracks had only about 100 soldiers, and hence very little involvement in quelling the uprising.

In 1922, the British Army handed over the barracks to the Irish Army, and it was renamed Griffith Barracks in memory of Arthur Griffith, the founder of the Sinn Féin political party in 1905.

During the Civil War following independence, the barracks came under attack on 8 November 1922, while the Irish Free State troops were on parade duty. Anti-Treaty troops occupied some of the houses at Upper Parnell Place on the south side of the Grand Canal and began sniping at the

1844 painting by Henry O'Neill, depicting the small private chapel in the Richmond Bridewell used by Daniel O'Connell. (Courtesy of Irish Christian Bothers)

barracks, which resulted in one fatality and numerous injuries. The army returned fire, causing some slight damage to the houses and injury to two of the snipers. The house owners later sought compensation from the new government and were awarded varying amounts. For example, P.J. Browner in No. 24 Upper Parnell Place was paid £3 plus legal costs because his roof was pierced by bullets. William Oates in No. 27 received £9 plus costs for a similar reason. W.H. Kelly in No. 28 received £90 plus costs for damage to his furniture (hit by rifle fire), and for alleged theft of jewellery. Edward McGuirk, a butcher from 69 Harold's Cross Road, received £31 10s plus costs because his mare was killed and his harness and van were damaged while his man was inside the barracks delivering meat – there is no mention of compensation for the family of the delivery man who was killed.

Thereafter, the barracks was only partly used for army purposes. In 1925, the Greenmount and Boyne Linen Co. took a lease from the Board of Works of four blocks, previously used as married quarters for thirty-six army families, and they remained here until 1963. The space was used as accommodation for their own employees and appropriately called Greenmount Quarters.

In the Second World War (the Emergency in neutral Ireland), the army was engaged in shooting cattle and digging trenches for burial during the 'foot and mouth' crisis of 1941, and also digging turf in the bogs around Timahoe (Laois), since no coal could be imported from England.

The sport of amateur boxing originated in British Army barracks, and the Irish Amateur Boxing Association was founded in Beggars Bush Barracks in 1911, with D.P. Mordaunt as its first president. Soon, boxing clubs were set up around Ireland, providing a welcome social outlet in working-class neighbourhoods. Competitions were still held in different army barracks until the association decided to build its own stadium on some land leased for ninety-nine years from 1939 in Griffith Barracks. The building committee comprised Major General W.R.E. Murphy and his wife, Revd John McLaughlin, Frank Aiken (minister for defence), Lieutenant-General Daniel McKenna, Niall D. McLaughlin, Alfred E. Jones (architect), Stephen S. Kelly (architect), Colonel Thomas McGrath, Commandant J.A. Farren, Commandant L. Breenan, John Coffey and Garda James Healy. The stadium opened in March 1939 for the National Senior Championships. The army retained a long building to the west of the new stadium as its own gym (which was built in 1899 as the drill shed for the 1st Battalion Infantry), and nowadays this houses three practice rings for the stadium. Besides

1844 painting by Henry O'Neill, depicting the dining room in the Richmond Bridewell used by Daniel O'Connell, associates and families. Daniel O'Connell sits on the right, sporting his signature green beret. (Courtesy of Irish Christian Bothers)

March 1939 at the opening of the National Stadium on the occasion of the National Senior
Championships in boxing. (Courtesy of National Stadium)

A boxing tournament on the 29 March 2001 in the National Stadium, which is sited on the
site of the governor's gardens attached to the former Richmond Bridewell.

boxing tournaments, the stadium has hosted many concerts and other events, including a Moving Hearts farewell concert in the 1980s and an ice-skating pantomime in the 1960s. The stadium was recently refurbished, including a new front facade and a new roof.

From 1946 to 1966, the Labour Court occupied the north block of the barracks.

In the 1960s and '70s, Dublin Corporation and the Eastern Health Board utilised some blocks for homeless people, and also the census was based here. During this period, the Army Reserves, FCA (Fórsa Cosanta Áitiúil) were also in occupation. By the late 1970s, the army had regained the use of most of the buildings, but a fire destroyed the East Block in 1979, leading to its demolition. In 1988, the film, *Act of Betrayal*, was shot here.

Business and Accounting Training, which was founded in 1974, bought the 7-acre army barracks in 1992, and now Griffith College is making great

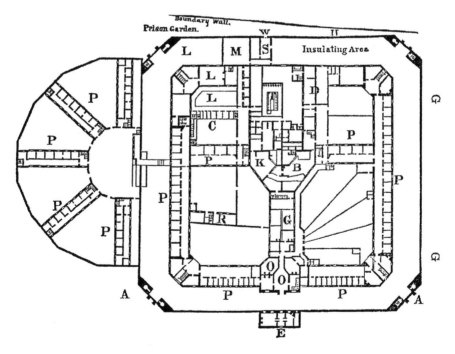

1860s plan of the Richmond Bridewell, with the following legend: A, Waste ground railed in; B, Bakehouse; C, Punishment Cells; D, Washhouse; E, Entrance; G, Governors Apartments; G-G, Governor's Garden; K, Kitchen; L, Lunatic Wards; M, Former Capstan Mill; O, Offices; P, Prisoners cells; T, Treadwheel (centre left-hand side); R, Workshops; S, Store. (Courtesy of Southampton University Digitisation Project online)

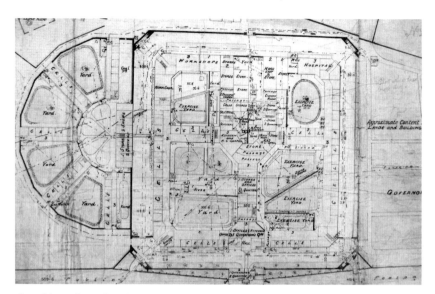

Plan of the Richmond Bridewell in 1889, immediately after the prison was passed to the War Department and re-named Wellington Barracks. (Courtesy of the Office of Public Works)

use of the former prison/barracks as a third-level college. In 2005, two five-storey blocks of student apartments were built alongside the canal, with basement car parking, and the following year a modern conference centre and design faculty were built nearby.

The north-east corner of the former barracks was acquired by the Eastern Health Board, who demolished the army married-quarters blocks and built Bellvilla in 1998, as a fifty-bed community unit for older persons. This is currently being extended.

Looking around the campus now, stone buildings date from the prison era, whereas red-bricked buildings date from British Army days. Historic portions to be admired include the north block, built of squared black-calp limestone, with ashlar-limestone window surrounds (yellow brick to the two upper floors of the rear elevation), and granite window sills. The large windows were originally fitted with louvres for privacy and iron bars for security. The impressive central staircase in the north block dates from British Army days, and likewise the fireplaces and red-brick chimney stacks. The west block and the two spurs are also original, but the large gap at the north end was an army alteration. The two limestone buildings on the east side of the campus (one housing the present students' union) were built in 1839 as part of the five-wing radial extension outside the east side of the original prison. These are not as impressive as the original prison, being of smaller dimensions and incorporating smaller windows. The limestone at ground floor of the two-storey building that separates them dates from the time of the prison, and the red brick first-floor addition from British Army days. Note the nearby stables. The three-storey red-bricked building towards the south-east of the original prison was built as soldiers' quarters (and for the army band), but the nearby Regimental Institute (recreation building with south-facing verandas) and many of the other single-storey brick buildings were recently demolished to make way for apartments and classrooms. The former 1893 army guardhouse at the north-west of the campus has been used since 1998 as the Griffith Barracks' Multi-Denominational School (primary school). During the British Army days, there was an education hut in the south-east corner of the barracks, and a church hut in the south-west corner. During the Irish Army days, there were two school huts in the south-west corner of the site. The two-storey house at the north-east corner was the quartermaster quarters in army times, and awaits refurbishment. Many numbered boundary stones can be seen built into the boundary walls all around the campus, with the letters WD (War Department).

Griffith Barracks in the 1950s, looking north. (Courtesy of National Library of Ireland)

The 1893 Army Barracks Guardhouse is now a primary school on the campus of Griffith College.

The front of Griffith College today.

FAMOUS PEOPLE

ROBERT EMMET

For many people, Robert Emmet was the most famous resident of Harold's Cross, although he only lodged under the assumed name of Hewitt for about a month in a house owned by Mrs Anne Palmer, before his arrest in 1803 by Major Sirr at the tender age of 25 years. After his execution in the same year outside St Catherine's church in Thomas Street, his body disappeared, and to this day no one knows where he is buried. There is also some confusion about the exact house in Harold's Cross where he was arrested, some people saying it was at the bottom of Mount Drummond Avenue, where a large house in tenements up until the 1970s was called Emmet House (Greenfield House before that). The house was in fact 5 Harold's Cross, beside the present 23 Harold's Cross Road, on the north side of the entrance to the present Le Vere Terrace. The small two-storey house faced the main Harold's Cross Road, and had a medium-sized garden, including a tree, in front. In later years, the back yards of 4 and 6 Armstrong Street would have abutted the side gable wall of the original old house, which was later demolished. To mark the bicentenary of the death of Robert Emmet, the Robert Emmet Association arranged for a limestone plaque to be unveiled on 25 August 2003 by the former Lord Mayor of Dublin, Councillor Mary Freehill, on the site of the original house at the corner of Le Vere Terrace. Phillip Emmet and some members of his family travelled up for the occasion from Kilpedder, County Wicklow – his family are direct descendants of Thomas Addis Emmet (the older brother of Robert Emmet). The bridge over the Grand Canal was always called Clanbrassil Bridge, or Harold's Cross

1890 watercolour of the 1803 capture of Robert Emmet in Harold's Cross by Major Sirr.
(Courtesy of The Allen Library)

Bridge, but when it was rebuilt in 1936 it was renamed Emmet Bridge, and a bronze bust of Emmet by Albert Power, in bass-relief, was erected on the east balustrade in 1938, with Gaelic inscription underneath.

Emmet's faithful servant, Anne Devlin, was badly tortured by the authorities about the activities of Robert Emmet, but she never broke her silence. Sadly, she was abandoned thereafter, and died a pauper in 1851. She is buried in Glasnevin Cemetery, and her friend Dr Richard Madden provided a simple headstone over her grave. In 1904, the Dublin Cemetery Committee erected a fine high cross over her grave. In addition, on 4 March 2004, the Robert Emmet Association unveiled a lovely bronze statue of her in Main Street, Rathfarnham.

JOHN STANISLAUS JOYCE

John Stanislaus Joyce, originally from Cork, was a rates collector in Dublin, where he met Mary Jane Murray while both of them were in the choir of the church of the Three Patrons, Rathgar. Mary Jane's family was living in 7 Upper Clanbrassil Street, and John Joyce decided to move to 15 Upper Clanbrassil Street. John and Mary Jane married on 5 May 1880 in Our Lady of Refuge church, Rathmines, just before Mary Jane's twenty-first

To commemorate the bi-centenary of the capture of Robert Emmet in Harold's Cross, the Robert Emmet Association organised a pageant on 25 August 2003. Here the actors march over Robert Emmet Bridge on their way to unveil a plaque at the corner of Le Vere Terrace, led by a very young Robert Emmet lookalike.

birthday. After the honeymoon, the Joyces settled at 47 Northumberland Avenue, Dún Laoghaire. The couple moved to 41 Brighton Square, backing on to No. 337 Harold's Cross Road, where James Joyce was born on 2 February 1882, the eldest of a family of ten children. James was baptised in St Joseph's church, Terenure. In 1884, the family moved to 23 Castlewood Avenue, Rathmines, and thereafter moved many more times – in those days, very few people bought houses, but rented instead. The unusual novel *Ulysses*, published by James Joyce in Paris in 1922, is set in Dublin on 16 June 1904 (Bloomsday), with two main fictional characters, Leopold Bloom and Stephen Dedalus, wandering around Dublin. In the novel there are many references to the Harold's Cross area, including a horse-drawn tram going over Emmet Bridge, Griffith Barracks ('cease to do evil'), Major Gamble in Mount Jerome, a boxing soldier from Portobello Barracks (Cathal Brugha), Fr Sebastian (Keens) in Mount Argus, in addition to Brighton Square, Kenilworth Square, and Harold's Cross Road. '52 Clanbrassil Street' is also mentioned, probably Lower, since Wesley Terrace was positioned between 49 and 57, Upper Clanbrassil Street. The year 2004 was the centenary of Bloomsday, and there were great celebrations in Dublin, which carried on for many months.

JOHN KEOGH

John Keogh, very active in the quest for Catholic Emancipation, lived for many years in Mount Jerome House (now part of the cemetery). After his return from France in 1802, Robert Emmet had supper in the Keogh home.

J.B. YEATS

In the years 1883 to 1887, the famous portrait artist John Butler Yeats, father of artist Jack, and poet William Butler Yeats, lived in 10 Ashfield Terrace, which is now 418 Harold's Cross Road, very near Brighton Square. John's most famous portraits of the Fenian John O'Leary hang in the National Gallery. Harold Leask, architectural author, also lived in this house in the first half of the twentieth century.

JONATHAN PIM

Jonathan Pim (Junior) lived at 1 Parnell Place Upper in the 1840s, now the site of an Applegreen petrol station. The Pims were the owners of the adjoining Greenmount Spinning Manufactory (later called the Greenmount and Boyne Linen Co.).

COUNTESS MARKIEVICZ

In 1912, Countess Markievicz, one of the leaders of Cumann na mBan, came to live at 49B Leinster Road, halfway between Harold's Cross and Rathmines, and from here ran a secret printing press. Her maiden name was Constance Gore-Booth (the family were big landlords based in Lissadell House, Sligo) and she married a Pole, Count Casimir Markievicz, but separated amicably from him. In 1918, she was elected for Sinn Féin as the first-ever woman MP at Westminister, in London.

LORD LONGFORD

Lord Longford, Edward Pakenham, famous for his association with the Gate Theatre in the 1940s and '50s, lived in Grosvenor Park at the corner of Leinster Road and Grosvenor Place, up until his death in 1961. Edward was the 6th Earl of Longford, and his headstone in Mount Jerome Cemetery (to the south of the old house) describes him as a poet and patriot, while his wife Christine (who died in 1980) is described as a writer and dramatist. Happy and sad masks, the symbol of the theatre, are carved on the sides of the headstone. The auctioneer described Grosvenor Park in 1962 as having 2 acres, 1 rood and 36 perches. There were four reception rooms and a cloakroom on the hall floor, four bedrooms and two bathrooms on the first floor, and three servants' rooms, kitchen and domestic quarters on the ground floor, in addition to central heating, a conservatory, greenhouse, enclosed yard with three garages, stables, workshop and more. The house was demolished in the 1970s and replaced with townhouses bearing the same name. Lord Longford was related to the founder of St Paul's Retreat, Mount Argus, Revd Paul Mary Pakenham.

THE KELLY AND ROWSOME FAMILIES

The Kelly family of *Dublin Opinion* fame lived for many years in 139 Harold's Cross Road, right up to the 1980s. While the Rowsome family, famous as traditional Irish musicians and bagpipe makers, lived for many years in 18 Armstrong Street.

WILLIAM HAYES

William Hayes (1840–1918), was the superintendent of the Sunday school in the Protestant church beside Mount Jerome Cemetery for fifty years in the latter half of the nineteenth century. The Hayes family lived at Mount Tallant House from 1844 to 1851, and then moved to Edmondstown Park (a big house) in Whitechurch, Rathfarnham. However, he is more famous as one of the three founders of the chemists Hayes Conyngham and Robinson (HCR) in 1897, although he had bought 12 Grafton Street for a druggist shop in 1864. The other partners were Henry Conyngham of Upper Baggot Street and Thomas Robinson of Dún Laoghaire. William was also one of the founders of the Pharmaceutical Society of Ireland in 1875. The HCR chain of chemists included a branch at Leonard's Corner up until the mid-1980s, and the chain was sold to Boots Chemist in 1997.

CECIL SHERIDAN

In the 1970s, Cecil Sheridan, the comedian, ran a gift and crafts shop called Cosy Cottage a few doors away from Cooney's (now Centra) grocers, in the centre of the village.

AODHAGAN BRIOSCU AND SEAN O'SIOCHAIN

Two of the founders of Gael Linn had strong connections with Harold's Cross, namely the architect Aodhagan Brioscu (Briscoe), whose family lived for many years in Westfield Road, and Sean O'Siochain who taught in Harold's Cross National School in nearby Clareville Road.

Comedian Cecil Sheridan in 1954, outside Robins Bros headstones, opposite the Holy Rosary church. Note the advertisement for the British film, *Lease of Life*. (Courtesy of Anthony Carberry)

JAMES CARROLL

James Carroll, plastering contractor, Lord Mayor of Dublin in 1957/58, lived in 73 Harold's Cross Road (opposite the hospice).

HENRY CROWLEY AND CHARLES MACKENZIE

Henry Crowley, an artist, was a nephew of the more famous artist Nicholas Joseph Crowley. Henry regularly exhibited at the Royal Hibernian Academy (RHA) in the 1860s, and lived at 72 Harold's Cross (now No. 228), also known as Mountain View Terrace. He worked mainly in landscapes, but one intriguing painting from 1861 is entitled 'The Bird's Nest' – could this be a reference to the Brethren girls' orphanage opposite his house? The Hugh Lane Gallery in Dublin has one of his paintings, entitled 'The Grandmother'. Henry died in 1869, aged 27 years.

Another landscape painter who resided in Harold's Cross was Charles Mackenzie, who attended the Dublin Society Schools, first the Landscape and Ornament School in 1769, and then the Figure Drawing School the following year. He sent fourteen paintings to an exhibition in the Parliament House (now Bank of Ireland) in 1801. The Dublin Society was called the Royal Dublin Society (RDS) in later years, and its art school became the Metropolitan College of Art, and is now the National College of Art and Design.

CECELIA MARGARET CAMPBELL

Cecelia Margaret Campbell (1791–1857) was a prominent Dublin painter whose works included many watercolours of the Harold's Cross locality in 1817. Her painter father, John Henry Campbell, was more famous, and likewise her husband, George Nairn, who specialised in animal pictures. Cecelia painted two scenes of Hen and Chicken Lane (later called Mount Drummond Avenue), which appears to include a stream, possibly a tributary of the Swan River. Other Harold's Cross landmarks which she painted were a lime kiln, and a lovely view of Clanbrassil Bridge (now called Emmet Bridge). She exhibited quite a few paintings at the Royal Hibernian Academy.

WILLIAM SHEPPARD

William Sheppard, landscape gardener and designer of St Stephen's Green and Harold's Cross Park, lived in 74 Kenilworth Square.

GEORGE RUSSELL (Æ)

George Russell (Æ), poet, lived for a while as a child in 67 Grosvenor Square. In the 1920s, his parties for the literary set, at 17 Rathgar Avenue opposite the Rathgar Schools, were famous.

HOWARD GRUBB

No. 51 Kenilworth Square, a fine three-storey detached house, was home in the 1890s to the famous astronomer Sir Howard Grubb (his telescope factory was in Observatory Lane, Rathmines, leading up to the present Leinster Cricket Club), while the famous le Brocquy artistic family also lived here in the middle decades of the twentieth century. Ernest Blythe TD was a neighbour at No. 50 during the same period.

LOUIS LE BROCQUY

Louis le Brocquy was born in 1916 in 4 Zion Road, Rathgar, to Albert and Sybil (née deLacy Staunton), followed by Noel, and then Melanie in 1919. The family moved to 51 Kenilworth Square in 1930, remaining here until the late 1970s. After finishing secondary school in 1933, Louis went to work in the family business, the Greenmount Oil Company in Harold's Cross, and studied chemistry at night classes in both Kevin Street Technical College and Trinity College Dublin. After five years in this business, Louis felt attracted to painting and went to the Continent, where he taught himself by studying the great artists in the major galleries. During the war years, Louis was back in Kenilworth Square with his parents, and around 1942 he painted *Tennis Courts in Kenilworth Square*. Thereafter his life revolved around London and France, although before his death in 2012 he and his artist wife, Anne Madden, also had a house in Portobello, Dublin.

MUBARAK HABIB

Most Harold's Cross residents probably never heard of Mubarak Habib, a 49-year old man from Somalia who made a one-minute guest appearance on 6 June 2012. In fact, he jogged through, carrying the Olympic Torch. The Olympics were held in London that year, and it was decided that the torch should travel from Northern Ireland down through the Republic of Ireland, as a gesture of goodwill. The torch was carried in relays by many special people. 15-year-old Ger Keelan was Young Person of the Year in 2007, after saving his father's life in a farm accident in Westmeath, and he carried the flame along Grove Road up from Portobello. Mubarak Habib, who was a volunteer with SARI (Sport Against Racism in Ireland), took over near Emmet Bridge, and carried the torch over the bridge and down Clanbrassil Street. All the local schoolchildren, dressed in their uniforms, lined the route and cheered the torch on its historic way.

On 6 June 2012, the Olympic Torch was carried over Robert Emmet Bridge by Mubarak Habib (in white tracksuit).

SELECTED SOURCES

ARCHIVES

National Archives
Ordnance Survey Mill Books
Ordnance Survey House Books
E.D. Files (Dept. of Education)
Lord Meath Index
Tithe Applotment Books
Griffith's Valuation
Census of 1901 and 1911
Landed Estates Court Rentals

National Library
Down's Survey 1654
Books of Survey and Distribution
Parliamentary Papers – Education, and Municipal Boundaries
Rathmines News/Dublin Lantern, 1895–1907

Lord Meath (Private Archives)
Eighteenth- and nineteenth-century estate maps and rental books

Representative Church Body Library
Records of Harold's Cross Anglican church

Valuation Office
Cancelled Books and Maps

Dept. of Defence Archives
Bureau of Military History 1913–1921

Our Lady's Hospice Archives
Congregation Annals

Various Jubilee Booklets
Children of Mary Bulletins 1934–1963
Annual Report for 2014

Mount Argus Archives
Various booklets and photographs

Central Catholic Library
Irish Catholic Directory, 1821 onwards

Irish Architectural Archive
Irish Builder Magazine
Photo Collection
Roseanne Dunne Collection

Catholic Diocesan Archives
1937 – Visitation Report
1938 – Souvenir Booklet

Charitable Commissioners
Religious Congregations

Dublin City Library and Archives
Thom's Directory, 1844–2016

Trinity College Map Library
Ordnance Survey Maps for 1837, 1869, 1882, 1907, 1936, 1967

Southampton University: www.dippam.ac.uk
Reports of the Inspectors-General on the General State of the Prisons in Ireland

Interview with Melanie le Brocquy

PUBLICATIONS

Anon, *Centenary of the Passionists in Ireland, 1856–1956*
Anon, *Greystones Presbyterian Church, 1887–1987*
Anon, *Our Lady's Hospice, Dublin, 1845–1945: A City set on a Hill*
Anon, *Sisters of St Clare: A Brief History* (1985)
Anon, *Sisters of Charity: Celebrating 150 Years* (1995)
Anon, *Souvenir of Church of Our Lady of the Rosary* (1938)
Arnold, Mavis, *Children of the Poor Clares* (Belfast; Appletree Press, 1985)
Brasch, R., *Reminiscences of a Roving Rabbi* (Sydney; Angus & Robertson, 1998)
Burton, Nathanael Joseph, *Letters from Harold's Cross* (Dublin; J.F. Fouler, 1850)
Donnelly, Nicholas, *A Short History of Some Dublin Parishes* (Catholic Truth Society of Ireland, 1905)

Elliott, Anthony, 'The Abbey of St Thomas' in *The Journal of the Royal Society of Antiquaries of Ireland*, Vol. XXII (1892), pp. 25-41

Forristal, Desmond, *The First Loreto Sisters* (Dublin; Dominican Publications, 1994)

Dublin Corporation, *The Rathmines Township, a Chronology* (1995)

Harrison, Richard, *Dublin Quakers in Business, 1800–1850* (MLitt thesis, 1987, Trinity College Dublin)

Lewis, S., *History and Topography of Dublin City and County* (London; S. Lewis & Co. 1837)

McCoole, Sinead, *No Ordinary Women* (Dublin; O'Brien Press, 2015)

Madden, R., *Life and Times of Robert Emmet* (New York; Kennedy, 1902)

O'Maitiu, Seamas, *Dublin's Suburban Towns, 1834–1930* (Dublin, Four Courts Press, 2003)

Mount Jerome Historical Project, 1996/97, *Mount Jerome, A Victorian Cemetery*

Raftery, Mary, *Suffer the Little Children* (Dublin; New Island, 1999)

Rowan, M.V., *An Apostle of Catholic Dublin, Fr Henry Young* (1944)

Wigham, H.A., *A Christian Philanthropist – Memoir of Richard Allen* (London; Hodder & Stoughton, 1886)

INDEX

Abattoir 143
Abbey Stained Glass Studios 47
Abbey Stream 162
Abbey of St Thomas 13
Abbey of Thomas Court and Donore 13
Acres Cross 8
Aiken, Frank 201
Aikenhead, Mary 95
Akmene 65
Albert Hall 106
Alderman Flanagan 18
Alexandra Guild House 57
Alexander Perry & Co 131
Allen family 35
Anne's newsagent 152
Apollo Cinema 127
Aquarius Youth Club 86
An Tur Gloine 43, 55
Arbutus Avenue 172
Ardee, Baron of 13
Army School of Music 187
Ascension, The 121
Ashfield House 53
Ashworth, Charles Herbert 170
Aughavanagh Road 66

Ball, Fanny 29, 78
Balmers sweets 155
Banks 144
Baptist Church 61
Barberstownland 16
Barony of Uppercross 8
Bas, Samuel le 68
Battalion, Fourth 22
Beardwood, James 96
Begg, Fr Des 48

Bellew, Jane 103
Bellvilla 204
Bergin Place 169
Beth Olam 66
Bethany Home 44
Birds Nest 38
Blackberry Parks 18
Bloomfield School 66
Blythe, Ernest 214
Board of Education 72
Booth Poole 138
Bosonnet jams 149
Bowen-Colthurst, Captain 183
Bowers Abattoir 143
Boxing Stadium 201
Boyne Weaving Co 129
Brabazon, William 13
Brady, Fr Kevin 48
Brethren 61, 62
Bretzel bakery 66
Brighton Square 177
Briscoe, Robert 66
British Pathe News 149
Brittains Car Assembly 138
Brocquy, Louis le 132, 214
Broe sculptors 45, 155
Brown, Fr 48
Brown & Polson 139
Buchan 162
Buckleys Orchard 147
Buggy Barracks 179
Burke Bros149
Burmah-Castrol 134
Business & Accounting Training 203
Button factory 137
Byrne, Alfie 160

Campbell, Cecelia 213
Capstan mill 193
Caritas 100
Carlisle Cricket Club 70
Carmelites, Discalced 73
Carmelite nuns 39
Casimir 177, 210
Cathal Brugha Barracks 180
Ceannt, Eamon 145
Cedar Court 40
Century House 57
Charles, Saint 116
Cherry Court 40
Cherry Orchard 134
Chicken Lane 170
Children of Mary 105
CIÉ 161
City Watercourse 162
Clanbrassil 160, 177
Clandaube Bridge 164
Clarkes Buildings 31, 173
Clareville Road school 85
Clarnico Murray sweets 139
Classic Cinema 141
Cloisters, The 40
Coade, J.J. 183
Colaiste Caoimhin 93
Colbert, Con 24
Collins, Michael 186
Columbarium Wall 42
Concannons bakery 152
Connor, Jerome 43
Cooneys grocers 153
Cooper, Rose 197
Corballis, John 28, 46
Cork Street Fever Hospital 35
Corners shop 153
Cranny family 23
Cross 22
Crowe, Eamon 23
Crowe, Fr Patrick 48
Crowe sculptors 44
Crowley, Henry 213
Crowley, Nicholas 103
Cruice, Mary 99
Cruz del Campo 7, 175
Cumann na nBan 23

Dark Lane 126
Davis, Thomas 43

Deghini, John A. 117
Delaneys cycles 156
Denmark Hill 67
Deveneys 153
Devlin, Anne 208
Dillon, John Blake 197
Discalced Carmelites 73
Dobbyn, Robert 133
Dockery, Fr Desmond 48
Dohertys Garage 151
Dolphins Barn brick 145
Domville, Sir Compton 8
Donnybrook 104
Donore 131
Double Mill 17
Douglas, James G. 129
Drummond, Thomas 43
Dublin Artisan Dwelling Company 169
Dublin Board of Sechita 65
Dublin Brick & Tile Co. 145
Dublin Central Tramways Co 164
Dublin Hampers 143
Dublin Metropolitan Police 44
Dublin Mosque 63
Dublin Oil & Grease Works 133
Duffy, Charles Gavin 197
Dunne, Ben 71

Earl of Meath Liberty 14
Earl of Meath Watercourse 162
Earley of Camden Street 98
Elliman, Louis 66
Elmville 141, 175
Emmet, Robert 207
ESB 130
Evans, John Hawker 55
Eyre Court 174

Fanagans Funeral Undertakers 124
Farrens butchers 152
FCA 187, 203
Findlater, Alex 43
FitzAldelm, William 13
Fitzpatricks Cottages 175
Flaggerfield 120
Flour mill 135
Flynns florist 45, 153
Fountain Head Bell Foundry 119
Franciscan Missionaries of Mary 40
Frongoch Internment Camp 25

Gaelic League 25
Gallows 7
Gamble, Major 45
Garda Siochana 116
Garrison church 187
Gaynor, Anna 100
General Cemetery Co. of Dublin 41
Gifford, Grace & Muriel 24
Gilbert Gilkes & Co. 130
Gogoleff, Fr Michael 58
Golden, Paul 67
Good Samaritan, The 55
Goodbody, T.P. & R. 131
Gordons Fuel Depot 144
Gowrans grocers 153
Grand Canal 160
Grand Canal Drainage Tunnel 161
Grangegorman 191
Great Comet 35
Green, The 20
Greenmount 96, 168
Greenmount and Boyne Linen Co. 127
Greenmount Oil Co. 131
Greenmount Quarters 200
Greenville Synagogue 65
Gresham vault 44
Greyhound Stadium 147
Griffith Barracks 189
Griffith College 189
Griffith, Sir Richard 43
Grimwoods Nurseries 189
Grosvenor Gardens 31
Grosvenor Hall 61
Grosvenor Square 176
Grotti, Revd Vincent 114
Grove Inn 150
Grubb, Howard 55, 214
Guinness, Arthur 43

Habib, Mubarak 215
Hamill, Charles 97
Hamilton, Sir William Rowan 43
Hangmans Lane 172
Hankerchief Tree 136
Harold Engineering 143
Harold family 7
Harold House pub 151
Harold's Cross Anglican church 50
Harold's Cross Button Factory 137
Harold's Cross Cottages 169

Harold's Cross Episcopal church 52
Harold's Cross Garage 140
Harold's Cross Improvement Association 20
Harold's Cross Laundry 135
Harold's Cross Musical Society 49
Harold's Cross National School 81
Harold's Grange 7
Harrisons Monumental Works 23
Hastings, Revd J.D. 52
Hathland 17
Hayes, Gabrielle 106
Hayes, William 211
HCR chemists 155
Healys grocers 152
Hells Lane 143
Hempthorn Land 18
Hen and Chicken Lane 8
Heritage Centre 103
Herzog, Chaim 66
Hill of Tara 199
Hill, Professor Edward 21
Holy Rosary Church 46
Honigbaum, Joshua 174
Horse Barracks 180
Hospice 95
Hospital of Charles Borromeo 98
Huguenots 43

Irish Amateur Boxing Association 201
Irish House 150
Irish Whiskey Distillery 132
Irish Women Workers Union 136

Jewish Progressive Congregation 69
Johnston, Francis 189
Jones, Alfred E. 201
Joyce, James 208

Kangley, Bro Mark 115
Katz, Joe 69
Keelan, Ger 215
Kenilworth Bowling Club 176
Kenilworth Cinema 141
Kenilworth Laundry 140
Kenilworth Motors 140
Kenilworth Square 177
Keogh, John 41, 210
Kernoff, Harry 67
Kilbrides pawnbrokers 155

Kilmartins turf accountants 152
Kirk, Thomas 43
Knutsford prison 24
Kosher Meat Products 66

Labour Court 203
Lancastrian Monitorial Teaching 72
Landed Estates Court 119
Lantern Inn 150
Larkfield Garrison 24
Larkfield Mills 23
Laundry, Harold's Cross 135
Laundry, Kenilworth 140
Lawlors drapery 152
Leask, Harold 210
Lennons sweets 153
Le Vere Terrace 173
Limekiln 168
Little Sisters of the Assumption 118
Lloyd & Ridley 137
Loader Park 119, 123
Longford, Lord 211
Longford Row 173
Lord Edwards Fife & Drum Band 130
Loreto Abbey 78
Lutman, Edward 133

McCauls pharmacy 155
McDermotts pub 152
McDonagh, Thomas 24
McDowell, Fr Kevin 48
McGarrys pub 151
McGee, Revd Robert James 52
McGough, Fr Percy 47
McGowans pub 151
Maccabi Sports Grounds 70
Machzikei Hadass 68
Mackenzie, Charles 213
Mageough Home 44
Magnet newsagent 152
Maltese Cross 164
Man of Achill pub 152
Manor Villas 177
Marian Shrine 178
Markievitz, Countess 210
Marleigh House 56
Marques, Dominic 193
Marrowbone Lane 24
Marymount 89
Massey, Alan & Rom 41

Mathers, Adeline 36
Mayer of Munich 32, 55
Mayfield Tennis Grounds 40
Maypole 7
Meadows Taylor, Colonel 55
Meath, Earl of 13
Mercantile Academy 74
Methodist church 60
Mikvah Baths 69
Milofsky 139
Misstears Medical Hall 155
Molyneux Asylum 44
Moriarity, Mary 48
Morris Tube Range 182
Mount Argus 114
Mount Argus Pools 124
Mount Drummond 170
Mount Harold House 47
Mount Jerome Cemetery 19, 41
Mount Jerome Monumental Works 44
Mount Tallant 39, 139
Mulcahy, Richard 184
Mullens Scrapyard 144
Mulvany, John Skipton 43
Murdocks hardware 152
Murphy, Major General 201

Murphy, Mike 140
Murphy & Gunn 141
Murray, Archbishop Daniel 30, 78
Murray, Mary Jane 208
Mushatt, Louis 155
Muslims 43, 63
MVP pub 152

National Stadium 201
Nelligan, David 43
Neville, Fr Ron 48
New Court 174
Noonan, Michael 86
Noyek, Sam 66, 69
Nun of Kenmare 33

O'Brien, Anna Maria 29
O'Brien, Catherine 55
O'Brien, D.D. 149
O'Brien, Denis 28
O'Brien, Maria 28
O'Brien, William Smith 197
O'Ceallaigh, Sean T. 22

O'Connell, Daniel 196
O'Connor Jewellery 143
O'Dalys tobacconist 27
O'Loughlin, Andy 124
O'Neill, Henry 197
O'Reilly-Hyland, Ken 134
Oatlands College 43
Old Court 55, 174
Old Mens Asylum 44
Olympic Torch 215
Orphan Walk 44
Orphanage, St Clares 28
Orphanage, Protestant 35
Osborne, Walter 43
Our Lady's Hospice 95
Our Lady's Mount 89
Our Lady of Refuge, Rathmines 46
Our Lady of the Rosary 38
Owen, Jacob 43

Paddy Walsh Cycles 153
Pakenham, Charles Reginald 114
Papermill Lane 177
Park, The 20
Parkview Avenue 175
Parnell 171
Parochial Hall 57
Passionist priests 114
Paul Mary, Revd 114
Pearse, Patrick 24, 115
Pearse, William 24
Peggy Kellys 150
Perrys Brewery 131
Petrie, George 43
Pim 127, 128, 130, 210
Pixie sweets 156
Plunkett, Archbishop 43
Plunkett, Count George Noble 23
Plunkett, Joseph Mary 24
Plunkett, Blessed Oliver 117
Plymouth Brethren 35
Poddle, River 162
Pollock, Mathew 43
Poor Clares 28
Portobello Barracks 18, 180
Portobello House 97
Posts & Telegraphs, Dept of 138, 157
Presbyterian Church 61
Protestant Orphanage 35
Punnet florist 153

Purdon, Thomas 190
Purser, Sarah 43

Quakers 63

Rathfarnham House 78
Rathgar National Schools 88
Rathgar Tennis Grounds 40
Rathland 9, 19, 120
Rathmines church 25
Rathmines Township 10
Rathnew Brickworks 145
Rectory 56
Red House 184
Renewable Leasehold Conversion Act,
    1849 16
Reservoir 164
Richmond Bridewell 189
Riding the Franchises 14
River Poddle 162
River Swan 163
Robins Bros 45
Robinson, Eilis & Sinead 27
Rocky Horror Picture Show 141
Rope Walk 172
Ropers Rest 131
Rosary Hall 49
Rose Grove 8
Rosie O'Gradys pub 151
Rowsome Pipe Quartet 23, 211
Royal Irish Constabulary 44
Russell, George 43, 214
Russian Orthodox Church 57

St Catherine's 51
St Clare's Convent 28, 75
St Clare's Orphanage 28
St Gabriel's Boys Club 124
St James' Hospital 27
St John's VAD 184
St Joseph's, Cavan 33
St Joseph's Geriatric Centre 99
St Kevin's Hospital 24
St Michael's Nurses Home 99
St Pancras 139
St Patrick's church 187
St Patrick's Guild 99
St Patrick's Infant Hospital 99
St Paul's Hall 125
St Paul's Retreat 114

St Peter & St Paul parish 58
St Peter's Free School 73
St Sepulchre, Liberty of 7
St Teresa's Monastery 38
St Thomas-á-Becket 13
St Victor 13
St Vincent's Hospital 95
Sadler, William 180
Sallys Bridge 18
Salmon barbers 154
Samuel Taca Hall 69
Sarsfield House 182
Scoil Iosagain 93
Scoil Mologa 86
Scripture Union 36
Secondary Top 92
Shaw, Robert 41
Shelbourne Football Club 148
Sheppard, William 214
Sheridan Bell Foundry 135
Sheridan, Cecil 212
Sheridan la Fanu, Joseph 43
Sisters of Charity 45
Skeffington, Francis Sheehy 183
Slige Chualann 8
Smiths Land 18
Solomons, Bethel 70
South Dublin Union 24
Spence family 55
Spencer, Fr Ignatius 116
Spinks, May 49
Steele, Honest Tom 197
Stephens, James 195
Stokes, Frederick 68
Stone Boat 162
Stratford College 66, 88
Stratford Lawn Tennis Club 176
Sundrive Park 145
Swan River 163
Sweeneys grocery 156
Synge, J.M. 43

Tailteann Games 184
Taylor Signs 138

Tayto 138
Terenure Synagogue 69
Theopan, Bishop 58
Thom, Alexander 43
Timmons, Rose 91
Tin Church 47
Toft Carnival 102
Tone, Wolfe 180
Tongue 162
Tonguefield 126
TR Motors 140
Trams 164
Tread-wheel 190
Tree of Knowledge 21
Trinity College Garden 21
Trustee chapels 51
Twinem sauces 149

United Nations 185
Uppercross Fusiliers 179
Usher, Sir William 8

Walsh, George P. 145
Waterworks 164
Watkins, Kathleen 23
Weld, Edmond 8
Wellington Barracks 198
Westbank, Greystones 36
Westfield Park 48
Westfield Road 177
Wharton Hall 61, 68
Wilde, Sir William 43
Wine, Louis 67
Wood Mills 17
Woodworkers & Hobbies Supply Centre
 139

Yeats, John Butler 210
Yeomanry 180
Young, Fr Henry 73

BEAT PMS THROUGH DIET

*The medically proven Women's
Nutritional Advisory Service Programme*

Maryon Stewart

with contributions from
Dr Alan Stewart and Dr Guy Abraham

VERMILION
LONDON

To daughters everywhere

IMPORTANT NOTE FOR SUFFERERS

There are many fairly technical terms used to describe the Pre-Menstrual Syndrome and the normal menstrual cycle. You may already be familiar with some of the more technical terms, whilst others will be new to you. I have prepared a brief Dictionary of Terms to refer to which begins on page 246. Please don't be afraid to use it as often as necessary. The better you understand the information, the more you will be able to apply it to your own life and symptoms.

If your symptoms occur at other times of the month, apart from during your pre-menstrual time, you should have a medical check-up with your own doctor. If your symptoms are very severe it would be advisable to have your nutritional programme supervised by your own doctor or a trained counsellor. If you get confused or need extra advice, the Women's Nutritional Advisory Service is there to help you. All letters receive a personal reply: their address is on page 254.

This revised edition first published in 1994

1 3 5 7 9 10 8 6 4 2

Text copyright © 1987, 1990 and 1994 by Maryon Stewart, Dr Guy Abraham

First published in the United Kingdom in 1987 by Century Publishing Co. Ltd

This edition published in 1994 by Vermilion
an imprint of Ebury Press
Random House, 20 Vauxhall Bridge Road, London SW1V 2SA

Random House Australia (Pty) Limited
10 Alfred Street, Milsons Point, Sydney
New South Wales 2061, Australia

Random House New Zealand Limited
18 Poland Road, Glenfield
Auckland 10, New Zealand

Random House South Africa (Pty) Limited
PO Box 337, Bergvlei, South Africa

Random House UK Limited Reg. No. 954009

A CIP catalogue record for this book
is available from the British Library

ISBN 0 09 178352 6

Illustrations by Mike Gordon

Typeset by SX Composing, Rayleigh, Essex

Printed and bound in Great Britain by Mackays of Chatham plc, Chatham, Kent

CONTENTS

Foreword by Leslie Kenton   vii
Introduction   ix

PART ONE   THE REALITIES OF PMS
Chapter 1   A problem as old as the hills   1
Chapter 2   Functioning normally   5
Chapter 3   PMS defined   12
Chapter 4   The making of PMS   14
Chapter 5   Anxious, irritable and uptight   19
Chapter 6   Bloating, weight gain and breast tenderness   40
Chapter 7   Sugar cravings, headaches and fatigue   47
Chapter 8   Depression, crying and thoughts of suicide   55
Chapter 9   Other symptoms – clumsiness, loss of sex drive
                and agoraphobia   71
Chapter 10   The social implications of PMS   83

PART TWO   NUTRITION AND OUR BODIES
Chapter 11   Why is PMS more common today?   93
Chapter 12   Medical treatments   111
Chapter 13   Nutritional treatments   118
Chapter 14   Nutrition and the body: vitamins and minerals,
                what they do   123

PART THREE   THE NUTRITIONAL APPROACH – A SELF-HELP MANUAL
Chapter 15   Choosing a nutritional plan   142
Chapter 16   A tailor-made nutritional programme – Option 3   156
Chapter 17   Nutritious recipes   193
Chapter 18   Stress or distress?   214
Chapter 19   The value of exercise and relaxation   218
Chapter 20   Other valuable therapies   229
Chapter 21   Other related problems   234
Chapter 22   Men who no longer suffer   240

PART FOUR   APPENDICES
1 Dictionary of terms 246   2 Food additives 249
3 Nutritional supplement suppliers 250   4 Recommended reading list 251
5 Useful addresses 253   6 Charts and diaries 256   7 References 260
Index 265   Further help 275

ACKNOWLEDGEMENTS

I would first like to acknowledge the researchers that have gone before us who collectively completed the groundwork that allowed us to begin our work from an advanced point. In particular I refer to early work by Dr Katharina Dalton, Dr Michael Brush, Dr David Horrobin, Dr Guy Abraham and Professor Shaughn O'Brien.

Special thanks are due to both Dr Alan Stewart and Dr Guy Abraham for their advice and support over the years. Without their technical support we would not have been able to provide such valuable help to so many women, and education on the nutritional approach to Pre-Menstrual Syndrome to so many doctors, nurses and medical organizations.

My heartfelt thanks also go to all the wonderful patients who have volunteered to share their case histories with us in this book. Their willingness to divulge intimate details so frankly in an effort to help others is highly appreciated.

Next I must thank the caring team that have worked at the Women's Nutritional Advisory Service, in particular Michele Apsey and Sarah Tooley. Without them this book would not have been possible.

I would also like to thank the following people for advice: Deryn Bell on osteopathy, Paul Lundberg on acupuncture and acupressure and Julia Swift on exercise.

Thanks are also due to Lavinia Trevor for her support and the benefit of her wisdom and to Rowena Webb and Anabel Briggs at Vermilion for their enthusiasm and professionalism.

Lastly, I must thank our wonderful nanny, Joanna John, for happily occupying the children whilst I put the third edition of this book together, and the children themselves, Phoebe, Chesney, Hester and Simeon, for unselfishly allowing me time out, and providing me with regular refreshments and cuddles.

Maryon Stewart

FOREWORD
BY
LESLIE KENTON

This is an extraordinary book. Not only does it tackle the very complex subject of Pre-Menstrual Syndrome (PMS) in a simple and straightforward way so that it becomes understandable to the average woman suffering from it, but it is also eminently practical. It tells you exactly how to go about finding the answer to your own difficulties.

PMS, with its symptoms of bloating, depression, irritability, fatigue and all the rest is not something 'normal' which you have to suffer from, month in month out. I have seen even the most resistant cases turn around through changes of diet, alterations in living habits and the judicious use of certain nutritional supplements. What Maryon Stewart has done so cleverly is to explain how to help yourself: first by making you aware of what your specific problems are, and then by helping you outline a self-directed lifestyle programme for solving them.

And Maryon Stewart can substantiate her claims too. Having already put into practice the natural approach to PMS set out in this book for 11 years, and having monitored its results on a thousand women through the Women's Nutritional Advisory Service, she knows what she is talking about. The methods work. And her advice about eating natural organically-grown foods, using simple techniques which can help you better manage stress, calling on well-planned nutritional supplements when necessary and even making use of natural treatments which you can carry out yourself to cope with acute problems is not only sound in relation to eliminating PMS. It can also be taken far beyond to form the basis of a total lifestyle for optimum health for women and men alike. *Beat PMS Through Diet* is a book to be read, used and then loaned to friends when they need it.

'After the birth of our first baby I began to experience intense mood swings. One moment I'd be rational and calm, then the next minute I would fly off the handle. My foul mood was lasting two weeks every month. During this time I'd feel bloated and constantly tired. I experienced the most incredible bouts of anger: I'd throw things – there was hardly a decent piece of china left in the house. I'd hit out at everything. All our kitchen equipment was dented and scratched.

I'd rant at my husband and the children. I never hit them, though once I remember raving at my husband with the bread knife in my hand and, at that moment, I could have killed him. Something wouldn't let me, thank God. Sometimes I'd get in the car and fly off down the road. I was lucky I never killed myself or anyone else. I usually clicked back to normal the moment my period started.

My GP suggested my problem was depression, but I knew it wasn't. Luckily for me, by chance I saw a copy of Beat PMS Through Diet in our local bookshop, bought it, read it and phoned up the Advisory Service to get some extra help. That was three years ago. I started on the new regime the next day, and felt better at once. My next period came and went with almost no ill effects. It was magical. The next time I suffered hardly at all. I couldn't believe that after 13 years I was back in the normal world! Both my husband and I agree that our marriage couldn't have lasted much longer if I'd gone on the way I was. I'm just thankful I found out what my problem was before I drove my family away.'

---

* Despite the fact that most of the patients who volunteered to tell their story in the book didn't object to my using their actual names, I felt it would be more appropriate to change their names and let them remain anonymous.

INTRODUCTION

The Pre-Menstrual Syndrome, or PMS, does not have the physical characteristics of an abscess or an ingrown toenail. Neither does it show up under a microscope like a diseased cell. The agony and the anguish suffered, not to mention the misery and the mental torture, cannot easily be measured.

Perhaps because PMS is relatively difficult to detect or quantify by an outsider the condition has taken far longer than it should have done to become recognized, and still longer to be treated effectively without the use of drugs. As a result, women have had to go on suffering unnecessarily.

'My doctor told me it was all in my mind. But I gain five inches (12cm) pre-menstrually around the middle. I told him indignantly that if it was anywhere it was all in the waist!'

'My monthly symptoms were diagnosed as "problems with my nerves". I was prescribed tranquillizers which I became too dependent upon.'

'I was told by my doctor that the solution to my symptoms is to have a baby. I'm single, I don't have a regular boyfriend, and I don't want a baby!'

'All part of being a woman' is a hot favourite, followed by 'PMS symptoms are a sign of a woman rejecting her femininity'.

The most inventive advice for overcoming PMS symptoms was the treatment prescribed by a doctor who advised his patient to join the Conservative Party and become a magistrate, as his wife had done previously!

To a non-sufferer this may sound amusing. However, to a woman with

PMS who is feeling wretched, in some cases suicidal, and certainly bitter that her life is being disrupted by this condition, it is really no laughing matter.

There exists now a wealth of evidence to show that PMS not only exists, but that it can be treated, to a large degree, quite naturally. From studies we have undertaken, for example, we have shown that in excess of 90 per cent of the PMS sufferers who follow our recommendations are significantly better within the first three months. The reasons why this approach is not widely recognized are that medical research on PMS has hitherto been scattered far and wide in medical journals around the world, and the medical profession are by their own admission not educated about nutrition; more of this later. By gathering this information together we were able to formulate a very simple, effective programme to help overcome Pre-Menstrual Syndrome.

In order to make this often life-saving information available to anyone and everyone in need, the Women's Nutritional Advisory Service was set up as an interim measure. For 11 years we have been helping thousands of women, not only in Britain, but indeed all over the world.

The Women's Nutritional Advisory Service has carried out a scientific survey of the symptoms, progress and treatment of 1000 women who have consulted them. Throughout the book you will find figures and charts which refer to this survey, unless stated otherwise, as for example, when particular studies were made of individual cases and groups.

We have also been able to provide a Medical Information Service which regularly supplies doctors and other health-care professionals with information about the nutritional approach to PMS. The ideal situation is that the nutritional approach to PMS becomes recognized as a valid part of orthodox medicine and is practised widely.

In the meantime, this book has been put together based on a very successful programme which the Women's Nutritional Advisory Service has been using for the last 11 years. I have hard facts to substantiate our claims, as you will see as you read on. The good news is that overcoming PMS consists mainly of SELF-HELP with a little education along the way.

The book will explain to you how you can solve the problem for yourself, according to your own individual symptoms. It is written in four parts. Part One deals with the realities of Pre-Menstrual Syndrome and the effect it has on individual and family life. Part Two covers nutrition in relation to our body. Part Three is devoted to diet and other means of self-help, and finally, in Part Four, you will find lists of useful information and addresses.

Consider your voyage through this book an adventure, and as we often say to the sufferers beginning our programme – 'May you never be the same again!' Good luck!

1

A PROBLEM AS OLD AS THE HILLS

Despite the fact that for the last few years we have been talking and writing about the Pre-Menstrual Syndrome (PMS) as if it has just been discovered, in reality it has been affecting women all over the world for many years.

I am often asked the question 'How come PMS is more common now than it was years ago?' My answer is that we talk about the condition far more now than we used to, and that there are many aspects relating to the twentieth-century diet and environment that seem to contribute significantly to the problem.

The whole event has become affectionately nicknamed 'The Curse'. It seems that this term derives from ancient times when a menstruating woman was considered by society to be unclean, and in some cases dangerous. In some primitive tribes menstrual blood was considered to be evil, and a menstruating woman had to remain shut away for fear that she would cast a spell on the menfolk or kill off whole herds of animals using her temporary 'witch's' powers. If a menstruating woman disobeyed this or similar rules and mixed with the menfolk, some tribes would even condemn her to death.

Certain religions still regard a menstruating woman as undesirable. In the Moslem religion a menstruating woman is not allowed to enter the mosque. As recently as the beginning of this century a Greek Orthodox woman was not permitted Communion during her period, and to this day in the Orthodox Jewish religion, menstruating women are not permitted to sleep with their husbands during their period.

1

Is it any wonder that complexes about the whole subject developed and that the subject became taboo? Who, with any degree of sanity, would have wanted to admit the fact that their period was due? It makes the mind boggle!

Despite the fact that women's often frenzied accounts of their unbearable pre-menstrual symptoms have been labelled as being 'all in the mind', i.e. a mental condition, past treatments included hysterectomies, electric shock treatment, and even, in tragic cases, lobotomies (an operation where part of the brain is removed). Traditionally Western medicine tends to regard a physical condition as one that we have no control over and that needs treatment by physical means using drugs and suchlike, and a mental condition as one where the person's personality contributes to the illness. This division is seen as being increasingly artificial.

The first recorded cases of PMS (or PMT, as it was then known) were in 1931, when Dr Robert T. Frank, an American physician working in New York reported 15 cases of Pre-Menstrual Tension. These women had symptoms of nervous tension, water retention and weight gain. Dr Frank found a high level of the hormone oestrogen present in these patients and felt that they were unable to excrete the oestrogen from their bodies pre-menstrually. The excess oestrogen, he felt, then irritated the nervous system, and thus symptoms developed.

Further work was done by other American doctors in this field. In 1938 Dr Israel, another American doctor, presented his theory that not all women had high levels of oestrogen, but they did have low levels of the hormone progesterone.

In 1943 Dr Biskind published a study which supported the theory that many pre-menstrual symptoms reported were similar to vitamin B deficiency symptoms. He found that treatment with vitamin B greatly improved symptoms, especially uncomfortable breast symptoms and heavy bleeding during menstruation, which are also symptoms of vitamin B deficiency. The cause was an overload of oestrogen pre-menstrually.

As early as 1944 Dr Harris observed women with pre-menstrual fatigue, nervousness and cravings for sweet foods. Further research along these lines continued in the 1950s.

The first scientific publication from the United Kingdom was in 1937 from a group of women doctors led by Dr McCance from King's College Hospital in London. Their detailed survey of 169 mainly professional women documented the presence of increased fatigue, headaches and mood swings occurring pre-menstrually and during the period. These doctors were uncertain as to the exact cause of these physical and mood changes. In 1953 Dr Katharina Dalton, a British doctor, began publishing

2

her work. She and Dr Raymond Greene renamed the condition 'Pre-Menstrual Syndrome', as they identified so many symptoms as being pre-menstrual. Dr Dalton is considered a pioneer in this field. She spent many years identifying the magnitude of the problem in prisons, hospitals, factories, offices and schools. She also studied the relationship between pre-menstrual symptoms and crime, alcoholism and drug abuse. Quite a few of her studies are mentioned later on in the text, as they served as a starting point for our own research. Dr Dalton supports the theory that pre-menstrually low levels of the hormone progesterone are present. Her treatment consists largely of progesterone supplementation.

During the 1970s and 80s there were many attempts to identify a hormonal abnormality – a deficiency in women with PMS when compared with those who did not suffer. Many minor abnormalities, including elevated or decreased levels of progesterone, oestrogen and other hormones, were described in numerous small studies. However, no consistent pattern has emerged and the considered medical wisdom is that the vast majority of sufferers do not have a hormone excess or lack but are perhaps unduly sensitive to the normal swings in hormone levels that occur throughout the menstrual cycle. To support this new concept there is some very good evidence that the most powerful hormonal treatments are highly effective in controlling PMS. The reason for this is that if you can switch off the ovaries then you lose the normal rise and fall of hormone production, abolish the menstrual cycle, cease having periods and thus prevent PMS. No ovaries equals no PMS. Of course you then have a whole host of other problems as a result of this type of treatment.

Other workers have tried to link different patterns of pre-menstrual symptoms with changes either in hormones or in body chemistry. Dr Guy Abraham, a leading researcher from the United States, has over the last twenty years looked in detail at the relationship between nutritional factors, hormone function and PMS. Certain patterns can sometimes be discerned, thus allowing a more rational use of dietary treatments, and sometimes drug or hormonal treatments.

These are covered in some detail later on and we also show the benefits we have obtained using a nutritional approach. Many family doctors and experts now agree that tackling dietary and lifestyle factors is the best first-line approach to treating PMS.

As you have probably gathered, despite the fact that the Pre-Menstrual Syndrome has been approached from many angles, confusion still exists on the subject. There are those schools who believe the condition should be treated with hormones, whilst others believe it is a psychological condition which should be treated with tranquillizers and anti-depressants.

3

As a group we haven't set out to prove whether it is in fact a physical or mental condition. *We know it is a real condition.* Instead, we approach it from the viewpoint that certain symptoms exist which may be overcome by making dietary changes and adjustments in lifestyles where necessary. Between us we have many years of experience and have been able to help tens of thousands of women around the world to overcome their pre-menstrual problems.

I aim to give you a good understanding of what happens to your body during your monthly cycle. I will then help you to identify what the symptoms may be due to and then, of course, how you can go about getting them sorted out.

2

FUNCTIONING
NORMALLY

THE NORMAL MENSTRUAL CYCLE

In order to understand what is going wrong with your menstrual cycle, it is important to have a fairly good understanding of what the normal menstrual cycle is.

The age at the onset of periods has been decreasing at a rate of three years per century. Periods begin between the tenth and sixteenth year in 95 per cent of European girls, and between the tenth and fifteenth year in American girls. The age at the onset of the menopause, when periods cease, has been increasing at a rate of three years per century as well. Menopause occurs between the ages of 40 and 55.

The menstrual cycle is a fertility cycle, a fascinating process that enables a woman to conceive a child. This cycle is repeated each month, and if fertilization does not occur the cycle ends with a menstrual period – the shedding of the lining of the womb in preparation for the next cycle. The cycle can vary in length from approximately 22 days up to 34 days. Anything between these numbers would be considered normal. The first day of bleeding, the day the period arrives, is referred to as the first day of the cycle.

THE ORGANS INVOLVED

There are specific organs which each play an important role in the menstrual cycle. They are designed to work together so that a woman can become pregnant and nourish the growing child throughout the nine months of pregnancy.

The uterus or womb, as it is more commonly known, is a hollow, pear-shaped muscular organ which is about three inches (7.5 cm) long in a non-pregnant woman. There are many layers of specialized muscle here which, as if by magic, can expand so that the uterus becomes many times its usual size during pregnancy. The growing child lives in the uterus until it is ready to be born.

The innermost layer of the uterus is a membrane called the endo-metrium. During the cycle it becomes filled with the blood supply which would be needed to nourish a pregnancy. If conception has not occurred the endometrium breaks down, and together with the blood leaves the uterus through the neck of the uterus, which is known as the cervix.

The cervix or neck of the womb is like a little ball towards the back of the vagina. It has a small opening which remains closed for most of the time. A few days before the egg is released by the ovary, the cervix begins to open. By the time the egg has left the ovary, the opening would have become wide enough to let the sperm swim up through it, in order to gain access to the egg.

For a few days each cycle, at the time of ovulation, the specialized cells in the cervix produce fertile cervical mucus, which allows the sperm to live during their journey to the uterus. At other times during the men-strual cycle the cervix produces infertile cervical mucus which prevents the sperm from surviving.

Once the menstrual blood passes through the cervix it flows into the vaginal canal, a four- to six-inch (10–15 cm) muscular tube which has the ability to widen during sexual intercourse and during labour. During inter-course the lining of the vaginal canal becomes engorged with blood. A slippery liquid is produced which is designed to make the experience of sexual intercourse more comfortable.

The two almond-shaped organs on either side of the uterus are called the ovaries. They contain thousands of immature eggs which are present in a baby girl even before birth! From puberty, usually, one egg will leave one ovary during each menstrual cycle. I say usually, as there are occasions when more than one egg becomes fertilized simultaneously, and multiple births result.

OVULATION

The process of the egg leaving the ovary is called ovulation. At about 12 to 16 days before menstruation, the ovary will release an egg. The egg is then usually picked up by one of the Fallopian tubes, which is where the egg and the sperm would meet if conception were to take place. The Fallopian tubes are a pair of very thin tubes, about four inches (10 cm) long, which are connected to each side of the uterus. The egg waits for the sperm in the Fallopian tube for between 12 and 24 hours. If no sperm arrive, the egg is then absorbed by the body. If the egg and the sperm do meet and join up, fertilization takes place, and the fertilized egg will then move down, over the next few days, into the uterus, where it becomes embedded in the lining. This fertilized egg then grows into a baby.

WHAT CONTROLS THE CYCLE?

It is important to understand that although we have looked at the various organs at work for us during the menstrual cycle, it is actually the brain that controls the ovaries. In fact, a particular part of the brain called the pituitary gland sends instructions to the ovaries to make them function. The pituitary gland will tell the ovaries when to produce eggs and release them. It also stimulates production by the ovaries of oestrogen and progesterone, two very special sex hormones. If no fertilization occurs, the pituitary gland will send a new signal for the ovaries to begin producing eggs again.

WHAT ACTUALLY HAPPENS DURING THE CYCLE?

Either just prior to your period arriving, or during your period, several eggs will begin to grow in the ovary. Each egg is surrounded by a sac which is called a follicle. The egg and the follicle grow together. The follicle produces oestrogen which, as you can see from the chart overleaf, is at its highest during the latter part of the first half of the cycle. Oestrogen is responsible for the production of fertile cervical mucus, the opening of the cervix to allow the sperm in to meet the eggs, and the building up of blood in the lining of the uterus, preparing for a fertilized egg.

The cervical mucus is usually very fertile indeed: it is reckoned that sperm can survive for as long as five days in the fertile cervical mucus, waiting for an egg to fertilize. The egg is released from the ovary anything from eight to 14 days from the first day of your cycle – the day your period begins. Ovulation tends to vary from person to person. Some women are aware that they are ovulating as they experience some short-lived pain or stinging sensations in the area of the right or left ovary.

The cells or follicle that protected the egg before it was released remain

THE NORMAL MENSTRUAL CYCLE

1 — *Period begins – lining of uterus comes away. Very little progesterone.*

2 — *Very little oestrogen.*

3
4
5 — *Eggs growing and follicles beginning to produce oestrogen.*
6
7 — *Oestrogen levels rising.*

8
9
10
11
12 — *Oestrogen levels high, stimulating the lining of the uterus to*
13 *thicken.*

14 — *Ovulation occurs approximately at this time. Oestrogen levels are high. Once the egg has left, the follicle begins producing progesterone.*

15
16
17

18
19 — *Oestrogen and progesterone levels high.*
20
21
22
23
24
25

26 — *Both progesterone and oestrogen levels falling now that conception*
27 *has not occurred.*
28

in the ovary after the egg has left. The follicle develops into a special gland known as the corpus luteum. Whereas the cells of the follicle were producing large amounts of oestrogen during the first half of the cycle, after ovulation they begin to produce the other important sex hormone, progesterone.

Progesterone is an important hormone at the beginning of pregnancy as it is responsible for producing infertile mucus, preventing sperm and other substances from harming a pregnancy. It is sometimes known as the pregnancy protecting hormone. It also closes the cervix and holds the lining of the uterus in place from ovulation until the next period begins, if fertilization has not taken place. Progesterone levels are sometimes low in women who suffer with PMS, and it has been demonstrated that balancing a woman's nutritional condition can raise the levels of progesterone again. This will be discussed later in the section on nutritional supplements on page 118.

After ovulation the body waits to see whether a pregnancy has occurred. Once it realizes that pregnancy has not occurred, the corpus luteum of the ovary stops working, and the levels of both oestrogen and progesterone fall. As progesterone has been holding the lining of the uterus in place, when this hormone level drops the lining of the uterus is then shed and a menstrual period occurs.

THE MAIN FACTS

Oestrogen controls the first half of the cycle until the egg leaves the ovary, and progesterone is in control of the cycle from the day the egg is released until the menstrual period begins.

The hormones produced by the ovaries have a profound effect on moods and behaviour – not surprising, since oestrogen is a stimulant of the nervous system. Low oestrogen levels cause depression, whereas high oestrogen levels can result in symptoms such as anxiety, irritability and nervous tension. The correct amount of oestrogen produces assertiveness, motivation and emotional stability. Progesterone, on the other hand, is a depressant, and has a calming effect. It is therefore obvious that for a woman to function normally throughout the menstrual cycle a proper balance of these hormones must be maintained.

I will be talking more about how the levels of oestrogen and progesterone are affected by a deficient nutritional state in Chapter 14 on vitamins and minerals, and our laboratory findings. Although it was previously thought that a woman had to take supplements of hormones in

9

HOW YOUR HORMONAL SYSTEM WORKS

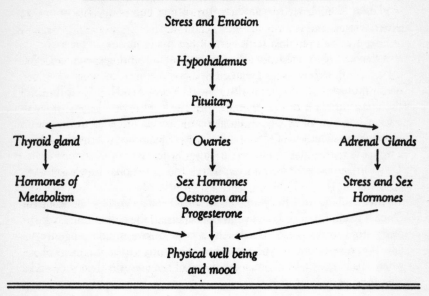

order to maintain her levels if she was deficient, it appears that this is not always so, as you will see.

EFFECTS OF NUTRITION
ON THE MENSTRUAL CYCLE

Nutrition affects the menstrual cycle in many ways. First, there are certain nutrients such as amino acids and vitamins that are necessary for the manufacture of brain hormones and the normal function of the pituitary gland, and which are also capable of influencing moods and behaviour.

Hormones are produced by the ovaries, adrenal glands and the thyroid gland. As already noted, the ovaries produce the sex hormones, oestrogen and progesterone. The adrenal glands produce both sex hormones and hormones related to stress. The thyroid gland produces its own hormones that control the body's rate of metabolism. These three glands – the ovaries, adrenals and thyroid – are all in turn controlled by a part of the brain, the pituitary which, if you like, is the conductor of the hormonal orchestra. It in turn is sensitive to a part of the brain called the hypothalamus which also influences appetite, temperature control and the 24-hour 'biological clock' that controls our eating and sleeping rhythms. It also contains another 'clock' that controls the 28-day menstrual cycle. Finally, it in turn is influenced by levels of stress and emotion. Thus it is that external stress and emotional factors can influence hormonal factors, and ultimately, one's physical sense of well-being and mood.

When an imbalanced diet exists or there are nutritional deficiencies the whole system may become disturbed or more sensitive. If there is a severe reduction in calorie (kj) intake and the body weight falls to an unhealthy level, the function of the pituitary gland will decrease and periods may cease altogether, or may continue but without ovulation. This is nature's way of protecting a woman from becoming pregnant when in an unhealthy state – a rather drastic form of contraception!

The hormones from the pituitary gland, thyroid gland, ovaries and adrenal gland all appear to be influenced slightly by the type of diet you eat, the balance of certain nutrients, exercise and stress. Vitamin B6, vitamin C, zinc, magnesium and other nutrients are subtly involved in the way in which the body responds to or processes the hormones that relate to the normal menstrual cycle. Making sure there is an adequate supply of these essential nutrients from the diet or from the use of supplements is one way to help combat PMS.

Finally, physical and emotional stress can have a powerful effect upon the menstrual cycle. For example, excessive or severe physical exercise, if continued on a regular basis, may cause the pituitary to 'switch off' the ovaries. Thus periods cease and the levels of the sex hormone oestrogen may fall. Such women put themselves at risk of fractures and thinning of the bones – osteoporosis. Emotional stress, such as the worry of becoming pregnant from having unprotected sexual intercourse, can itself lead to the delay or the missing of a period, which in turn causes increased worry and stress – not an uncommon experience at some time in one's life.

So a healthy diet and the avoidance of physical and mental stresses play an important part in health, and especially in the control of Pre-Menstrual Syndrome.

3

PMS DEFINED

PMS, or Pre-Menstrual Syndrome, is the term used to describe a collection of physical and mental symptoms that occur before a period starts and cease with or shortly after the arrival of a period.

WHEN DO SYMPTOMS BEGIN AND END?

- Most commonly symptoms begin from a week to a few days before menstruation begins, and then diminish as the period begins.

- Sometimes symptoms occur at the time of ovulation (mid cycle), then disappear until a few days pre-menstrually, when they recur until the onset of the period.

- Symptoms may begin at the time of ovulation, around the middle of the cycle, gradually increasing in severity until the period begins. It is not uncommon for symptoms to persist to the first day or two of the period.

WHAT IS THE DIFFERENCE BETWEEN PRE-MENSTRUAL SYNDROME AND PRE-MENSTRUAL TENSION?

- Pre-Menstrual Tension was the original name given to the collection of symptoms relating to tension and anxiety first reported by Dr Frank in the 1930s. Thus the condition became known as 'PMT'.

- Further research was done, particularly by Dr Dalton, who went on to discover further types of symptoms. She renamed the condition Pre-Menstrual Syndrome (PMS).

THE MOST COMMON PMS SYMPTOMS

Have a look at these symptoms. You might be surprised to realize that they are all associated with Pre-Menstrual Syndrome.

Nervous tension	Agoraphobia	Hayfever	Thoughts of
Mood swings	Bad breath	Fatigue	suicide
Irritability	Sensitivity to	Confusion	Sensitivity to
Anxiety	light	Forgetfulness	noise
Depression	Disorientation	Crying	Excessive thirst
Headache	Restlessness	Dizziness	Hostility
Migraine	Mouth ulcers	Tremors and	Sugar cravings
Insomnia	Acne	shakes	
Swollen breasts	Backache	Fainting	Weight gain
Tender/sore breasts	Heart poundings	Asthma	
Swollen abdomen	Cramp pains	Loss of interest	Diarrhoea
Bloated feelings	Wind	in sex	Cystitis
Craving for food	Generalized aches	Constipation	
Swelling of	Increased physical	Clumsiness	Boils
extremities	activity	Eczema	Hives
Heavy aching legs	Restless legs	Painful joints	Swollen ankles

JUST KNOWING THAT IT IS PMS

We are often told by patients that just knowing they have an identifiable, not to mention treatable, condition brings much relief in itself. It was a real surprise to me initially to discover women in all walks of life, with varying educational backgrounds, who were under the impression that their symptoms were in one of the following categories:

- All part of being a woman.
- Part of the ageing process.

- Early senile dementia.

- A psychological problem.

- A character fault.

- Schizophrenia.

The chances are that you may have been under an illusion that you fit in to one of these categories. I have lost count of the numbers of women who describe themselves as 'Jekyll and Hyde', i.e. two quite separate people during their menstrual cycle. They all seem to be acutely aware of the change as it occurs some time after ovulation. To a woman, they feel quite powerless to overcome the symptoms.

THE DIFFERENCE BETWEEN
PMS AND PERIOD PAINS

Characteristic	PMS	Period pains
1. Time of onset	3–14 days before period	One day before and/or on first day or two of period
2. Improvement	Approximately the onset of the period	Some time during or at the end of the period
3. After childbirth	Symptoms worsen	Symptoms improve

4

THE MAKING OF PMS

There are a number of factors that may cause or contribute to PMS symptoms. It is very important to examine these thoroughly in order to get the situation into perspective.

GYNAECOLOGICAL OR HORMONAL PROBLEMS

If you have been experiencing problems for some time it is important to consult your doctor for a full check-up. Certainly if you have symptoms that are persistent all month through, there may be other complications present. Here is a small checklist for you to look at to see whether there need be cause for any concern:

- Heavy or irregular periods.

- Abdominal pain.

- Excessive weight gain or weight loss.

- Facial hair growth.

- Persistent severe headaches.

- Current vaginal discharge, soreness or irritation.

- Breast lumps or tenderness throughout the menstrual cycle.

- Milky discharge from the nipples.

If any of these are a current problem it would be advisable to get them checked out, for peace of mind if nothing else. You will then establish whether you have other medical problems as well as PMS, or pure PMS.

FACTORS IN THE CAUSATION OF PMS

1. Difficulty with relationships.

2. Problems with work.

3. Problem children to cope with.

4. Disturbed night's sleep.

5. Financial difficulties causing friction and worries.

6. Strained relations with husband or partner.

7. Inadequate or incorrect diet.

8. Environmental pollutants.

9. Social poisons.

10. Oral contraceptive pill.

11. Increasing age, especially age 30–40.

12. After childbirth.

13. Lack of exercise.

14. Operations and physical illnesses.

EXAMINING PMS SYMPTOMS

WHAT ACTUALLY CAUSES PMS

In Chapter 2, 'Functioning Normally', hormonal changes throughout the menstrual cycle were described. Whilst major disturbance of hormone levels is not the sole explanation for PMS, certain variations in hormone levels or sensitivity to hormones may well be part of the cause. This in turn can be influenced by stress, dietary factors and nutritional state.

If you are confused about the cause of PMS, don't worry, as most medical scientists and researchers are just as perplexed. Dr Guy Abraham, former Professor of Obstetrics and Gynaecology at the University of California in Los Angeles, has attempted to unravel the causation of PMS by dividing the symptoms into four groups, as detailed below. This somewhat artificial classification does help us to develop possible explanations as to the cause of different aspects of PMS symptoms. Disturbances in the

16

levels of oestrogen and progesterone have been described in some sufferers with different types of PMS, but these are not universal changes. Furthermore, many women will experience symptoms from more than one sub-group.

PMS A (ANXIETY)

This is the most common sub-group. Symptoms are recorded in about 80 per cent of sufferers. The symptoms in this group are:

Nervous tension.
Mood swings.
Irritability.
Anxiety.

PMS H (HYDRATION)

This is the second sub-group. It is estimated that symptoms occur in 60 per cent of sufferers. The symptoms in the sub-group are as follows:

Weight gain.
Swelling of extremities.
Breast tenderness.
Abdominal bloating.

PMS C (CRAVING)

This is the third sub-group. Symptoms probably occur in 40 per cent of sufferers. There are six symptoms in this sub-group:

Headache.
Craving for sweets.
Increased appetite.
Heart pounding.
Fatigue.
Dizziness or fainting.

PMS D (DEPRESSION)

Of all four sub-groups, this is the one least commonly found on its own. Perhaps 20 per cent of sufferers have PMS D. There are five symptoms in this category:

Depression.
Forgetfulness.
Crying.
Confusion.
Insomnia.

Each group seems to have different factors involved, except that in-adequate diet and stress can be common to all of them. Although some women only suffer with one sub-group of symptoms, it is just as common to be suffering from any combination of sub-groups at the same time. Many severe sufferers seem to have symptoms in all four sub-groups initially.

In the next four chapters I will examine in greater detail each one of these sub-groups of symptoms and look at how the symptoms affected the lives of some of the women who contacted the Women's Nutritional Advisory Service. Rather than describing how PMS might affect various aspects of your life, I decided that the subject might become more alive if it was talked about by sufferers themselves. I have selected patients whose symptoms span a broad spectrum of the Pre-Menstrual Syndrome. By look-ing into their lives you may well recognize familiar situations.

5

ANXIOUS, IRRITABLE AND UPTIGHT

PMS A (ANXIETY)

The main symptoms of PMS A are nervous tension, anxiety, irritability and mood swings, beginning as early as two weeks before the period and becoming progressively worse as the period approaches.

There are several possible factors, both hormonal and dietary, that might cause pre-menstrual anxiety. Some doctors think that an excess of the hormone oestrogen or an increased sensitivity to it may trigger changes in brain chemistry, resulting in anxiety. The average diet, high in fat and relatively low in fibre, can increase the levels of this hormone. Also, high levels of oestrogen slow down the rate at which the stimulant caffeine is broken down by the liver. This is why some women become more sensitive to tea and coffee when they are pregnant or when taking the oral contraceptive pill.

A lack of vitamin B and possibly the mineral magnesium can also cause changes in the chemistry of the nervous system that can aggravate feelings of anxiety and irritability. Interestingly it seems that some women (and men) who are prone to anxiety and panic attacks are more sensitive to caffeine and genuinely have a more sensitive body metabolism which makes them very susceptible to the effects of a lack of vitamin B or magnesium.

A comparison of caffeine consumption in Chinese nurses and workers in a tea factory revealed a strong association between increased caffeine consumption and the severity of pre-menstrual symptoms. We conducted our own survey in the United Kingdom with *Fitness* magazine which was published in 1992. 377 women took part. Caffeine consumption was nearly two and a half times higher in PMS sufferers compared with non-sufferers.

On average a mug of tea contains 100 to 130 mg and a mug of coffee between 150 and 250 mg of caffeine. In excess of 250 mg of caffeine can produce symptoms of anxiety, irritability, headache, increased passage of urine and a shaking feeling. Insomnia and palpitations can also occur. It is therefore advisable that these ever popular beverages are limited to just one or two cups or mugs per day and that caffeine-free alternatives are used. More details about these can be found on pages 107-108.

A final and important factor is hyperventilation. This mouthful simply means over breathing. Often when one becomes anxious it is natural to increase the rate and depth of respiration. This provides more oxygen to the bloodstream but also removes more of the waste gas carbon dioxide. This lack of carbon dioxide causes a change in body chemistry which can actually aggravate or cause a variety of symptoms, including numbness and tingling of the fingers, hands and around the mouth, muscle cramps, headaches, light-headedness, increased anxiety, physical and mental fatigue and confusion. The solution is to relax, reduce the rate and depth of breathing and if symptoms are severe to breathe in and out of a paper bag for several minutes. Where these symptoms chronically occur, formal advice and breathing exercises may need to be given by a physiotherapist or psychologist.

ABOUT THE SYMPTOMS

The symptoms in PMS A can at least be disturbing, and at worst feel like a tidal wave of personality change. They are amongst the most common symptoms in PMS.

A staggering 97 per cent of women in our survey of 1000 PMS patients, who were suffering moderately to severely, complained that they suffered to some degree with irritability pre-menstrually, 73 per cent of them with severe irritability, 96 per cent reported mood swings, 62 per cent severe, while 95 per cent reported nervous tension, 60 per cent severe, and 91 per cent reported anxiety, 54 per cent severe.

Degree of irritability suffered out of a sample of 1000 women				
Not Affected	Mild	Moderate	Severe	Total Affected
2.5%	3.2%	20.8%	73.5% -	97.5%

As you can imagine, the implications of these figures are fairly devastating. No wonder so many women report Jekyll and Hyde syndrome! Let us look more closely at how PMS A affected the lives of some of our patients.

PMS HITS HOME!

Many women were also reporting wild feelings of violence and aggression pre-menstrually. Their nervous tension seemed to reach uncontrollable peaks, at which time they would lash out at children and husbands or boy-friends. To a woman, they reported that this behaviour was uncharacteristic of them, and that it was having disastrous effects on their families.

The chart below shows to what degree violent and aggressive feelings were a problem. We were very concerned indeed by the result of our research.

Just under 80 per cent of the women studied felt violent or aggressive pre-menstrually. This obviously had serious repercussions on their partners, and on their children in particular.

Sample of 1000 women who admitted being violent/aggressive whilst suffering from PMS				
Not Affected	Once	More Than Once	More Than Six Times	Total Affected
20.6%	4.7%	27.7%	47.0% -	79.4%

" Pauline's Story "

Pauline experienced extreme violent and aggressive feelings pre-menstrually. She actually used to strike her husband and her daughter. She relates her experiences here very frankly.

Pauline is a 35-year-old mother and housewife who has had PMS since she was 13 years old.

'I used to be able to cope when I was in my teens but as I became older, my symptoms became really dreadful. I used to feel groggy for the whole week before my period. I had terrible migraine headaches and my head felt like it was full of cotton wool. Towards the end I'd have to spend the last few days in bed as I had no energy. I also had severe insomnia, dizziness and forgetfulness.

Eventually I started hitting my one-year-old daughter. I knew it was wrong but I couldn't control myself. I even hit my husband. I tried to carry on with life pre-menstrually but the very thought of going out of the house sent me into fits of the shakes. I was very frightened of meeting people. In fact, I was terrified!

I was given so many treatments for PMS. First my doctor prescribed different types of pill. Then I had Valium and I wasn't sleeping. That's when the depression started. Then I had anti-depressants. I felt like a junkie with my "uppers and downers".

Hormone treatment made me feel worse, and so finally I was referred to a psychologist who prescribed narcosis (i.e. being sedated and put to sleep) which lasted three days. This failed to help, and so the psychologist suggested giving me a course of ECT. I was very frightened, really desperate, I felt as though I was cracking up. It wasn't any wonder that my marriage split up. I even attempted suicide.

I just felt like I wanted to shut the door and be on my own, and yet I didn't want to be on my own, it was most peculiar.

I disliked myself

I just felt a mess pre-menstrually. An absolute mess. I really didn't like myself at all. The thing was that in my teens I could cope with it, because it was every few months and only for a day or two before my period. I was slimmer then and I had long blonde hair. As I got older and had Emma I just felt like a slob because everything had gone, everything had dropped, my skin was really terrible and itchy and my hair was greasy.

Relationships

Steve and I had been married for ten years before he started retaliating. So he'd put up with me for a long time. He'd put up with a lot. I've thrown things down the stairs at him and even hit him right across the face in front of our daughter. He's 5 ft 10 ins (1 m 75 cm) and quite reserved and easy-going usually.

I can remember a day when he happened to mention the curtains I'd just hand-sewn were not wide enough. I flew into a rage and kicked him, then flew upstairs and cried. When I came down we started arguing and fighting over something else. That's when he started hitting back.

My terrified little daughter

Emma was a wonderful, active child and began talking by eight months. By twelve months she would answer back and be deliberately defiant. I could only put up with her for so long pre-menstrually and then I'd hit her. I knew I shouldn't have done that. I realize it now because she was only twelve months old. She's been smacked much more than she should have been.

She was growing up to be a frightened little girl. She just didn't know which way her mummy was going to be. She was very frightened of me, so much so, she didn't want to be left alone in the house with me, especially when I was pre-menstrual. That is a dreadful way for a child to be.

PRE-MENSTRUAL SYNDROME QUESTIONNAIRE

Name: Pauline Solent   Age: 35   Height: 5' 5"   Weight: 9st 10lb

MARITAL STATUS: Single _____ Married _✓_ Divorced _____ Widowed _____
(Please tick where applicable)

PRESENT CONTRACEPTION: None _✓_ Pill _____ I.U.D. _____ Other _____

Your periods come every _31–33_ days   Your periods last _7_ days

Your periods are: Light _____   Moderate _____   Heavy _✓_

Number of Pregnancies: _1_   Number of Miscarriages: _____

Birth weight of children:
1st child _6lb 4oz_ 2nd child _____ 3rd child _____ 4th child _____

SYMPTOMS	WEEK AFTER PERIOD (Fill in 3 days after period)				WEEK BEFORE PERIOD (Fill in 2-3 days before period)			
	None	Mild	Moderate	Severe	None	Mild	Moderate	Severe
PMS - A								
Nervous Tension				✓				✓
Mood Swings	✓							✓
Irritability			✓					✓
Anxiety			✓					✓
PMS - H								
Weight Gain	✓				✓			
Swelling of Extremities	✓				✓			
Breast Tenderness	✓							✓
Abdominal Bloating	✓							✓
PMS - C								
Headache				✓				✓
Craving for Sweets	✓							✓
Increased Appetite	✓				✓			
Heart Pounding	✓							✓
Fatigue			✓					✓
Dizziness or Fainting			✓					✓
PMS - D								
Depression				✓				✓
Forgetfulness	✓							✓
Crying			✓					✓
Confusion	✓							✓
Insomnia				✓				✓
OTHER SYMPTOMS								
Loss of Sexual Interest				✓				✓
Disorientation	✓				✓			
Clumsiness	✓							✓
Tremors/Shakes	✓							✓
Thoughts of Suicide		✓						✓
Agoraphobia			✓					✓
Increased Physical Activity	✓				✓			
Heavy/Aching Legs	✓				✓			
Generalized Aches	✓							✓
Bad Breath	✓				✓			
Sensitivity to Music/Light	✓							✓
Excessive Thirst	✓							✓

FOLLOW UP
PRE-MENSTRUAL SYNDROME QUESTIONNAIRE

Name: _Pauline Solent_____ Age: _35____ Height: _5' 5"____ Weight: _9st 2lb____

MARITAL STATUS: Single _____ Married _√_ Divorced _____ Widowed _____
(Please tick where applicable)

PRESENT CONTRACEPTION: None _√__ Pill_____ I.U.D._____ Other_____

Your periods come every___31–33___days   Your periods last___5–7___days

Your periods are: Light_____ Moderate___√___ Heavy_____

SYMPTOMS	WEEK AFTER PERIOD (Fill in 3 days after period)				WEEK BEFORE PERIOD (Fill in 2-3 days before period)			
	None	Mild	Moderate	Severe	None	Mild	Moderate	Severe
PMS - A								
Nervous Tension	√				√			
Mood Swings	√				√			
Irritability	√				√			
Anxiety	√				√			
PMS - H								
Weight Gain	√				√			
Swelling of Extremities	√				√			
Breast Tenderness	√				√			
Abdominal Bloating	√				√			
PMS - C								
Headache	√				√			
Craving for Sweets	√				√			
Increased Appetite	√				√			
Heart Pounding	√				√			
Fatigue	√				√			
Dizziness or Fainting	√				√			
PMS - D								
Depression	√				√			
Forgetfulness	√				√			
Crying	√				√			
Confusion	√				√			
Insomnia	√				√			
OTHER SYMPTOMS								
Loss of Sexual Interest	√				√			
Disorientation	√				√			
Clumsiness	√				√			
Tremors/Shakes	√				√			
Thoughts of Suicide	√				√			
Agoraphobia	√				√			
Increased Physical Activity	√				√			
Heavy/Aching Legs	√				√			
Generalized Aches	√				√			
Bad Breath	√				√			
Sensitivity to Music/Light	√				√			
Excessive Thirst	√				√			

Hormone treatment

After my overdose my doctor decided to try me on a hormone treatment. Shortly after I started on hormones I developed very severe breast tenderness. My breasts literally stood out and they were so sore and uncomfortable. I kept taking them for two months but the problem just intensified. I ended up taking pain killers every day to try to ease the pain.

I decided to stop taking the hormone treatment but that was easier said than done. I had awful withdrawal symptoms even though I came off them gradually. First I took two per day, then one, then every other day. The symptoms were so awful and, Oh my head! I've never known anything like it. I couldn't bear to put a foot down in front of me. The food cravings I had were unbelievable. I vowed I would never take another tablet for the rest of my life.

Relief at last

I read about the Women's Nutritional Advisory Service in the local newspaper. I was at my wits' end at the time at the thought of spending another weekend in bed with terrible sweats and shakes. I felt like it was the last resort before I accepted the ECT. Fortunately, they managed to sort me out in the first five days, it was unbelievable!'

Pauline suffered very severely with PMS, to the point where she was at times a danger to herself and certainly a liability to her family. Her whole life revolved around her pre-menstrual symptoms. She was, sadly, unable to lead a normal life and on the point of having psychiatric treatment, ECT, when she contacted us. (ECT, electroconvulsive therapy, electric shock treatment, kills brain cells and these do not regenerate.)

The chart from her first questionnaire has been copied on page 24. This she completed when she first contacted us. You will notice that quite a few symptoms in each category were severe pre-menstrually. She was, in fact, suffering with all four categories of PMS listed. However, most of the symptoms in PMS A, the first category, were so severe that they were still present the week after her period. We soon discovered that this was largely due to her nutritional state and her diet. I will explain this more fully in the Diet section on page 142. She admits herself that she responded exceedingly quickly to a change in diet and nutritional supplements of vitamins and minerals.

Previous diet

'I used to drink nine or 10 cups of tea per day and I used a lot of salt both in my cooking and at the table. I ate lots of convenience foods like pre-packed pies and tinned foods and I ate a fair amount of cheese, milk and wholemeal (wholewheat) bread. Also, I could easily eat four or five biscuits a day.

New diet

I think the diet suggested by the Women's Nutritional Advisory Service is wonderful. I found it a little difficult at first but I think that's because my head was so peculiar pre-menstrually that I couldn't take it all in.

When the programme arrived I drove to my mum's and we sat down together and read through it so that we understood it fully. She then came with me to the supermarket and I bought lots of leeks, fresh vegetables and fruit, salad and fish. I had to cut out wholewheat and all foods containing yeast. I was given lists of foods to avoid and lists of food to concentrate on. I eat loads of fresh food now and feel wonderful. My friends all know I'm on a special diet. It's become a way of life.'

Pauline's follow-up questionnaire after six months on page 25 looks dramatically different. All her pre-menstrual symptoms are gone completely.

End result

'I don't have any symptoms any more. My life has changed dramatically. I feel much more at ease and I never shout, unless I am very angry.

My agoraphobia has gone completely. I can go out with confidence and I feel great in myself. I can do all the things I couldn't do before. I can go anywhere.

Steve and I get on really well now, so much so we are even planning to have another baby, which I could never have coped with before. I had no intention of having any more children, in fact I'd given away all the baby equipment. I am truly delighted with the results of my programme. My husband thinks it's wonderful too.'

From a letter Pauline sent at the end of her programme you can tell she is now coping with life and feels normal again.

Dear Maryon,

I am very fit now and I have just spent a hectic week in London with my six-year-old daughter – who is a handful. I feel marvellous. She's been *better as I have practically put her on my diet (except she does have some sweets), and she watches my diet.*

Thanks again for giving me my life back after 20 years.

Yours ever so grateful
Pauline Solent

" Ruth's Story "

Ruth was another victim of violent and aggressive feelings which she acted on pre-menstrually. Classically, she didn't experience any of these feelings once her period arrived.

Ruth is a 39-year-old who is a housewife and a mother of two children. Her PMS began after the birth of her first baby, although she feels it may have been simmering beforehand.

'PMS *totally changed my character when I had it, and I had it for half my life. It began two weeks before my period, sometimes more. It would disappear on the first day of my period and I immediately felt a sense of relief. Then a week after my period it began to build up again.*

I became very irritable, very tired, snappy and aggressive, which is not a bit what I'm like normally. I would shout at my husband, literally scream at him. I think I still have sore throats as a result. I used to go to my room and have a screaming fit to keep it to myself. But people would aggravate me easily. Obviously when you have small children they tend to get on your nerves when you are tired. I felt like a lump of lead at the time and I know I had very little patience with my older daughter who was my only child when it was at its worst. She suffered, I'm sure. I would scream at her and hit her at times which was very upsetting for me afterwards because I know a child of seven couldn't possibly understand.

I vowed it wouldn't happen next month

Although my husband was understanding and sympathetic, it's very difficult to have a normal relationship with someone when they are aggressive and not well. There is no doubt about the fact that the presence of PMS symptoms placed a strain on our marriage.

I suppose everybody has irritating habits and normally I would just take them in my stride. But at PMS times my husband would aggravate me to the point where I'd scream at him. Unfortunately it was over stupid, insignificant things.

Very often I'd take it out on the children instead of my husband. This was because I knew he had such high standards of self-discipline and I think he felt that I ought to have been able to do something about my own behaviour. I always vowed that next month I was jolly well going to, it was mind over matter etc., but it never seemed to work.

I hated myself

When pre-menstrual I felt I was awful, I really hated myself. When I started hitting my daughter, I felt like I had really failed myself. I felt like a worm. Really dreadful. I cannot explain how I felt. My usual philosophy is that if children are treated right they respond and they are not naughty. I tried to explain to my doctor but he didn't understand. I remember shouting at him "you don't understand" but he just threw his hands up in horror and walked out of the surgery.

My daughter locked herself away from me

I think my daughter was quite frightened of me actually. I am normally placid but of course I wasn't, as my symptoms were occurring more often than not when I was at my worst.

The problem would usually begin over a trivial matter which now I would brush aside or cope with calmly. Then I would just feel so tight inside and, of course, it would then become a big thing. Of course with children if you build it up they build it up also, and it all gets out of hand. I would sometimes grip her and shake her, poor girl. It was a dreadful way to treat a child. She would often go off and lock herself in her bedroom because she was afraid of me.

I never did her any bad damage, but it was awful to me as I would never normally strike a child. I don't agree with bashing children when they are naughty, particularly as she probably wasn't even that naughty. It just got out of hand.

Previous treatments

The first time I went to the doctor about my PMS, and I have been to several doctors about it over the years, it was thought a good idea for me to take the Pill to remove the "tension" beforehand. This was after the birth of my first child, about 14 years ago. The Pill caused me awful headaches and I had to come off it.

PRE-MENSTRUAL SYNDROME QUESTIONNAIRE

Name: Ruth Sears   Age: 39   Height: 5' 11"   Weight: 12st

MARITAL STATUS: Single _____ Married _√_ Divorced _____ Widowed _____
(Please tick where applicable)

PRESENT CONTRACEPTION: None_____ Pill_____ I.U.D. _√_ Other_____

Your periods come every __28__ days   Your periods last __5__ days

Your periods are: Light_____ Moderate _√_ Heavy_____

Number of Pregnancies: __3__   Number of Miscarriages: __1__

Birth weight of children:
1st child _7lb 15oz_ 2nd child _8lb 10oz_ 3rd child_____ 4th child_____

SYMPTOMS	WEEK AFTER PERIOD (Fill in 3 days after period)				WEEK BEFORE PERIOD (Fill in 2-3 days before period)			
	None	Mild	Moderate	Severe	None	Mild	Moderate	Severe
PMS - A								
Nervous Tension	✓							✓
Mood Swings	✓							✓
Irritability	✓							✓
Anxiety	✓						✓	
PMS - H								
Weight Gain	✓						✓	
Swelling of Extremities	✓				✓			
Breast Tenderness	✓				✓			
Abdominal Bloating	✓						✓	
PMS - C								
Headache	✓				✓			
Craving for Sweets	✓							✓
Increased Appetite	✓							✓
Heart Pounding	✓				✓			
Fatigue	✓							✓
Dizziness or Fainting	✓				✓			
PMS - D								
Depression	✓							✓
Forgetfulness	✓							✓
Crying	✓				✓			
Confusion	✓							✓
Insomnia	✓				✓			
OTHER SYMPTOMS								
Loss of Sexual Interest	✓							✓
Disorientation	✓						✓	
Clumsiness	✓						✓	
Tremors/Shakes	✓				✓			
Thoughts of Suicide	✓				✓			
Agoraphobia	✓				✓			
Increased Physical Activity	✓				✓			
Heavy/Aching Legs	✓				✓			
Generalized Aches	✓				✓			
Bad Breath	✓				✓			
Sensitivity to Music/Light	✓				✓			
Excessive Thirst	✓				✓			

I realized I couldn't continue to suffer, by which time my original doctor had left the practice. The new doctor prescribed vitamin B6. He wanted to try the natural approach first before prescribing progesterone. Although I thought that the vitamin B6 was helping at first, it didn't make the slightest difference to my symptoms.

I saw a specialist who examined me thoroughly and could find nothing physically wrong. He said it was a hormonal imbalance and prescribed hormone treatment. I was never very happy about taking hormones, I would rather have taken more natural things. They did help my symptoms though, to the point where I could function to some degree. But PMS reared its ugly head again. It would pop up now and then. It was not fully quashed. Life wasn't what I would describe as being bearable, but it was more under control than before.

My husband then read an article in the newspaper about the nutritional programme for PMS being so successful and suggested I follow that up.'

Ruth struggled for 14 years with her symptoms. Again, it affected a large portion of her life. She admits her family suffered a great deal because of her behaviour pre-menstrually. And in common with all the other sufferers mentioned, she was unable to control herself. When her period began all her symptoms went.

She suffered severely with three categories of PMS: PMS A, the nervous and uptight symptoms, PMS C, craving for sweet foods etc., and PMS D, particularly depression, confusion and forgetfulness. She had tried many treatments before to help ease her symptoms, but she was unable to control the situation. Long-term hormone treatment did help to ease things a bit, but she was unhappy taking them.

Her first chart is opposite.

Diet helped

'I really had no idea that diet was an important factor in controlling PMS. I thought it was a question of hormone balance being wrong. And the only way to put it right was to put in more hormones, the right kind of hormones, rather than eat different things.

I used to drink quite a bit of coffee, add lots of salt to my food, and I had a lot of sugary foods. I used to try to eat a high fibre and low fat diet because I was always trying to get my weight down. I did have a weakness for chocolates and biscuits, in fact I used to crave them especially pre-menstrually.

Name: Ruth Sears   Age: 39   Height: 5' 11"   Weight: 12st

MARITAL STATUS: Single _____ Married _√_ Divorced _____ Widowed ____
(Please tick where applicable)

PRESENT CONTRACEPTION: None_____ Pill_____ I.U.D. _√_ Other_____

Your periods come every__28__days   Your periods last__5__days

Your periods are: Light_____ Moderate___√___ Heavy_____

SYMPTOMS	WEEK AFTER PERIOD (Fill in 3 days after period)				WEEK BEFORE PERIOD (Fill in 2-3 days before period)			
	None	Mild	Moderate	Severe	None	Mild	Moderate	Severe
PMS - A								
Nervous Tension	√				√			
Mood Swings	√				√			
Irritability	√				√			
Anxiety	√				√			
PMS - H								
Weight Gain	√				√			
Swelling of Extremities	√				√			
Breast Tenderness	√						√	
Abdominal Bloating		√			√			
PMS - C								
Headache	√				√			
Craving for Sweets	√				√			
Increased Appetite	√				√			
Heart Pounding	√				√			
Fatigue		√			√			
Dizziness or Fainting	√				√			
PMS - D								
Depression	√				√			
Forgetfulness	√				√			
Crying	√				√			
Confusion	√				√			
Insomnia	√				√			
OTHER SYMPTOMS								
Loss of Sexual Interest	√				√			
Disorientation	√				√			
Clumsiness	√				√			
Tremors/Shakes	√				√			
Thoughts of Suicide	√				√			
Agoraphobia	√				√			
Increased Physical Activity	√				√			
Heavy/Aching Legs	√				√			
Generalized Aches	√				√			
Bad Breath	√				√			
Sensitivity to Music/Light	√				√			
Excessive Thirst	√				√			

I read an article in the newspaper about the Women's Nutritional Advisory Service dietary recommendations, so I was semi-prepared when I received my programme. Being asked to cut out grains shocked me a bit. It was the most complicated part of the diet, I found, as so many things contain wheat.

I did stick to the diet to the letter for the first three months. I even had a special meal prepared when we attended a formal dinner. No one asked why, and I didn't want to mention the reason. They were all very discreet about it. It didn't cause a problem.

My symptoms completely vanished on the programme. It was absolute magic. Even my long-standing problem of thrush cleared up when I was avoiding wheat and foods containing yeast.

I am back on all the usual foods now. I no longer have the intense sweet cravings and I feel I know where to draw the line. I still take Optivite, a vitamin supplement which I think is marvellous, and my symptoms haven't returned.

I'm delighted to say that my life has been transformed since starting on the programme. I followed the suggested diet very closely for six months and took the recommended vitamin and mineral supplements. In fact, I still take the supplements but have been able to moderate my diet. It seems amazing to me that such strong, violent symptoms could be controlled by changing my diet and taking some vitamin pills.'

Her follow-up questionnaire (opposite) reflects her progress. Most symptoms are completely under control. Just a bit of mild breast tenderness pre-menstrually remains.

End result

'Since undertaking the nutritional programme to overcome my PMS, I can honestly say my symptoms have disappeared. I think they have really vanished, like absolute magic. I am overwhelmed by it. My life is now back to normal. There is no comparison in me now. I am a completely different woman. Back to what I was before.'

Ruth's letter to me at the end of her programme was interesting as she points out that it is sometimes genuinely difficult to come off treatment — even it it isn't really working. Trying a new approach does often involve courage, especially when so many other treatments have failed previously.

Dear Maryon,

I am enclosing my follow-up questionnaire and must take the opportunity to tell you how absolutely the course has changed my life. I couldn't have believed that just vitamins, minerals and a change of diet could have such a dramatic impact.

Having had quite severe symptoms it was an act of courage and determination to break off the progesterone treatment and step into the blue on your programme. I'm glad I did.

Ruth Sears

Here is another example of how PMS A symptoms affected the life of a young single woman, who was also diagnosed as having irritable bowel syndrome.

Nadine is a 25-year-old single woman who works as an advertising executive. She has been suffering with PMS since she was 15 years of age and feels that her life has been pretty disrupted as a result.

" Nadine's Story "

'I felt trapped like a victim, trapped in the philosophy of being a woman and stuck with it. I was very fed up with the suffering every month, it was like being in a biological prison. I was very frightened.

PMS just meant misery to me, it made my life difficult and extremely unpleasant. That's the best way I can explain it. The fact that I had no idea what it was, made matters worse. From the age of 15 I was extremely unpleasant pre-menstrually, to my mother in particular. I would start shouting at her. I was very aggressive and argumentative before my period. Unfortunately, I wasn't aware of the pattern at the time.

My social life was affected by my symptoms and at work I just got a reputation for being an extremely rude person. In fact, previously at college I had been nicknamed "The Misery".

I used to take my frustrations out on my boyfriend. I'd lash out at him with my fists, then I would throw things around the room. That was the worst thing, feeling so aggressive and throwing things around. He would try to calm me down by cuddling me. He knew if he rode the storm that I would calm down eventually when my period came.

My tummy problems were so severe I was diagnosed by my doctor as having irritable bowel syndrome, caused by stress. I felt that that was a *very convenient diagnosis to make when he didn't really know what the problem was and he wanted to get rid of me. "Tell them it's stress and they'll go away."*

I felt pretty awful. I tried to help myself by taking some vitamin B6, then I tried evening primrose oil and zinc, and finally my doctor prescribed progesterone suppositories. None of the treatments were successful, though.

It wasn't until I read articles in magazines about the work that the Women's Nutritional Advisory Service was doing that I came to realize that I was suffering from PMS. Up until then I was just aware that my symptoms were getting worse and worse and I didn't know what to do about them.'

Nadine is a young, single woman who has not had any children. Nevertheless, at the time she came to us she had been suffering with PMS symptoms for some 10 years. Her main problem areas were the tension and anxiety symptoms, and the swelling and bloating symptoms, as you can see from her chart overleaf.

Understandably, she was frightened about the effect that her ever-recurring symptoms had on her body and on her life. All areas of her life were disrupted because of her symptoms, and despite trying a series of treatments, both independently, and through her doctor, her symptoms showed no sign of easing off. The thought of going through her whole life suffering in this manner had been pretty uncomfortable to Nadine.

Diet

'My previous diet obviously wasn't right, in retrospect. I had a very bad stomach problem, in fact I was diagnosed as having irritable bowel disease. I had loads of unpleasant tests and was told that the condition was due to stress.

I used to get terrible diarrhoea and pain cramps in my tummy. The doctors told me to eat more bran, which I have since found out aggravates the condition.

I didn't know that diet could play such an important role. I did wonder sometimes though. I did a degree in Food Science and there was a small amount of information on the effects that diet could have on the body. Although I had my suspicions, I didn't know how to go about finding out more. I did try looking for papers but I didn't really find many and I didn't find anything to connect diet to PMS or my irritable bowel problem.

I used to eat up to four slices of wholemeal (wholewheat) bread per day

PRE-MENSTRUAL SYNDROME QUESTIONNAIRE

Name: Nadine Morris   Age: 25   Height: 5' 2"   Weight: 10st 4lb

MARITAL STATUS: Single __✓__   Married _____   Divorced _____   Widowed ____
(Please tick where applicable)

PRESENT CONTRACEPTION: None_____   Pill_____   I.U.D._____   Other __✓__

Your periods come every __27–35__ days   Your periods last __4–5__ days

Your periods are: Light_____   Moderate __✓__   Heavy_____

Number of Pregnancies: __1__   Number of Miscarriages: __1__

Birth weight of children:
1st child_____   2nd child_____   3rd child_____   4th child_____

SYMPTOMS	WEEK AFTER PERIOD (Fill in 3 days after period)				WEEK BEFORE PERIOD (Fill in 2-3 days before period)			
	None	Mild	Moderate	Severe	None	Mild	Moderate	Severe
PMS - A								
Nervous Tension	✓							✓
Mood Swings	✓							✓
Irritability	✓							✓
Anxiety		✓						✓
PMS - H								
Weight Gain	✓						✓	
Swelling of Extremities	✓				✓			
Breast Tenderness	✓						✓	
Abdominal Bloating		✓						✓
PMS - C								
Headache	✓				✓			
Craving for Sweets	✓					✓		
Increased Appetite	✓					✓		
Heart Pounding	✓				✓			
Fatigue	✓				✓			
Dizziness or Fainting	✓				✓			
PMS - D								
Depression	✓				✓			
Forgetfulness	✓				✓			
Crying	✓					✓		
Confusion	✓				✓			
Insomnia	✓				✓			
OTHER SYMPTOMS								
Loss of Sexual Interest	✓				✓			
Disorientation	✓				✓			
Clumsiness		✓						✓
Tremors/Shakes	✓				✓			
Thoughts of Suicide	✓				✓			
Agoraphobia								
Increased Physical Activity		✓			✓			
Heavy/Aching Legs	✓				✓			
Generalized Aches	✓				✓			
Bad Breath	✓				✓			
Sensitivity to Music/Light	✓				✓			
Excessive Thirst	✓							✓

FOLLOW UP
PRE-MENSTRUAL SYNDROME QUESTIONNAIRE

Name: <u>Nadine Morris</u> Age: <u>25</u> Height: <u>5' 2"</u> Weight: <u>9st 9lb</u>

<u>MARITAL STATUS:</u> Single <u>√</u> Married <u> </u> Divorced <u> </u> Widowed <u> </u>
(Please tick where applicable)

<u>PRESENT CONTRACEPTION:</u> None<u> </u> Pill<u> </u> I.U.D.<u> </u> Other<u> √ </u>

   Your periods come every<u> 28–35 </u>days Your periods last<u> 4–5 </u>days

   Your periods are: Light<u>   </u> Moderate<u> √ </u> Heavy<u>   </u>

SYMPTOMS	WEEK AFTER PERIOD (Fill in 3 days after period)				WEEK BEFORE PERIOD (Fill in 2-3 days before period)			
	None	Mild	Moderate	Severe	None	Mild	Moderate	Severe
PMS - A								
Nervous Tension	√				√			
Mood Swings	√				√			
Irritability	√				√			
Anxiety	√				√			
PMS - H								
Weight Gain	√				√			
Swelling of Extremities	√				√			
Breast Tenderness	√				√			
Abdominal Bloating	√				√			
PMS - C								
Headache	√				√			
Craving for Sweets	√				√			
Increased Appetite	√				√			
Heart Pounding	√				√			
Fatigue	√				√			
Dizziness or Fainting	√				√			
PMS - D								
Depression	√				√			
Forgetfulness	√				√			
Crying	√				√			
Confusion	√				√			
Insomnia	√				√			
OTHER SYMPTOMS								
Loss of Sexual Interest	√				√			
Disorientation	√				√			
Clumsiness	√				√			
Tremors/Shakes	√				√			
Thoughts of Suicide	√				√			
Agoraphobia	√				√			
Increased Physical Activity	√				√			
Heavy/Aching Legs	√				√			
Generalized Aches	√				√			
Bad Breath	√				√			
Sensitivity to Music/Light	√				√			
Excessive Thirst	√				√			

and have a bowl of bran. I also drank about five cups of tea per day, an extra ¾ of a pint (450 ml) of milk per day, and other dairy foods.

On my programme I was asked to cut out grains, dairy products, yeast-based foods, tea and foods containing sugar. I stuck to the diet to the letter. It was inconvenient at first because it was so different. It took me a week or two to adapt and then it became easier.

Miraculously, soon after I began the diet my tummy problems just cleared up. I now know through trial and error that wheat and dairy products are irritants and will cause my diarrhoea to return.

I have relaxed my diet now that I am so much better. I am still fairly strict with myself most of the time. I can get away with drinking alcohol occasionally and sometimes I do eat processed foods or crisps.

End result

Now that I have followed the nutritional programme, I have learned so much. My body has recovered from all the ailments, including my PMS and the irritable bowel syndrome. All the remaining traces of agoraphobia which I had previously suffered from in my late teens and early twenties have disappeared, and my skin condition has improved. My energy has just soared and I feel that I have come from being a poorly, lethargic person suddenly to someone who is healthy all the time. I am my usual bouncy self once again and I get on well with people. I don't experience the miseries any more, I am relieved to say.

I honestly feel that the Women's Nutritional Advisory Service has transformed my life. I used to think life was terrible. Now I find life pleasurable. I feel healthier than I have ever done, at least since I was a child. I can't thank them enough.'

Nadine had no symptoms whatsoever left at the end of her six-month programme, as you can see from her chart.

An extract from a letter explains how Nadine felt about her programme.

'I wanted to make some additional comments regarding the programme, apart from those in the accompanying questionnaire.

First of all, I'd like to thank you for such detailed information and guidance in your letter of recommendations. The programme has made the biological and physiological aspects of womanhood a great deal easier to cope with. My periods are much less painful and lighter. The gruesome week before my period, which was always so unbearable, is now like the other two weeks. I no longer suffer from any breast tenderness, which used to be so severe, and no longer suffer with bloatedness. I no longer hate everything and everybody including myself, and I no longer feel violent or aggressive, which is a very great relief. I also don't wreck everything around me through clumsiness, as that's gone too.

All in all, the programme has transformed me and my life quite remarkably and I am grateful for the work you and your colleagues have done to enable me to live without dreading the onset of each period. More significantly, I feel that the diet and discovery of foods that I am allergic to has improved my whole life, not just my PMS.

For about seven years I have suffered with irritable bowel syndrome, more recently it became so bad that I was referred to a specialist who, after various unpleasant tests, pronounced it was caused by stress. Ironically most doctors have prescribed increased intake of wholewheat products and bran, no wonder I wasn't getting any better! Admittedly, when I am in a stressful situation my symptoms return, but they last only as long as the stress. Previously, the irritable bowel symptoms were with me constantly and just became unbearable when I was under stress.

I know this isn't entirely relevant to your work on PMS but at the same time many of my female contemporaries seem to suffer from irritable bowel syndrome too and I wonder how many women are being inappropriately treated and dismissed with mutterings of "it's psychosomatic"?

I hope my comments have been some help in your work to relieve the misery of PMS. I for one am a very grateful and satisfied customer!'

Yours sincerely
Nadine

6

BLOATING, WEIGHT GAIN AND BREAST TENDERNESS

PMS H (HYDRATION)

PMS H sufferers complain of weight gain pre-menstrually. The hands and feet often swell so that rings and shoes become too tight. The face often becomes puffy and the waistline expands so that clothes feel too tight. The abdomen can become bloated and tender and the same applies to the breasts.

The manifestations of these symptoms are mostly physical, in that women report feeling very uncomfortable and often sore. Because of their increased size many women feel self-conscious and get very touchy and introverted. Surprisingly, most women who suffer from PMS H only gain up to 3–4 pounds (1–2 kg) pre-menstrually. Approximately 20 per cent seem to gain far more than this. I have personally seen women who gain up to 12 pounds (5.4 kg) before their periods. They literally change dress size and need to have two sets of underwear to cope with their increased breast size.

Symptoms due to excess fluid retention can easily be worsened by eating the wrong diet. A high intake of sodium or ordinary salt, which is the norm in the United Kingdom, is the commonest cause of fluid retention in women. It appears that some women are particularly prone to develop fluid retention whereas others can eat salty foods with impunity. Thus part of the programme for those with fluid retention symptoms is to greatly reduce the intake of salt from that used in the cooking, that added to food at the table and from salty foods. Nowadays, like our consumption of sugar, at least two-thirds of the salt we eat is 'hidden' in common foods such as bacon, ham, sausages, other preserved meat products, cheeses, most butters and margarines, bread, tinned foods like tinned tuna and veget-ables, salted crisps and nuts and most savoury snacks and convenience meals.

Good old plain fruit and vegetables, meat, fish, beans and rice are all low in sodium and have good levels of potassium. A good intake of potassium and magnesium from the diet may help minimize the effects of too much sodium. Fortunately there are many low-salt (sodium) versions of tinned and other foods now available.

Consuming a lot of carbohydrate-rich foods and sugar, including that from soft drinks, which many women drink in substantial quantities pre-menstrually, can also lead to fluid retention. Curiously, drinking a lot of water, low-calorie drinks and even tea and coffee without sugar does not cause this problem. Losing weight if you are overweight may also help with fluid retention symptoms.

However, some women who complain of pre-menstrual abdominal bloating and puffy fingers do not have an increase in body water and salt content. It may be that their perception of their body changes and they just 'feel' different.

THE DEGREE OF SUFFERING

In our survey we found that 90.8 per cent of the women complained of abdominal bloating to some degree, (72 per cent severe to moderately).

Of the women studied 86.8 per cent had pre-menstrual breast tenderness (67 per cent severe to moderate sufferers).

Weight was gained by 84 per cent (52 per cent severe to moderately) and 54 per cent complained of swelling of the extremities (33 per cent severe to moderate).

**Degree of pre-menstrual
breast tenderness
suffered out of a sample
of 1000 women**

Not Affected	Mild	Moderate	Severe	Total Affected
13.2%	19.9%	31.6%	35.3% -	86.8%

**Degree to which
abdominal bloating
affected a sample of
1000 women pre-menstrually**

Not Affected	Mild	Moderate	Severe	Total Affected
9.2%	18.5%	39.3%	33.0% -	90.8%

WEIGHT LOSS

Whilst conducting our follow-up consultations during the programme and in our clinics, we began to notice that many overweight women who were previously unable to lose weight were enthusiastically reporting weight loss. This began occurring even after the first month, without even 'dieting' to lose weight. In fact, their intake of food during the programme was in many cases greater than usual.

Because of this somewhat unexpected outcome, we decided to monitor a group of 50 PMS sufferers who were also overweight, through the first three months of their programme. (Thirty-six of the women were at least 10 per cent overweight and 14 of them were obese, which means greater than 33 per cent above normal body weight.) The symptoms complained of most severely to begin with were weight gain, fatigue, abdominal bloating, craving for food, in particular sweet foods, and anxiety.

After three months on their programmes there was an 84 per cent reduction in severe symptoms.

The overweight group of 36 women lost an average of 7 pounds (3 kg) and the obese group of 14 women lost an average of 13 pounds (6 kg) in this three-month period.

We can't say precisely why this amount of weight loss had occurred, particularly when the women had previously found it difficult to lose weight. However, the common denominator seems to be that they were all on a healthy diet that had been balanced according to their individual needs. We therefore suspect that this must have had a positive effect on their metabolism with the result that they began to shed excess weight.

This is certainly an area we would like to research further. But in the meantime it's a gift horse that won't be looked in the mouth by PMS H sufferers.

" Dee's Story "

Dee is a full-time mother of two from Dunstable in Bedfordshire.

'Whenever I was invited out I had to check my diary twice, once to see whether I was free and the other to see how near to my period it was. If the date was anything up to 16 days before my period I knew that I would be so bloated I wouldn't be able to fit into any of my usual clothes. I had one outfit that fitted pre-menstrually and that was it. My husband would ask about my new dress or skirt that I had bought only days before, and I'd have to admit that it didn't fit now. I am usually a size 12, but pre-menstrually I gained four inches around my waist. I also suffered with

*headaches, insomnia, continual tiredness and sore throats, and found it
very difficult to cope.*

*I actually didn't realize that I was suffering with PMS until I read a
feature on the Women's Nutritional Advisory Service. The article listed all
my symptoms. All at once I felt I had a reason for feeling as I did.*

Diet reduced my bloating

*I contacted the WNAS and followed their postal programme. They
thought the fluid retention was related to my salt and caffeine intake. I
had previously been snacking on crisps and drinking lots of strong tea. I
followed the programme written for me, and had my monthly consultations
during the programme. I noticed a real improvement within ten days, and
within three months my symptoms had disappeared. At last I feel I'm in
control of my body. It's a pain not to eat everything I'd like, but feeling
good all month is easily worth that – and I only need one wardrobe of
clothes.*

" Rebecca's Story "

Rebecca is a 38-year-old divorcee with two children who works as a
teacher.

'*Looking back, I think my symptoms began increasing in severity after the
birth of my children. Certainly, the last ten years have been the worst. I
suffered for years before I even knew what I was suffering from. I'd never
heard of "PMS". My doctor was unsympathetic, and so I thought it was
just part of my make-up and therefore something I had to suffer.*

*My husband was very unsympathetic towards me during my pre-
menstrual times. He couldn't believe I could be all right one minute and
then suddenly have symptoms which involved him making adjustments. He
really doubted that my symptoms actually existed. It caused a lot of
misunderstandings and arguments. For example, I remember a time when
I asked him to turn the record player down as it was giving me a
headache, and he just grudgingly said, "Well, you were quite all right this
morning". I just used to feel depressed, isolated and confused because I
didn't really know why I was feeling so different pre-menstrually.*

My symptoms would occur 10 to 12 days pre-menstrually. The most physically noticeable thing was that I'd gain four to five pounds (2–3 kg) in weight; my abdomen felt really bloated. I'd get cravings for food, in fact I just couldn't seem to get satisfied no matter what I ate. Apart from that I'd feel very irritable, exhausted and fairly afraid of my dizziness and fainting attacks, particularly when I went shopping or stood up for any length of time.

I looked terrible pre-menstrually, which didn't help. I had puffy eyes surrounded by dark shadows. Another thing was that I used to always feel cold, an inner cold. I would have to go to bed and crawl under the duvet with a hot-water bottle, but still wouldn't be able to overcome the cold; my teeth would still be chattering.

Life was really very difficult at the time and the stress of a broken marriage made things even worse. I found it difficult to work pre-menstrually as I couldn't concentrate. My head was so fuzzy and I couldn't formulate my ideas properly.

I had previously tried several different treatments for PMS, none of which were of any lasting value. I tried taking vitamin B6 on its own, but it didn't work. I also had some acupuncture and visited a medical herbalist. I put myself on to a course of Efamol evening primrose oil, but found that this only helped initially.

Scatterbrain!

I was so forgetful. One day I put my handbag on the roof of the car whilst I loaded it and then I drove off without moving it! I can honestly say I felt terrible pre-menstrually. I didn't like myself at all.

Wrecked marriage

My marriage broke down. I know that my PMS symptoms aggravated the situation. They caused a lot of misunderstandings. We had awful rows. He simply didn't believe my symptoms existed. I think he thought I'd made them up to suit myself and to inconvenience him. He had no understanding of the situation and I felt so isolated in it. I got very confused and tense as a result which aggravated my behaviour, so it was a vicious circle.'

Rebecca had severe symptoms in all four categories, pre-menstrually, whereas she had practically no symptoms at all at any other time of the month.

Rebecca also had 'before' and 'after' laboratory tests during her treatment which are detailed on page 138.

'When I heard about the nutritional approach to PMS, I decided to give it a go. I have been under Dr Stewart for over a year now. He has been measuring levels of vitamins and minerals in my body. I discovered I had an added complication of severe food allergies which we have also been working on, and a thyroid problem which is now being treated. My symptoms are down to a bearable two days per month now and I hope that I will be able to overcome them completely as time goes on.

Robert, with whom I now live, is very understanding and tolerant. Whenever I couldn't cope with a situation, he would just help me to do something. I'm sure it's due to his support that I have made it through.'

7

SUGAR CRAVINGS, HEADACHES AND FATIGUE

PMS C (CARBOHYDRATE CRAVING)

In this sub-group of PMS, one to two weeks before the period the appetite increases. Cravings for food begin, particularly for sweet foods and chocolate. Often stress intensifies the situation. Satisfying the cravings is a vicious circle. A typical example is as follows.

The day starts with either no breakfast or just a couple of cups of tea or coffee and a few cigarettes. This may stimulate the body's metabolism and one's energy for a short while, but the problems begin by mid-morning. By this time the energy level tends to fall, and symptoms of nervousness, anxiety, palpitations, light headaches, hunger and cravings for food, particularly sweet foods, set in. Another cup of tea or coffee with sugar, or with a sugary or chocolate snack, may delay symptoms for a while but nothing short of a good wholesome meal will resolve these symptoms.

Some of these symptoms may be due to a fall in the level of sugar (glucose) in the blood – known as hypoglycaemia. As the brain and nervous system rely upon glucose for their source of energy, a fall in its level can cause a whole host of nervous system symptoms. The body compensates by producing adrenaline, which increases the level of glucose in the blood, but aggravates symptoms of anxiety, palpitations, sweating and shaking.

Such symptoms may be improved by the next meal. Often the mid-morning or mid-afternoon fatigue or sweet cravings are relieved by a wholesome lunch, supper or snack.

Not all women will have such marked symptoms, nor indeed will there always be marked swings in blood sugar levels. Often one just feels better if one eats three good meals a day, a couple of healthy snacks, and has a regular, not too hectic lifestyle.

Headaches can also be caused by excessive intake of tea and coffee. Fatigue can be affected by the balance of minerals, such as iron and magnesium. Any women with persistent fatigue should certainly see her doctor for examination and appropriate blood tests, particularly to check for anaemia or reduced activity of the thyroid gland.

GOOD FOOD REGULARLY, PLEASE!

So often the cravings for sweet foods, sugary snacks and chocolate are the result of an irregular and inadequate diet. Women with PMS C – carbo-hydrate cravings – may also experience headache, increased appetite, heart pounding, fatigue, and dizziness and fainting. These symptoms can be due to the swings in blood sugar levels and over-reliance on social stimulants: caffeine from tea, coffee, cola, chocolate, alcohol, cigarettes and even marijuana. Three good, regular meals, two wholesome in-be-tween-meal snacks and cutting down on sugar and social stimulants are all essential to treat PMS C.

THE DEGREE OF SUFFERING

In our study we found that 77 per cent of the women were suffering with cravings for sweet food, just over 60 per cent severe to moderately. There were 93 per cent who reported suffering with fatigue pre-menstrually, 82 per cent severe to moderately; 77 per cent reported headaches pre-menstrually, 74 per cent general increased appetite, 53 per cent heart pounding and 50 per cent dizziness and fainting.

❝   Geraldine's Story   ❞

Geraldine is a 33-year-old mother of three who works as a nursing auxiliary. She had had PMS since 1983, after the birth of her third baby.

She had severe symptoms in all four categories. She felt 'possessed' pre-menstrually and hardly recognized herself. She was withdrawn from life and disgusted with her own behaviour. Her eating habits were particularly erratic pre-menstrually. In particular she craved chocolate, which she felt immensely guilty about.

'I thought sometimes I could just sit zombie-like and not talk to anybody. I wanted to go to the doctor and ask him to take my children and put me in a white jacket and stick me in a room somewhere. In fact, it even makes me feel bad talking about it.

Post-natal depression

When my third child was three months old I suddenly developed post-natal depression. It hit me really hard as I had never experienced it before. I didn't feel aggressive towards the baby, I just knew there was something wrong with me. I used to sit staring into space for hours. There were jobs that needed doing and the whole house was disintegrating, but I just couldn't do anything. I felt awful all the time and I had no energy or enthusiasm. I was overweight and depressed.

My doctor prescribed anti-depressants. I don't know if they helped or not. They helped me to sleep, but I was afraid I wouldn't wake up. They made me feel zombie-like.

I realized I had PMS during a sticky patch in my marriage. I felt I was reacting to everything and that some problem had to be present in order to make me feel so bad.

49

Black cloud overhead

Whereas I hadn't felt aggressive with post-natal depression, I felt absolutely horrendous when I had PMS. I used to feel I had an individual black cloud hanging over me. I'd wake up in the morning knowing that awful feeling was there and that there was nothing I could do to make it go away. I just knew I had days ahead of me feeling so awful.

I didn't want to participate in my usual activities pre-menstrually. I belong to an amateur dramatics society, but I just didn't feel I could do anything like that. You need to give a lot of yourself in things like that, and I didn't feel capable of doing what I was supposed to do. My memory just went, and I would literally go blank, and that applied to everything, not just my drama.

I felt like a zombie and wanted to withdraw from life. I was disgusted with my behaviour towards the children, who, as a result, are quite afraid of me. To compensate I'd then eat vast quantities of chocolate for comfort which would only serve to make my symptoms worse.

I often found myself hiding away to eat in private. I found the amount I was eating an embarrassment. If you fancy a bar of chocolate you go off and buy one and that's fine. But I could eat four or five bars at once, and then eat the same amount again. You can't get rid of that many sweet papers. So you gradually ease them out of your pocket, or wrap them in something else, and throw them in the bin. The children would notice I'd had more than one bar; I couldn't pull the wool over their eyes. I wasn't aware that I was being silly at the time, I just used to sit and eat and then feel so sick afterwards.

I knew I wouldn't do any housework in the days to come, and that I wouldn't want to do anything with the children. I would be unbearable to my husband and I wouldn't bother to cook.

My doctor again prescribed anti-depressants. But knowing they made me feel zombie-like, I didn't want to take them any more. I was also prescribed diuretics. Unfortunately they seem to stop my bladder working properly, because I can't make it to the loo in time. So they were really out anyway.

I also tried vitamin B6, evening primrose oil, multi-vitamins, ginseng and progesterone pessaries.

At the time I felt life wasn't really worth living. I existed from situation to situation. It was a very stressful time. I had one good week in four. It was unbearable for the family; it was really horrible. I thought I was going round the bend, totally insane and that no one could help me at all. I didn't really know who to contact as I'd tried all my doctor had to offer. I then read an article in a women's magazine about the nutritional approach to PMS and the work the Stewarts were doing.'

PRE-MENSTRUAL SYNDROME QUESTIONNAIRE

Name: <u>Geraldine Ellis</u>   Age: <u>32</u>   Height: <u>5' 9"</u>   Weight: <u>10st 7lb</u>

<u>MARITAL STATUS:</u> Single _____   Married _√_   Divorced _____   Widowed _____
(Please tick where applicable)

<u>PRESENT CONTRACEPTION:</u>   None_____   Pill_____   I.U.D._____   Other _√_

   Your periods come every <u>28</u> days   Your periods last <u>7–8</u> days

   Your periods are: Light_____   Moderate _√_   Heavy_____

   Number of Pregnancies: <u>3</u>   Number of Miscarriages:_____

Birth weight of children:
   1st child <u>7lb 3oz</u>   2nd child <u>8lb 1oz</u>   3rd child <u>8lb 11oz</u>   4th child_____

SYMPTOMS	WEEK AFTER PERIOD (Fill in 3 days after period)				WEEK BEFORE PERIOD (Fill in 2-3 days before period)			
	None	Mild	Moderate	Severe	None	Mild	Moderate	Severe
PMS - A								
Nervous Tension	√					√		
Mood Swings	√						√	
Irritability	√							√
Anxiety	√				√			
PMS - H								
Weight Gain	√						√	
Swelling of Extremities	√							√
Breast Tenderness	√					√		
Abdominal Bloating	√						√	
PMS - C								
Headache	√						√	
Craving for Sweets	√							√
Increased Appetite	√							√
Heart Pounding	√				√			
Fatigue	√							√
Dizziness or Fainting	√				√			
PMS - D								
Depression	√							√
Forgetfulness	√						√	
Crying	√							√
Confusion	√						√	
Insomnia	√						√	
OTHER SYMPTOMS								
Loss of Sexual Interest	√							√
Disorientation	√				√			
Clumsiness	√						√	
Tremors/Shakes	√				√			
Thoughts of Suicide	√					√		
Agoraphobia	√							√
Increased Physical Activity	√				√			
Heavy/Aching Legs	√						√	
Generalized Aches	√					√		
Bad Breath	√				√			
Sensitivity to Music/Light	√				√			
Excessive Thirst	√				√			

FOLLOW UP
PRE-MENSTRUAL SYNDROME QUESTIONNAIRE

Name: Geraldine Ellis   Age: 32   Height: 5' 9"   Weight: 10st

MARITAL STATUS: Single _____   Married __✓__   Divorced _____   Widowed _____
(Please tick where applicable)

PRESENT CONTRACEPTION: None_____   Pill_____   I.U.D._____   Other__✓__

   Your periods come every___28___days   Your periods last___7–8___days

   Your periods are: Light_____   Moderate___✓___   Heavy_____

SYMPTOMS	WEEK AFTER PERIOD (Fill in 3 days after period)				WEEK BEFORE PERIOD (Fill in 2-3 days before period)			
	None	Mild	Moderate	Severe	None	Mild	Moderate	Severe
PMS - A								
Nervous Tension	✓				✓			
Mood Swings	✓				✓			
Irritability	✓				✓			
Anxiety	✓				✓			
PMS - H								
Weight Gain	✓					✓		
Swelling of Extremities	✓					✓		
Breast Tenderness	✓					✓		
Abdominal Bloating	✓						✓	
PMS - C								
Headache	✓				✓			
Craving for Sweets	✓					✓		
Increased Appetite	✓				✓			
Heart Pounding	✓				✓			
Fatigue	✓				✓			
Dizziness or Fainting	✓				✓			
PMS - D								
Depression	✓				✓			
Forgetfulness	✓				✓			
Crying	✓				✓			
Confusion	✓				✓			
Insomnia	✓				✓			
OTHER SYMPTOMS								
Loss of Sexual Interest	✓				✓			
Disorientation	✓				✓			
Clumsiness	✓				✓			
Tremors/Shakes	✓				✓			
Thoughts of Suicide	✓				✓			
Agoraphobia	✓				✓			
Increased Physical Activity	✓				✓			
Heavy/Aching Legs	✓				✓			
Generalized Aches	✓				✓			
Bad Breath	✓				✓			
Sensitivity to Music/Light	✓				✓			
Excessive Thirst	✓				✓			

One of Geraldine's particular weaknesses was her craving for sweet food pre-menstrually and her excessive indulgence. Later on in Chapter 11, I will be talking about the detrimental effects of excessive amounts of sweet food, particularly in relation to PMS symptoms.

On her first chart Geraldine's worst symptoms were in the sub-groups PMS C and PMS D, although she did have severe symptoms in all four categories.

Like the majority of women, Geraldine was lacking in education about the importance of a correct diet. This is hardly surprising considering how little we learned at school about nutrition as a subject. Until recent times very little attention has been placed on the role of nutrition in relation to women's health.

'I knew a bit about diet, but had no idea that changing my diet could bring me back to normal, and that's what it has done. Although I didn't know that I was sensitive to any foods, I had a good idea what was and what wasn't a sensible diet. My trouble was temptation. It's much easier to buy chocolate, which is available wherever you go, than it is to go home and make fish cakes with sesame seeds on them or things like that which you know are much better for you. I did eat healthy things, but I also ate a load of rubbish.

I try to stick to the diet. I feel much better when I do. I know I shouldn't eat chocolates, processed food, salty food or wheat. I did try some Stilton cheese and crisps, but I blew up like a balloon shortly after eating them. I now know that chocolate makes me depressed and, of course, I put on weight if I eat rubbish.

End result

Since I've been following the nutritional programme I feel so much better. My children notice the difference in me; I am no longer nasty to them. It has made me feel so much better in myself. I personally feel fine, although I could still do with losing weight.

I still have my marital problems. But I know that we have got things wrong marriage-wise, I know they are not related to PMS. I haven't got that aggressiveness inside me so much and I haven't got that awful feeling, that black cloud hanging over my head. That was the worst thing.'

Geraldine's follow-up chart verifies her story. Apart from a few remaining mild symptoms at the time of writing, she felt that she had overcome her PMS.

Another victim of chocolate cravings was Anita Walker. Her addiction to chocolate was no secret. It ran her life. She admits that she had little control over it. When you read her story, she could so easily be talking about a drug or alcohol.

ANITA WALKER – SUGAR CRAVINGS

'I am actually embarrassed to tell you about my sugar cravings. I would eat masses of chocolate bars, I could eat two bags of fun-size chocolate bars, or seven or eight ordinary bars and half a cake, and then eat my tea.

The more I ate, the worse my cravings would be, it was a vicious circle. I would feel OK for a bit after eating all that, and then I would feel awful. Especially more irritable, and especially more aggressive!

I didn't recognize that this was happening pre-menstrually at the time. I felt as though the toxins were building up and I would have to go to bed early, feeling fat and sick and having eaten myself into a stupor.'

I'm hardly surprised that Anita felt embarrassed to relate this part of her story. She was a real 'chocoholic'. Fortunately, we were able to relieve her of these cravings early on in her programme. Over the years we have had great success treating cravings for sweet food. If this is your main problem you may be interested to read about the latest research and how to overcome the problems in the book *Beat Sugar Craving*. See page 251 for details. In the Self-Help section on page 182 I will explain how Anita also managed to overcome her thrush.

8

DEPRESSION, CRYING AND THOUGHTS OF SUICIDE

PMS D (DEPRESSION)

Depression is a common pre-menstrual symptom and usually is present with other symptoms such as anxiety and breast tenderness. Our own research has shown that those most likely to suffer from pre-menstrual depression are more often overweight and do less exercise than those who do not suffer so badly with this problem.

The balance of certain nutrients has an important influence on both hormone and brain chemistry. Magnesium, for example, influences how the ovaries respond in the normal menstrual cycles, and many other nutrients are also important in this respect. It is also known that in people with severe depression the chance of finding some degree of B vitamin deficiency is much higher than would be expected in the general population. These nutrients have been used successfully in treating both PMS and depression.

In our study we found that 94 per cent of the women suffered from pre-menstrual depression, 83.8 per cent severe to moderately. This, we felt, was a frighteningly high number, and in view of the possible consequences of depression, not something that should be taken lightly.

Degree to which 1000 women suffered depression pre-menstrually				
Not Affected	Mild	Moderate	Severe	Total Affected
6%	10.2%	29.9%	53.9% -	94%

In 1959 Dr Katharina Dalton published a study in the *British Medical Journal* which showed that the time of admission to hospital of depressed patients coincided with the menstrual period, the pre-menstrual phase, and ovulation.

The balance of hormones – or whatever determines their balance, seems to be crucial in controlling mood. We are beginning to learn how diet and lifestyle can influence our hormones and our moods.

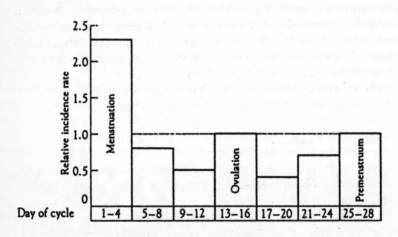

Time of admission of 185 patients with depression.
(From Dalton K. (1959). Br. Med. J.; 1:148–149.)

SUICIDAL

Many women who were suffering with PMS D reported that they felt suicidal, indeed it was because we were coming across so many women who felt suicidal that we decided to embark on the study of 1000 women.

Tragically, we found that 41 per cent of them had previously contemplated suicide pre-menstrually, 35 per cent of them several times and 5.8 per cent had actually attempted suicide pre-menstrually. That is a staggering 58 women out of 1000 that were chosen.

Suicidal tendencies out of a sample of 1000 women				
Once	More than once	More than six times	Total	Attempted
6.0%	23.3%	12.1%	41.4%	5.8%

A group of French doctors have linked attempted suicide in the premenstrual phase with low levels of the hormone oestrogen. However, some of the women had normal or even high levels of this hormone. For some an imbalance in this hormone might affect brain chemistry and thus mood. A healthy diet, exercise, nutritional supplements and controlling stress are the types of approaches that can help normalize hormone and body chemistry and thus decrease pre-menstrual depression.

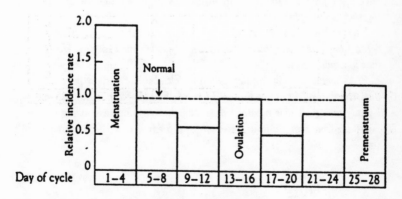

Time of acute psychiatric admission in 276 patients.
(From Dalton K. (1959). Br. Med. J.; 1:148–149.)

Again in 1959 Dr Dalton looked at the timing of 276 acute psychiatric admissions in four London hospitals. According to her findings, which were published in the *British Medical Journal*, 46 per cent of the patients were admitted between the 25th day of their cycle and the 4th day of their new cycle.

Also 53 per cent of attempted suicides, 47 per cent of admissions for depression and 47 per cent of schizophrenic patients were admitted during these eight days of the menstrual cycle.

" Sally's Story "

Sally is a 38-year-old woman who works as a recruitment consultant. She was married previously, but is now divorced.

Sally seriously contemplated taking a whole bottle of pills when she was pre-menstrual. Fortunately, she saw the light in time and relates the story to us as if she were talking about someone else.

'I really thought I was mentally ill, mentally inadequate; I thought I was cracking up. I was frightened to tell people how I felt because they might have thought I was a loony.

I did seriously contemplate suicide once. It was a bad time for me anyway as I was under a lot of stress. Being pre-menstrual was the last straw and I did contemplate taking a whole bottle of pills. Fortunately, I have some faith in God and I'm sure that's what eventually pulled me together and stopped me.

I felt that I was unbalanced and I couldn't stand the pain that the depression inside was causing any more. I just wanted to go to sleep so that it would all end.

PMS meant the pain of depression. I felt absolute despair pre-menstrually and I cannot express in words how desolate this made me feel. I really thought I was mentally ill. I thought my mind was taking over. Anything and everything was too stressful for me, and I felt I just couldn't cope.

Stress

I would say stress definitely did influence my symptoms. When I was under stress I tended to get a runny tummy, therefore I don't suppose I got the full benefit of my food. It's like a vicious circle to me. When I'm under stress I don't eat, and then as a result I feel even more stressed.

However, since I have been following the programme I am definitely less affected by stress. I seem much more able to cope with stressful situations, which I certainly wouldn't have been able to cope with before.

I tried vitamin B6. It wasn't any help, but I think I know why. I discovered on the programme that I have a sensitivity to yeast, and the B6 tablets I was taking were yeast-based. I found that the B6 would perk me up and then I would drop down mentally and have a terrible bloated tummy.

I also tried evening primrose oil, which helped with the breast symptoms. I was prescribed anti-depressants, which were no help at all. They just made me feel out of control. They controlled a bit of the depression, but they just made me void of other emotions.

I didn't really recognize my symptoms as PMS. That was the worst thing, looking back. I just knew I was suffering with depression and agoraphobia regularly, in fact towards the end, most of the time. I only had one good week after my period, the rest of the time was distressing. When I first saw the Women's Nutritional Advisory Service questionnaire and realized that agoraphobic symptoms could be part of the Pre-Menstrual Syndrome it gave me a great sense of relief. I felt a bit better just knowing that my symptoms were part of PMS. It gave me a far greater understanding of my suffering.

I thought I would give the nutritional approach to PMS a try as I felt so unwell, and I was so sick of taking anti-depressants and sleeping tablets. I had to do something as I honestly felt I was cracking up.'

Imagine having to live with the secret that you thought you were mentally ill. As a divorcee, Sally had to fend for herself.

Her job and her income were exceedingly important and she obviously thought these were threatened by her severe symptoms. She had tried several solutions, like our other patients, but did not find her symptoms lessened.

She suffered pre-menstrually with severe symptoms in all four categories, as her chart shows. She also had pre-menstrual agoraphobia, which was a terrific handicap in her working and social life.

The power of diet

'I used to eat lots of bread, cakes, animal fats including lots of butter and drink a substantial amount of tea and coffee.

PRE-MENSTRUAL SYNDROME QUESTIONNAIRE

Name: <u>Sally Noone</u>   Age: <u>38</u>   Height: <u>5' 3"</u>   Weight: <u>9st</u>

MARITAL STATUS: Single _____   Married _____   Divorced _✓_   Widowed _____
(Please tick where applicable)

PRESENT CONTRACEPTION: None_____   Pill_____   I.U.D._____   Other_✓_

Your periods come every __29__ days   Your periods last __3__ days

Your periods are: Light_____   Moderate_✓_   Heavy_____

Number of Pregnancies:_ – _   Number of Miscarriages:_ – _

Birth weight of children:
1st child_____   2nd child_____   3rd child_____   4th child_____

SYMPTOMS

SYMPTOMS	WEEK AFTER PERIOD (Fill in 3 days after period)				WEEK BEFORE PERIOD (Fill in 2-3 days before period)			
	None	Mild	Moderate	Severe	None	Mild	Moderate	Severe
PMS - A								
Nervous Tension			✓					✓
Mood Swings			✓					✓
Irritability			✓					✓
Anxiety			✓					✓
PMS - H								
Weight Gain	✓							✓
Swelling of Extremities	✓				✓			
Breast Tenderness	✓						✓	
Abdominal Bloating		✓						✓
PMS - C								
Headache		✓				✓		
Craving for Sweets	✓							✓
Increased Appetite	✓							✓
Heart Pounding		✓						✓
Fatigue			✓					✓
Dizziness or Fainting	✓							✓
PMS - D								
Depression		✓						✓
Forgetfulness		✓						✓
Crying			✓					✓
Confusion		✓						✓
Insomnia		✓						✓
OTHER SYMPTOMS								
Loss of Sexual Interest				✓				✓
Disorientation		✓						✓
Clumsiness		✓					✓	
Tremors/Shakes	✓							✓
Thoughts of Suicide	✓							✓
Agoraphobia	✓							✓
Increased Physical Activity	✓							✓
Heavy/Aching Legs		✓				✓		
Generalized Aches		✓					✓	
Bad Breath	✓							✓
Sensitivity to Music/Light	✓							✓
Excessive Thirst	✓							✓

FOLLOW UP
PRE-MENSTRUAL SYNDROME QUESTIONNAIRE

Name: Sally Noone___ Age: _38___ Height: _5' 3"___ Weight: _8st 9lb___

MARITAL STATUS: Single _✓_ Married_____ Divorced_____ Widowed_____
(Please tick where applicable)

PRESENT CONTRACEPTION: None_✓_ Pill_____ I.U.D._____ Other_____

Your periods come every___28___days   Your periods last___3___days

Your periods are: Light_____ Moderate___✓___ Heavy_____

SYMPTOMS	WEEK AFTER PERIOD (Fill in 3 days after period)				WEEK BEFORE PERIOD (Fill in 2-3 days before period)			
	None	Mild	Moderate	Severe	None	Mild	Moderate	Severe
PMS - A								
Nervous Tension	✓					✓		
Mood Swings	✓				✓			
Irritability	✓					✓		
Anxiety	✓					✓		
PMS - H								
Weight Gain	✓				✓			
Swelling of Extremities	✓				✓			
Breast Tenderness	✓					✓		
Abdominal Bloating	✓					✓		
PMS - C								
Headache	✓				✓			
Craving for Sweets	✓					✓		
Increased Appetite	✓				✓			
Heart Pounding	✓				✓			
Fatigue	✓					✓		
Dizziness or Fainting	✓				✓			
PMS - D								
Depression	✓					✓		
Forgetfulness	✓				✓			
Crying	✓				✓			
Confusion	✓				✓			
Insomnia	✓				✓			
OTHER SYMPTOMS								
Loss of Sexual Interest		✓			✓			
Disorientation	✓				✓			
Clumsiness	✓					✓		
Tremors/Shakes	✓				✓			
Thoughts of Suicide	✓				✓			
Agoraphobia	✓				✓			
Increased Physical Activity	✓				✓			
Heavy/Aching Legs	✓				✓			
Generalized Aches	✓				✓			
Bad Breath	✓				✓			
Sensitivity to Music/Light	✓				✓			
Excessive Thirst	✓				✓			

I had no idea that my symptoms could be diet-related until I read an article in a magazine. I realized at that point that it was likely that something in my diet might be making me feel so bad.

The diet recommended was a bit bewildering at first, probably because it's so different. I was asked to come off grains for a short period, and to omit all foods with a yeast base from my diet. I had to cut down my junk food intake, including sugary foods, i.e. biscuits, cakes, puddings. Also to cut down on salt, alcohol and dairy products.

There are many alternative foods to eat and I soon got used to the diet. In fact I feel I have now revamped my whole way of eating, and I enjoy my food more. I found that I have a sensitivity to wheat, sugar and chocolate. If I eat them I get a reaction the next day. I get a mild sort of dizziness and windy stomach. I know now that it is going to be over within 24 hours, whereas before I would get so upset and confused because I wouldn't know what was causing it. To tell the truth, when my tummy used to swell, I really thought I had cancer.

My symptoms disappeared on the programme. The depression cleared within one week and the remaining symptoms gradually disappeared during the first three months. So much so, I decided I no longer needed to follow the recommendations. Coming off the diet and reverting to my previous diet brought the symptoms back. I went back on to the programme recommended, and within a short space of time my symptoms were under control again. I've proved to myself that the diet works for me.

I have been taking Optivite since I started the programme. That, the exercise and the diet have done so much good for me. I really think that Optivite is the best thing since sliced bread.

End result

Now that I have been through the programme, I am much more stable. I am able to stick at my job and maintain my concentration. I have a very stressful job, but I am now able to work hard and I feel very happy. PMS does not affect me any more. The programme has changed my life. I can cope better with everything. I would say I am a thousand times better. I no longer feel exhausted after little effort. I am so delighted. Looking back, it's like looking at a different person.'

Once again you can see that Sally's symptoms have gone from severe to mild in just a few months. She feels her life has returned to normal because she followed the nutritional programme, which is reflected in her final chart and letter as follows.

Dear Maryon,

I am writing to let you know that there is a marked change in my life. I feel that I have come through the proverbial 'long dark tunnel' out of despair into sunlight. If only I had known about the yeast allergy years ago and trusted my instinct about magnesium, the before and after picture shown on the symptom tables would not have been so acutely marked!

I think because I had hidden all the symptoms and bottled them up, my family are not really aware of the change I feel inside. There was certainly scepticism from one branch of my family when I tried to explain it to them, and why I was being 'faddish' about my food. The knowledge that certain foods will send me back into the downward spiral of depression is enough to ensure that I steer clear of any of them, and keep to the new regime.

I am getting to be a bore with some of my friends. As soon as they start complaining about any of the symptoms I used to have, I try to analyse their diet for them and I also give them your address – whether they want it or not!

I do hope you manage to get the message across to all the women who need it – for anyone else to suffer the way I did, and not to know the way out – well, it is criminal and so much more must be done.

Sally Noone
(a convert)

PMS D can be very severe indeed. We have dealt with some very sad cases, where women felt suicidal, depressed and that life was not worth living pre-menstrually.

The first example I will give you is the story of Anita Walker.

" Anita's Story "

Anita is a 36-year-old mother of two children who works as a personnel assistant. Her PMS began when she was 17 years old, but became worse about eight years ago after having children and a miscarriage. She has also had a hysterectomy due to excessive bleeding and fibroids.

'I ended up with only four or five normal days per month. The rest of the time, apart from my period, I'd get fatter and fatter. I'd feel tired and

irritable and couldn't concentrate, to the point where I didn't know what day of the week it was.

I attacked my husband with a knife on several occasions. I kept away from the baby as I was terrified of baby battering; I knew I could so easily have done it.

I remember feeling suicidal and not knowing where I was. I'd find myself out in the street yelling in the middle of the night, this happened pre-menstrually. It was like being Jekyll and Hyde. I'd be totally irrational and make stupid decisions. The week after, I'd look back and wonder why on earth I acted that way.

One night, a week before my period, feeling nobody cared, I thought I just couldn't go on any more. I felt fat, depressed and I didn't think life was worth living for a week to ten days before my period. I was utterly desperate. I got this bottle of wine and my nice collection of sleeping pills that my doctor had doled out. I just quietly swallowed the lot, and the next thing I knew I was waking up in hospital, wondering what I was doing there.

No connection was made there between my condition and PMS. They just told me to go away, not to be a silly girl, and to stop upsetting my family. No treatment offered by my doctor made any lasting impact on my symptoms.

What about me?

I never liked myself pre-menstrually. I really did feel worthless as a human being. I was aware that eating junk food and giving in to my cravings made me far worse. If I had some "sinful" foods in the cupboard I would eat them all pre-menstrually, and then tell myself that I deserved to feel awful, because that was all I was fit for. It felt like I was punishing myself. I felt utterly fatigued. I'd go to bed at 8 p.m. each night, feeling dead, and then wake up the next morning feeling equally awful.

I always used to feel I wasn't doing my job properly. I think I inherited this from my mother. Looking back I think she suffered too. There were times when my father would come home to find us throwing things around the kitchen at each other. We'd be fine for a couple of weeks and then it would all start up again.

What about them?

I really hated everybody when I was pre-menstrual. I used to turn my anger on to myself as I couldn't bear to see the effect it had on others. I felt like I literally changed character, like Jekyll and Hyde.

The suicidal feelings I had were both strange and positive. I couldn't talk myself out of them, despite the fact that I really knew, deep down, that suicide was not a good solution. I felt so determined at times, I really felt I would have succeeded if I hadn't been found.

I must emphasize that these feelings and suicidal tendencies only occurred pre-menstrually. I felt utterly dreadful pre-menstrually, like a jibbering wreck.

I think stress aggravated the situation. Both my husband and I are in high-pressure jobs. I've been attending relaxation classes which I find helpful. I don't find it easy to unwind; there is a part of me that remains burning away, probably because I tend to lack confidence and so I'm always pushing myself. I used to burn out at PMS times, but I don't any more.

Apart from all the drugs and sleeping tablets I was given, I also tried diuretics, which were prescribed by my doctor as I used to put on seven pounds (3 kg) pre-menstrually. They helped a little bit initially, but by the end of the day my symptoms would be back and I felt as if I was getting nowhere.

My doctor then prescribed Primolut N in massive doses and all it succeeded in doing was make me gain even more weight. There was a time, five or six years ago, when I tried another hormone treatment, but I didn't get on very well with that either. I felt I was given too much, and it seemed to exaggerate my symptoms. I had a Well Woman test at the time and they said how enlarged my uterus was, and that it was probably due to the hormones.

It was through the media that I learned about the nutritional approach to PMS.'

Anita was a classic case of pure PMS. She had practically no symptoms after her period, and very severe symptoms in all four sub-categories of PMS pre-menstrually, which you can see on her first chart.

Again, from the sound of her symptoms she might well have been classified as a psychiatric patient. After all, screaming in the street in the middle of the night and suicidal feelings are not classified as socially acceptable behaviour.

Although she was taking prescribed sleeping tablets and hormones, she was unable to function properly. Consequently she found it unbelievably difficult to keep herself together at work. It was a wonder she managed to hold down her job at all under the circumstances. You can see how severe these symptoms were from her first chart overleaf.

PRE-MENSTRUAL SYNDROME QUESTIONNAIRE

Name: Anita Walker   Age: 36   Height: 5' 4½"   Weight: 11st

MARITAL STATUS: Single _____ Married __✓__ Divorced _____ Widowed _____
(Please tick where applicable)

PRESENT CONTRACEPTION: None_____ Pill_____ I.U.D. __✓__ Other_____

    Your periods come every___28___days   Your periods last___7___days

    Your periods are: Light_____ Moderate_____ Heavy___✓___

    Number of Pregnancies:___4___ Number of Miscarriages:___2___

Birth weight of children:
    1st child_7lb 3oz_ 2nd child_8lb 2oz_ 3rd child_____ 4th child_____

SYMPTOMS

SYMPTOMS	WEEK AFTER PERIOD (Fill in 3 days after period)				WEEK BEFORE PERIOD (Fill in 2-3 days before period)			
	None	Mild	Moderate	Severe	None	Mild	Moderate	Severe
PMS - A								
Nervous Tension	✓							✓
Mood Swings	✓							✓
Irritability	✓							✓
Anxiety	✓							✓
PMS - H								
Weight Gain	✓							✓
Swelling of Extremities			✓					✓
Breast Tenderness	✓							✓
Abdominal Bloating		✓						✓
PMS - C								
Headache	✓						✓	
Craving for Sweets	✓							✓
Increased Appetite	✓							✓
Heart Pounding	✓					✓		
Fatigue	✓							✓
Dizziness or Fainting	✓					✓		
PMS - D								
Depression	✓							✓
Forgetfulness	✓							✓
Crying	✓						✓	
Confusion	✓							✓
Insomnia	✓							✓
OTHER SYMPTOMS								
Loss of Sexual Interest	✓					✓		
Disorientation	✓							✓
Clumsiness	✓							✓
Tremors/Shakes	✓							✓
Thoughts of Suicide	✓							✓
Agoraphobia	✓					✓		
Increased Physical Activity	✓					✓		
Heavy/Aching Legs	✓							✓
Generalized Aches	✓							✓
Bad Breath	✓							✓
Sensitivity to Music/Light	✓					✓		
Excessive Thirst	✓							✓

FOLLOW UP
PRE-MENSTRUAL SYNDROME QUESTIONNAIRE

Name: Anita Walker   Age: 36   Height: 5' 4½"   Weight: 10st 12lb

MARITAL STATUS: Single _____   Married _✓_   Divorced _____   Widowed _____
(Please tick where applicable)

PRESENT CONTRACEPTION: None_____   Pill_____   I.U.D. _✓_   Other_____

Your periods come every___21___days   Your periods last___7___days

Your periods are: Light_____   Moderate____✓____   Heavy_____

SYMPTOMS	WEEK AFTER PERIOD (Fill in 3 days after period)				WEEK BEFORE PERIOD (Fill in 2-3 days before period)			
	None	Mild	Moderate	Severe	None	Mild	Moderate	Severe
PMS - A								
Nervous Tension	✓				✓			
Mood Swings	✓					✓		
Irritability	✓					✓		
Anxiety	✓					✓		
PMS - H								
Weight Gain	✓				✓			
Swelling of Extremities	✓				✓			
Breast Tenderness	✓				✓			
Abdominal Bloating	✓				✓			
PMS - C								
Headache	✓				✓			
Craving for Sweets	✓				✓			
Increased Appetite	✓				✓			
Heart Pounding	✓				✓			
Fatigue	✓				✓			
Dizziness or Fainting	✓				✓			
PMS - D								
Depression	✓				✓			
Forgetfulness	✓				✓			
Crying	✓				✓			
Confusion	✓				✓			
Insomnia	✓				✓			
OTHER SYMPTOMS								
Loss of Sexual Interest	✓				✓			
Disorientation	✓				✓			
Clumsiness	✓				✓			
Tremors/Shakes	✓				✓			
Thoughts of Suicide	✓				✓			
Agoraphobia	✓				✓			
Increased Physical Activity	✓				✓			
Heavy/Aching Legs	✓				✓			
Generalized Aches	✓				✓			
Bad Breath	✓				✓			
Sensitivity to Music/Light	✓				✓			
Excessive Thirst	✓				✓			

'When I began the nutritional PMS programme, I was taking both Primolut N and Mogadon. Very soon after I was able to stop taking both of the drugs. I no longer felt I needed them.

The new diet

I made all the dietary changes suggested and stuck to them rigidly. In fact, I changed the whole family's diet. My son turned out to have some allergies which had been causing behavioural problems. My husband also turned out to have a problem. One day when he was under a lot of stress, he went out to lunch. He ate a lot of bread and pasta and had some alcohol with the meal. On the train on the way home his bladder stopped working and an ambulance had to be called as he was in a terrible state of near-collapse. He was rushed to hospital and was subsequently diagnosed as having a massive dose of thrush. He said it was the most awful thing in his life, the swelling and the irritation were so bad.

I took him off wheat and yeast-based foods and I am now very particular about our diet.

The whole family now look and feel better. You can see it, they sort of "glow" somehow. They are not black around the eyes as they used to be, their hair shines and they have a lot more energy. Maybe that's partly because they have a lot more green vegetables and other fresh raw foods.

We now watch each other's plates and occasionally, if he's suspicious, Mark, my son, will check through my bag!

Come home Mum, all is forgiven

We can actually hold a conversation now. We have good discussions and I really think my family are coming around to thinking I'm a worthwhile person again, probably because I myself consider I am. I can actually say we are back to having a normal married life. David is delighted we live life normally and feels it's great that we are still together, which is lovely. We all joke about my former behaviour. They are much more responsive now, but then again I suppose I am, too.'

After six months Anita had her PMS well and truly under control. She had some remaining mild symptoms which she finds comparatively easy to live with – although within another few months these too should disappear.

The comparison between her two questionnaires clearly shows the progress that Anita felt she made during the six months on the programme, and her letter outlines how her life has since changed.

Dear Maryon,

A very big thank-you to your team for saving a life and a marriage.

As you know, when I wrote to you, I had tried everything I knew and everything my doctor knew to relieve the pain of my PMS. So I wrote to you and will always be glad I did, as the nutritional programme helped so much.

I felt that the hysterectomy without the nutritional programme would not have made such a difference. I can be certain that my speedy recovery was certainly thanks to good nutrition and definitely to the vitamin supplement, Optivite; I took six a day then.

When I wrote to you my only fear was 'What if this fails too?' I almost didn't post the letter when I contemplated the consequences of this: certain divorce, Ben taking the children away because of my emotional instability (and I would have agreed with him) and my certain self-destruction. Happily we can be sure now that this will not happen. As I said, you saved a life and marriage.

Whoever said 'you are what you eat' was so right. I do tend to think I am cured and slip back occasionally to bad eating habits. I then feel tired, cross and lethargic. I suffer this for a day or two and say, look, you're 'going off' again, you're not cured at all. Then I realize what's happening, check back on what I've eaten, and within 36 hours can be all right again; the power of food!

I do enjoy the 'high' of constant energy and health and most of all the joy of not having to take drugs. I will recommend your Service to all who have difficulties. I am battling with my GP at present to recommend his patients to you but he sees it all as 'black magic'. He says I'm better because I think I'm better! He's only got to read my notes. The only time I have seen him since my hysterectomy last year was to talk to him about you. I have not consulted him for anything else.

Again, my thanks and that of my family.

Anita Walker

PAULINE'S SUICIDAL FEELINGS

'One day I felt so awful. I had pre-menstrual insomnia and was desperate to get some sleep. I decided I was going to have a good long sleep. I took all the tablets and then after a while I became panic-stricken and chickened out. I called my husband and told him what I'd done. I can't remember much, except he was trying to keep me awake. When the doctor arrived he said, "We've had problems with you threatening to do this before, haven't we? It's your periods isn't it, you always get like that." This was because I'd said I felt like doing it many times in the past.'

9

OTHER SYMPTOMS – CLUMSINESS, LOSS OF SEX DRIVE AND AGORAPHOBIA

After the first year of providing nutritional help to women, it became obvious that there were other pre-menstrual symptoms that were affecting them severely. We made additions to the chart to assess the most common extra symptoms (see chart overleaf).

CLUMSINESS

Clumsiness was the most troublesome additional symptom to our 1000 patients outside the four sub-groups. Eighty-three per cent of sufferers reported being clumsy pre-menstrually, nearly 56 per cent severe to moderately.

The cause of pre-menstrual clumsiness is uncertain, but it may reflect a disturbance in the finer aspects of nervous system function, which might occur pre-menstrually. This can be caused by changes in brain chemistry, hormonal chemistry, lack of certain nutrients, excessive intake of tea, coffee, cigarettes or alcohol. The presence of pre-menstrual clumsiness suggests that there may well be a substantial physical, rather than psychological, component to such women's pre-menstrual symptoms.

71

Degree to which clumsiness affected a sample of 1000 women pre-menstrually

None	Mild	Moderate	Severe	Total Affected
16.6%	27.5%	36.1%	19.8% -	83.4%

SEX DRIVE

Out of a sample of 1000 PMS sufferers with sexual relationships 67 per cent reported decreased interest in sex and frequency of sexual intercourse pre-menstrually. Only 1.5 per cent reported increased sexual activity pre-menstrually.

OTHER SYMPTOMS	WEEK BEFORE PERIOD					WEEK AFTER PERIOD			
Loss of Sexual Interest	✓					✓			
Disorientation	✓					✓			
Clumsiness	✓					✓			
Tremors/Shakes	✓					✓			
Thoughts of Suicide	✓					✓			
Agoraphobia	✓					✓			
Increased Physical Activity	✓					✓			
Heavy/Aching Legs	✓					✓			
Generalized Aches	✓					✓			
Bad Breath	✓					✓			
Sensitivity to Music/Light	✓					✓			
Excessive Thirst	✓					✓			

Do you have any other PRE-MENSTRUAL SYMPTOMS not listed above?

1. _____

2. _____

3. _____

4. _____

5. How much weight do you gain before your period? _____

We were concerned to see such a large number of women reporting similar distressing problems, so we decided to follow the progress of a group of 50 severe PMS sufferers, who also had severely decreased sex drive, through a three-month diet and supplement programme to see whether there was any improvement.

After three months these women were asked whether their interest in sex had altered. Fifty per cent of them reported that there had been a complete return to their libido (sex drive) and a further 38 per cent reported a significant but not full improvement to their libido. Only 12 per cent reported no change in libido at all.

The results were obviously very encouraging. Considering neither we nor the women had anticipated improvement in this area initially, it was considered by all to be an added bonus. In most cases the women did not associate their decreased libido with their PMS, and furthermore did not feel that reduced libido was a symptom, but merely a reflection of the state and stage of their relationship. Needless to say, many husbands and partners were satisfied with this particular result.

**Improvement in sex drive
of 50 women who had
previously reported a decrease**

Little or no improvement	Significant but not full return to libido	Complete return of libido		Total improvement
12%	38%	50%	-	88%

" Geraldine's Story "

Geraldine, who explained about her intense chocolate craving problems in the PMS C section, also feels her problems with her relationships and sex life were magnified because of her symptoms.

'My relationship with my husband was definitely affected by my pre-menstrual symptoms. I think, in all fairness, we began going through a sticky patch before I had any of the symptoms, but in those days I didn't lash out and hit him. I'd just get worked up. With PMS I just started hitting out in anger. About the most frustrating thing is that he wouldn't row back. He'd just go quiet and go off, we could never discuss it.

I didn't want him to come anywhere near me pre-menstrually, let alone sexually. I didn't want him to cuddle me, touch me, talk to me or be there. I'd go right into myself and would really rather not have any contact with anyone at all.

A lot of the problems with my husband stem from PMS. I'd feel much worse than crabby, it was unbelievably horrible. The other issues would creep in once I'd started to get worked up, and it became very complex.'

AGORAPHOBIA

On our extended symptom list is the condition of agoraphobia, the exaggerated fear of going out alone. This was eventually added to the list as it seemed to be mentioned far more often than we had anticipated. At about this time we were contacted by a marvellous lady who was running a national group for agoraphobic sufferers. She had some amazing facts and figures about agoraphobia, including statistics on the incidence of PMS-suffering agoraphobic women.

Firstly, we were surprised to learn that 88 per cent of agoraphobia sufferers are women. Out of a sample of 94 agoraphobic women 91 per cent also suffered with PMS!

By coincidence, we had several severe PMS sufferers who also suffered severely with agoraphobia on our programme at this time. Many of them were making excellent progress, not only with the overcoming of their PMS symptoms, but their agoraphobia had also disappeared on the programme.

I'll never forget one joyous phone call I had from a lady in Jersey, who had taken herself out for the day for the first time in eight years. She had gone to have her hair permed and buy some clothes.

As she had previously only gone out accompanied by her husband or a neighbour, when her husband arrived home and found her missing he became understandably worried. After a while he began knocking on neighbours' doors to see whether she had gone visiting. By the time she casually wandered home her husband and neighbours were out in the street looking for her. They couldn't believe her new hair-do, and her husband wasn't sure whether to laugh or cry when he saw how many packages she had! He told me she's been costing him a fortune in evening entertainment ever since! Well, she has got eight years to make up for.

Agoraphobia is a very nasty condition: being afraid to go out is both anti-social and isolating for the victim, and can place an awful strain on a family. Here is the story of a woman who had been perfectly well until she underwent surgery for the purpose of sterilization. The change in her health was so unexpected that it had dramatic repercussions on her life.

" Jane's Story "

Jane was a 36-year-old mother of three children who was trying to work part time at the time she contacted the Women's Nutritional Advisory Service. I say 'trying to work' as for six years she had been severely agoraphobic pre-menstrually.

'It was six years ago that I went to my front door and discovered I couldn't walk through it. I was pre-menstrual at the time, and had noticed symptoms had begun after my sterilization.

I couldn't go out alone, not to the shops or to the bingo, which I had always taken in my stride. I really thought I was suffering from a very serious illness. I saw my doctor and he diagnosed nervous tension. I didn't believe him though, because I'm not the nervous type.

My doctor prescribed Valium, but it was no help. In fact it made me feel worse because it gave me panic attacks. I was on Valium for six months and then had great difficulty stopping. I went back to the doctor when I was pre-menstrual and just threw the tablets at him. I told him to never, ever prescribe me any kind of tablets like that again, as they made me feel so ill.

Previously, I would have been described by my family and friends as practical, hard-working and always full of fun and laughter. I was frightened and bewildered by the changes in myself. I found myself losing new friends as they grew tired of hearing my constant tales of woe.

I was at the doctor's every other week with my list of symptoms. He referred me to a psychiatrist at one point who insisted I was as strong as a horse and that the condition was all in my mind. I was gaining four to five pounds (2–3 kg) in weight pre-menstrually, suffering with severe breast soreness, pounding headaches, edginess and irritability and then the agoraphobia would start. I was sure it wasn't all in my mind.

After recovering from the effects of the Valium I had been taking, we decided to move so that I could be near my supportive family. My new doctor suggested hormone therapy as he said it was usually prescribed for women who were going through the menopause early, but I was only 36 years old! When I read contra-indications of the hormones I decided that as an overweight, over-35 smoker I should not be on these hormones.

I had now reached an impasse. My doctor had given his advice and I had refused to take it. Coincidentally, a few days later I saw an article in the newspaper about Maryon Stewart and the work she was doing at the Women's Nutritional Advisory Service. When I read the article I couldn't believe it. Here was someone describing me and my symptoms, saying that she had helped other people in similar situations.

I was like an old woman at 36

I was suffering three out of every four weeks. I felt very uptight and niggly all the time. Plus I felt really frustrated and frightened that I couldn't get to the bottom of the problem.

The only way I could get out during the day was on the arm of an elderly neighbour in her seventies, who walks with the aid of a walking stick. There was I, half her age, clinging to her. Talk about the blind leading the blind! We'd even have to stop off on the way at my friend's shop because I was shaking so much.

I tried to forget it, but life was far from normal. I began to wonder if I would ever feel right again.

My miserable family

I was sheer hell to live with. For five years I had lived a life of misery and so had my family. My husband was very good, considering what I put him through. I used to deliberately row with him pre-menstrually and pick holes in things. I was very agitated and always looking for an argument. He would avoid me at this time of my cycle. Sexual relations were a real problem in view of how I felt pre-menstrually, plus the fact that I was so tired, I just wasn't up to it.

My husband had to take me everywhere. I was utterly dependent on him. You can't have a normal relationship under these circumstances. But at least I am lucky that he was so supportive.'

Jane's problem areas were PMS A, H and C as well as her agoraphobia. She was literally a shadow of her former self. Her 'before' and 'after' charts and a letter to us are here for you to examine. She also comments on the dietary changes she had to make on the nutritional programme.

Dear Maryon,

As you know, when I first contacted you, I described all my symptoms of PMS. One was of being unable at certain times of the month (i.e. just before and after each period) to leave the house. I experienced severe anxiety and panic attacks going shopping, and doing my evening job was sheer terror with the feeling of passing out, sickness and sweating. Fortunately, my husband took me to and picked me up from the school where I do two hours' cleaning. During the day when I had to go shopping, the feelings were so severe I used to wait for my children to come home from school, then send them to do any shopping I needed.

However, after following your diet recommendations, the attacks lessened to such a degree I go out now without even thinking about it.

I started a new part-time office job. It started a day before my period was due and yet that week I didn't experience any problems at all. I went to town shopping after work, came home, cooked, cleaned, did my evening job and although I felt tired, at no time did I suffer from any feelings of panic or anxiety.

I went completely off the diet and ate and drank all the things I shouldn't have: within 48 hours I suffered really bad stomach ache and diarrhoea. All the feelings returned, so I am now back sticking strictly to

PRE-MENSTRUAL SYNDROME QUESTIONNAIRE

Name: Jane Moor   Age: 36   Height: 5' 6"   Weight: 11st 11lb

MARITAL STATUS: Single _____ Married _✓_ Divorced _____ Widowed _____
(Please tick where applicable)
PRESENT CONTRACEPTION: None _✓_ Pill _____ I.U.D. _____ Other _____

    Your periods come every __26–30__ days   Your periods last ___4___ days

    Your periods are: Light __✓__ Moderate _____ Heavy _____

    Number of Pregnancies: ___3___   Number of Miscarriages: ___–___

Birth weight of children:
    1st child _____ 2nd child _____ 3rd child _____ 4th child _____

SYMPTOMS	WEEK AFTER PERIOD (Fill in 3 days after period)				WEEK BEFORE PERIOD (Fill in 2-3 days before period)			
	None	Mild	Moderate	Severe	None	Mild	Moderate	Severe
PMS - A								
Nervous Tension	✓						✓	
Mood Swings	✓						✓	
Irritability		✓						✓
Anxiety			✓					✓
PMS - H								
Weight Gain	✓						✓	
Swelling of Extremities	✓					✓		
Breast Tenderness	✓							✓
Abdominal Bloating	✓							✓
PMS - C								
Headache			✓					✓
Craving for Sweets	✓					✓		
Increased Appetite	✓					✓		
Heart Pounding	✓						✓	
Fatigue	✓							✓
Dizziness or Fainting			✓				✓	
PMS - D								
Depression	✓					✓		
Forgetfulness	✓				✓			
Crying	✓				✓			
Confusion	✓				✓			
Insomnia	✓						✓	
OTHER SYMPTOMS								
Loss of Sexual Interest			✓				✓	
Disorientation	✓				✓			
Clumsiness			✓				✓	
Tremors/Shakes		✓				✓		
Thoughts of Suicide	✓				✓			
Agoraphobia			✓					✓
Increased Physical Activity	✓					✓		
Heavy/Aching Legs	✓						✓	
Generalized Aches	✓						✓	
Bad Breath	✓				✓			
Sensitivity to Music/Light	✓				✓			
Excessive Thirst	✓				✓			

FOLLOW UP
PRE-MENSTRUAL SYNDROME QUESTIONNAIRE

Name: Jane Moor   Age: 36   Height: 5' 6"   Weight: 11st 5lb

MARITAL STATUS: Single _____   Married __✓__   Divorced _____   Widowed _____
(Please tick where applicable)

PRESENT CONTRACEPTION: None _✓_   Pill_____   I.U.D. _____   Other_____

Your periods come every__26–30__ days   Your periods last____4____days

Your periods are: Light____✓____   Moderate_____   Heavy_____

SYMPTOMS

	WEEK AFTER PERIOD (Fill in 3 days after period)				WEEK BEFORE PERIOD (Fill in 2-3 days before period)			
	None	Mild	Moderate	Severe	None	Mild	Moderate	Severe
PMS - A								
Nervous Tension	✓				✓			
Mood Swings	✓				✓			
Irritability	✓					✓		
Anxiety	✓				✓			
PMS - H								
Weight Gain	✓					✓		
Swelling of Extremities	✓				✓			
Breast Tenderness	✓					✓		
Abdominal Bloating	✓					✓		
PMS - C								
Headache	✓				✓			
Craving for Sweets	✓					✓		
Increased Appetite	✓				✓			
Heart Pounding	✓				✓			
Fatigue	✓					✓		
Dizziness or Fainting	✓				✓			
PMS - D								
Depression	✓				✓			
Forgetfulness	✓				✓			
Crying	✓				✓			
Confusion	✓				✓			
Insomnia	✓				✓			
OTHER SYMPTOMS								
Loss of Sexual Interest	✓				✓			
Disorientation	✓				✓			
Clumsiness	✓				✓			
Tremors/Shakes	✓				✓			
Thoughts of Suicide	✓				✓			
Agoraphobia	✓					✓		
Increased Physical Activity	✓					✓		
Heavy/Aching Legs	✓					✓		
Generalized Aches	✓					✓		
Bad Breath	✓				✓			
Sensitivity to Music/Light	✓				✓			
Excessive Thirst	✓				✓			

your diet. Although I still have a queasy tum and headache, I can see myself getting back to normal.

The diet really works, I feel a new woman after six years of living in sheer hell.

Jane Moor

Dietary changes

'I already knew I was allergic to eggs when I began the programme. It seems to run in my family. I was astonished, though, to be asked to give up all grains execpt brown rice, all sugar, tea and coffee and reduce my intake of dairy products.

I followed the diet rigidly for the first three months I felt on top of the world. I lost weight, which was great, and was able to go out alone for the first time in six years. I got so much better that I am now able to hold down a full-time job. I have let the diet slip a bit more recently. You tend to take it all for granted when you are feeling really well. Plus it takes extra time and effort shopping for and preparing special food. I know that once I tighten my diet up again I will feel 100 per cent again.'

All Jane's long-standing severe symptoms either cleared up completely or became very mild and 'livable' with. Diet was a major factor in her case, as she has proved to herself.

CRIME OR ILLNESS?

Finally in this section, I return to the subject of violence. As violence in general is on the increase in our society I feel this is an area which is certainly worthy of fuller discussion.

As early as 1845 menstrually-related disorders were accepted by the courts as a defence for a criminal act. In that year there were three recorded examples:

- Martha, a servant who, without motive, murdered her employer's child, was acquitted on the grounds of insanity caused by 'obstructed menstruation'.

- A woman was acquitted of murdering her young niece on the grounds of insanity stemming from disordered menstruation.

- A woman servant was accused of theft and was acquitted at Carlisle quarter sessions on the grounds of temporary insanity 'from suppression of the menses'.

So you see, it's not such a new problem. We probably talk openly about it now, whereas years ago it would have been hushed up. More recently there have been other famous cases where PMS has been a large part of the defence.

Dr Dalton reported in *The Lancet* in 1980 the case of a 28-year-old worker in the food industry who was accused of fatally stabbing her girlfriend. Following the stabbing she was admitted to prison and noted to be menstruating. Although she was imprisoned, it was acknowledged that she had severe PMS which was subsequently treated. In 1982 she was freed on probation on the grounds of PMS.

There have been several other similar cases over the past few years. There was the case of Anna Reynolds who battered her mother to death in June 1986. She was convicted of murder in February 1987, and subsequently at appeal the charge was reduced to manslaughter on the basis of diminished responsibility whilst suffering with Pre-Menstrual Syndrome. Debra Lovell was another victim of PMS who became a human fireball after soaking herself in paraffin whilst she was pre-menstrual.

In November 1988 a teenage mother, Donna Kelly, suffering from PMS unintentionally killed her seven-week-old son by shaking him when he would not stop crying. The verdict recorded was not guilty as it was appreciated that Donna Kelly had previously been a loving mother who did not have the intention to kill her baby.

In May 1989 a mother of four killed her son after he 'wound her up'. She walked free from the Old Bailey after the judge said she was sick, rather than evil.

And then there was the case of Nicola Owen who made medical and legal history by becoming the first woman successfully to use PMS as a mitigating plea in the courts, when she was discharged from the Old Bailey where she faced arson charges.

This evidence that some women become more vulnerable, unpredictable and even lose control pre-menstrually and around the time of the onset of their period, confirms the fact that the Pre-Menstrual Syndrome is a common condition which can be life-threatening and should most certainly be taken seriously.

It does, however, mean that PMS may be considered a plausible excuse for an offence. This, I am only too aware, is a very sensitive subject. Like any other scapegoat, it has and will, I'm sure, continue to be used in the courts as a means of reducing or escaping sentence.

Although, at the Women's Nutritional Advisory Service, we have encountered our share of criminal cases, I feel it is important to take a stand on this issue. There is no way that we condone any crime, or believe that a woman should be excused for her actions due to PMS. However, it is acknowledged that PMS can be a contributing factor which should be considered along with all the other factors in each individual case.

Each person, be they male or female, has the responsibility to look after their own body. There is evidence now, for example, that indicates that poor diet is related to delinquency and even dyslexia.

Rather than excusing women with PMS for their actions, or adolescents who offend for their behaviour, it would be better to help them overcome the problem by at least correcting their nutritional state. The upsetting and frustrating fact is that much education is needed, both for the public and also for the medical profession. Just knowing which foods help and which foods may harm would be a great start. Having some basic understanding of how diet can affect one's state of mind, for instance, would be invaluable.

We hope that over the next few years doctors will be taking all this into consideration, much more so than they are generally doing at present.

In the meantime, the courts have the difficult task of deciding where to draw the line. There should certainly be the facility for them to check on a woman's nutritional state and have her assessed for PMS. This assessment usually would take three months to confirm as three consecutive cycles need to be charted in order to confirm the diagnosis of PMS.

The fact that a woman may be a danger to herself or society has to be dealt with in a routine way by the courts. When PMS is presented as a defence or mitigation, and the diagnosis confirmed, then effective treatment should be sought whilst the woman is serving her sentence, if she has been convicted.

It is very important that when PMS is used as a defence or mitigation, appropriate treatment is instituted. It then becomes the woman's personal responsibility to follow the appropriate diet or take the appropriate treatment to ensure that her pre-menstrual symptoms are properly controlled. PMS could then not be used as a defence or mitigation should she then re-offend.

10

THE SOCIAL
IMPLICATIONS
OF PMS

RELATIONSHIPS AT HOME AND AT WORK

It was not surprising that as a result of these severe symptoms, we were recording that 95 per cent of our survey of women reported that their home lives and relationships with family and friends were affected by their PMS symptoms.

**Degree to which a sample
of 1000 women felt that their
home life/relationship with
family/friends was affected
due to PMS symptoms**

Not Affected	Mild	Moderate	Severe	Total Affected
4.9%	12.7%	36.1%	46.3% -	95.1%

You will have read in earlier sections about how some family lives were affected. I have added two quite different examples here to make the point in its own right, as the family and our immediate circle are so very important.

Anita, who suffered severely with all four sub-groups, and actually attempted suicide, explains how she felt her home life was affected.

ANITA'S PROBLEMS AT HOME

'From about 1982 I used to get so bad-tempered. I remember one day I was having an ordinary discussion with my husband and he made a comment which I took the wrong way. I started attacking him with a knife. Then I'd start attacking everybody else in the house except the baby, who I made a point of keeping away from.

I firmly believe that if we hadn't been having difficulties with our son at the time, my husband would have left me. I think he had got to the point where he couldn't take any more. My marriage was really under severe pressure. He was definitely on the point of saying "That's it".

I have two children and I think they have both been affected by my premenstrual behaviour. They learned to watch me carefully to see the mood I was in. This is because I would often attack them verbally and be cruel. Then afterwards I would pick them up and cuddle them. I couldn't always keep myself under control. They didn't understand. I think they have forgiven me now, but they still watch me. I don't think they can believe I'm not going to flip on them.'

Geraldine, whose worst problem was her secret chocolate binges, took her anger and frustration out on her daughters.

GERALDINE'S FEELINGS OF ANGER

'I feel really aggressive towards the children, especially the older ones. I smack them in instances where it's not really deserved. I tend to take it out on the oldest daughter, even if she hasn't done anything to justify it.

The worst thing with the children is not so much the aggressiveness, because when I feel that way I try to keep away from them, but the sarcasm. I can be really horrible, and it's awful because it takes away all their self-confidence.

After being really awful I'd just go into the bedroom and lean my head on the wall and think, "Fancy saying something like that?" I'd feel really *wicked and go into floods of tears. Sometimes I'd blame them and ask them how they could do this to me. I'd tell them that they were making me ill and accuse them of being horrid to me. Then I'd complain that they didn't do a thing around the house and threaten to get a maid. By this time they would be staring at me, absolutely rigid with fright. All the time, at the back of my mind I'd know I was being a bitch and feel crumby, really crumby because basically I love my girls to death and I don't want to say such awful things to them.'*

PERSONAL RELATIONSHIPS

It is exceedingly difficult to maintain a loving relationship when you are experiencing severe symptoms of irritability, nervous tension and aggression. I so often see women whose personal and sexual relationships have fallen apart as a direct result of their PMS. Penny and Liz are two good examples of how symptoms stood in the way of a harmonious personal life. The good news is that they both, like the majority of our patients, were able to restore their relationships once over their symptoms. It is not uncommon for men to thank us for giving them back the girl they married!

" Penny's Story "

Penny is a 40-year-old director of a small publishing and public relations company who works and lives with her partner.

'I knew that unless I took some drastic action, I would lose my boyfriend. My ex-husband used to take the stance of ignoring me until the mood was over. However, John would not accept that I would be so moody with him one minute and then pick up the telephone and speak perfectly normally to clients. At work I seemed to be able to control myself for short periods of time. I was able to switch on this false smile and air of calmness. But once amongst those I loved and trusted, I'd let rip about how I really felt inside. When John first moved in with me he was staggered to discover the effect that PMS had on me. At first he tried to arrange business trips away to coincide with my PMS days, but because my cycle was irregular planning them wasn't easy.

Our relationship nearly snapped

Each month it was as if the normal, happy me disappeared for up to ten days, and was replaced by an irritable, moody and very clumsy woman. My PMS symptoms nearly broke up our relationship. I'd snap at John and be really rude when his children came to visit.

I knew from early on that I was suffering from PMS. It started when I stopped taking the contraceptive pill when I was 33. In desperation I tried all the remedies I'd read about, but they made no difference at all. Then I spotted an article suggesting that PMS could be helped by diet. I was very sceptical, but concerned enough about my relationship with John to give it a try.

Diet brought me back to normal

I followed the diet that was tailor-made for me, took specific vitamin and mineral supplements, and did some moderate exercise. It took three months to overcome my symptoms. The moodiness and snappiness subsided, and thankfully I was normal and happy all the time again.

John and I are now on an even keel.'

John is obviously delighted that Penny found a solution, and feels that PMS affects men every bit as much as it does women. He says, 'Having been through some tough times at the start, I'm convinced that many marriages must fail not because the couple aren't right together, but because PMS comes between them.'

❝ Liz's Story ❞

'I suffered with PMS for about four years and was gradually worsening. It became so bad I sought help from my GP. The worst symptoms I suffered were mainly terrible food cravings - particularly for sweet things. I could go through not just one bar of chocolate but half a dozen at one sitting. That made me feel terribly bloated abdominally, I had terrible breast tenderness and I felt really really depressed.

I don't know how he put up with me!

My PMS symptoms affected the relationship I have with my husband on a month to month basis – in between times I would be fine, but at that time of the month I would completely change and because of my mood swings and depression it did put a strain on things. I didn't want to cook, I didn't want to go out – I was really withdrawn into myself. I could go from being happy one minute and dress to go out, and because I was so bloated and my skirt wouldn't fasten, I would stomp into a rage and I just wasn't going out and it wasn't for discussion. I don't know how he put up with me – he was very supportive, but it did put a great strain on things.

I tried various treatments from vitamin B6 tablets to water tablets and I eventually went on to hormone therapy, none of which I found very helpful at all. I really didn't want to be taking drug treatment in the long term. I was more interested in finding a more natural method but did not seem to find it through my GP.

When I followed the Women's Nutritional Advisory Service programme that was sent to me through the post, and I followed all the recommendations I received over the telephone, there was a vast difference even within the first month. I followed the programme for about six months and got continued help and support from the telephone helpline and by letter. Any problems I had, or any worrying symptoms, I could just phone up and chat things through.

I'm feeling a lot better now. I'm virtually symptom-free. I carried on with the diet, the exercise and the supplements, and I'm really, really grateful for the help and support I was given by the WNAS.'

PRODUCTIVITY AND EFFICIENCY AT WORK

Another incredible statistic that emerged from the study on 1000 PMS sufferers was the degree to which their work suffered as a result of their symptoms. 92.7 per cent reported that their productivity and efficiency decreased pre-menstrually.

They further reported that they were, to a large degree, 'not there mentally' for an average of five days per month! This means that they produce very little work during this period of time.

" Ifey's Story "

Ifey is a 29-year-old barrister who suffered with PMS for 17 years.

'My worst PMS symptoms were nausea. I always felt nausea and in the latter years I would be continuously vomiting, which I found the hardest thing to deal with. Apart from that I used to feel very depressed. I'd be very weepy, upset and emotional for no apparent reason. I used to put on weight and become very bloated.

PMS affected my work

I always felt I wasn't functioning properly and wasn't doing my best workwise. I'm a barrister and I need to be able to concentrate and I need to be able to think very quickly, but when I was suffering from my symptoms, I wasn't able to do that and consequently it affected my work. I'd always hope that when my symptoms came I had a case that was easy to deal with and didn't involve a lot of work or concentration.

Altogether I had suffered with PMS for 17 years. I had been to several gynaecologists to get help with my symptoms. Initially my GP had told me that I would continue to have these symptoms until I had my first child; since I started my period when I was 11 that wasn't very helpful. I was put on the pill at the age of 16 and I took the pill for 10 years to deal with the symptoms; but it wasn't very helpful. It was only helpful in so much as it would suppress symptoms during exam times.

My symptoms vanished overnight

When I went on the PMS programme I was told I would have to cut out chocolate from my diet, which I found very hard because I love chocolate. Also I was told to avoid foods containing wheat and alcohol before my symptoms arrived, to exercise and to take the recommended supplements. Having done that for a month, and I stuck regularly to the programme, my symptoms just vanished overnight. It was just absolutely amazing. Normally the symptoms would be there, but I had no symptoms whatsoever, it was just like a miracle, and after 17 years of suffering it was just brilliant!'

A labour force survey conducted in 1992 found that there were just over 11 million working women in the UK. Over nine million were employed and the remainder were self-employed. Given these figures the cost to industry due to lack of production must be vast, and probably not a statistic that has been properly considered. It wouldn't register as sickness or absenteeism as these women appear to be at work in the normal way. Unless specifically asked for, this information would not appear. Indeed, even asking for it may not produce the truth as there are so many women who would be in fear of losing their jobs. As it is, they feel they are teetering on the edge of disaster at work because of their general behaviour pre-menstrually. **81.6 per cent** of 1000 women felt that their work or career had been adversely affected by their PMS. So keeping a low profile is the least line of resistance.

Effects on productivity/efficiency pre-menstrually out of a sample of 1000 women		
Same	*Decreased*	*Increased*
6.2%	92.7%	1.1%

In 1993 the results of a study we undertook on work efficiency were published. It was to my knowledge the first study of its kind in the UK. In conjunction with Kimberly-Clark, the makers of Kleenex and Simplicity products, we were able to work with 47 of their staff who were suffering with PMS. The group was split into two, with half the women making dietary changes and taking Optivite, and the other half just making dietary changes. There was an improvement in work efficiency in both groups with a trend towards increased benefit in the group taking the nutritional supplement as well. As a group all the women reported an increased sense of well-being and energy levels.

A look at case histories of women who came to the Women's Nutritional Advisory Service proves the point. First there was Sally, a divorcee in an executive position.

" Sally's Story "

'I have a very responsible, full-time position. My job involves dealing with people and quite a lot of travel. I found it very difficult to cope pre-menstrually. I felt emotionally unstable and frightened to go out of the house. It made me a liability, really. The moods I experienced gave me feelings of dislike for people I worked with for no apparent reason. Especially my manager.

I would be extremely bad-tempered and unable to concentrate. I had this persecution complex and felt that everybody was against me and scheming. If something went wrong I felt that it was other people's fault and that they were getting at me.

I would sometimes think "sod the lot of them, it's all their fault". I'd try to work, feeling so agitated and ill. I pushed myself to work even harder and faster, which made me even more tired and exhausted.'

Anita, a PMS D sufferer who had attempted suicide, had more than her share of problems at work.

" Anita's Story "

'My work was certainly affected. I would forget things. Forget appointments and forget to put things in the diary. I just couldn't concentrate for that time of the month. In fact I was only normal for one week in four. For three weeks I'd feel so tired and work would take me much longer than usual. It would take me one to two hours to do half-an-hour's work. Consequently, for at least two weeks per month I'd have to work late to get my work done. Even then I'd still have to check all the work again when I wasn't pre-menstrual.'

DRIVING ABILITY

Many of the symptoms discussed have broad repercussions on the sufferer herself and on her family and friends. However, the seriousness of PMS comes right home when a statistic appears that could affect us all. We asked 1000 drivers who suffer with PMS whether their driving ability was affected pre-menstrually. An astounding **76.9 per cent** said their driving ability decreased before their period. Many women stop driving before their period is due as they have previously had so many accidents pre-menstrually. The two main factors that seem to affect driving ability are lack of concentration and poor coordination. Amazingly, the women report that as soon as their period arrives, their driving ability returns to normal.

Driving a car, or any vehicle for that matter, is a real responsibility and not to be taken lightly. We advise severe sufferers to keep off the road until their symptoms have gone, or are under control. Placing lives at risk is no joke. Here are two examples of many who experienced diminished driving skills pre-menstrually.

" Anita's Story "

'I have had several accidents and near-misses, all of which were during my pre-menstrual time. Once, when I was delivering a parcel, I went straight into the back of the car in front of me which was stationary. I didn't even see that he had stopped. Another time I was going to turn right, I saw something coming in the opposite direction and yet I carried on despite the fact that I'd seen the chap. I knew I hadn't got the speed to get past him, but I carried on nevertheless. I made lots of stupid decisions because I didn't have my mind on what was going on around me. I felt very vague and as if I was driving along in a metal box detached from reality. I have an excess on my insurance policy as a result of these accidents.'

" Ruth's Story "

'If I was feeling aggressive generally pre-menstrually, then I would be aggressive behind the wheel. I can remember once, there was a stupid man in a van in front of me at a junction. He was over the white line on the middle of the road. He was going right and I was going left, I was feeling all steamed up. I was alone in the car. I mounted the pavement to get past him, revving up hard and hooting the horn. In fact I scraped my car all along his mudguard. Then I zoomed off. That was typical of how I used to feel. I have still got the car with the mark.'

11

WHY IS PMS MORE COMMON TODAY?

As I have already mentioned, PMS seems to be more common today than in years past. This is undoubtedly partly because it is talked about now in a way that was inconceivable 30 or 40 years ago. But it is probably also due to changes in our lifestyle, diet and possibly our use of hormones and drugs. It is extremely hard to pinpoint any one factor as being a clear-cut cause of PMS. But though the case may not be proven, it may be useful to look at some of these factors and their relationship with PMS and other common diseases that have become the hallmark of the twentieth century.

It is estimated that in 1993 the NHS bill for the taxpayer was £37 billion. In the USA in the last 20 or so years, the medical bill has increased from $27 billion to over $200 billion! The awful fact is that, despite these amounts of money being spent, some of us have been getting sicker.

Cardiovascular disease is still the biggest killer in developed countries and undoubtedly the commonest preventable cause of early death in young to middle-aged men and women. Approximately 170,000 people die each year in the United Kingdom from heart attacks and strokes. There has been little improvement, as yet, in these figures, though the United States and Finland have begun to achieve a substantial fall in their incidences of heart disease. Smoking, lack of exercise, obesity, high blood pressure and high blood cholesterol are all well-documented risk factors and these last three are all influenced by diet.

Cancer too, it appears, is on the increase. There seem to be three main factors for this. The first is age. With a few exceptions the incidence of most cancers rises steeply with age from about 40 years onward. In times past many people did not live long enough to be at risk of developing cancer. Secondly, it is highly likely that there has been a true increase in the rate of cancer this century, regardless of age, and that this reflects the increased use of chemicals in the environment. Many industrial chemicals, pesticides and even drugs linger in the environment for years. Finally, the type of food we eat also influences cancer risk. Consumption of smoked and pickled foods is associated with an increase in some cancers, especially of the stomach and oesophagus, whilst a high intake of fresh fruit and vegetables may well protect against many types of cancer. These protective foods are rich in vitamin C, E and carotene – vegetable vitamin A – which help limit the damage to tissues by cancer-inducing chemicals.

'Mental' illnesses are also on the increase and this too may be influenced by our diet, consumption of alcohol, medical and illicit drugs. Obviously social factors, education and life skills are also all important in helping us cope with times of stress or ill-health. The stresses and strains of twentieth-century living have not made it easy for some of us to cope, and for many women, working and raising a family is particularly stressful.

Allergic problems have also become much more common in the last 40 years. The reasons for this are not clear but include family or genetic factors, chemicals in the environment, dietary habits and the pattern of feeding in childhood.

What, I hear you ask, has this pessimistic view of the state of our health got to do with PMS? Quite simply, it appears that the development of PMS is very much influenced by the same factors: diet, exercise or lack of it, and possibly environmental chemicals. It is possible that these diverse conditions have common causative and aggravating factors.

In 1986 the Women's Nutritional Advisory Service completed a national street survey on 500 women in Britain. We found that 73.6 per cent of them suffered in varying degrees with PMS. This figure is considerably more than estimates of 30–60 per cent made during the previous 30 years.

By now you must be wondering why the diseases are becoming more common, and you might well ask. Our twentieth-century lifestyle brings many relatively new experiences to us, some of which we are not well equipped to handle. The diets most of us know are very far removed from that of our ancestors. Our bodies were not built to cope with refined and processed foods, very often empty of nutrients. We have had to live with pesticides and insecticides being sprayed on our crops, growth hormones and antibiotics pumped into animals, and environmental pollution and acid rain as the finishing touches. Many of us over-eat and under-exercise, and women nowadays tend to lead far more stressful existences. So it is logical, really, that we can't honestly expect our 'machines' to go on indefinitely without breaking down when we don't treat them with respect. We generally treat our cars better than we do our bodies – you wouldn't dream of putting the wrong fuel in your petrol tank, would you?

Before I launch into the tale of woe about our diet, let me say that although you will probably come to realize that we are faced with certain problems concerning our diet, with good education we *can* find ways around them. I will of course be discussing various solutions in the Self-Help section on diet in Part Three.

A GOOD LOOK AT OUR DIET

In order to look at diet more closely we need to examine how our habits have changed during this century.

- We have increased our consumption of sugar. The UK has become one of the world's largest chocolate and sweet eaters, with the average person consuming some 188 lb or 85 kilos each per year. We currently spend over £4 billion per year on chocolate alone.

- Our diet is particularly high in saturated fats (animal fats). It is thought that this has much to do with our also having a high incidence of heart disease and breast cancer.

- We eat far too much salt – 10 to 20 times more than our bodies really require per day. Salt can contribute to blood pressure problems and pre-menstrual water retention.

- We often drink far too much coffee and tea which can impede the absorption of essential nutrients. On average we consume four cups of tea and two cups of coffee per day, but many people exceed this.

- We consume volumes of foods with a high level of phosphorus, which again impedes absorption of good nutrients. Examples of these foods are soft drinks of low or normal calorie types, processed foods, canned, packaged, pre-packed, convenience foods and ready-made sauces.

- Alcohol consumption has almost doubled in the United Kingdom since the end of the Second World War. On average, women drink about the equivalent of one unit per day (equal to one glass of wine). Not much, you may think, but enough to have a slight adverse effect on the outcome of pregnancy! Also, about one-third of women are teetotal or consume very little alcohol so someone is having their share.

- Unbelievable as it may seem, we actually eat less food than we did thirty and more years ago. It seems that women of today actually expend less energy than those of a generation or two ago and this has resulted in a 10 to 15 per cent reduction in food intake. This means that our intake of essential nutrients has also fallen, particularly if we eat refined or convenience foods. The motor car and lack of exercise has almost certainly been a factor in the decline in energy expenditure.

- Many of the foods available contain chemical additives in the form of flavour enhancers, colouring and preservatives. Whilst some of these are not harmful, some of them *are*, and our bodies are certainly not designed to cope with them.

- Our water contains certain pollutants which are thought to be a risk to public health.

- Our meat has become contaminated with antibiotics and growth hormones.

- Nitrate fertilizers have been used to obtain fast-growing and abundant crops. It is now recognized that nitrates are harmful and can produce cancer, at least in animals.

- Almost all of our fresh fruit, cereals and vegetables are sprayed with pesticides at least once. In addition, milk and meat may retain the pesticides from feed given to livestock.

Smoking

Smoking tobacco has become a widespread habit among Western societies. In 1922 in the United Kingdom, for example, 20–34-year-old women smoked an average of fifty cigarettes per year, but by 1975 this had risen to an average of just over three thousand cigarettes per woman, per year. Despite the more educated classes reducing their cigarette consumption, smoking has become relatively more common amongst women, in those who are less well educated.

Alcohol

Since the 1940s alcohol consumption has doubled in the United Kingdom. On average, women consume one unit of alcohol per day, and men three units (one unit = 1 glass of wine, 1 pub measure of spirits, 1 small sherry or vermouth, or half a pint of normal strength beer or lager). These average levels are now the maximum recommended daily intakes for women and men respectively. Whilst many of us may be teetotallers, or drink substantially less than this, there will be those who regularly consume more. Some women may go on pre-menstrual alcohol binges.

For every £1 spent on food in the United Kingdom, some 75p is spent on alcohol and tobacco. Just think how the quality of the food in the United Kingdom could improve if only half the money spent on alcohol and tobacco was spent on purchasing better quality food.

Drugs

Western societies have become drug-oriented. In the 12 months of 1991 in the United States nearly £35 billion was spent on medicines by a population of 250 million, and in the UK it was £3.5 billion or £69 per man woman and child. Doctors issue some 15 per cent more prescriptions than they did a decade ago. In England only, over 425 million prescriptions were written in 1992, nearly 10 million for anti-depressants, amounting to £81 million. Not surprising in view of the power and influence that drug companies have been allowed to assume in the education of doctors.

In the last year there has been tremendous concern by medical practitioners worldwide about the excessive use of benzodiazepene tranquillizers and sleeping tablets. It is now recommended that these drugs, which include Valium, Mogadon and Ativan, are used as a temporary measure for only a few weeks. Those who have been taking them long-term should, if at all possible, have their dosage and frequency gradually reduced under medical supervision.

The Pill

The oral contraceptive birth control pill has been a popular and effective method of contraception. The initial forms of the birth pill had high levels of oestrogen, which were known to cause some disturbance in vitamin and mineral balance, increase the risk of vaginal thrush, and in some women precipitate significant depression and migraine headaches. These side-effects are less likely with the new lower dose, or phased dosage oral contraceptive pill. However, problems can certainly arise. Whilst the oral contraceptive pill can help some women's pre-menstrual symptoms, and is a useful way for treating mild PMS, particularly in those women who require contraception, it can also aggravate some PMS symptoms. There is no way of determining this, other than by trial and error. If you find an oral contraceptive pill that suits you, all well and good. However, some women will find that practically any form of the Pill aggravates their pre-menstrual symptoms.

Vitamin and mineral intake

Our diet this century has gone through, and continues to go through, several substantial changes. By the end of the 1970s there was evidence, from certain surveys, of a deterioration in the quality of the UK diet, particularly since the Second World War. A high intake of sugar, refined foods, animal fats and alcohol had meant a relatively poor intake of essential vitamins and minerals.

Some fifteen vitamins, twenty-four minerals and eight amino acids have been isolated as being essential for normal body function. They are synergistic, which means that they rely upon each other in order to keep the body functioning at an optimum level. When one or more is in short supply, alterations in body metabolism occur. Minor deficiencies can often be tolerated, but major or multiple deficiencies result in the body becoming inefficient, whith the development of symptoms and possibly disease.

There is, however, some heartening recent evidence. All the good advice from numerous individual experts and expert committees, government ones included, has finally got through to *some* of the British public. Many of us have increased our intake of fruit and vegetables and this greatly offsets the potential fall in intake from eating refined foods or eating smaller amounts of food in general. However, this has not happened with the unemployed or those who come from families where the main wage-earner is unskilled. From the recent dietary survey of British adults in the UK, the single biggest factor that determined nutrient intake was not age, sex, illness, or whether on a diet or not, but whether the person was unemployed. Like it or not, it seems that we already have a nutritional underclass who don't have the money and the knowledge to improve their diets. Fats and sugar are cheap calories, and when you are hungry calories are more important than fibre or vitamins and minerals.

Let us now turn our attention to certain specific nutrients which may contribute to symptoms of PMS.

THE NITTY GRITTY REVIEW
OF SPECIFIC NUTRIENTS

Some nutritional factors may be of particular importance to PMS. In the United Kingdom, the Department of Health has instructed the Committee on the Medical Aspects of Food to investigate the nature of the UK diet, and what the appropriate intakes of calories, fats, fibre, vitamins and minerals should be. A similar governmental review by the Food and Drug Administration in the USA was also undertaken in the 1980s.

In 1991 the Department of Health in the UK published its report on Dietary Reference Values for Food Energy and Nutrients for the United Kingdom. This report was prepared by an august group of scientists and doctors who set guidelines for intakes for most of the known essential nutrients. It followed another important report, The Dietary and Nutritional Survey of British Adults. These two reports and similar reports from the United States have allowed a more detailed assessment than ever before of the nutritional adequacy for the adult population in these two developed countries.

Vitamin B

The B group of vitamins, and in particular vitamin B6, have been used for many years to treat PMS. In the UK the new recommended average intake for women of child-bearing age is 1.2 mg per day, exactly the level found in an independent nutrition survey (the Booker Health Report 1985) and less than the value of 1.7 mg from the recent government survey. According to these figures, hardly anyone should be deficient in this nutrient. But several surveys using blood tests have revealed that some 10 to 20 per cent of adults, especially women, appear to have a mild deficiency. This seems more likely in those with problems such as depression and anxiety, as well as PMS. However, deficiency of this nutrient does not explain PMS as many of those with a mild deficiency have no symptoms at all.

Folic acid, another of the B vitamins, was found to be slightly low in between eight and 40 per cent of adult women. Young women seemed particularly at risk. These figures are almost certainly an overestimate of the problem and comparable surveys from the US give values less than half these, but still with no cause for complacency.

Deficiency of these two B group vitamins and the others (B1, B2, B3 and B12), which occur less frequently, can all affect energy level, mood, skin quality, hormone function and appetite. A poor intake may contribute in part to some women's PMS. Certain aspects of our modern diet deserve further comment.

Many refined foods are low in B complex vitamins. For example, a McDonald's Big Mac hamburger is known to contain only a fraction of the vitamin B6 that it should do. Presumably, substantial quantities are lost in preparation, cooking and storage. In fact, you would have to eat sixty Big Mac hamburgers a day, in order to achieve an intake of 1.2 mg of vitamin B6 – a current conservative allowance.

Thus, for some of us whose diets do not contain good quantities of fresh and wholesome foods, the intake of B vitamins may be low.

Magnesium

Magnesium is a key mineral in the treatment of PMS. It has now been shown in several medical studies that women with PMS have low levels of magnesium in their red blood cells, and finding a mildly reduced level of magnesium in the blood is now the most consistent reported abnormal finding in women with PMS. Once again, however, not all women with a low level of blood magnesium will have PMS.

Intakes of this mineral in the UK are generally below optimum levels: aproximately 15 per cent of all women in the UK of child-bearing age eat a diet deficient in magnesium, and many others consume only borderline amounts – a low intake (i.e. likely to lead to deficiency) has been defined in the UK as less than 150 mg per day; the recommended intakes and actual intakes in the United States are higher but without any cause for complacency. It may come as no surprise to you to learn that vegetables, fruit and all unrefined or unprocessed foods are rich in this mineral and that refined foods are poor sources. Eating a diet low in protein and high in salt, sugar, alcohol and possibly coffee may contribute to increased losses of magnesium. Like the B vitamins, magnesium has an effect on energy production, mood, muscle function and hormone metabolism. Curiously there are no physical or skin signs of a deficiency.

Magnesium is definitely an important piece of the puzzle of PMS.

Iron

It is probably better known that menstruating women have an increased need for the mineral iron; in fact, iron levels are at their lowest four days pre-menstrually. This time there *is* an RDA (Recommended Daily Allowance) in the UK for iron, which is 12 mg per day; this is somewhat lower than the RDA for the USA, which is 18 mg.

The Booker Health Report showed that 60 per cent of females between the ages of 18 and 54 have iron levels below the recommended daily allowance. In another study in 1984, it was found that a group of 15–25-year-old women consumed only 75 per cent of the RDA for iron, so many are at risk of deficiency.

Consuming a cup of tea with a meal will reduce the absorption of iron from all non-animal foods in the diet.

Zinc and other trace minerals

Zinc, like iron, is an essential mineral which is required in tiny amounts but also plays an important part in many aspects of the body's normal functioning. It is needed for normal hormone production, certain aspects of brain chemistry, for healthy skin and good resistance to infection. The average daily intake of this mineral for women of child-bearing age in the UK is 7.6 mg per day, which compares favourably with an average recommended daily intake of 5.5 mg. However, like iron and magnesium, a significant percentage, at least five, consume less than the recommended minimum of 4.0 mg per day. Furthermore, the absorption of this mineral is easily upset by alcohol, tea, probably coffee, bran, unleavened breads, chapattis, and many other foods. So a considerable percentage of women may be getting insufficient zinc. Any ill-effects are likely to be slight and subtle, but a deficiency certainly could be a contributing factor to some PMS symptoms.

We are not certain about other trace nutrients. If you are eating a healthy diet with plenty of fruit and vegetables and not smoking or drinking then you are likely to have a good intake of the trace nutrients such as selenium, chromium, copper and manganese. A lack of chromium or selenium may occasionally be relevant for some women with PMS. For example, a lack of chromium does have an influence on the action of insulin and the control of blood sugar. Chromium can enhance the effect of insulin, and correcting a deficiency has been shown to improve blood sugar control. This can be important for some women who are either very overweight or eat a diet very high in sugar and refined foods which are depleted of chromium.

IT'S A POOR SHOW

It seems astonishing to consider that such important nutrients are acknowledged to be in such short supply, and yet not a great deal is being done to reverse the trend. Three out of four of these nutrients do not even have a Recommended Daily Allowance in the UK.

When you read the section on Vitamins and Minerals in Chapter 14, pay particular attention to these four important nutrients, notice what their function is in the body and what happens to us if we don't get them in sufficient quantities. Is it any wonder that our bodies are slowly going to seed when we are not providing them with the essential materials they need in order for them to function properly?

In the Self-Help section, I concentrate on foods that contain a high level of these particular nutrients as well as a few others. I will help you to work out a diet for yourself which will provide you with good amounts of the essential nutrients that you are most likely to be short of.

Other barriers

Not only may we be taking in insufficient amounts of vitamins and minerals, but the value of many of these nutrients is impaired by factors like alcohol, tea, coffee and tobacco.

Another thing to bear in mind which severely lowers the nutritional value of food is the cooking process. For example, boiling a cabbage rids it of about 75 per cent of its vitamin C. Baking or frying food can destroy up to 50 per cent of other vitamins. Commercially frozen vegetables can also be lacking in some nutrients by as much as 47 per cent though usually they are the next best thing to fresh ones, since canning can result in up to 70 per cent of the nutritional content being lost. It appears that processing food does little to enhance our health at the end of the day.

A good example of the effect of processing on nutrient content, is the nutrient content of some of McDonald's foods. I am sorry to keep using them as an example, but at least they are one of the few fast-food manufacturers who have had the nerve to assess the nutrient content of their own products.

By now you no doubt realize that a 'normal healthy diet' is somewhat of a myth. Although it is possible to eat a nutritious diet, you need to be fairly educated on the subject before you can even make a start. Then, as you can see, there are numerous hurdles to be overcome.

Whilst all these facts do seem depressing, there is a light at the end of the tunnel. In the Self-Help section on diet I will be concentrating on which types of foods to buy, and suggesting methods of preparation that will preserve the nutrients in your food.

TIMES DO CHANGE

Is it any wonder women suffer with PMS! One hundred years ago, meat, animal fat and sugar were a much smaller part of our diets than today. The consumption of cereal fibres has also dropped by as much as 90 per cent. These are important factors in relation to PMS, as you will see.

It has become far more difficult to eat a 'normal healthy diet'. However, if you concentrate on avoiding the nutrient-deficient and contaminated foods listed below, you will be making changes for the better in your diet, which will not only help your PMS, but will help you feel healthier all round. There is less you can do to combat the unhealthy effects of the polluted environment, but I make some suggestions below.

The diet of our ancestors. When we examine the diet of our ancestors, we then begin to realize that it is not 'natural' to eat meat in the quantity that the majority of us do today. Evidence shows that diet approximately three million years ago consisted largely of hard seeds, plant fibre, some roots and stems – a diet high in vegetable matter similar to that of the Guinea baboon today.

Animals today are bred to be fat. Modern meat contains some seven times more fat than the wild meat our ancestors ate. Our ancestors' meat also contained five times more of the good polyunsaturated fats than today's meat, which is high in the potentially harmful saturated fats. The ancient diet was also richer in vitamins and minerals and polyunsaturated fats, and many times richer than the modern diet. It was a diet which was largely composed of fresh raw foods.

Antibiotics. Because antibiotics are being so widely used on animals, the conditions that would normally be treated by antibiotics are becoming resistant to them. Apart from being used as a medicine for individual sick animals, they are given to whole herds as a preventive measure, and they are again used for growth promotion.

My advice is to try to use organic or additive-free meat where possible, meat which has not been subjected to drugs, growth promoters or contaminated foods. Organic and additive-free meat is becoming more and more available. Certainly local farms and even supermarkets often keep stocks. If you can find 'clean' meat, it can be included in your diet approximately three times per week. An alternative is to limit one's meat intake to moderate quantities of good-quality lean meat, or to become a vegetarian. It's the fat in the meat that will carry much of the pollutants, so avoid it – and also rely more on fish. When eating chicken, don't eat the skin and don't make the gravy from the fatty part of the juices, pour it off first.

Fat consumption. Britain has the honour of having the highest incidence of heart disease in the world. This was not so in the past, when other countries such as Finland and Australia were way ahead. Something drastic must have happened to change statistics so dramatically.

It seems that the saturated fats increase the level of cholesterol which leaves the bloodstream and settles down in the arteries, resulting in a gradual blockage of those supplying the heart, brain and other organs. This leads to heart attacks, strokes and poor circulation. Smoking accelerates the process.

By 1966 the Australian and US rate of heart disease began to decline, but that was not so for Britain, whose casualties were on the increase.

In other countries such as Finland, for example, who were previously 'top of the coronary pops', a national nutritional education campaign was undertaken. The result now is that they are a much healthier nation with a far lower incidence of heart disease than many other countries.

The sweet facts. Over the past 100 years there has been a 25-fold increase in world sugar production. This is a real change from the days when sugar was an expensive luxury that we locked away for high days and holidays, and was only consumed by the wealthy. Refined sugars simply didn't exist for our ancestors. Their diet consisted mainly of vegetables, fruit, cereals and some wild meat. It wasn't until this century that we developed an addiction to the sweet and sticky sugar family.

We clearly don't need refined sugar. What seems to have been overlooked is that our bodies can change complex carbohydrates and proteins into the sugar they require. Sugar contains no vitamins, no minerals, no protein, no fibre, no starches. It may contain tiny traces of calcium and magnesium if you're lucky, and it certainly provides us with loads of calories (kjs), 'empty calories'.

It is actually a fair skill these days not to consume large amounts of sugar, because it is added to so many foods. What do you think the following have in common? Cheese, biscuits, fruit yogurt, tomato sauce, baked beans, pickled cucumbers, muesli, beefburgers, Worcester sauce, pork sausages, peas, cornflakes and Coca-Cola – well, they can all contain sugar. Coca-Cola contains some eight teaspoonfuls per can.

There are some more nutritious alternatives which I will discuss in the Self-Help section. The food manufacturers are beginning to understand that their consumers are waking up, and the majority actually don't want to be dumped on. For now my advice is to read the labels carefully when you are shopping: I guarantee you will have a few surprises!

Water

Our most important nutrient is water, and sadly it is becoming one of our major sources of pollution. Not only is the water contaminated with lead, aluminium and copper, we now have nitrates to contend with as well. Nitrates are chemicals used in fertilizers to promote crop growth.

Why are nitrates harmful? Well, they go through chemical changes and at the end of the day turn into nitrosamines which are believed to be strong cancer-producing chemicals.

Toxic minerals

Toxic minerals in the form of lead and mercury are in the soil, the air and the water, as well as being present in our food. During this century their levels have been rising rapidly, and at times to a point where our bodies have not been able to cope.

Lead. Lead pollution has been much discussed in the media over the past few years. High lead levels are acknowledged to be linked to low birth weight and low intelligence in children. As a result of extensive research on lead, many countries have removed lead from petrol and are trying to keep lead levels down in cities. However, it is far more difficult to remove it from the water supply as the filtering systems at water purification plants can't always cope with the load.

Helpful tips to avoid the toxins

- Concentrate on eating a nutritious diet, particularly high in zinc, magnesium, calcium and vitamins C and B.

- Take a well-balanced multi-vitamin supplement and some extra vitamin C if you are at particular risk.

- Scrub all fruit and vegetables with a brush to clean off as many toxins as possible, and remove the outer layers of lettuce and cabbage, etc. Don't peel fruit and vegetables unless you don't like the peel – very often the bulk of the nutrients is just under the skin. Use organic vegetables and salad stuff or grow your own where possible, without using chemicals.

- Water filters tend to filter out a good deal of the toxic metals. Water purifiers can be bought in healthfood shops, but they aren't so efficient. Every so often the filter needs replacing – and it's amazing what collects in it. Rather the toxic deposits collect in the filter than your body!

Avoid:

- Spending too much time near busy roads if the local exhaust fumes contain lead (which may be easier said than done).

- Copper and aluminium cookware unless with a non-stick lining.

- Alcohol, as it increases lead absorption.

- Refined foods which give the body little protection against toxins.

- Antacids which contain aluminium salts.

Food additives

Whilst, of course, there are some perfectly harmless substances added to food, the number of potentially harmful additives is significant. Many additives have been shown to cause hyperactivity in children, asthma, eczema, skin rashes and swelling. It's obviously important to be able to differentiate between the safe and not-so-safe additives.

After being bombarded by warnings about additives is it any wonder that some of us have at one time or another avoided all foods containing them? Understandably, 'additive' has become a dirty word in some circles. But it's important to understand that some additives are, in fact, beneficial! For example: beneficial additives include riboflavin – vitamin B2 – and calcium L-Ascorbate which is vitamin C, and the many preservatives which help keep our food from spoiling.

WHICH ADDITIVES ARE SAFE?

Fortunately, there is now no need to remain confused about which additives are safe and which are potentially harmful. Look in Appendix 2 on page 249 for details of booklets and books on additives which will help you to pick out the dangerous additives from the safe ones.

Coffee

Over the last 10 years reports have begun to filter through about the health hazards attached to coffee consumption. Probably one of the reasons why these facts are now coming to light is that increasing amounts of coffee are being consumed. Since 1950 the consumption of coffee in the UK has increased fourfold and according to the US Department of Agriculture, in 1984 10.4 lb (4.6 kg) of coffee were consumed per person in the USA. Many people become quite addicted to it unknowingly, and couldn't give up the habit easily.

We now know that coffee worsens nervous tension, anxiety and insomnia. So obviously, no matter how much we may enjoy it, drinking coffee to excess is not a healthy habit. In fact, coffee contains caffeine which is a mental and physical stimulant. This can be of benefit of course, but even with 2–4 cups per day, adverse effects can be experienced. These include anxiety, restlessness, nervousness, insomnia, rapid pulse, palpitations, shakes and passing increased quantities of water. Regular coffee drinkers not only enjoy the flavour, but in many cases come to rely on the stimulation to get them through the day. If you cannot get going without your first fix of the day, you know what I mean!

Weaning yourself off coffee can sometimes be a fairly traumatic experience. It can sometimes produce symptoms not unlike a drug withdrawal, in particular a severe headache, which may take several days to disappear. However, rest assured they do eventually go completely, as long as you manage to abstain from coffee.

Ways to go about giving up coffee

- Cut down gradually over the space of a week or two.

- Use decaffeinated coffee instead of coffee containing caffeine, but limit yourself to 2–3 cups per day.

- Try alternative drinks like Barleycup or Bambu which you can obtain from healthfood shops.

- If you like filter coffee, you can still use your filter, but with decaffeinated versions or with roasted dandelion root instead of coffee. You can obtain dried roasted dandelion root from good healthfood shops. It may sound a bit way out, but it has a very pleasant malted flavour.

Tea

The British are famous for their tea consumption. Tea, like coffee, contains caffeine, about 50 mg per cup, compared to coffee's 100 mg per strong cup. Tea also contains tannin, which inhibits the absorption of zinc and iron in particular. Excess tea produces the same effects as coffee, and you can also experience a withdrawal headache. Tea can also cause constipation.

By drinking a cup of tea with a meal you can cut down the absorption of iron from vegetarian foods to one-third. Whereas, a glass of fresh orange juice with the same meal would increase iron absorption by two times because of its high vitamin C content. Vegetarian and vegan women need their intake of iron to be readily absorbed. Therefore, drinking anything other than small amounts of weak tea may mean they risk becoming iron deficient.

'Herbal teas' don't count as tea as such. It's really a confusing name. Most herbal teas are free of caffeine and tannin and just consist of a collection of herbs. Unlike regular tea, they can be cleansing and relaxing.

Alcohol

Alcohol is causing far greater problems to our society than most of us realize. It is the drug most seriously abused. Young people tend to begin drinking at an earlier age than was the case in previous generations. Public attitudes to drinking have become much more liberal and gradually alcohol has become widely socially accepted, without an appreciation of its adverse effects.

A major factor explaining the rise in alcohol consumption appears to be the decline in the real price of alcohol. It's not alcohol itself that has gone down in price, but the amount of work necessary to earn the cost of a drink.

Before I go any further I must state that I am not addressing alcoholics as such in this section but 'social drinkers'; those who like to have a few drinks, two or three times a week, can be jeopardizing their health. Anything above the national average for women, that is one glass of wine or half a pint of beer or one sherry or vermouth per day, means running some degree of health risk. Men consume on average three times this amount, and are recommended to halve it.

Alcohol in excess destroys body tissue over the years, and can cause or contribute to many diseases. For example, cardiovascular diseases, digestive disorders, inflammation and ulceration of the lining of the digestive tract, liver disease, brain degeneration, miscarriages, damage to unborn children and malnutrition, are some of the conditions associated with the long-term use of alcohol. In particular, certain vitamins and minerals are destroyed or lost from the body, including vitamin B1, thiamin, magnesium, zinc, vitamin B6, pyridoxine, calcium and vitamin D. All of these nutrients are particularly important to PMS sufferers, as you will see in Chapter 14.

As most of these conditions come on gradually, we often don't see the real dangers of alcohol. There is no impact like that of an accident, or the drama of an ambulance arriving to carry you off. But instead, there is a slow process of destruction which conveniently escapes our awareness.

Amongst those PMS sufferers who like a regular drink are those who increase their consumption considerably before their period. If this happens to you, then you will be well aware of the social problems that go with it, such as mood swings and personality changes. When this occurs others around become affected, and relationships may be strained at home and at work. It is a fact that one-third of the divorce petitions cite alcohol as a contributory factor and one-third of child abuse cases are linked to heavy drinking by a parent. Local courtrooms are always having to deal with people who committed offences whilst under the influence of alcohol. Offences that might never have been committed, were it not for that 'one for the road'!

Old habits die hard

The type of food you eat is usually determined by you. However, there are many other factors that influence your 'preferences' through your life. The two main influential factors are:

1   Your parents, who introduce you to your initial diet, based on their preferences and their knowledge about diet.

The chances are that you continue to eat many of the foods introduced to you by your parents through your life. Habit patterns are quite hard to change, and a very important factor, of course, is that you've got to want to change them.

2   The exposure to the media which we all have in the form of advertisements on television, in magazines, billboards, etc. Now, the second factor, the power of persuasion via the media, might be highly desirable – if it was good food that was being promoted. If the media were dedicated to educating the public about a good, wholesome, nutritious diet, a more valuable asset we could not wish for! In reality they are there to persuade

us, on behalf of the food industry, that fast foods, processed foods, or convenience foods, call them what you will, are desirable. They would have us believe that coffee is sexy and that we should switch to cola-based drinks for energy.

Rather than being a help educationally, they are often a great hindrance. Considering how much television we watch, is it any wonder that the hypnotic powers of the media begin to affect many of us, who would otherwise be influenced by common sense and our own good judgement?

Take one positive step at a time

I am sorry to bombard you with so many depressing facts all at once. We the consumers definitely need more information about the food we eat and the environmental factors we are subjected to.

Probably the first step towards reversing the effects of the twentieth century on your body is for you to acknowledge the value of that body if you haven't already done so. After all, we only have one body to last us through a lifetime, so it's important to treat it with respect.

It's up to you how often you expose your body to alcohol, cigarettes, drugs and additives, and how physically fit you keep through exercise. Making one change at a time is better than not changing at all. I will be concentrating on how to go about making changes in the Self-Help section of the book, Part Three.

As for environmental pollution, there are now many worthwhile national and local groups running campaigns to help overcome these problems. You will find a list of these in Part Four. If you are concerned about your local situation, you can always contact the government representative for your area for help and advice.

If you have been neglecting your body to some extent, now may be the time to take stock. Don't expect your doctor to piece you back together again when you have fallen apart through 'environmental wear and nutritional tear'!

It's up to each one of us to look after our bodies to the best of our abilities and to treat them as well as any other of our treasured possessions.

12

MEDICAL TREATMENTS

There are now many different treatments for PMS. The last seven years in particular have seen a flourish of medical publications reporting the effects of a wide variety of different treatment approaches. Their conflicting findings can create more confusion than clarification for both the sufferer and the doctor.

It is understandably hard to imagine why so many different treatments, both hormonal and non-hormonal, can all appear to be effective in treating one condition. Much of the confusion arises because many of the studies conducted have involved only small numbers of women, and have only been performed once, which is really insufficient to prove anything. Also, some of the studies haven't assessed PMS symptoms thoroughly, or explored the possible side-effects of treatment in detail. As a result, we are still in the dark about how effective many of these preparations are in the treatment of PMS.

That said, if we are careful in interpreting these trials, then they can usefully increase our understanding of PMS, and improve the care we can offer to sufferers, especially those with symptoms which may have proved difficult to treat. In an attempt to put the technical findings in perspective, the rest of this chapter is therefore a brief review of the different hormonal and non-hormonal treatments that have ever been tried in PMS. For the technically minded, the relevant references given in the appendix of the book are on page 262.

HORMONAL TREATMENTS FOR PMS

Many of the hormonal treatments that have been put forward as treatments for PMS have been based on the notion that PMS was due to a lack of a particular hormone. Research of the last ten years has, as we have already seen, laid that idea firmly to rest. Even so, some of the more powerful hormonal preparations have been shown to be effective. How could this be? The production of true pre-menstrual symptoms is undoubtedly linked to the normal hormonal cycle. Any treatment that abolishes or suppresses normal hormone production by the ovaries will alter pre-menstrual symptoms for the better, especially if the symptoms are severe to start with. The difficulty with using these types of treatments is that they can produce considerable side-effects, both in the short and long term.

Coming off hormonal preparations may not be easy as they rarely correct the underlying reasons for pre-menstrual symptoms, and the symptoms are likely to return with a vengeance when you stop taking them. Additionally, they are often very expensive. On balance, there seems little justification for using many hormonal products, though we appreciate they may occasionally be useful for individual patients.

PROGESTERONE PREPARATIONS

Progesterone is one of the two main hormones produced by the ovaries. It was once believed that deficiency of this hormone was the cause of PMS, but this is now known not to be the case.

Progesterone pessaries (Cyclogest)

Progesterone, in the form of a pessary inserted into the vagina, has been one of the most popular treatments for PMS. However, seven different scientific studies showed no evidence of any benefit. The latest of these studies by Dr Freeman and colleagues from the University of Pennsylvania involved 168 women. Those who were given progesterone showed no benefit when compared with women who took a placebo (inactive agent). The progesterone which is normally given for 10 to 14 days before the onset of menstruation can no longer be considered as an effective treatment for PMS.

Progesterone tablets

The natural hormone, progesterone, is not active by mouth. Thus for oral preparations synthetic progesterones, known as progestagens, need to be given. Dydrogesterone is one such synthetic progestagen that has been tried in PMS. It has shown modest success in two out of four trials, when compared with placebos. It may also be effective for painful periods and endometriosis, and is particularly suited for women who have PMS and one or both of these conditions together.

Norethisterone is another synthetic progesterone used in the treatment of PMS, though it has not been subjected to much scientific scrutiny. It is effective in the treatment of heavy periods, or delays periods that occur too frequently, and is again best reserved for women who have these problems in addition to PMS.

THE ORAL CONTRACEPTIVE PILL

There are many different types of Pill. Since they were first used in the 1960s, the dosage of oestrogen and progesterone that they contain has fallen dramatically, and with it the risk of side-effects.

The Pill has a variable effect on PMS. In some women it may make it worse, and in others it may improve it; in many it makes little or no difference. It cannot be considered a routine treatment for PMS, but it may be worth trying in women with mild to moderate PMS who require this type of contraception. It should be noted that the Pill can aggravate migraine headaches, and cause an increase in blood pressure in some sensitive women. Women who are overweight, smoke or who have high blood pressure probably should not consider the Pill as an option anyway.

OESTROGEN PREPARATIONS

Oestrogen can come in forms other than the oral contraceptive pill and some of these have been tried in PMS.

Oestrogen implants which are inserted under the skin of the abdomen by a small operation under local anaesthetic have been popularized by Mr John Studd from King's College Hospital, London. He and his colleagues have found them to be highly effective in the treatment of PMS, but they cannot be used long-term because of side-effects, and because the body adapts to the artificially high levels of oestrogen.

Oestrogen given in the form of a patch which slowly releases the hormone into the bloodstream is an elegant and more gentle way of administering this hormone. This may also be an effective treatment for PMS, but is best reserved for women who are approaching the menopause.

When taking oestrogen, you will also need to take progesterone in order to maintain your monthly bleed, unless you have had a hysterectomy.

TESTOSTERONE – THE MALE HORMONE

It may surprise you to know that this hormone, in the form of an implant, has been tried in the treatment of PMS, with some benefit for depressive symptoms but not for physical complaints. It is not a routine treatment.

OTHER HORMONE-RELATED PREPARATIONS

There are a number of other powerful drugs which influence hormone metabolism that have been used in PMS. They can often produce side-effects and are best reserved for special situations.

Danazol:

This drug blocks or interferes with the action of many sex hormones. It can be useful in situations where there is a hormone excess, but anything other than small doses can lead to side-effects, including excessive hair growth, deepening of the voice and other changes. Low doses can be effective in PMS, and are also useful in the treatment of endometriosis, heavy periods and pre-menstrual breast tenderness, if all else fails.

Bromocriptine:

This is another powerful drug which blocks the effect of the hormone, pro-lactin, from the pituitary gland. It too can be used for pre-menstrual breast tenderness, and in small doses to help PMS, but again it is not suitable for long-term treatment of PMS.

Others

Certain drugs can treat PMS very successfully, by switching off the pituitary gland's stimulus to the ovaries. In this way the ovaries go into 'retirement' and a false menopause is achieved. This abolishes the pre-menstrual symptoms, but not surprisingly replaces them with hot flushes and the risk of osteoporosis. This is really a last-ditch treatment, and has no place for the majority of sufferers.

DRUG TREATMENTS FOR PMS

Just as almost every kind of hormonal treatment has been used in the treatment of PMS, so has almost every type of drug been tried. Many of these treatments have not established themselves as routine therapies.

Diuretics (water tablets)

This in the past has been a popular treatment, particularly in the treatment of pre-menstrual fluid retention and breast tenderness. Many older types of diuretics are effective in the short term, but lead to a loss of the important minerals, magnesium and potassium. Magnesium may be low in some 50 per cent of women with PMS, so further losses would not be desirable. Diuretics are not expected to help mood changes. One type of diuretic, called Spironolactone, has been shown to be moderately helpful, but its manufacturer no longer recommends it for long-term use in young patients.

Most of the symptoms of fluid retention should respond to a diet that is low in sodium (salt) and, if necessary, restricted in calories.

Pain-killers

These can be useful for painful periods, migraine and other headaches that occur just before or with the period. One type of pain-killer, available on prescription only, is Mefenamic acid, which when taken for two weeks before the onset of menstruation may help PMS symptoms. If you experience very painful periods you should ask your doctor for a gynaecological assessment.

Anti-depressants

This type of drug has never been used much in the treatment of PMS. Some of the newer types of anti-depressants may, however, be temporarily helpful in the treatment of severe pre-menstrual depression, especially if you are experiencing suicidal feelings.

Sleeping tablets, sedatives and anti-anxiety drugs

The over-use of these drugs by the medical profession has been of particular concern to many patients over the last 30 years. They have no role in the treatment of PMS, except perhaps occasionally for short-term use in the treatment of anxiety or insomnia. One type of anti-anxiety drug, Buspirone, has shown some benefit in one small trial in PMS. The method of assessing its benefit was, however, limited.

All of these types of drugs should be used with great caution, if at all, and patients should always be given advice about other measures to limit or control anxiety.

Antibiotics

Extraordinary as it may seem, there has even been a trial of antibiotics in PMS! This involved giving an old, established antibiotic, Doxycycline, to a group of women aged 25 to 35 years, 77 per cent of whom also had evidence of vaginal infection. The reduction in PMS symptoms was accompanied by a clearance of the associated vaginal infection. Other doctors have related PMS to vaginal infection with *Candida albicans*, a yeast that causes thrush. The message here is simple. If there is evidence of vaginal or other infection, then treat it. In doing so one may help PMS as well.

Other treatments

Many other treatments have been reported as being tried in PMS, including lithium (a drug used to treat certain mental illnesses). Three studies showed no benefit; Naltrexone (a drug used to counteract the side-effects of morphine) showed benefit in one small study when given at mid-cycle; and an anti-allergy treatment showed benefit in one study, especially in those with an allergic tendency.

Let me finish this chapter with a few conclusions which I hope will help you make sense of the situation.
1. Do not accept a treatment as proven to be effective unless it has shown benefit in at least two studies.
2. Powerful hormone and drug treatments probably are effective, but at the cost of significant short- or long-term side-effects. They are best reserved as a last resort.
3. All treatments can, and should ideally always, be combined with self-help and nutritional treatments.
4. Many of the above treatments are best suited to those women who have

PMS with associated problems, including period pains, vaginal infection, gynaecological problems, or who are approaching menopause.

5. Many experts now agree that a nutritional approach to PMS is indeed the best first-line treatment. As the nutritional approach is so effective, there will usually be no need to make use of hormonal and drug treatments.

13

NUTRITIONAL TREATMENTS

Thankfully, in the last few years nutritional treatments for PMS have been taken more seriously. This has come about because of the wider appreciation that many existing medical treatments are not as effective as was once thought and often produce undesirable side-effects, whereas research has shown the value of some nutritional preparations which, as a rule, have no side-effects.

A wide variety of nutritional products have been assessed for PMS, including individual vitamins and minerals, combinations of vitamins and minerals, and evening primrose oil, which contains some specialized fats with vitamin-like qualities. The reason why most of these nutrients were tried in the first place was because of the way in which they are known to influence the function of either hormones or the chemistry of the brain and nervous system, and thus, potentially, the body's metabolism, for the better. But how effective are they?

VITAMIN B6 (PYRIDOXINE)

This has been the most popular nutritional preparation for PMS in years past. Studies conducted in the UK, the Netherlands and Australia have, surprisingly, not found that deficiency of this vitamin is a particular feature of women with PMS, though mild deficiency is quite common in people experiencing anxiety, depression and other mental symptoms. However, it is now known that vitamin B6 influences the action of the hormone oestrogen in the body, as well as being important in the normal function of the nervous system and the processing of protein-rich foods.

At least 13 studies comparing placebo tablets with different doses of vitamin B6, ranging from 50 to 500 mg per day, have been performed. The results are very mixed and a group of Dutch experts who reviewed all of these studies concluded that there was little evidence to support its use. This is perhaps a rather harsh judgement as it may still have a modest beneficial effect for some, and its cheapness means that it should not be discarded completely. If it is to be taken, then a dose of 100 mg per day, every day of the month, is recommended. If it is going to be effective, then there should be improvement within two months. The evidence points to vitamin B6 being more effective if combined with other nutrients.

VITAMIN E

This has long been a popular supplement since it was shown to prevent miscarriages in pregnant rats! Actual deficiency in humans is exceptionally rare, but vitamin E can influence the body's metabolism of fats, which in turn can influence hormone and nervous system chemistry.

Three studies of vitamin E have been performed, all of which have been conducted in the United States. Two of the three studies showed benefit with, curiously, the most effective dosage being 300 to 400 IU (International Units) per day, rather than a higher dose. This may be because different dosages have different effects on female hormones. Certainly it is worth considering; it may help depressive symptoms the most.

MAGNESIUM

Magnesium has, until recently, been a neglected nutrient. For much of this century it has only been considered worthy for use as a laxative. However, it is known to be essential for muscle, nerve and bone function and structure.

The typical diet of developed civilizations can be low in this nutrient if there is over-reliance on convenience foods; an excellent dietary source is green vegetables. This mundane mineral, severe deficiency of which is only rarely encountered, is proving to be one of the most effective bedside treatments in increasing the rate of survival in those suffering from acute heart attack.

It had been suggested by French workers in the 1970s that a mild lack of magnesium might contribute to anxiety and related symptoms. Dr Guy Abraham, from the United States, together with his colleague, Dr Lubran, was the first to show that many, but not all, women with PMS have evidence of a mild deficit of this mineral – a reduced concentration was found in the red blood cells of sufferers when compared with healthy women. This finding has been confirmed in a number of studies including two of our own, and now is perhaps the most consistent abnormal finding in women with PMS.

Unfortunately, only one trial of magnesium alone has been undertaken, and this was by a group of Italian doctors who administered 375 mg per day of this nutrient for two months. There was a significant rise in the level of magnesium and an accompanying fall in the level of pre-menstrual symptoms reported. This important study deserves repetition. Certainly, magnesium is a very promising preparation. It is particularly useful for constipation – it is interesting to note that severe constipation in young women is associated with quite marked hormonal abnormalities.

Magnesium comes in different forms, the most convenient being a tablet. Liquid preparations and crystals of magnesium sulphate (Epsom Salts) are only really useful as laxatives.

MULTI-VITAMINS

Rather than buy them individually, it would seem tempting to use nutritional supplements that combine several nutrients in one preparation. This idea has its merits. It is known that many individual nutrients interact, requiring the presence of their fellows to function properly, and that when someone is deficient in one nutrient, they are likely to be lacking in others as well.

A number of multi-vitamins, usually with minerals, have found their way on to the marketplace in different countries around the world. Virtually all of these preparations have been used without being assessed scientifically. The only preparation of this type that has been subjected to trials published in proper medical journals is Optivite. This preparation is a comprehensive multi-vitamin and mineral supplement that contains substantial amounts of vitamin B6, other vitamins, magnesium and other minerals. It has been the subject of several open or preliminary trials and, more importantly, it has been assessed in four scientific trials where it has been compared with placebo or 'dummy' tablets. The conclusion of these trials from both the United Kingdom and the United States is that it is an effective treatment for PMS when given over three menstrual cycles. The most effective dosage is six tablets a day, every day throughout the menstrual cycle. The effectiveness of this particular supplement may be enhanced by combining it with dietary modification and also exercise. This has very much been our experience at the WNAS in our many years of using this and other nutritional preparations. Interestingly, there is evidence from one American study that Optivite, when combined with dietary changes, does produce a potentially beneficial effect on the metabolism of female sex hormones.

EVENING PRIMROSE OIL

In the 1980s, evening primrose oil became an increasingly popular supplement, and has been the subject of many trials in PMS and other conditions. The particular attraction of EPO is that this oil is rich in an essential fat called gamma-linolenic acid, low levels of which have been recorded in some women with PMS. This interesting fat, and its chemical relatives, does have some influence on hormone metabolism and many aspects of body health. It seems that some individuals may lack the ability to make sufficient amounts of gamma-linolenic acid from other fats in the diet, such as those provided by sunflower and other vegetable oils. Such individuals are particularly likely to benefit from supplements of EPO. This has been the case in the skin condition eczema, where a lack of these fats appears to influence skin quality.

The evidence from scientific trials shows that EPO may be of particular benefit for pre-menstrual breast tenderness, but may not be so helpful for other symptoms. Like Optivite it is best taken when following a healthy diet, as alcohol and a lack of many other nutrients interferes with this delicate area of body metabolism.

The most effective dose of evening primrose oil is 3 to 4 g per day, usually as six to eight 500 mg capsules taken every day through the menstrual cycle. It needs to be taken for four to six cycles, as breast symptoms can be quite stubborn.

The effectiveness of other plant oil preparations, such as blackcurrant seed, starflower oil or borage oil in PMS, is not known as trials have not been conducted. They cannot therefore be recommended.

SIDE-EFFECTS OF NUTRITIONAL PREPARATIONS

No review of the above supplements is complete without mentioning that all of them can produce side-effects, though these are rare and usually much less serious than those that occur with drug-based preparations.

Very high doses of vitamin B6 (pyridoxine) can produce mild nerve damage, causing numbness or tingling in the hands or feet. This has only definitely been described at doses of 500 mg or more per day, as a single nutrient, on a regular basis. Optivite at the effective dosage of six tablets per day provides 300 mg per day of pyridoxine in a slow-release preparation. Nerve damage with this preparation, even at higher doses, has not been reported in any of its numerous trials, nor in the many years of its use, either in the US or the UK.

The main side-effect of magnesium is diarrhoea, which quickly alerts the user to reduce the dose. Magnesium should not be taken by those with poor kidney function, unless under medical supervision, as excessive amounts may accumulate in the body.

Evening primrose oil should not be taken by anyone suffering with epilepsy, as occasionally this condition may be worsened by its use. Again, medical advice should be sought.

All nutritional products may occasionally cause minor symptoms such as nausea, slight abdominal discomfort, diarrhoea or headache. If this occurs they should be stopped for a few days and then tried again at a lower dose. Alternatively, you should obtain some professional advice.

It is unlikely that you will need to take any of these or other nutritional preparations at high or full dosage in the long term. If they prove to be effective, the dose can be reduced, and if not effective, then they should be stopped and a different treatment tried. Some women do find that it is helpful to continue with a modest dose of some supplements, such as vitamin B, Optivite, Femvite (one or two tablets per day) or evening primrose oil (one or two capsules per day) in the longer term. These dosages are safe and reasonable.

We find scientifically based supplements to be a very useful nutritional prop in the short term. Once the symptoms are under control the dosages can be cut back, and very often ex-sufferers can manage with their new diet and exercise alone.

14

NUTRITION AND THE BODY: VITAMINS AND MINERALS, WHAT THEY DO

THE BODY

One thing we have in common is that we all have a body! Our body is nothing more nor less than a highly complicated biochemical machine, the function of which, like any engine, is dependent up on the quality of its food or fuel supply. The body is composed of many different organs and tissues which have important and essential functions and interactions. For example, if you want to move your arm, a tiny electrical message passes from the brain, through the nervous system and down the nerves to the muscles in your arm, which then contract. The degree of stretch or tension in a muscle is relayed, via other nerves, back to the brain, so that the muscle does not over-, or under-stretch in performing the movement that you originally intended.

There are factors that affect the healthy function of nerves, muscles and all other parts of the body. *Firstly, you need to inherit a good and healthy metabolism.* The thousands of chemical processes that take place within each and every cell are mainly determined by the genetic material in the centre of the nucleus of the cell. This genetic material is a master plan or blueprint. It holds the key to which chemical reactions need to take place in order for that cell to function. It determines whether a cell is a muscle cell, nerve cell, skin cell, red blood cell, or any other type of cell. Almost everyone has healthy genes, and thus the possibility for their body to be completely healthy and function efficiently. However, there may be subtle individual variations in metabolism, which determine the strengths and weaknesses of one's physical constitution. This may explain why some people are sensitive to some types of dietary change or nutritional deficiencies, and others are not – why some women may develop Pre-Menstrual Syndrome, and others, despite eating an 'unhealthy' diet, may not.

Secondly, some disease states can lead to the development of PMS.

Finally, and most importantly, there must be a healthy diet, giving an adequate supply of those nutrients necessary for the normal functioning of each individual cell. A lack of any one nutrient leads to changes in the cell's metabolism, which in turn will result in changes in the individual's health.

THE DIET

Many people, when they hear the word diet, think of a weight-reducing or slimming diet. The word diet simply refers to the type of food that a person is eating. Every one of us has a diet of some kind, unless we are starving to death. Certain components of a diet are essential, and many of these terms may be familiar to you. The essential nutrients include proteins, fats, carbohydrates, fibre, water, vitamins, minerals and essential fatty acids. Other factors that are also essential for life include a certain degree of heat and light. First, we should have a brief word about what each of these nutrients does, and why they are essential.

Proteins. These are the building blocks of a body. A protein is in fact a group of smaller building blocks called amino acids, which in turn are composed of individual chemicals. Proteins are found in large quantities in tissue such as muscle, skin and bone. In these tissues protein serves a mainly structural function, contributing to the shape of the body, and its ability to move. Other proteins perform highly specialized functions, such as hormones which influence metabolism, and antibodies which help to fight infection.

We all make our own proteins, mainly in the liver, but to do this, must have a steady supply, from our diet, of amino acids, which are in turn derived from the proteins that we eat. Thus, it is essential for us to eat good-quality proteins, such as fish, eggs, nuts, seeds, wholegrains, peas, beans and lentils and lean additive-free meat. A lack of protein in the diet would lead to loss of muscle function and performance, and to a multitude of changes in the body's metabolism.

Fats. These are providers of energy, and, apart from two essential fats (discussed below), are really not necessary to the body at all. However, every type of protein contains some fat, whether it is an animal or vegetable source of protein. This fat can be burnt by the body to provide energy. The liver and muscle cells in particular can make substantial use of fats in this way. Fats also provide a structural role in forming the walls of each individual cell.

The specialized fat, cholesterol, is used to form the male and female hormones, vitamin D and other important hormones in the body. Our bodies can usually make twice as much cholesterol as we eat. So often a raised level of cholesterol in the blood is caused not by eating too much cholesterol, but a faulty metabolism and a high-fat, high-sugar diet. We certainly do not need to increase our intake of animal fats, as I'm sure you will appreciate after reading the section on fats in Chapter 11, page 103.

Essential fatty acids. These are specialized fats, whose importance is becoming increasingly realized. There are two essential fatty acids, linoleic and linolenic acid. As their names suggest, they are very similar in chemical structure, and both of them are of the polyunsaturated type (i.e. not cholesterol-forming). These perform two main roles. First, they are a structural component of the walls of many cells, and thus contribute to the cellular skeleton of the body. Secondly, these two essential fatty acids can be transformed into a wide variety of different chemical compounds which appear to play a part in hormone function and inflammation. Disturbance in the metabolism of these essential fatty acids has been described in one group of women with PMS. However, this has not been confirmed by a second study. Even so, supplements of evening primrose oil, Efamol, have been shown to be effective in the treatment of pre-menstrual breast tenderness, as well as in the skin condition, eczema. It remains to be seen what role these nutrients play in PMS-causation.

Carbohydrates. Carbohydrates, too, are a source of energy. They can be divided into two categories: simple and complex. Simple ones include glucose, fructose (fruit sugar), sucrose (ordinary or table sugar), and lactose (milk sugar). Glucose and fructose are in fact the simplest sugars, consisting of only one type of sugar each. Sucrose and lactose, on the other hand, contain two different types of sugar joined together, and thus are sometimes known as di-saccharides (two sugars).

125

Polysaccharides (literally, many sugars), are the 'complex' carbohydrates most usually found in vegetables. These consist of many interlinked sugar sub-units, and in order for them to be used by the body, they must be broken down into simple, single-sugar units by the digestive processes in the gut. Vegetables, wholegrains, nuts and seeds are high in these complex carbohydrates.

The refining of sugar cane and sugar beet to make table sugar, sucrose, results in a loss of some of these complex carbohydrates, and a loss in the vitamins, minerals and fibre present in the original plant. When we eat these carbohydrates they are converted by the digestive processes and the body's metabolism to the simple sugar, glucose, which is a major form of energy in the body. Glucose is essential for the brain, as it can only use this form of fuel. However, one does not have to eat glucose or sucrose, table sugar, in order for the brain and nervous system to have an adequate supply: the liver can make glucose from fats or proteins, as well as from other types of sugars, so while glucose is essential for life, it is a mistake to believe we have to add it to the diet. However, some form of carbohydrate, preferably the complex or unrefined carbohydrates, are necessary for an adequate supply of energy.

Fibre. Fibre is the undigestible carbohydrate residues found in food. Natural or unprocessed foods are usually high in fibre and include wholegrains, nuts, seeds and fruit. Some types of carbohydrate cannot be digested by the human body, and so pass through the stomach and digestive tract to the large bowel. Here, fibre absorbs water and other waste materials, and forms our waste product, faeces. A lack of fibre in the diet often leads to constipation, but it is now realized that fibre has other important functions. Lack of fibre is also associated with such conditions as gallstones, varicose veins, obesity, heart disease and diabetes. Of particular relevance is the fact that fibre binds with cholesterol and hormones that are secreted by the liver into the gut. A high-fibre diet may help in expulsion of excessive quantities of cholesterol and unwanted female sex hormones, but more of this later.

Water. This is of course essential for health. Our bodies are composed of 60–70 per cent water, and many bodily functions are dependent upon water. Water is necessary for vitamins, minerals and other chemicals to dissolve in. The amount of urine produced by the kidneys is largely dependent upon the amount of water consumed. An adequate water intake is necessary to clear waste materials through the kidneys, and to allow normal metabolic processes to take place. Water can sometimes be retained by the body, particularly if the intake of salt (sodium) is high. Both salt and water need to be cleared by the kidneys, and their ability to do this may vary from individual to individual. Women who have suffered with pre-menstrual water retention for years, have managed to overcome the condition by making changes to their diet and taking additional supplements.

VITAMINS

Vitamins are the best-known essential nutrient. Indeed, their name was derived from the term 'vital amines' (a type of chemical). They are named as letters of the alphabet, A, B, C, D, E, and K, and members of the B group are further subdivided by numbers into vitamins B1, 2, 3, 5, 6, 12 and Folic acid. The vitamins themselves, as a whole, are divided into two groups. The water-soluble vitamins include members of the vitamin B complex and vitamin C, and the fat-soluble group includes vitamins A, D, E and K.

Vitamins are vital but only in tiny or trace amounts, unlike proteins, carbohydrates and fats, which are necessary in substantial quantities. These trace amounts of vitamins help modify and control essential cellular reactions. Each vitamin which has particular relevance to the development of pre-menstrual symptoms is described in more detail below.

Vitamin A. This comes in two types : retinol (animal-derived), and beta-carotene (vegetable-derived). Deficiency of vitamin A is very rare indeed, and usually only occurs with a grossly inadequate diet or with severe impairment of digestive function. A lack of vitamin A usually results in an impairment of vision at night, or when in the dark. If deficiencies continue, there are further eye, as well as skin changes.

Recently, a number of studies have demonstrated that either poor intakes of vitamin A, or low blood levels, especially of beta-carotene, are associated with a future increased risk of certain types of cancer, including lung cancer. High intakes of fruit and vegetables rich in vitamin A may thus prove to have a cancer-protective effect.

Vitamin B complex. This is a group of several vitamins with certain things in common. They are all water-soluble, their metabolisms are often inter-related, and they are frequently found together in the same types of foods. Factors that lead to deficiency often, but not always, produce a deficiency of several of the vitamins in this group. Deficiency very often produces mental changes which have many similarities with those of Pre-Menstrual Syndrome.

127

Vitamin B1, Thiamin, is essential for the normal metabolism of sugar. Requirements for this vitamin increase if the diet is high in sugar, refined carbohydrates, and alcohol. Some subtstances which destroy thiamin are found in tea, coffee and raw fish. Good sources of this vitamin are wholegrains, most meats (preferably additive-free or organic) and beans. Any food that is refined is usually quite substantially depleted in thiamin. A lack of thiamin results in anxiety, depression, irritability, changes in behaviour, aggressiveness and loss of memory.

Vitamin B2, Riboflavin, is required for the metabolism of proteins, fats and carbohydrates, particularly in the liver. Deficiency rarely occurs as this vitamin is present in such a wide range of foods, including milk, cheese, meat, fish and some vegetables. Deficiency does not usually produce any mental symptoms. However, vitamin B2 is necessary for the metabolism of vitamin B6 (pyridoxine).

Vitamin B3, Nicotinic Acid or Nicotinamide, is essential for the metabolism of carbohydrates and the release of energy from them. It is found in brown rice, wheatgerm, peanuts and liver. Deficiency rarely occurs unless there is a very poor diet or a high intake of alcohol. In deficiency states, dry scaling and redness appear in light exposed areas, particularly the backs of hands, face, neck and top of the chest. Mental deterioration and diarrhoea are also features, but severe deficiency is very rare. Requirements are between 12 and 15 mg a day. B3 is present in yeast, liver, meat, poultry, legumes, wheat flour and corn. Eggs and milk contain a niacin equivalent called tryptophan.

Vitamin B6 comes in three different varieties: pyridoxine, pyridoxal and pyridoxamine. Pyridoxine is the sort normally used in vitamin supplements, and is also generally used in the treatment of Pre-Menstrual Syndrome. Vitamin B6 requires a supply of vitamin B2 – riboflavin – and magnesium before it is chemically active. Vitamin B6 plays a crucial role in the metabolism of proteins and in the normal metabolism of certain chemicals involved in the brain that control mood and behaviour. Good sources of vitamin B6 include most animal and vegetable proteins, especially fish, egg yolk, wholegrain cereals, nuts and seeds. Bananas, avocados, meat and some green leafy vegetables are also high in this nutrient. A McDonald's Big Mac hamburger contains only 0.02 mg of pyridoxine, which is only 1–2 per cent of that required per day. In fact, it does not contain enough vitamin B6 for the metabolism of the protein contained in the hamburger! Thus a diet containing a significant quantity of such depleted foods, will undoubtedly lead to vitamin B6 deficiency. Other factors which

128

seem to affect it adversely include alcohol and smoking. Deficiency of vitamin B6 produces anxiety, depression, loss of sense of responsibility and insomnia.

Some 15 per cent of women of child-bearing age in the UK have been found to have laboratory evidence of mild vitamin B6 deficiency.

Vitamin B12 and Folic acid. These two types of vitamin B are very important, particularly for the formation of blood and the functioning of nerves. Deficiencies tend to be rare. Vitamin B12 is found almost exclusively in animal produce, especially meat. Long-term vegetarians can be at risk of deficiency unless they take supplements.

Lack of Folic acid can occur from a poor diet, especially if you do not consume plenty of green, leafy vegetables. The name Folic acid comes from foliage, a major source of this important nutrient.

Increased requirements of vitamin B12 and Folic acid occur during pregnancy. Supplements of Folic acid are often given during pregnancy and vitamin B12 should be given to pregnant and breast-feeding mothers if they have been long-term strict vegetarians.

Vitamin C. Almost everyone knows that vitamin C deficiency causes scurvy, and we all think of scurvy as a disease of sailors in the past, and perhaps the extreme deprivation of Victorian times. Indeed, vitamin C deficiency is quite rare but still does occur in some elderly folk. However, in modern times, some people are at risk of having a lower level of vitamin C than is desirable for health. Smoking, in particular, reduces vitamin C levels substantially. The recommended daily intake in this country is only some 40 mg per day, about the amount in an apple.

The increased intake of vitamin C may improve certain aspects of metabolism. In particular, the absorption of iron is helped by the presence of vitamin C in the food. Vitamin C is also necessary for the normal production of sex hormones and the breakdown of excess cholesterol in the body.

Deficiency of vitamin C produces depression, low energy and hypochondria, a condition in which the victim imagines he or she has a variety of different illnesses and complaints. Sometimes, an early sign of vitamin C deficiency is the presence of small pinpoint bruises under the tongue. This seems to be particularly common in smokers.

Vitamin E. Vitamin E is also known as tocopherol, from the Greek words meaning 'child-bearing'. The name is given because rats deprived of vitamin E are unable to bear healthy offspring. Like vitamin C deficiency, vitamin E deficiency is also rare. There are no obvious symptoms or signs of its deficiency, but lack of it is likely to be caused by long-standing digestive problems. Supplements of vitamin E have also been used to treat Pre-Menstrual Syndrome and breast tenderness with some success. It is probable that extra vitamin E is not correcting a deficiency, but improving some aspect of metabolism. The normal daily requirements are in the region of 8–10 mg, which can usually be obtained from dietary sources such as vegetable oils, nuts, green vegetables, eggs and dairy produce.

Like vitamin A, recent evidence has appeared to suggest that low levels of vitamin E in women may be associated with an increased risk of breast cancer in later years. Again, ensuring a good intake of foods rich in such a vitamin may help you achieve good health, not only today, but also for your future tomorrows.

Vitamin D. Vitamin D is necessary for normal healthy bones and teeth. Most of us make adequate vitamin D if our skin is exposed to sunlight. Some can also be provided by the diet as in cod liver oil and dairy produce. Margarine in this country has vitamin D as well as vitamin A added to it. Vitamin D helps the body's absorption of calcium from the diet. In particular, it assists in the normal uptake of calcium into the bones and teeth to make them strong. Too much vitamin D can be toxic, more than 400 international units per day should not be consumed without medical advice.

MINERALS

Minerals are essential components, and may be divided into two types. First there are those minerals which are required in substantial bulk quantities. These include calcium, phosphorus, magnesium, sodium and potassium. They play a large part in the formation of bones and cells. Some other minerals are required in only small amounts and are called trace elements. These include iron, zinc, copper, chromium, selenium and a variety of others. Their main function, like many vitamins, is to help stimulate the complex chemical reactions that take place in the body. A lack of these trace elements, rather like a lack of vitamins, can have a very wide-ranging dire effect upon the body's metabolism. Often the chemical reactions that control energy level and mood, as well as hormone function, can be adversely influenced.

Calcium and Phosphorus. These two minerals often go together, particularly in bones and teeth. It is important to have a good balance of calcium and phosphorus in the diet and the ratio of 2:1 is often recommended. Too much phosphorus will block the absorption of calcium and too much calcium will block the absorption of phosphorus. It is very rare that our diets lack phosphorus, but a lack of calcium is not so uncommon. Good sources of calcium include all dairy products, many nuts, especially Brazils and almonds, bony fish such as sardines, sprats and whitebait, beans, peas, lentils, wholegrains and some green vegetables, especially watercress. In fact, you do not have to eat dairy produce to get an adequate source of calcium but the rest of your diet must be very well balanced indeed. Recommended intakes vary between 700 mg and 1300 mg per day. The absorption of calcium is blocked by bran. Bran contains phytic acid, a substance that combines with calcium, preventing its absorption. (Indian chapattis may also have a similar effect.)

Many convenience foods contain phosphates in the form of food additives: soft drinks, including the low-calorie (kj) variety, are notoriously high in phosphate. As a high level interferes with calcium or magnesium balance, these products should be avoided as much as possible.

Magnesium. Magnesium seems to be a particularly important mineral as far as PMS is concerned. Firstly, magnesium, like calcium, is essential for healthy bones as well as nerves and muscles. Lack of magnesium produces poor appetite, nausea, apathy, weakness, tiredness, mood changes and muscle cramps. Good sources of magnesium include most wholefoods, e.g. wholegrains, beans, peas, lentils, nuts, seeds and green vegetables. Water, particularly some bottled waters and tap water from a hard water area, can contain substantial quantities of this mineral, too.

In 1981 Dr Guy Abraham showed that a low level of magnesium was commonly found in women with PMS. Most of the magnesium is inside cells where it is busily involved in chemical reactions. Hence it is the level of magnesium inside the cells – red blood cell magnesium – and not the magnesium in the water compartment of blood that is often low. We repeated his work on magnesium deficiency in 105 women with PMS and showed that some 45 per cent of women had evidence of magnesium deficiency. We don't know precisely how important this deficiency is, but it seems likely that it has an effect on our mental function, the control of the levels of blood sugar and energy, and also the metabolism of some hormones. Unfortunately, there may be no obvious physical signs of magnesium deficiency and so it is easily missed.

Like calcium, requirements increase substantially during pregnancy and while breast-feeding, and it is often after a pregnancy and breast-feeding that the worst cases of magnesium deficiency are seen. This may well explain why some women's pre-menstrual problems begin shortly after childbirth. Indeed, magnesium deficiency is also associated with some other problems such as poor contractions of the womb during labour,

131

elevated blood pressure during pregnancy and pre-eclamptic toxaemia. These conditions can be treated by injections of magnesium, an approach often used in the US, but not so much in the UK.

It is important that women with PMS consume a diet rich in magnesium. Sometimes your doctor can arrange for a simple red cell magnesium test to be performed at the local hospital and this may serve as a guide to the use of magnesium supplements.

Sodium and Potassium. These two minerals form an interesting pair. Both sodium and potassium are essential for the normal functioning of almost all cells in the body, particularly nerves and muscles. Since the use of more convenience foods, our diets have had markedly increased levels of sodium. Although table salt and sea salt (both are sodium chloride) represent a substantial source of sodium in our diets, most of the sodium we consume is found in convenience and other tinned, frozen or prepared foods.

Potassium is found mainly in fruit and vegetables, particularly tomatoes, bananas, figs, citrus fruits and almost all green leafy vegetables. Most of the potassium is found inside the cells rather like magnesium, and most of the sodium is found outside the cells. It is the balance of sodium and potassium that is important. This balance has to be maintained: if it is not, then the body may retain water. Too much sodium in the diet is indeed the commonest cause of fluid retention in many women, particularly in the week or so before the start of a period.

Water tablets, known as diuretics, will get rid of this excess fluid retention, but after a while the system gets used to them and the fluid retention returns, sometimes even worse than before. As well as getting rid of the excess water in the body, diuretics have the effect of ridding the body of useful potassium and magnesium, which makes the situation worse.

The answer: reduce sodium intake in the diet by not having salt at the table, not using it in the cooking, and avoiding any salty foods. It is difficult, on the contrary, to consume too much potassium, and problems only arise in patients with kidney disease.

Iron. Iron is one of the most important trace minerals. We all know that iron is necessary for healthy blood and a lack of it results in anaemia. Iron is necessary for the formation of the blood pigment haemoglobin. What is not widely appreciated is that iron is also found in high concentrations in muscles and in the brain. It is necessary for the uptake of energy by muscles as well as for certain aspects of mental function in the normal brain. Iron deficiency is probably the most common deficiency in the world. Women, of course, have increased needs for iron because of their monthly blood-loss due to menstruation. Women who have heavy periods, such as those using the coil, often have increased requirements.

Good sources of iron include wholefoods such as peas, beans, lentils, nuts, seeds and wholegrains, eggs, meat and to a lesser extent fish. The iron from animal sources is easily absorbed, whereas iron from vegetarian sources may not be so well absorbed, particularly if tea and coffee are consumed at the same meal. Vitamin C in the diet may greatly assist the absorption of iron from vegetarian foods.

The features of iron deficiency include fatigue, tiredness, digestive problems, poor quality nails, and recurrent infections, especially thrush. Although 15 per cent of women of child-bearing age are at risk of developing these problems due to iron deficiency, only one-quarter of these women will actually be anaemic. This means that to detect iron deficiency the doctor must not just measure the haemoglobin level but actually measure the level of iron in the blood for a protein associated with iron called ferritin. If you think you are iron deficient *don't* rely upon your own doctor just doing a test to see if you are anaemic. The iron level or ferritin level must be measured and any deficiency treated. Of course, the most sensible thing to do is to eat a well-balanced diet and avoid the factors that can lead to iron-deficiency. It is a good idea not to drink tea or coffee immediately after meals, but only drink it two hours before or after eating.

Any women with continually heavy periods should have this problem looked into. In fact iron deficiency can even be a cause of heavy periods. Now you can see how important a trace mineral can be!

Zinc. Zinc, like iron, affects many different aspects of metabolism, particularly those involved in growth, and resistance to infection. It is necessary for healthy skin, normal hormone production and normal mental function. Adequate quantities can be obtained from wholegrains, nuts, peas, beans, lentils and meat. Like iron, zinc absorption may be blocked by tea and coffee as the tannin from the drink binds with it, preventing its absorption. You know what strong tea can do to the inside of a white teacup – imagine what it does to the inside of your intestines!

Anyone regularly consuming substantial quantities of alcohol, i.e. more than two glasses of wine or a pint of beer per day, is at risk of developing zinc as well as vitamin B deficiencies. Women on the Pill can have lower levels of zinc, as can those who make long-term use of diuretics – water pills. Often a useful clue to a lack of zinc is poor quality skin such as excessively dry or greasy facial skin, particularly at the sides of the nose. Eczema, acne and psoriasis may also suggest a deficiency of this important mineral. Interestingly, the metabolism of zinc and vitamin B6 are closely related, which explains why the skin changes produced by these two deficiencies can have a similar appearance.

Chromium. Chromium is a fascinating trace mineral. Only minute quantities are required: a lifetime's supply of chromium only weighs one-sixth of an ounce (5 g), and the body will only use 1 per cent of that. Yet even this tiny amount of chromium plays a crucial part in the control of blood sugar metabolism. A lack of chromium can lead to poor blood-sugar control, which in turn can lead to fluctuating energy levels and the dreaded sugar cravings. They are a classic feature of some women's pre-menstrual symptoms, as we have seen.

In severe cases of chromium deficiency a diabetes-like state can occur, particularly in older people. Chromium supplements can have a marked effect in this situation, and can also help improve poor blood-sugar control

VITAMINS AND MINERALS – DO YOU LACK THEM?

	Food Sources	What They Do
Vitamin B6	Meat, fish, nuts, bananas, avocados, wholegrains.	Essential in the metabolism of protein and the amino acids that control mood and behaviour. Affects hormone metabolism.
Vitamin B1 Thiamin	Meat, fish, nuts, wholegrains and fortified breakfast cereals.	Essential in the metabolism of sugar, especially in nerves and muscles.
Vitamin C Ascorbic acid	Any fresh fruits and vegetables.	Involved in healing, repair of tissues and production of some hormones.
Iron	Meat, wholegrains, nuts, eggs and fortified breakfast cereals.	Essential to make blood – haemoglobin. Many other tissues need iron for energy reactions.
Zinc	Meat, wholegrains, nuts, peas, beans, lentils.	Essential for normal growth, mental function, hormone production and resistance to infection.
Magnesium	Green vegetables, wholegrains, Brazil and almond nuts, many other non-junk foods.	Essential for sugar and energy metabolism, needed for healthy nerves and muscles.

in people who are not diabetics. Eating large quantities of carbohydrates such as table sugar increases the loss of chromium in the urine. There are no outward signs of chromium deficiency, unless you count the presence of old sweet wrappers in the bottom of your handbag! We have seen no end of 'little miracles' as a result of increasing chromium intake: it really is very useful in helping to control the sugar cravings. Eating a sensible diet is the best way to prevent chromium deficiency. Foods which contain a good quantity of chromium are green vegetables, root vegetables, eggs, scallops, shrimps, rye and some fruit.

That ends all you really need to know about vitamins and minerals. It may be useful to summarize this vital information and indicate how you can recognize any deficiencies.

Deficiencies

Who is at Risk	Symptoms	Visible Signs
Women, especially smokers, 'junk-eaters'.	Depression, anxiety, insomnia, loss of responsibility.	Dry/greasy facial skin, cracking at corners of the mouth.
Alcohol consumers, women on the Pill, breast-feeding mothers, high consumers of sugar.	Depression, anxiety, poor appetite, nausea, personality change.	None usually! Heart, nerve and muscle problems if severe.
Smokers particularly.	Lethargy, depression hypochondriasis (imagined illnesses).	Easy bruising, look for small pinpoint bruises under the tongue.
Women who have heavy periods (e.g. coil users), vegetarians, especially if tea or coffee drinkers, women with recurrent thrush.	Fatigue, poor energy, depression, poor digestion, sore tongue, cracking at corners of mouth.	Pale complexion, brittle nails, cracking at corners of mouth.
Vegetarians, especially tea and coffee drinkers, alcohol consumers, long-term users of diuretics – water pills.	Poor mental function, skin problems in general, repeated infections.	Eczema, acne, greasy or dry facial skin.
Women with PMS! (some 50 per cent may be lacking), long-term diuretic users, alcohol consumers.	Nausea, apathy, loss of appetite, depression, mood changes, muscle cramps.	Usually NONE! so easily missed; muscle spasms sometimes.

As a general rule vitamin and mineral deficiencies are caused by a poor diet or the presence in the diet of agents such as alcohol, tea, coffee, cigarettes, poor-quality food, or an excessive consumption of carbohydrates. These increase the need for nutrients from the remaining healthy foods that are consumed. If you have any symptoms or signs of deficiencies which persist despite a healthy diet, or despite taking nutritional supplements for a period of three months, then it is important to consult your medical practitioner. In the Self-Help section on diet, beginning on page 142, more attention will be given to the foods which are high in essential vitamins and minerals and how to have a diet with sufficient quantities of each.

TRIED AND TESTED

The value of the nutritional approach to PMS can be measured in a laboratory. Here are three examples of patients who had 'before' and 'after' laboratory tests. These tests allow us to measure vitamin and mineral levels to verify precise deficiencies which can then be treated.

GERALDINE ELLIS

Geraldine had mainly been troubled by PMS D, and episodes of recurrent thrush. In the past, taking the oral contraceptive pill had aggravated her thrush and worsened her feelings of depression, but stopping the Pill had not stopped the thrush. Similarly, nutritional deficiencies can pre-dispose to thrush, especially a deficiency of iron, and Geraldine was quite severely iron-deficient. The level of iron in her blood was 2 micromols per litre, normal range being 11–29. She was iron-deficient even though she was not anaemic. Iron is necessary, not just for making the blood pigment haemoglobin, but also because it helps to strengthen muscles and improves the digestive system and the ability of cells to fight infection.

Treatment with supplements of iron, multi-vitamins and a further course of anti-fungal treatment to control her thrush resulted in a substantial improvement in Geraldine's pre-menstrual symptoms, clearance of her thrush and correction of the iron deficiency itself. She also had a low level of magnesium in the red cells so required an additional magnesium supplement.

SANDRA PATTERSON

Sandra was a 29-year-old, single girl for whom Pre-Menstrual Syndrome carried a very special significance: on two occasions pre-menstrually she had inadvertently shoplifted. In her pre-menstrual confusion she had forgotten to pay for goods as she left the shop. The mistake was picked up by the store detective before she herself had time to return to the shop and pay for them. The courts put her on probation the first time and Sandra decided she must do something about the Pre-Menstrual Syndrome. She started taking Efamol evening primrose oil, 500 mg capsules, four per day. This controlled her pre-menstrual symptoms extremely well, so well in fact that after a few months she stopped them altogether. Unfortunately, the next month her PMS returned and with it her second shoplifting episode. The court was now beginning to find her story hard to believe.

In fact, the laboratory investigations showed that Sandra had some marked nutritional deficiencies of zinc and vitamin B6. The activity of vitamin B6 in her blood was 46 per cent below an optimum level, the normal range being up to 15 per cent below – this indicated a severe deficiency. Similarly, the level of zinc was also depressed by some 25 per cent. Both zinc and vitamin B6 deficiencies may have influenced mental function and mood. Both play a crucial part in the metabolism of essential fatty acids, a specialized form of which is found in evening primrose oil. Thus it was that evening primrose oil was controlling Sandra's symptoms, without correcting all the underlying nutritional deficiencies. When an appropriate supplement of zinc and vitamin B6 was combined with her evening primrose oil, her pre-menstrual symptoms once again disappeared completely. With a better diet she was able to reduce her need for nutritional supplements. Fortunately the court took a lenient attitude on the second occasion, and she is now well aware of the responsibility she has to look after herself.

REBECCA HARLEY

Rebecca had a long history of Pre-Menstrual Syndrome and low energy levels which showed a significant improvement when her nutritional problems were treated. Investigations showed her to have a very low level of magnesium. The red cell value was 1.5 millimols per litre, normal range being 2–3. Treatment with magnesium supplements, multi-vitamins (especially vitamin B6) and avoiding salt and wheat, made a substantial reduction in her symptoms of PMS H, fluid retention, abdominal bloating, as well as her other symptoms of anxiety, depression and fatigue. However, the fatigue was persistent and she had a rather puffy facial appearance. This suggested that the thyroid gland might be underactive. First tests were normal, but repeat tests a few months later showed that the thyroid was indeed beginning to fail. The pituitary gland, at the base of the brain, normally produces a thyroid stimulation hormone known as TSH. The TSH level had increased to 5.2 micro units per litre, when the normal value should be less than 5. Thus the pituitary gland was producing slightly increased amounts of hormone to try to stimulate the failing thyroid. Treatment with small quantities of thyroid hormone made a dramatic difference to Rebecca's symptoms. Initially, her magnesium level rose to 2.55 millimols per litre, thus showing full correction of the deficiency. An underactive thyroid should always be considered in women with Pre-Menstrual Syndrome, especially PMS H symptoms which do not respond to other treatment. An underactive thyroid may be the underlying cause not only of PMS, but also of heavy periods, a lack of periods, weight gain, decreased energy level, depression, mental sluggishness and dry skin.

RESULTS OF THE WOMEN'S NUTRITIONAL ADVISORY SERVICE PROGRAMME FOR PMS

Over the years the WNAS has conducted a number of studies to assess the value of the WNAS programme. The two most important questions that we have tried to answer are: *How easy or difficult is the programme to follow*, and *How successful is it?*

The first study we conducted was in 1985. Looking at 382 women who were sent a postal programme, we found that at least 245 of them followed the programme either completely or to a reasonable degree. Thus we knew that at least two-thirds of women found the programme acceptable. Further analysis showed that the more closely the programme was followed the more successful the outcome. In those who followed it completely (150 women) 91 per cent of the symptoms marked as severe in the pre-menstrual week reduced to either none, mild or moderate. Overall, 87 per cent of these women felt that they had benefited considerably by three months.

Of the 150 women, 93 were already taking other treatment for their PMS, usually vitamin B6 alone, hormonal treatments, diuretics or anti-depressants. 75 per cent of these 93 women were able to stop all their previous treatment, 16 per cent reduced the dosage and 9 per cent continued unchanged.

In 1988 we looked at a further group of 200 women who had completed all their questionnaires on the postal programme. Again, the degree of improvement depended very much on how closely the programme was followed, particularly for the dietary side of their treatment. 96 per cent of those who had followed the programme reported that they were signifcantly better within the first three months. We also found that women who were overweight lost between eight and 13 pounds, depending on how large they were to start with, without trying! It is now known that even modest weight loss in those who are overweight and have period problems can have a powerful corrective effect on hormonal abnormalities.

In 1990 we conducted a survey of 100 women who began the postal programme and we tried to contact them all so that we had as true a result as possible about the results of the programme. We were able to contact 88 of the 100 women. 69 of them had followed the programme. The reasons why the others had not were: pregnancy, other illnesses such as appendicitis, family stress including divorce and a death in the family, or because the programme was considered too difficult. This last was the case for 10 women. So we knew from this that the programme could be followed by some 70 per cent of women and that the success rate in them was also about 70 per cent. This compared very favourably with the outcome of most drug and hormone trials on PMS.

We tried to learn some lessons from these studies. Firstly, we realized that we had to be as scientific as possible about the supplements, and for many years we have limited our use to those preparations that are scientifically proven to be of value in PMS. Secondly, the diet has to be as easy as possible whilst still being thorough, and this means giving a good number of alternatives. This has become much easier over the years as caffeine-free, salt-free, low-fat foods have appeared on the supermarket shelves. Finally, the better the support from the WNAS the better the degree of improvement.

It was also obvious to us that there will always be some women whom we will be unable to help. As I have said elsewhere, certain medical and gynaecological problems can cause PMS, which will not fully improve until the problems themselves are corrected. We now include a number of questions on our questionnaire to try and identify those who would be well advised to have a gynaecological check.

Our latest analysis has been of those women who attended our clinics in London and Sussex during 1992. These women received detailed, tailor-made advice about their diets with many diet sheets and sample menus, advice about nutritional supplements, some of which were prescribable by their GPs, and advice to exercise. Every effort was made to help women make the necessary changes to their diets. Each woman who attended one of the clinics was either seen again or reported on their progress by telephone. The minimum duration for assessment was two months and most were assessed at three or four months.

Out of a total of 75 women, two women who attended did not actually have PMS but had depression that lasted throughout the month, and they were referred back to their family doctor. The remaining 73 were considered to have moderate to severe PMS and they were all given appropriate advice. Within the first week, two of the women considered that the diet was too difficult for them to follow because of their lifestyles. They both travelled extensively and ate almost all their meals away from home. A further two women could not be contacted because they had moved or were travelling abroad.

This left 69 women, two of whom became pregnant within the first month and were thus excluded from the analysis. (Pregnancy is not a side-effect of the programme!) All of them were asked to complete detailed questionnaires detailing the severity of their symptoms and the degree to which they followed the programme. We found that 97 per cent of the women had complied with the recommendations made, and 82 per cent were significantly better after an average of three to four months. These improved compliance figures almost certainly reflect the greater degree of co-operation that can be achieved in a clinic setting than with a postal programme, and also refinements made to the programme over the years. When we looked further at the relationship between the degree of success and the degree of adherence to the different parts of the programme, again we found that the best improvement was obtained in those who followed the programme most carefully, especially the dietary side.

Only one of the women needed to take a drug, an anti-depressant, because of severe depression in addition to her PMS. Four of the 69 women were also found to have other health problems that had not been previously investigated, and these were: repeated miscarriages, deafness due to a hormone sensitivity, a hormone abnormality related to ovarian cysts, and some unusual food intolerances. All such women needed to be referred to their GP and on to a specialist for further assessment and treatment. Sometimes, therefore, PMS may mask other conditions that require treatment in their own right.

The overall message, I am delighted to say, is that it is a very effective programmme, and that not only does it help to overcome the majority of PMS symptoms, it also provides an education about diet, and a getting-to-know-what-your-body-likes-and-dislikes process, which most of us have missed out on in the past. Energy levels improve, women experience a great sense of wellbeing, and it has a wonderful knock-on effect for the husbands and children, both in dietary and social terms.

15

CHOOSING A NUTRITIONAL PLAN

The Nutritional Approach to PMS is one which involves making dietary and lifestyle changes. It may span a very broad spectrum, in that mild sufferers only need to make a few dietary changes, whilst the moderate and severe sufferers need to follow a more specialized diet and perhaps even change their lifestyle to some degree.

In order to accommodate all PMS sufferers, I have prepared three options for you to choose from:

Option 1 Basic dietary and health recommendations – for mild sufferers.

Option 2 A specialized dietary plan – for moderate sufferers.

Option 3 A tailor-made nutritional programme – for moderate and severe sufferers.

Be guided by the severity of symptoms when making your choice of option, and not the convenience of one regime as opposed to another!

The closer you stick to the recommendations, the better your chances of rapid improvement. It's worth bearing this in mind as you go along, especially if you find it hard going making some of the changes.

OPTION 1 – BASIC DIETARY AND HEALTH RECOMMENDATIONS

1. **Reduce intake of sugar and 'junk' foods.** This includes sugar added to tea and coffee, sweets, cakes, chocolates, biscuits, puddings, jams,

marmalade, soft drinks, ice cream and honey. Consumption of these foods may cause water retention and block the uptake of essential minerals.

2. **Reduce intake of salt, both added during the cooking and at the table.** Also reduce the intake of salty foods, e.g. salted nuts, kippers, bacon, etc. This causes fluid retention and may contribute to other PMS symptoms.

3. **Reduce intake of tea and coffee.** Consume no more than one or two cups of tea and coffee per day. There are many pleasant herbal teas and substitutes for coffee from healthfood shops.

4. **Eat green vegetables or salad daily.** A good helping of either of these should be obtained and eaten every day. Both of these contain important vitamins and minerals useful in the treatment of PMS symptoms.

5. **Limit your intake of dairy products.** They interfere with magnesium absorption, a mineral which is often deficient in PMS sufferers. Restrict yourself to only one serving a day to be safe.

6. **Reduce intake of tobacco and alcohol.** These aggravate some PMS symptoms.

7. **Use good vegetable oils.** A good-quality vegetable oil, such as sunflower or safflower seed oil, should be used for any cooking, or for making salad dressings. Similarly, a sunflower seed margarine should be used rather than butter or other margarine.

8. **Eat plenty of wholefoods.** By 'wholefoods' we mean foods, usually of vegetable origin, which have not been processed or refined, e.g. wholemeal bread and cereals, such as rye, oats, barley and millet. Food such as nuts and seeds are high in vitamins and minerals as too are the important vegetable oils. If eating meat, make sure that it is lean, and eat fish and poultry too. Certain fish, e.g. herring and salmon, contain some essential oils which are helpful in maintaining skin quality and may be of some value in preventing pre-menstrual breast tenderness.

9. **Have regular exercise.** Physical exercise is of proven value in the treatment of pre-menstrual symptoms. Certainly those with a sedentary job, particularly those who do not get into the fresh air, should

take regular physical exercise. Exercise, fresh air and exposure to sunlight are important factors in maintaining health, just as important as ensuring a healthy diet and taking vitamin and mineral supplements.

10. **Take a walk.** In moments of pure desperation or impending aggression, please do immediately take a walk. Get out of the house and change your environment. Walk quietly, taking notice of the things around you. Do this until you feel a bit better.

OPTION 2 – A SPECIALIZED DIETARY PLAN

As well as following the broad dietary recommendations outlined in Option 1 you will need to select a diet that will help your particular symptoms. Once you have worked out which vitamins and minerals you need to concentrate on from the chart below, you can then go on to refer to the food lists and menus that apply to you.

BROAD DIETARY REQUIREMENTS FOR PMS AND OTHER RELATED SYMPTOMS

PMS A – nervous tension, mood swings, irritability and anxiety. Sufferers need high vitamin B6 and magnesium diets.

PMS H – weight gain, swelling of extremities, breast tenderness and abdominal bloating. Sufferers need high vitamin E, vitamin B6 and magnesium diets.

PMS C – headache, craving for sweets, increased appetite, heart pounding, fatigue and dizziness or fainting. Sufferers need high vitamin B6, magnesium and chromium diets.

PMS D – depression, forgetfulness, crying, confusion and insomnia. Sufferers need high vitamin B6, magnesium and vitamin C diets.

Acne/skin problems. A diet high in zinc is needed.

Smokers. Need high vitamin C diets.

Anaemic/heavy periods. Need high iron diets.

If, for example, you decide you are suffering with PMS A (Anxiety) and PMS C (Sugar Cravings) you will need to concentrate on a diet high in vitamin B6, magnesium and chromium. You simply refer to the relevant food lists on pages 149-155 when selecting the foods to include in your daily diet. I have also prepared a sample daily menu (see below) plus a sample menu plan for one week. These are designed to give you a guide to balanced menu planning. They are not something you have to follow, but you might like to use them as a starting point.

WHERE TO SHOP

I will be suggesting that you eat plenty of salads, vegetables and fruit. You will have realized from Chapter 11 in Part Two that many of these foods are contaminated with chemicals. Fortunately, most of the large super-markets are now beginning to stock organic produce. Although this is a little more expensive, if you can possibly manage to buy it, you'll be better off. That is, unless you grow your own organic produce, which makes even more sense.

Whilst there are many vegetarian suggestions and recipes included, I have catered for meat- and fish-eaters as well. Again, because of the chemicals and drugs in meat, I would suggest you try to find a butcher who will buy additive-free meat for you from an organic farm.

Changing over to a full range of organic produce is going to take some time. Currently the demands by retailers for organic produce cannot be met. As more and more farmers switch, there will be plenty to go round.

SAMPLE DAILY MENU

Breakfast

Muesli *or* Jordan's Oat Crunchy with a piece of chopped fruit (e.g. a banana, some grapes, berries, etc.)
with milk or yogurt

Followed by:
One or two slices of wholemeal toast *or* Ryvita
with low sugar jam *or* marmalade

Alternatively:
2 scrambled eggs *or* omelette with grilled tomatoes and mushrooms
or boiled or poached eggs
Wholemeal toast or Ryvita and low sugar spreads

Mid-morning snack

See **Snack list** below.

Lunch

Cold meat *or* fresh or tinned fish with salad platter *or* sandwiches
or
Pasta and vegetables
or
Jacket potato with a nutritious filling – for example:
    Tuna and sweetcorn with a little sour cream and black pepper
    Prawns
    Baked beans
    Curried chicken
or
Home-made soup and salad and wholemeal bread or Ryvita

Tea-time snack

See **Snack list** below.

Dinner

Poultry/fish/meat or vegetarian protein served with three portions of vegetables.
Fresh fruit or a fresh fruit salad
or
choose an appropriate sweet from the dessert section or from the *Beat PMT Cookbook*

Snack list

Ryvita and fruit spreads *or* peanut butter
Jordan's 'Fruesli' bar *or* Oat Crunchy bars
Scones and low sugar jam
Pasta *or* bean salad

Raw vegetables and dips like humus, taramasalata *or* guacomole
Fresh fruit, nuts *or* seeds
Yogurt and fruit

Beverages

Coffee substitutes. Barley Cup, Caro, Bambu, dandelion coffee, chicory, or up to two cups of decaffeinated coffee per day.
Herbal teas. Rooibosch Eleven O'clock tea (with milk). This herbal tea 'look alike', available from healthfood shops, contains a mild, natural muscle relaxant and may help alleviate tension and ease period pains. It is favoured by many of our patients and is definitely worth a try. Other suggestions are bramble, raspberry and ginseng, mixed berry, lemon verbena, fennel and wild strawberry. These days most healthfood shops sell single sachets so that you can 'buy and try' without being saddled with a whole box of tea bags that you absolutely detest.
Cold drinks. Bottled water with or without fruit juice, mineral water, Appletise, Aqua Libra, or Citrus Spring.

A SAMPLE MENU PLAN FOR ONE WEEK

See above for **Beverages**. As your calorie requirements increase by 500 calories per day in the pre-menstrual week, make sure you have a mid-morning and mid-afternoon snack each day of that week in order to keep your blood sugar levels constant. (See **Snack list** on page 178.)

B = Breakfast   L = Lunch   D = Dinner   S = Sweet
Recipes in Chapter 17, page 193.

DAY 1
B   Orange juice
    Muesli (home-made) with
      milk
L   Broccoli soup
    1 slice of wholemeal
      (wholewheat) bread
D   Mackerel with herbs (foil-
      baked)
    Brown rice salad

    Apple and celery salad
S   Baked pears with raisins

DAY 2
B   Fresh grapefruit and orange
      salad with sunflower seeds
    Toast and dried fruit conserve
      or sugar-free jam (jelly)
L   Stuffed peppers (bell peppers)

Banana
D   Roast chicken
    Cabbage
    Turnips
    Swede (rutabaga) and carrot
      mix
    Sliced fried potatoes
S   Slice of date and walnut cake

DAY 3

B   Apple juice
    Poached egg and toast
L   Lentil and vegetable soup
    Avocado with crab meat or
      prawns (shrimps)
    Green bean salad
    Fresh orange
D   Lamb paprika
    Brown rice
S   Stuffed baked apple

DAY 4

B   Wholewheat pancakes (crêpes)
    ½ quantity dried fruit
      conserve
    ½ grapefruit
L   Jacket potatoes with tuna
    Bulgar (cracked wheat) and
      nut salad
    Orange and cucumber salad
    Slice of melon
D   Steamed fish with garlic,
      spring (green) onions and
      ginger
    Stir-fried vegetables
S   Rhubarb fool

DAY 5

B   Orange juice

Scrambled eggs and tomatoes
  with toast
L   Grilled sardines
    1 slice wholemeal
      (wholewheat) bread
    Beanshoot salad
    Grapes
    2 slices of Ryvita
D   Nut roast
    Brown rice
    Waldorf salad
S   Fresh fruit salad

DAY 6

B   Grapefruit juice
    Yogurt with sliced apple and
      raisins
L   Nutty parsnip soup
    Cheese omelette
    Red cabbage, apple and bean
      salad
    Plums
D   Liver with orange
    Leafy green vegetables
    Boiled potatoes
    Cauliflower and carrots
S   Ginger bananas

DAY 7

B   Apple juice
    Poached haddock
    Tomatoes and mushrooms
L   Cauliflower and leeks in
      cheese sauce
    Slice of bread
    Orange
D   Vegetarian goulash
    Brown rice
S   Fresh fruit salad

NUTRITIONAL CONTENT OF
FOOD PER 100 g (4 oz)

Foods containing vitamin B6

Cereals

	mg
Wholemeal (wholewheat flour)	0.50
Wheat bran	1.38
Soya flour low fat	0.68

Meat

Bacon (lean)	0.45
Gammon (lean)	0.37
Beef forerib (lean only)	0.33
Minced (ground) beef (stewed)	0.30
Lamb breast (roast lean only)	0.22
Veal (roast)	0.32
Chicken (roast meat only)	0.26
Duck (roast meat only)	0.25
Turkey (roast meat only)	0.32
Liver (stewed)	0.64

Fish

Cod (baked)	0.38
Cod (grilled)	0.41
Salmon (steamed)	0.83
Plaice (steamed)	0.47
Herring (grilled)	0.57
Kipper (baked)	0.57
Mackerel (fried)	0.84

Fruit

Bananas (raw)	0.51
Apricots dried (raw)	0.17
Prunes dried (raw)	0.24
Raisins dried	0.30

Vegetables and pulses

	mg
Butter (lima) beans (raw)	0.58
Haricot beans (raw)	0.56
Mung beans (raw)	0.50
Red kidney beans (raw)	0.44
Broccoli tops (boiled)	0.13
Brussels sprouts (boiled)	0.17
Cabbage red (raw)	0.21
Cauliflower (boiled)	0.12
Avocado pear	0.42
Leeks (boiled)	0.15
Potatoes (boiled and baked)	0.18

Nuts

Hazelnuts	0.55
Peanuts	0.50
Walnuts	0.73

Other

Tomato purée (paste)	0.63
Bovril (Miso)	0.53
Marmite (Miso)	1.3

Foods containing magnesium

Cereals

Wheat bran	520
Wholemeal (wholewheat) flour	140
Oatmeal (raw)	110
Porridge (rolled) oats	30
Soya flour (low fat)	290
Wholemeal (wholewheat) bread	230
Muesli	100

Dairy	mg
Dried skimmed (skim) milk	117
Fresh whole milk	12

Meat

Beef (lean cooked)	11
Lamb (lean cooked)	12
Chicken meat (roast)	24
Sheep's heart (roast)	35

Fish

Cod (baked)	26
Herring (grilled)	32
Kipper (baked)	48
Pilchards (canned)	39
Salmon (steamed)	29
Sardines (canned in oil)	52
Winkles (boiled)	360
Crab (boiled)	48

Fruit (raw)

Pineapple (fresh)	17
Apricots (fresh)	12
Apricots (dried)	65
Bananas	42
Blackberries	30
Dates (dried)	59
Figs (dried)	92
Raisins (dried)	42
Passion-fruit	39
Sultanas (golden raisins)	35
Prunes (dried)	27

Nuts

Almonds	260
Brazil	410
Walnuts	130
Peanuts	180

Vegetables and Pulses	mg
Butter (lima) beans (boiled)	33
Haricot beans (boiled)	45
Mung beans (raw)	170
Chick peas (dahl) (cooked)	67
Spinach (boiled)	59
Sweetcorn (boiled)	45
Potatoes baked (with skins)	24
Avocado pear	29

Beverages/drinks

Infusion sachet	6
Indian tea	250

Other

Black treacle (molasses)	140

Foods containing zinc

Cereals

Wheat bran	16.2
Wholemeal (wholewheat) flour	3.0

Dairy

Milk whole	0.35
Dried whole milk	3.2
Dried skimmed (skim) milk	4.1
Cheddar cheese	4.0
Parmesan cheese	4.0
Yogurt	0.60

Eggs

Egg (boiled)	1.5
Egg yolk (raw)	3.6
Egg (poached)	1.5

Meat

	mg
Bacon (cooked)	0.8
Beef (lean roast)	6.8
Lamb (cooked)	1.4
Lamb chops (lean only grilled)	4.1
Pork (grilled lean only)	3.5
Chicken (roast meat)	1.4
Turkey (roast meat)	2.4
Liver (fried)	6.0

Nuts

Almonds	3.1
Brazils	4.2
Hazelnuts	2.4
Peanuts	3.0
Walnuts	3.0

Fish

Cod (baked)	0.5
Plaice (fried)	0.7
Herring (grilled)	0.5
Mackerel (fried)	0.5
Salmon (canned)	0.9
Sardines (canned in oil)	3.0
Tuna (canned)	0.8
Crab (boiled)	5.5
Prawns (shrimps) (boiled)	2.1
Oysters (raw)	45.0
Mussels (boiled)	2.1

Vegetables and Pulses

Butter (lima) beans (boiled)	1.0
Savoy cabbage (boiled)	0.2
Cabbage red (raw)	0.3
Lentils split (boiled)	1.0
Peas fresh (boiled)	0.5
Lettuce	0.2
Spinach (boiled)	0.4
Sweetcorn (boiled)	1.0

Other

	mg
Ginger (ground)	6.8

Foods containing iron

Cereals

Bemax (wheat germ)	10.0
Wheat bran	12.9
Rice	0.5

Meat

Beef (lean cooked)	1.4
Rumpsteak (boneless sirloin) (lean only grilled)	3.5
Lamb (lean roast)	2.5
Lamb kidney	12.0
Pork lean (grilled)	1.2
Pig liver (stewed)	17.0
Veal	1.2
Chicken (dark meat)	1.0
Chicken (liver fried)	9.1
Bovril (Miso)	14.0

Eggs

Egg whole (boiled)	2.0
Egg yolk (raw)	6.1

Fish

Mackerel (fried)	1.2
Sardines (canned in oil)	2.9
Trout (steamed)	1.0
Crab (boiled)	1.3
Prawns (shrimps) (boiled)	1.1
Cockles (boiled)	26.0
Mussels (boiled)	7.7
Oysters (raw)	6.0
Scallops (steamed)	3.0

Nuts	mg
Almonds	4.2
Brazils	2.8
Coconut (fresh)	2.1

Dairy

Cheddar cheese	0.40

Vegetables and Pulses

Haricot beans (boiled)	2.5
Mung beans (raw)	8.0
Red kidney beans	6.7
Avocado pear	1.5
Lentils (boiled)	2.4
Butter (lima) beans (boiled)	1.7
Parsley	8.0
Spring greens (cabbage) (boiled)	1.3
Leeks (boiled)	2.0

Fruit

Apricots	0.4
Bananas	0.4
Blackberries	0.9
Dates (dried)	1.6
Figs (dried)	4.2
Sultanas (golden raisins) (dried)	1.8
Prunes (dried)	2.9
Raisins (dried)	1.6
Strawberries	0.7

Foods containing vitamin C

Dairy

Milk fresh whole	1.5
Natural yoghurt	0.4

Vegetables	mg
Asparagus (boiled)	20
Runner beans (boiled)	5
Broad (sava) beans (boiled)	15
Broccoli tops (boiled)	34
Brussels sprouts (boiled)	40
Cabbage red (raw)	55
Radishes	25
Spinach (boiled)	25
Watercress	60
Cauliflower (boiled)	20
Spring greens (cabbage)	30
Avocado pear	15
Leeks (boiled)	15
Lettuce	15
Mustard and cress	40
Onions (raw)	10
Spring onions (scallions) (raw)	25
Parsley	150
Parsnips (boiled)	10
Peas fresh (boiled)	15
Peppers (bell peppers) green (boiled)	60
Potatoes (baked)	5-16

Meat

Lamb kidney	9.0

Fruit (raw unless otherwise stated)

Apples	10
Apples (baked with sugar)	14
Apricots (fresh)	7
Banana	10
Blackberries	20
Blackcurrants	200
Gooseberries green (stewed)	31
Grapes (white)	4
Grapefruit	40
Guavas (canned)	180

Fruit (continued)

	mg
Lemons (whole)	80
Lychees	40
Oranges	50
Orange juice (fresh)	50
Peaches (fresh)	8
Pears (eating)	3
Pineapple (fresh)	25
Plums	3
Raspberries	25
Rhubarb (stewed)	8
Strawberries	60
Coconut (fresh)	2
Grapefruit juice (unsweetened)	28

Note: Nuts generally have only a trace of vitamin C

Foods containing vitamin E

Oils

Cod liver oil	20.0
Sunflower seed oil	48.7
Peanut oil	13.0
Olive oil	5.1

Meat

Lamb (cooked)	0.18
Lamb kidney	0.41
Pork (cooked)	0.12
Chicken (roast meat only)	0.11

Eggs

Egg (boiled/poached)	1.6

Fish

Cod (baked)	0.59
Halibut (grilled)	0.90
Herring (grilled)	0.30

	mg
Mussels (boiled)	1.2
Salmon (canned)	1.5
Tuna (canned in oil)	6.3

Nuts

Almonds	20.0
Brazils	6.5
Hazelnuts	21.0
Peanuts	8.1

Fruit

Blackberries (raw)	3.5
Blackcurrants	1.0

Vegetables

Asparagus (boiled)	2.5
Broccoli tops (boiled)	1.1
Brussels sprouts (boiled)	0.9
Parsley	1.8
Spinach (boiled)	2.0
Avocado	3.2

Foods containing calcium

Cereals

Brown flour	150
Oatmeal (uncooked)	55
Soya flour	210
Wholemeal (wholewheat) bread	23
Brown bread	100
Muesli	200

Fish

Haddock (fried)	110
Pilchards (canned in tomato sauce)	300
Sardines (canned in oil)	550

Fish (continued)

	mg
Sprats (fried)	710
Tuna (canned in oil)	7
Shrimps (boiled)	320
Whitebait (fried)	860
Salmon (canned)	93
Kipper (baked)	65
Plaice (steamed)	38

Fruit

Apricots (dried)	92
Blackberries (raw)	63
Figs (dried)	280
Lemons (whole)	110
Rhubarb (stewed)	93
Tangerines	42

Dairy

Milk	120
Milk dried (skimmed/skim)	1190
Cheddar cheese	800
Parmesan cheese	1220
Cottage cheese (ricotta)	800
Yogurt (natural)	180

Vegetables and Pulses

Carrots (raw)	48
Celery (raw)	52
Parsley (raw)	330
Spinach (boiled)	600
Watercress	220
Turnips (boiled)	55
French beans (boiled)	39
Haricot beans (boiled)	65
Broccoli tops (boiled)	61
Spring greens (cabbage) (boiled)	86

Nuts

	mg
Almonds	250
Brazil nuts	180
Peanuts	61

Foods containing chromium

The following foods are known to contain chromium.

Meat

Calf liver	55
Chicken	15
Lamb chops	12
Pork chops	10

Eggs

Hens' eggs	16

Fish

Scallops	11
Shrimps	7

Cereals

Rye bread	30

Dairy

Milk	1
Butter	13

Fruit

Apple	14
Banana	10
Orange	5

Fruit (continued)

	mg		mg
Strawberries	3	Lettuce	7
		Mushrooms	4
		Parsnips	13
Vegetables		Potatoes	24
Cabbage	4	Spinach	10
Carrots	9		
Fresh chilli	30		
Green beans	4	**Other**	
Green (bell) peppers	19	Brewer's yeast	112

Foods containing polyunsatured fats

Certain fish contain essential oils, similar to those found in vegetables. These oils are helpful in maintaining skin quality and may also be of value in preventing pre-menstrual breast tenderness.

Herring
Mackerel
Pilchard
Salmon
Sardines
Sprats
Whitebait

How to begin

In the next chapter 'A tailor-made nutritional programme' you will find details about charting your symptoms and keeping daily diaries as a record of your progress. I suggest you do the following:

Complete a chart before you begin so that you have a clear picture of your symptoms.

- Follow the specialized diet for a period of three months.

- Keep daily diaries of all your symptoms. These are provided on page 256 at the end of the book.

- Complete another chart after three months. This can then be compared with your first chart to measure your progress.

16

A TAILOR-MADE NUTRITIONAL PROGRAMME – OPTION 3

The tailor-made nutritional programme is designed to help overcome severe symptoms. Having said that, I feel I should also point out that it is a tough programme, and if your symptoms are extremely severe, you may need help initially. If you can't manage to work out your own programme or you feel you need support, you can contact us at the Women's Nutritional Advisory Service.

Before getting too enthusiastic, it's important to understand that 'The Nutritional Programme' involves quite a bit of work. It's not a magic pill or potion that works overnight in your sleep, but an organized regime that requires a substantial amount of will-power to start with.

At the Women's Nutritional Advisory Service we try to work out the best programme for each individual, according to their symptoms and their existing lifestyle. A *realistic* regime stands a good chance of being followed, whereas an idealistic programme that would work wonders in theory is useless if left in a drawer and forgotten about because it's just too difficult to face or follow.

In order to work out each individual's programme, we need a fair amount of information. As I don't have your chart in front of me I can't work out your programme in the usual way. What I *can* do is to set you a series of questions, and then explain to you, according to your answers, how you go about working out your own programme. I will be unveiling some 'trade secrets' in the course of this section of the book, and hopefully most aspects of the Pre-Menstrual Syndrome will have been covered.

YOUR PERSONAL NUTRITIONAL PROGRAMME

This programme is designed to help moderate and severe sufferers over their symptoms. If you feel your symptoms fit into the definition of moderate or severe on page 160, you would be best advised to follow this more specialized tailor-made nutritional plan. Make a start in completing the chart and the diary provided on pages 159 and 257. Once you are satisfied with your answers, usually after one full cycle, you can begin compiling your own programme.

If you prefer to begin immediately without waiting for the forms to be completed, then I suggest you follow Option 2 – A Specialized Dietary Plan on page 144. Once your precise programme has been formulated you can implement the additional recommendations and make any changes that are needed.

To avoid confusion, remember that recommendations according to your symptoms should be followed in the long term for best results, rather than continuing to follow the general recommendations made in previous chapters. The reason I make this point is that you may find the two sets of instructions conflict in some areas. An example is that the general recommendations suggest eating plenty of whole grains. However we often find that severe symptoms may be aggravated by certain grains and we may therefore suggest that these are omitted from the diet for a specific period of time in some cases. I have covered this in much fuller detail in the section on food allergies on page 171.

A STEP-BY-STEP GUIDE
TO WORK OUT YOUR OWN PROGRAMME

STEP ONE – HOW TO CHART YOUR SYMPTOMS

Begin by completing the first Pre-Menstrual Syndrome Chart on page 159. This should ideally be completed in two parts.

The left-hand column deals with how you feel normally when you are not pre-menstrual. *This column should be completed three days after your period has started or when you feel at your best.*

The right-hand column deals with how you feel pre-menstrually when your symptoms are at their worst. *This column should be completed two days before your period is due or when you feel at your worst.*

SYMPTOMS	WEEK AFTER PERIOD (Fill in 3 days after period)				WEEK BEFORE PERIOD (Fill in 2-3 days before period)			
	None	Mild	Moderate	Severe	None	Mild	Moderate	Severe
PMS - A								
Nervous Tension	✓							✓
Mood Swings	✓							✓
Irritability	✓							✓
Anxiety	✓							✓
PMS - H								
*Weight Gain	✓							✓
Swelling of Extremities			✓					✓
Breast Tenderness	✓							✓
Abdominal Bloating		✓						✓
PMS - C								
Headache	✓						✓	
Craving for Sweets	✓							✓
Increased Appetite	✓							✓
Heart Pounding	✓				✓			
Fatigue	✓							✓
Dizziness or Fainting	✓				✓			
PMS - D								
Depression	✓							✓
Forgetfulness	✓							✓
Crying	✓						✓	
Confusion	✓							✓
Insomnia	✓							✓
OTHER SYMPTOMS								
Loss of Sexual Interest	✓					✓		
Disorientation	✓							✓
Clumsiness	✓							✓
Tremors/Shakes	✓							✓
Thoughts of Suicide	✓							✓
Agoraphobia	✓							
Increased Physical Activity	✓				✓			
Heavy/Aching Legs	✓							✓
Generalized Aches	✓							✓
Bad Breath	✓							✓
Sensitivity to Music/Light	✓				✓			
Excessive Thirst	✓							✓

Do you have any other PRE-MENSTRUAL SYMPTOMS not listed above?

1. _____

2. _____

3. _____

4. _____

*5. How much weight do you gain before your period? 7–10lbs

158

SYMPTOMS

	WEEK AFTER PERIOD (Fill in 3 days after period)				WEEK BEFORE PERIOD (Fill in 2-3 days before period)			
	None	Mild	Moderate	Severe	None	Mild	Moderate	Severe
PMS - A								
Nervous Tension								
Mood Swings								
Irritability								
Anxiety								
PMS - H								
*Weight Gain								
Swelling of Extremities								
Breast Tenderness								
Abdominal Bloating								
PMS - C								
Headache								
Craving for Sweets								
Increased Appetite								
Heart Pounding								
Fatigue								
Dizziness or Fainting								
PMS - D								
Depression								
Forgetfulness								
Crying								
Confusion								
Insomnia								
OTHER SYMPTOMS								
Loss of Sexual Interest								
Disorientation								
Clumsiness								
Tremors/Shakes								
Thoughts of Suicide								
Agoraphobia								
Increased Physical Activity								
Heavy/Aching Legs								
Generalized Aches								
Bad Breath								
Sensitivity to Music/Light								
Excessive Thirst								

Do you have any other PRE-MENSTRUAL SYMPTOMS not listed above?

1. _____

2. _____

3. _____

4. _____

*5. How much weight do you gain before your period? _____

159

In order to work out your score, you must place a tick by each symptom in both columns. On page 158 is an example of a completed chart. You can see how the symptoms become far more severe pre-menstrually (on the right-hand side of the chart).

Severity of symptoms

You will notice that on the chart you are asked to assess whether your symptoms are mild, moderate or severe. Each of these categories has a numerical score as follows:

0 = None.
1 = Mild.
2 = Moderate.
3 = Severe.

Mild, moderate and severe defined

(1) Mild   Means that symptoms are present but they do not interfere with your activities. You feel all right, but are aware that some physical and emotional changes are taking place as your period approaches.

(2) Moderate Means that symptoms are present and they do interfere with some activities, but they are not disabling. You feel well below par and maybe even cancel arrangements. The family would be aware your period is on its way, maybe even before you are.

(3) Severe Means that symptoms are not only present, they interfere with all activities. They are severely disabling and it's likely that life would be pretty hard to cope with until the symptoms pass.

Using Anita's first chart on page 158 as an example, let's go through it section by section so that you can understand how it works.

PMS A, H, C and D

PMS A – Anxiety. In order to 'qualify' for PMS A your score must be 4 or above for this section. To get your final score you subtract the score for the week after your period from the score for the week before your period.

Anita scored 0 after her period and 12 pre-menstrually. Therefore, her overall score is 12, so she certainly does qualify for PMS A.

The reason for subtracting one score from another in this fashion is to attempt to get the *actual* pre-menstrual score. For example, if you have moderate regular headaches all month and they become severe pre-menstrually your real pre-menstrual headache score is only 1, as this symptom only moved from mild to moderate. Compare this to another person who usually has no headaches, but has severe pre-menstrual headaches: the pre-menstrual headache score would be 3 here.

Not to subtract the usual situation for the rest of your cycle from the pre-menstrual situation would create a false picture.

This method of scoring applies to all four categories.

PMS H – Hydration. For PMS H you also need a score of 4 to qualify. Anita scored 3 after her period and 10 before her period, giving her a total score of 7. She therefore qualifies.

PMS C – Sugar craving. For PMS C there are six symptoms. You will need an overall score of 6 to qualify. Anita scored 0 after her period and a score of 11 before her period. Her overall score was therefore 11.

PMS D – Depression. And finally for PMS D, a score of 5 is necessary as there are five symptoms listed in this category. Anita scored 0 after her period and 14 pre-menstrually. Her total score here was 14. She qualified with honours!

Once you have completed your chart you can go on to work out your scores using this example.

Each category has been dealt with separately. You may find that only one of the four categories applies to you. However, it is perfectly possible to be suffering from several categories, or in fact all four.

Now fill in your first chart and see how you fare.

You will notice an additional section on the chart. This is made up of other symptoms which have been reported repeatedly by patients.

Is it really pre-menstrual?

The best way to assess your symptoms in order to confirm that they are pre-menstrual is to keep daily diaries as I mentioned previously. After two or three months you will see a definite pattern emerging which will serve to confirm the diagnosis of PMS. Two diaries have been provided for this purpose beginning on page 258. Please feel free to photocopy the diaries if you wish.

If, after three months, it seems that your scores are low and your symptoms seem to be persisting all month rather than pre-menstrually, then it would be best to have a full medical consultation and physical examination to determine whether there is some other problem.

Diaries

It is not only a good idea, but essential that you keep daily diaries. In fact, some doctors feel that it is necessary to keep a diary for three months in order to confirm the diagnosis of PMS. There are several reasons for this:

- To keep a check on your symptoms.

- To confirm that you have PMS.

- To show a pattern of when the symptoms occur each month.

- To have as a record so that you can judge whether improvement is occurring, without having to rely on your memory.

The form we use is called the Menstrual Symptomatology Diary (MSD), and was designed by Dr Abraham to enable sufferers to keep an ongoing record of their symptoms. The diary should be filled in at the end of each day, throughout the cycle. There are a few things to remember when you do this:

The first day of your cycle is the day your period begins. Whether your period comes every 22 days or 32 days is irrelevant here. The day bleeding begins, you start a new diary calling this *Day 1*.

There is an example of a completed diary opposite.

Now you should start filling in the diary and continue to fill it in at the end of each day.

After a few months you should see a very definite pattern emerging. The most likely pattern is for you to experience few symptoms once your period has arrived until at least ovulation, that is, mid cycle. So you will fill in only noughts in the diary. If you have any symptoms at ovulation, indicate them vertically, according to their severity. As your period approaches, the number you fill in will probably get higher, at least for the symptoms that bother you.

MENSTRUAL SYMPTOMATOLOGY DIARY

Month: January

GRADING OF MENSES

0–none	3–heavy
1–slight	4–heavy and
2–moderate	clots

GRADING OF SYMPTOMS (COMPLAINTS)

0–none
1–mild-present but does not interfere with activities
2–moderate-present and interferes with activities but not disabling
3–severe-disabling. Unable to function.

Day of cycle	1	2	3	4	5	6	7	8	9	10	11	12	13	14	15	16	17	18	19	20	21	22	23	24	25	26	27	28	29
Date	13	14	15	16	17	18	19	20	21	22	23	24	25	26	27	28	29	30	31	1	2	3	4	5	6	7	8	9	10
Period	1	2	3	3	2	1	0	0	0	0	0	0	0	0	0	0	0	0	0	0	0	0	0	0	0	0	0	0	0

PMS - A

Nervous tension	1	0	0	0	0	0	0	0	0	0	0	0	0	0	0	0	0	0	0	1	0	1	1	2	2	3	3	3	2
Mood swings	0	0	0	0	0	0	0	0	0	0	0	0	0	0	0	0	0	0	1	2	1	2	2	3	2	3	2	2	3
Irritability	0	0	0	0	0	0	0	0	0	0	0	0	0	0	0	0	0	0	0	1	1	2	2	2	2	2	3	3	3
Anxiety	0	0	0	0	0	0	0	0	0	0	0	0	0	0	0	0	0	1	1	0	0	2	3	3	2	2	2	3	2

PMS - H

Weight gain	0	0	0	0	0	0	0	0	0	0	0	0	0	0	0	0	0	0	1	1	1	2	2	2	3	2	2	3	3
Swelling of extemities	0	0	0	0	0	0	0	0	0	0	0	0	0	0	0	0	0	0	0	1	1	1	1	2	2	2	2	2	2
Breast tenderness	0	0	0	0	0	0	0	0	0	0	0	0	0	0	0	0	0	0	1	1	1	1	2	2	2	2	2	2	2
Abdominal bloating	1	0	0	0	0	0	0	0	0	0	0	0	0	0	0	0	1	1	2	2	2	1	2	1	1	2	2	2	

PMS - C

Headache	0	0	0	1	0	0	0	0	0	0	0	0	0	0	0	0	0	0	0	0	0	0	0	0	2	0	0	1	
Craving for sweets	0	0	0	0	0	0	0	0	0	0	0	0	0	0	0	1	2	2	0	1	2	3	3	3	2	1	2	2	
Increased appetite	0	0	0	0	0	0	0	0	0	0	0	0	0	0	0	3	2	2	1	0	0	2	2	2	2	2	2		
Heart pounding	0	0	0	0	0	0	0	0	0	0	0	0	0	0	0	0	0	0	0	0	0	0	0	0	0	0	0	0	0
Fatigue	1	1	2	1	0	0	0	0	0	0	0	0	0	0	0	0	0	0	2	2	3	3	3	3	3	3	3	3	
Dizziness or faintness	1	0	0	0	0	0	0	0	0	0	0	0	0	0	0	0	0	0	0	0	0	0	0	0	0	0	0	0	

PMS - D

Depression	1	0	0	0	0	0	0	0	0	0	0	0	0	0	0	0	0	0	1	1	1	2	2	2	3	3	3	3	3
Forgetfulness	0	0	0	0	0	0	0	0	0	0	0	0	0	0	0	0	1	0	3	2	3	3	3	3	3	2	2	3	
Crying	0	0	0	0	0	0	0	0	0	0	0	0	0	0	0	0	1	0	1	2	1	2	3	3	3	3	2	3	3
Confusion	1	0	0	0	0	0	0	0	0	0	0	0	0	0	0	0	1	2	2	2	2	2	3	3	2	2	2	2	
Insomnia	1	1	0	0	0	0	0	0	0	0	0	0	0	0	0	0	0	1	1	1	1	2	2	2	1	3	3	3	

PAIN

Cramps (low abdominal)																													
Backache																													
General aches/pains																														

NOTES:

STEP TWO – PLANNING YOUR DIET

Making changes

Unfortunately there seems to be some truth in the saying 'old habits die hard'. If you set out bearing this in mind you won't get disillusioned along the way. Following the programme usually involves making quite a few changes in both diet and lifestyle. To be realistic, it does take a while to adjust fully. The first month is usually the most rocky. The new routine may cause a bit of confusion here and there at first and a few surprises along the way. If it seems difficult, remember, it is important to persist until you are out of the woods.

Forewarned is forearmed

Withdrawal symptoms may occur during the first few days on the programme, and can sometimes last for as long as two weeks. Whilst you shouldn't definitely expect these, it's worth bearing in mind that they are very common. Depriving the body of things which it has grown used to sometimes causes it to 'bite back'. It may seem a strange concept that this should occur as a result of dietary changes. However, it is fairly similar to the mechanism of withdrawing from drugs or alcohol. Due to the possible withdrawal symptoms from certain foods and drinks, it is better not to begin this diet in your pre-menstrual phase. Make a start after your period has arrived.

Giving up tea and coffee, for example, may trigger off a number of changes in the body. These may cause you to feel tired or uptight, anxious and on edge. Headaches may occur and, more often, the desire to eat seems to persist. You will be pleased to hear that all this tends to settle down within days, certainly within a couple of weeks. Once you have passed this stage, if it happens to you at all, life becomes much easier, and before long you will notice new habit patterns forming. So much so that patients often prefer *not* to return to their former habits, simply because their tastes have changed! For example, they lose their desire for salty food and regular cups of strong coffee.

The general consensus of opinion is that it is worth persevering, for there is a light at the end of the tunnel. Our research proves this conclusively. When the Women's Nutritional Advisory Service had been in existence for one year we decided it would be desirable to get some scientific feedback on our results. We looked at the results of a group of women who had been on the programme. They had made dietary changes, taken nutritional supplements and regularly exercised. After three months 89 per cent of the women reported that they felt significantly better and there was a 91 per cent reduction in severe symptoms.

We are also reminded that our efforts are worthwhile by the constant flow of grateful letters we receive from patients. From reading the case histories in Part One you will have had a taste of the magnitude of the original problems and then read about incredible changes that took place. The letters we receive from women who have completed the programme often read like fairy stories. It is no wonder we are keen to see the natural approach to curing PMS being widely used!

If I haven't put you off – let's get down to it! We'll deal with dietary aspects first of all, then supplement recommendations. Just a word before we begin: it is not advisable to start following your programme during your PMS week. The reason for this is that the body can be put under strain initially when making dietary changes and it is not a good idea to have to cope with this pre-menstrually.

First of all, decide from your chart which are your main pre-menstrual symptoms. Refer to the section 'PMS and Other Related Symptoms' on page 144 and decide which vitamins and minerals you should be concentrating on in particular. Then read through the food lists starting on page 149 to familiarize yourself with the foods high in the relevant nutrient. If you are suffering severely, it's likely to encompass most of the food groups.

LET'S PUT YOU UNDER THE MICROSCOPE

Some of your symptoms fall into categories which you have now been able to identify, but for severe PMS sufferers there are often other factors which play a major part in their condition. In order to determine whether any of these factors apply to you personally, you will need to examine several groups of symptoms. I have put certain symptoms into groups to make this simpler.

On this page there is a skeleton chart for you to complete as you go along. As you read through the sections that follow, make a note of each recommendation which you feel applies to you. By the time you have finished reading the whole of Part Three of this book you should have your programme noted down for easy reference. A copy of this can be pinned up in your kitchen to remind you of the Dos and Don'ts.

PERSONAL NUTRITIONAL PROGRAMME
SUMMARY OF RECOMMENDATIONS

Diet section

1.

2.

3.

4.

5.

6.

7.

8.

9.

10.

Supplement section

1.

2.

3.

4.

5.

GENERAL RECOMMENDATIONS

There are general recommendations that should be implemented by all severe sufferers, almost regardless of which categories of PMS they suffer from. The fact that you need to cut out certain food groups now does not mean this will remain so for ever. It is simply a way of giving your body a rest and allowing it to recover. I will explain later how to go about re-introducing some of the foods into your diet.

1. Cut out caffeine

Caffeine is addictive, although we do not readily believe it to be so. It is present in tea, coffee, chocolate and cola-based drinks.

Caffeine and some other similar substances tend to aggravate PMS A symptoms, i.e. anxiety, irritability, mood swings and nervous tension. It also affects breast symptoms, and the PMS D symptoms of depression and insomnia.

It is advisable to cut caffeine out completely, and to consume only small amounts of decaffeinated coffee, as this contains other chemicals which may have an effect on PMS symptoms. Fortunately, there are many pleasant alternatives which you will find in healthfood shops.

- There are many varieties of herb tea, some fruity and some more herby in taste, most of which are caffeine-free. The most 'tea-like' substitute we have found is 'Redbush' or 'Rooibosch' tea. This can be made with or without milk. Many former tea addicts have found that after a week or two it tastes far more pleasant than ordinary tea. You will need to shop around and experiment to find teas that suit your palate.

- Dandelion coffee is certainly worth a try. It comes in instant form and in roasted root form. I like to use the root, which I put through my coffee filter.

- There are numerous other cereal alternatives you could try, all of which you should find in a good healthfood shop.

2. Reduce your dairy produce consumption

Milk, cheese, cream and yogurt tend to make PMS symptoms far worse, particularly PMS A symptoms. Keep your total daily dairy consumption down to the equivalent of one glass of milk per day. If you have a portion of cheese or a yogurt, bear in mind you have very little milk left from your allowance. There are many non-dairy sources of calcium, which you will find mentioned on the calcium food list. So there is no fear of becoming calcium-deficient.

3. Keep your salt intake to a minimum

Salt may play a part in Pre-Menstrual Syndrome. Either in the cooking or added at the table, salt leads to increased water retention which tends to aggravate many of the PMS symptoms. You should also avoid eating salty foods. A diet low in salt is a good idea for many reasons, as well as being of value in the treatment of some of your symptoms. If you have an irresistible desire for salt, try using a salt substitute high in potassium salt, rather than the commonly available sodium salt. You will find that after you have been avoiding salt for three or four weeks you no longer miss it, and will begin to taste the food itself.

4. Keep your sugar intake low

Sugar is an important dietary factor in Pre-Menstrual Syndrome. Sugar and sweet foods such as cakes, biscuits, cookies, puddings, jam (jelly), soft drinks and ice cream are high in calories (kjs) and low in important vitamins and minerals. It is deficiencies in some of these vitamins and minerals which play such a part in pre-menstrual symptoms, particularly vitamin B6 and magnesium. Having a lot of sugar in your diet may also contribute significantly to fluid retention and therefore should be avoided.

It is not widely appreciated that 'junk food' contains a lot of phosphorus, which is known to block the uptake of certain trace minerals. Without these important trace minerals PMS symptoms tend to get worse. By 'junk food' we mean processed food, refined food, prepared food, i.e. packet soups, cakes, etc. and anything that contains added sugar, such as sweets (candy), cakes, biscuits (cookies), chocolates and soft drinks.

Coming off sugar can be difficult. However, there are a number of good alternatives.

- Sweeteners can be used in drinks.

- Low-sugar or sugar-free fruit juice and nut bars can be found in many healthfood shops and used in place of sweets.

- Concentrated apple juice is a good sweetener when cooking. Small amounts of molasses may also be used as it is high in the B vitamins and magnesium.

- There are sugar-free jams (jellies) available in healthfood shops. These are made with fruit and apple juice.

- Watered-down fruit juice is a good substitute for soft drinks as it contains no extra sugar or colouring agents etc.

Unfortunately, honey consists mainly of sugar, and only one or two teaspoons should be consumed a day if you can't resist it. Similarly, small amounts of refined sugar – one teaspoon per day - may also be allowed. The same goes for brown sugar, as it has more or less the same effect on your metabolism.

There are specific supplement recommendations for sugar cravings which are mentioned on pages 183 and 188.

5. Limit your intake of alcohol

As I mentioned in Chapter 11, regular alcohol consumption can have devastating consequences on the body. Alcohol is known to block absorption of certain trace minerals and to knock out B vitamins from the system. Without these you are far more prone to pre-menstrual symptoms. Try not to consume more than two or three alcoholic drinks per week. Fortunately, there are now alcohol-free wines and beers on the market, so you need not refuse a drink.

6. Reduce cigarette smoking

Smoking may affect the levels of certain vitamins, particularly vitamin C, and also aggravate pre-menstrual breast tenderness as well as PMS A symptoms. It is advisable, therefore, that your cigarette consumption be substantially reduced. You may find it easier to cut down on smoking once you have been on the programme for a few weeks. If you don't succeed at first, try again after a month.

7. Eat your greens!

Green leafy vegetables are the major source of some important vitamins and in particular contain the mineral magnesium which plays a substantial part in the correction of pre-menstrual symptoms. It is vital, therefore, that you have a good helping of salad or green leafy vegetables every day. The greens should preferably be lightly cooked in the minimum of water to preserve their vitamin and mineral content. By careful attention to your diet, your need for vitamin and mineral supplements should be reduced.

8. Eat plenty of raw feed

Uncooked food is usually far more nutritious than food that has been cooked. In many cooking processes as much as half of the nutrients are lost. Raw food has a much higher fibre content, too. Aim to eat at least one, and preferably two raw meals per day. Eat plenty of salad stuff, fruit and raw vegetables, all of which are easy to prepare and fairly portable, if you are eating away from home. An excellent book to refer to is *Raw Energy* by Leslie and Susannah Kenton which is mentioned on the Recommended Reading List on page 252.

9. A note to vegetarians and vegans

Vegetarians who do not eat meat or fish, and vegans who only consume vegetable produce may need to pay particular attention to certain aspects of their diet, so that they do not become nutritionally deficient. Whilst there are many vegetarians who take great care over their diets, there are still too many who try to exist on lettuce leaves and the like. Apart from all the recommendations made so far, vegetarians and vegans should concentrate on the following.

Make sure you have an adequate balance of proteins in your diet.

No single vegetarian protein contains all the appropriate nutrients required, so it's important to combine the different types of vegetable proteins in your vegetarian meals. Vegetarian proteins include: nuts, seeds, peas, beans, lentils, whole grains, brown rice, sprouted beans and soya bean products.

Whilst beans are particularly nutritious, they often cause abdominal wind. Soaking them for 24 hours before cooking them and de-husking them may reduce the problem.

10. Iron and Zinc

Ensure you have an adequate intake of the minerals iron and zinc. You can check on this by referring to the iron and zinc food lists which can be found on pages 150-152.

MORE SPECIALIZED PROBLEMS: SECTIONS 1–8

I have split this section up into symptom groups. After reading through the group of symptoms, there are recommendations. If these symptoms apply to you, make a note of the recommendation on your personal chart. If the symptoms don't apply to you, then simply pass on to the next section.

Do you suffer with any of the following? (tick applicable boxes)

Abdominal bloating	☐	Depression	☐
Excessive wind	☐	Mouth ulcers	☐
Constipation	☐	Fatigue	☐
Diarrhoea	☐		

If you ticked any two of these symptoms it would be *desirable* for you to follow these recommendations.

If, however, you ticked three or more it is *advisable* for you to read through the recommendations carefully, mark them on your chart, and apply them.

SECTION 1: SENSITIVITY TO GRAINS

There is evidence to show that the symptoms mentioned in sections 1 to 8 may be related to food sensitivity. Research suggests that a significant percentage of the population produce antibodies to some foods. In our experience, this may be only a temporary state of affairs that occurs when we are not in very good nutritional shape. Finding the right kind of diet for your body will help to overcome your symptoms. It is therefore worth avoiding certain groups of foods temporarily if you suffer with the symptoms in this section. Try to follow the recommendations closely – you will reap the benefit.

WHOLEWHEAT AND GRAINS: ALTERNATIVES

Many symptoms such as irritability, abdominal bloating, constipation, diarrhoea, excessive wind, irritable bowel, fatigue and depression can be aggravated by eating foods containing wheat and other grains. Certain people react to wheat, oats, barley and rye, and all foods made from them or containing them. They are therefore better off avoiding them altogether initially, until the symptoms are under control. It sounds a bit drastic, but there are lots of alternative foods that can be used instead, so don't despair.

Bread

There are now many alternatives to ordinary bread, some of which can be purchased and others which you need to bake yourself. Both chemists and healthfood shops usually have some stocks of the alternative grain products; in our experience the chemists are usually the most reasonably priced. Behind the counter in the pharmacy you will usually find a stock of products kept for people with gluten allergy. Ask the pharmacist for help, as they sometimes have to order products in on request.

Look out for some of the following products:

- Ener G white or brown rice bread (which toasts nicely)

- Glutafin wheat-free bread and rolls and Glutafin crackers

- Rice cakes

Home-made bread. Whilst I have not been very successful in making bread with alternative flours, some of our patients have successfully experimented. Look out for the recipes for potato and rice bread, and buckwheat and rice bread, on pages 210–211.

Pasta

Although you will need to avoid the pasta made with wheat, there are many reasonable alternatives you can try. Most of these are available from healthfood shops, the Chinese supermarket or the pharmacist.

- **Pastariso** make brown rice spaghetti, which is very acceptable slightly undercooked. They also do a range of other pastas. Although some healthfood shops do stock it, it is easier to order it from the chemist.

- **Glutafin** have a range of pasta which is sometimes available in health-food shops, and again can be ordered from the chemist.

- **Rice noodles** are available in a wide variety from Chinese super-markets. There are wide flat rice noodles that resemble tagliatelli, spaghetti-like noodles, and the very skinny variety that only need soaking in a covered pan in boiling water for a few minutes. You will probably find that these are cheaper than the alternative pastas available from healthfood shops and chemists.

Breakfast cereal

Any rice or corn cereals will be fine, even the ordinary Rice Krispies and Cornflakes from the supermarkets. Add some chopped fruit and some crumbled nuts, perhaps a few seeds and a little dried fruit to your cereal to make it a bit more wholesome. There are some alternative mueslis available, but they are usually very expensive for only a small packet.

Home-made cakes

If you enjoy cooking there are plenty of very acceptable biscuits, cakes, pastries, sponges and pancakes you can make using alternative flours. If you have never used any of the alternative flours before it may take you a little time to find the consistency that you like.

Sponge. Brown rice flour is probably the best for making sponge. Make it up to the weight given in the recipe by mixing it with a little ground almond and a raising agent (cream of tartar and bicarbonate of soda).

Raising agents. As baking powder contains wheat, you will need to use an alternative. Either use a combination of one part of bicarbonate of soda to two parts of cream of tartar, or use Glutafin wheat-free baking powder.

Savoury pancakes. These can be made with pure buckwheat flour, which is part of the rhubarb family and tends to be quite heavy, or buckwheat mixed with a little white rice flour, which is very light.

Sweet pancakes are best made with a combination of brown rice flour, or ground rice, and cornflour, purchased form a healthfood shop or Chinese supermarket. Use half cornflour and half rice flour to replace the normal quantity of flour in the ordinary pancake recipe.

Breadcrumbs or batter. A crisp coating for fish or meat can be made with maize meal, which can be found in the healthfood shop. Coat the fish or meat with maize meal, then with beaten egg, and once again with maize meal. You can then bake, grill or even fry the food which should emerge with a crispy coat.

Biscuits. There are varieties of biscuits that you can make using brown rice flour, or ground rice, and ground nuts or coconut. If you make plain biscuits you can flavour them with lemon or ginger. Our recipes for almond macaroons and coconut biscuits are very acceptable, and at the same time more nutritious than the average biscuit as they are full of eggs and nuts. It's an idea to make some and keep them in the freezer so that you can take a few out when you really feel you need something sweet to eat.

There are many other flours that you can use in your cooking. Gram flour made from chickpeas, potato flour, soya flour, tapioca flour, and millet flour are all good examples. Glutafin make flour mixes for bread, pastry and cakes, as do True Free, and these are available in some health-food shops.

Shop-bought cakes and biscuits

Acceptable cakes and biscuits can now be purchased in healthfood shops and ordered from most chemists.

Glutafin have a range of biscuits including digestives, and Rite-Diet have a range of biscuits and cakes. The coconut biscuits are the least sweet, and the banana or lemon cakes are worth trying too.

Snacks

It's nice to have something to crunch on when you are avoiding wheat. There are lots of corn products available, but do remember to read the labels as some have added wheat. Try corn chips, crisps, and wafers, and look in the Mexican section of the supermarket. Also, poppadoms are fine, and little mini spiced poppadoms are nice to nibble on or dip.

ASSESSING FOR GRAIN SENSITIVITY

You will need to become a nutritional detective by doing the following:

- Stop eating all the grains mentioned earlier (wheat, oats, barley, rye) for at least a month, preferably six weeks. You can eat one slice of French bread per day if you are desperate! But it's better to try to manage on rice crackers or rice cakes instead. This may seem strange as refined bread is nowhere near as nutritious as wholemeal bread. However, during the refining process most of the grain has been removed and therefore the degree of aggravation caused by this is far less than by a wholegrain loaf.

- After a month or six weeks, or longer, when you feel that your symptoms have diminished, try introducing the various grains one by one to your diet. Begin just after a period, so that you don't confuse any reaction with PMS symptoms. Choose one grain, e.g. rye in the form of Ryvita. Introduce this into your diet and eat this for several days. If you have no reaction after five days, choose another grain and repeat this process. DO NOT MIX the grains initially because if you do get a reaction you won't know exactly what you have reacted to! Continue to do this with all the grains, providing you don't have reactions to any one of them. Try wheat last as it is the most common grain to cause problems.

Once you get used to using the alternatives you shouldn't find the diet difficult to stick to. If you are going to avoid eating certain groups of foods for any length of time, it is important to arm yourself with all the alternative foods you can muster. It is not a weight-loss diet (although you might find that you lose weight if you are overweight) and you can literally eat as much as you like of the foods on your list. Never allow yourself to get hungry and never miss a meal. It's important to keep up a steady flow of good nutrients in order to allow your hormone and brain chemical metabolism to function at an optimum.

What to do if you have a reaction

The reactions may include diarrhoea or constipation, excessive wind, abdominal bloating, headaches, weight gain, fatigue, confusion, depression, mouth ulcers, rash, irritability and palpitations.

1. Once you have established what you have reacted to, make a note of it and avoid eating this food at all for now. This doesn't mean that you won't be able to eat this food again ever, but it is best avoided for now.

2. Wait until things have settled down again and then try again with another grain.

I appreciate that cutting out all grains is a severe measure. I suggest you begin by just cutting out wholewheat products. You will need to do this for at least four to six weeks to see whether there is any improvement. You can remain on small amounts of white or French bread.

Constipation

If constipation is a particular problem you might like to try taking some linseed. You can find some very palatable forms of it at your healthfood shop such as Linusit Gold. It is pleasant to eat and can easily be included in your breakfast cereals or salad.

Foods containing grains

It's surprising how many foods contain grains. Before I began 'label reading' I would never have believed the extent to which grains are used. It's a good exercise to go around the supermarket, reading labels on packets to get an idea of this for yourself. Sometimes labels aren't as explicit as they might be and they just contain the words 'edible starch'. This has to be regarded with suspicion if you are on a grain-free diet. Labelling of food in healthfood shops is usually more reliable and precise.

Wheat. The most obvious foods containing wheat are bread, biscuits, cakes and flour made from wheat etc., but wheat is often present in prepared sauces, soups, and processed foods in general. Gluten-free products are not particularly recommended on a wheat-free diet as some of them still contain wheat.

The following list will give you a rough idea of what to look out for, but I suggest you make a practice of reading labels thoroughly before buying anything.

- Bread, particularly wholemeal, wheatmeal, etc. as these contain more of the natural wheat.

- Cakes, biscuits, pasta, spaghetti, macaroni etc. – pastry, pies, buns, bran (except rice or soya bran), and many breakfast cereals and sausages.

Oats. Porridge, oat cookies and oat flakes.

Rye. Rye bread (which may also contain wheat), Ryvita.

Barley. Often found in packet/tinned soups and stews, barley beverages.

Corn. Corn on the cob, corn starch, corn (maize), oil and popcorn.

There are many lovely recipe books available with further ideas listed in the Recommended Reading section on page 251.

I have prepared some sample menus to give you an idea of the scope possible. There are also a few recipes included in the recipe section on page 193 as a guideline.

GRAIN FREE ALLERGY DIET

SAMPLE DAILY MENU – WHEAT, OATS, BARLEY AND RYE FREE

Breakfast

Cornflakes or Rice Krispies with:
    a piece of chopped fruit (e.g. a banana, some grapes, berries etc.)
    a few crumbled pecan nuts
    a tablespoon of pine nuts
    a tablespoon of raisins (if not avoiding yeast)
with milk *or* yogurt

Followed by:

One or two slices of alternative toast with low sugar jam or marmalade

Alternatively:

2 scrambled eggs *or* omelette with grilled tomatoes
or boiled or poached eggs
Alternative crackers and low sugar spreads

Mid-morning snack

See **Snack list** overleaf.

Lunch

Jacket potato with a nutritious filling, for example:
  Tuna and sweetcorn with a little sour cream and black pepper
  Prawns
  Baked beans
  Curried chicken

or

Cold meat *or* fresh or tinned fish with salad

or

Rice noodles, *or* alternative pasta, and vegetables

or

Home-made soup and salad

Tea-time snack

See **Snack list** overleaf.

Dinner

Poultry/fish/meat or vegetarian protein served with three portions of vegetables.

Fresh fruit or a fresh fruit salad, or choose an appropriate sweet from the dessert section in this book starting on page 208 or from the *Beat PMT Cookbook*.

Snack list

raw vegetables and dips like humus, taramasalata or guacamole
fresh fruit, nuts or seeds
yogurt and fruit
alternative crackers and spreads
corn chips
mini poppadoms
rice salad with fruit and nuts

Beverages

Coffee substitutes. Dandelion coffee, chicory, or up to two cups of decaffeinated coffee per day.

Herbal teas. Rooibosch Eleven O'clock tea (with milk). This herbal tea 'look alike', available from healthfood shops, contains a mild, natural muscle relaxant and may help alleviate tension and ease period pains. It is favoured by many of our patients and is definitely worth a try. Other suggestions are bramble, raspberry and ginseng, mixed berry, lemon verbena, fennel and wild strawberry. These days most healthfood shops sell single sachets so that you can 'buy and try' without being saddled with a whole box of tea bags that you absolutely detest.

Cold drinks. Bottled water with or without fruit juice, mineral water, Appletise, Rio, or Citrus Spring.

B = Breakfast   L = Lunch   D = Dinner   S = Sweet

For recipes, see Chapter 17, page 193.

A SAMPLE MENU PLAN FOR ONE WEEK

DAY 1

B   Orange juice
    Buckwheat pancakes (crêpes)
    Dried fruit conserve
L   Fresh avocado and tomato
        soup
    Jacket potato with cheese
D   Cold mackerel fillets or
        Prince's Mackerel in Spicy
        Tomato Sauce
    Green salad

Brown rice salad
S   Baked stuffed apples

DAY 2

B   ½ grapefruit
    Mushroom omelette
L   Sliced turkey
    Orange and beanshoot salad
    Banana

D   Stir-fry vegetables and brown
rice
S   Grain-free carrot cake

DAY 3
B   Apple juice
Orange and apple salad with
millet flakes and nuts
L   Stuffed tomatoes
Waldorf salad (using
sunflower seeds and nuts)
D   Grilled trout
Green leafy vegetables
Carrots and parsnips in herb
sauce (thickened with
potato flour)
Boiled potatoes
S   Banana cream

DAY 4
B   ½ grapefruit
Hot fruit breakfast
L   Tuna omelette
Salad
D   Rosemary and garlic lamb
Brown rice
Jacket potato garnished with
(bell) peppers and parsley
S   Slice of apple cake

DAY 5
B   Orange juice
Buckwheat pancakes (crêpes)

with tomatoes, (bell)
pepper and herbs
L   Leek soup
Jacket potato with prawns
(shrimps)
Plums
D   Roast chicken
Leaf greens
Carrots
Sprouts and turnips
Boiled potatoes
S   Dried fruit compote and
yogurt

DAY 6
B   ½ grapefruit
Smoked haddock
Mushrooms, tomatoes
L   Green salad
Rice salad and dressing
Apple
D   Liver and onions
Green vegetables
Sauté potatoes
S   Fruity cakes

DAY 7
B   Cornflakes
Banana, sliced
Crumbled pecan nuts
1 tbsp raisins
Yogurt or milk
L   Savoury buckwheat pancakes
(crêpes) with salmon, tuna
or mackerel filling
D   Colourful lentils and salad
S   Fruit jelly

Snacks

With attention focused very much on food, you may get the 'munchies' for a few weeks. There are a number of things to eat between meals which will prevent you from dipping into the cookie jar!

1. Rice crackers or rice cakes from the healthfood shop. The crackers are particularly nice spread with peanut butter, sesame spread or sugar-free jam (jelly), all these from healthfood shops, too.

2. Sesame seeds or other seeds from healthfood shops are pleasant to nibble between meals.

3. Unsalted nuts can be eaten freely, but limit intake of peanuts, which are somewhat indigestible.

4. Fruit of your choice.

5. Rice biscuits or sesame biscuits and healthfood bars that don't contain wheat. Watch out for the sugar, though!

SECTION 2: SENSITIVITY TO YEAST

Do you suffer from any of the following symptoms?

Thrush (more than two episodes in the last five years)	☐	Cracking at the corners of your mouth	☐
		Depression	☐
Itchy bottom	☐	Excessive wind	☐
Bloated abdomen	☐	Cystitis	☐

Two or more episodes of thrush and/or any other two symptoms certainly qualify you for the yeast-free diet.

YEAST SENSITIVITY

Yeast problems in the gut are very common it seems, and they can produce or aggravate a wide variety of symptoms. Everyone has the yeast bug in their gut in harmless quantities (*candida albicans*), but in many people it gets triggered into rapid growth, producing toxins which then affect us, often without our realizing.

A few of the symptoms are of the emotional, mental and physical variety. These are also often 'allergic' type symptoms.

The more obvious yeast conditions are thrush in the vagina or in the mouth, cystitis, abdominal bloating and flatulence.

Many PMS symptoms seem to be aggravated by the yeast bug, *candida*. The vague symptoms of confusion, fatigue, lethargy, depression, poor memory, the feeling of 'not really being there' etc. – the list seems endless.

There are several actions that can be taken to prevent this problem continuing.

Avoiding yeast in food

It is surprising how many foods contain yeast. Yeast is used frequently in food preparation processes, in which case it is generally marked on the label of the product. However, yeast is a fungus which grows on food, particularly left-over food, even if well covered. It is also particularly fond of foods with an acid-base like citrus fruits and vinegar.

The following list is a guide to foods high in yeast, which you should try to avoid if you want to reduce the PMS symptoms mentioned above.

1. All foods containing sugar or honey, as yeast thrives on sugary or starchy food.

2. All bread, buns, biscuits, cakes etc.

3. Most alcoholic drinks often depend on yeasts to produce the alcohol, especially beer.

4. Citrus fruit juices – only fresh home-squeezed juice is yeast-free.

5. Malted cereals, malted drinks.

6. Pickles, sauerkraut, olives, chilli peppers.

7. Blue cheese (Roquefort).

8. Mushrooms and mushroom sauce.

9. Hamburgers, sausages and cooked meats made with bread or breadcrumbs. Yeast extract (Miso).

10. All fermented foods.

11. Dried fruits.

12. Left-over or stale food.

13. Vitamins. All B-vitamin preparations are likely to be derived from

yeast unless otherwise stated; but most manufacturers do make some B-vitamin preparations which are free of yeasts.

Other contributory factors

Apart from dietary changes there are a few other areas to check. The Pill can make yeast problems worse and should be avoided. Advice should be sought from the Family Planning Clinic for an alternative method of contraception. If the symptoms persist you may need to consult your doctor.

Hints for beating thrush

- Wear cotton underwear instead of nylon.

- Douche with live yogurt for immediate relief.

- Get your sexual partner treated as well, as it is highly likely that you would pass it back and forwards to each other.

There are some very helpful books on the subject of yeast problems on page 251.

ANITA'S THRUSH PROBLEMS

'I had continual thrush. I had been under my doctor for this problem and we had tried everything but nothing handled it. I had oral tablets, pessaries to insert in the vagina, creams etc. I tried using live yogurt and even baby oil; I changed my underwear and even stopped wearing tights. Nothing made an impression on the thrush until it was suggested that my diet was continually aggravating the thrush and I went on the nutritional programme. I was asked to stick to the recommendations strictly and my thrush cleared up completely. Wheat does make a difference to me. I'm okay now if I have one or two slices of bread or a small amount of cereal, but if I go beyond that I'll start to bloat. The minute I had a little alcohol as well back would come my thrush. So when I get the feeling I'm going to develop it, I cut out all foods containing yeast. I used to be absolutely plagued with thrush. It has totally vanished now, I haven't had any re-occurrence for at least 18 months.'

GERALDINE'S THRUSH PROBLEMS

'I had thrush all the time before I went on the programme. The hospital gave me a prescription and told me to use it for three months and not to have any sexual contact with my husband whatsoever in the meantime! Our marriage was already going through a very rough phase at this point, and I'd already tried this treatment before. I tried using the treatment again. It helped for a bit, but as soon as I stopped it the thrush was worse than ever. I had more pessaries and even went into hospital where it was suggested I paint the affected area violet. Diet certainly did help. Once I cut out sugary foods and other yeast-based foods it made a tremendous difference and the thrush began to clear up by itself.'

SECTION 3: HEADACHES

Do you suffer from the following?

Migraine headaches? ☐

Regular pre-menstrual headaches? ☐

Migraine symptoms may be aggravated by cheese, alcohol, oranges, tea, coffee, chocolate, fermented foods, potted foods and pastes, yeast and wholemeal (wholewheat) bread, smoked and preserved food and yeast extract. It is therefore advisable to avoid these foods where possible for at least a period of two to three months to see whether it makes any difference to your symptoms.

Make sure any vitamin supplements you take are yeast-free.

SECTION 4: SUGAR CRAVINGS

Do you suffer with excessive sugar cravings? There are several things you can do if sugar cravings are a problem.

- Sugar cravings could well improve by taking particular supplements, including vitamin B complex, magnesium and the mineral chromium. Chromium deals with sugar balance in the body, and thus plays an important and effective role in controlling sugar cravings.

- Eat a diet rich in foods containing chromium (see page 154).

- Whilst you are experiencing the sugar cravings, eat little and often. In other words, have five or six smaller meals per day, rather than three larger ones. This will help your blood sugar to remain constant and prevent you from having the extreme sugar cravings.

SECTION 5: IRON DEFICIENCY

Do you suffer with the following?

Heavy periods ☐   Cracking at the corners ☐
                                 of the mouth

Fatigue ☐   A sore tongue ☐

Heavy periods alone can cause iron deficiency. The other symptoms mentioned above may serve to confirm this. IUDs can sometimes cause heavy bleeding, so if you have a coil, it might be advisable to have a check-up and possibly consider an alternative method of contraception.

With any of the above symptoms you would be wise to ask your doctor to check your serum iron, to see whether you may need some iron supplements. In the meantime you should concentrate on eating iron-rich foods (see page 151).

SECTION 6: ZINC DEFICIENCY

Do you suffer with any of the following?

Acne ☐   Eczema ☐

White spots on your nails ☐   Poor hair growth ☐

Split brittle nails ☐   Infertility ☐

Any combination of the above symptoms may indicate that you need to increase your intake of zinc. This can be done by concentrating on foods rich in zinc and initially by taking a zinc supplement.

SECTION 7: FATTY ACID DEFICIENCY

Do you have any of the following?

Dry rough pimply skin on
  the upper arms or thighs ☐   Dandruff ☐

Red greasy skin ☐   Dry flaky skin ☐

                                          Eczema ☐

These symptoms may indicate that you are short of essential fatty acids. If you feel this may be so, you can refer to the Food List on essential fats on page 155. Evening primrose oil capsules may be helpful, as is cold pressed linseed oil when taken orally.

SECTION 8: BREAST TENDERNESS

Do you suffer with severe breast tenderness or lumpy breasts pre-menstrually? There are a number of preventive measures you can take:

- Eat a low salt diet.
- Cut out tea and coffee.
- Cut out cigarettes, or at least cut down.
- Restrict your dairy produce intake.
- Keep alcohol consumption to a minimum.
- If taking the contraceptive pill it might be worth changing your Pill or using an alternative method of contraception.

TAKE ONE STEP AT A TIME

There are many new ideas for you to absorb. If you don't feel you can make the necessary changes all at once, then make them gradually. The closer you follow the recommendations, the better off you are likely to feel after you have overcome any withdrawal symptoms that may occur at the very beginning.

It's quite normal to feel sceptical about the value of making such drastic changes. It is only when you start to feel better that you are likely to believe that this is a workable solution.

WILL YOU BE ON A RESTRICTED DIET FOR EVER?

There seems to be a definite difference between a 'food allergy' and a 'food sensitivity'. More often than not we find that severe PMS cases are suffering with food sensitivity rather than actual allergy, although there are cases where women are violently allergic to certain types of food.

Realistically, if you are suffering with severe symptoms, you need to give your body a complete rest for a minimum of two to three months. We often find it takes as much as six months to a year before the body is really back to normal, and can once again cope fully with foods that have been eliminated.

If you notice unpleasant side-effects occurring when you begin to reintroduce the grains, one by one, or products containing yeast, discontinue them for another month or two, before attempting to reintroduce them again. Usually, the very fact that there is so much progress occurring is an incentive to continue with the nutritional programme.

Occasionally we have found that some unfortunate souls have what seems to be a permanent allergy to a particular food, which when reintroduced continues to make them feel very unwell. In these cases the women themselves usually decide that it is better to be well and do without the food in question than to suffer unnecessarily.

It is probably better not to reintroduce foods to your diet during your pre-menstrual week. I usually suggest waiting until your period is over and you are feeling at your best.

CHEATING

One for one, the women who go through the programme cheat at some point. Not only do we expect it, we also think it is a positive step. It's only when you have put the system to the test yourself that you really begin to follow it because you believe in it, rather than following it because someone else said it might work.

I have to smile when I think of the stories I'm told about broken diets. I've been through restricted diets myself, so I know what happens. It goes like this. You begin to feel so well on the diet, in fact you've almost forgotten how rotten you felt initially. Amazing how the memory of pain and discomfort evaporates!

You begin to doubt that you really have food sensitivities, perhaps it's just a coincidence that you felt 'unwell' at the time you were eating your favourite restricted food. So you decide to blow the diet. You eat and enjoy one or two days' helpings of the forbidden 'fruit'. Sometimes the symptoms return within an hour or two, sometimes they creep on within a day or so; either way, you have the symptoms back again and you remember what feeling so unwell was like. You now realize that dietary factors and your symptoms are clearly related. So it's back on the diet with a far more self-determined resolution not to cheat!

IN THE LONG TERM

Once you have been following the dietary and supplement recommendations closely for three or four months, and you have noticed substantial improvement, you can then start to relax a bit. As long as you follow the basic recommendations most of the time, the occasional indulgence shouldn't hurt. Make sure it's only occasional to begin with, and preferably not in the pre-menstrual week. As a general rule, supplements should not be necessary in the long term. They should be taken until you feel that your symptoms are well under control. This may take as little as three or four months or as long as nine months to a year.

Occasionally, months after completing your programme, symptoms may recur. Times of great stress and general illness may, in some circumstances place extra nutritional demands on your body and this may bring on some of the old symptoms. Should this happen to you, identify which PMS category they fall into and take the appropriate dietary action. Use your original programme to help you.

Again, as symptoms reduce, gradually return to the maintenance recommendations and reduce the supplements gradually. It is important to do this in stages as abrupt withdrawal can often lead to recurrence of symptoms.

Do remember to take action quickly with any symptoms so that they can be relieved quickly.

STEP 3 – CHOOSING YOUR SUPPLEMENTS

We never advise women to take random supplements without some sort of advice. Our bodies are fairly sensitive mechanisms which have specific needs. Too much of a particular nutrient can cause imbalances and consequently other problems in the long term.

Before considering supplements, have a look at the chart called 'Physical Signs of Vitamin and Mineral Deficiency' on page 189: you might recognize some of the signs of vitamin and mineral deficiency which you have had for years but accepted as being 'normal'.

PHYSICAL SIGNS OF
VITAMIN AND MINERAL DEFICIENCIES

There are several useful supplements that can be tried in conjunction with each other. Assuming your symptoms are fairly severe and you are looking for the most effective treatment I will first sugest the optimum regime to begin on, regardless of cost. I will then go on to discuss cheaper, and finally, still cheaper alternatives. As you decide which supplements to try, make a note of their name and the daily dosage on your personal tailor-made programme.

MULTI-VITAMIN AND MINERAL SUPPLEMENTS

The first and most basic supplement to take is a multi-vitamin and mineral supplement which contains goodly amounts of the essential nutrients mentioned.

The most tried and tested multi-vitamin and mineral supplement for PMS is an American supplement, formulated by Dr Guy Abraham, Optivite for Women. It has been through several American clinical trials and has been shown to raise progesterone levels. It is available in the USA and the UK.

The Women's Nutritional Advisory Service has conducted two trials on Optivite, the results of which are detailed on page 191.

We usually recommend that four tablets be taken per day during the first few months. After this, reduce down to two per day until mid cycle, increasing to four per day during your pre-menstrual time. Sometimes, in severe cases, six tablets should be taken per day. If your symptoms are moderate, then a lower dosage may be used.

Another multi-vitamin and mineral supplement that performed well in a clinical trial is Femvite. This new supplement is based on WNAS research and is considerably cheaper than Optivite. It is currently available from Nutritional Health (mail order) and is expected to be available from chemists and healthfood shops by late 1994.

There are certain situations when other supplements need to be taken alongside your multi-vitamin and mineral tablets, some of these are listed on the chart on page 190.

PHYSICAL SIGNS OF
VITAMIN AND MINERAL DEFICIENCY

Sign or Symptom	Can be Caused by Deficiencies of:
Cracking at the corners of the mouth	Iron, vitamins B12, B6, Folic acid
Recurrent mouth ulcers	Iron, vitamins B12, B6, Folic acid
Dry, cracked lips	Vitamin B2
Smooth (sore) tongue	Iron, vitamins B2, B12, Folic acid
Enlargement/prominence of taste buds at tip of the tongue (red, sore)	Vitamins B2, or B6
Red, greasy skin on face, especially sides of nose	Vitamins B2, B6, zinc or essential fatty acids
Rough, sometimes red, pimply skin on upper arms and thighs	Vitamin B complex, vitamin E or essential fatty acids
Skin conditions such as eczema, dry, rough, cracked, peeling skin	Zinc, essential fatty acids
Poor hair growth	Iron or zinc
Dandruff	Vitamin C, vitamin B6, zinc, essential fatty acids
Acne	Zinc
Bloodshot, gritty, sensitive eyes	Vitamins A or B2
Night blindness	Vitamin A or zinc
Dry eyes	Vitamin A, essential fatty acids
Brittle or split nails	Iron, zinc or essential fatty acids
White spots on nails	Zinc
Pale appearance due to anaemia	Iron, vitamin B12, Folic acid, essential to consult your doctor

Problem	Type of Supplement	Daily Dosage	Available from
*PMS, A, H, C, D	Optivite or Femvite	2–6 tabs daily	Boots, chemists, healthfood shops and Nutritional Health (mail order)
*Breast problems	Efamol/Efamast evening primrose oil Natural Vitamin E	4-8 500 mg capsules daily 400 IUs daily	Chemists, healthfood shops, Nutritional Health (mail order) and prescription
Extreme nervous tension, drug withdrawals	Strong Vitamin B complex	1–2 tabs daily	Healthfood shops
*Sugar cravings	Normoglycaemia/ Sugar Factor	1–2 tabs daily	Nutritional Health (mail order)
*Eczema	Efamol/Epogam evening primrose oil	4-8 500 mg tabs daily	Boots, chemists, healthfood shops, Nutritional Health (mail order) and prescription
Dry, rough skin/ dandruff	Cold pressed linseed oil	2 tbsp with fruit juice at night	Healthfood shops
*Period pains/ palpitations insomnia	Magnesium chelate or magnesium hydroxide mixture	2 500 mg tabs daily or 15 ml taken as 5 ml 3 times daily	Healthfood shops and chemists

*Available by mail order through Nutritional Health,
  PO Box 926 Lewes, East Sussex BN7 2QL.

IMPORTANT POINTS

- Never take supplements without the consent of your GP if you have a current medical problem.

- Always begin taking your supplements gradually. For example, if you are due to take two or four per day of a particular supplement, begin taking them one tablet per day and gradually build up to the optimum dosage over the period of a week or two. Take them after meals unless otherwise specified.

How to cut down on your supplements

- Cut down on the dosage very gradually over a period of months rather than weeks, but keep taking the supplements each day of your cycle.

- Once you have reduced the dosage gradually, if you feel that your symptoms are well under control you can leave the supplements off altogether the week after your period.

- After another couple of months you can remain supplement-free for two weeks after your period.

- You might prefer to keep taking supplements pre-menstrually, or to cut them out completely and only take them at times of great stress. Some women prefer to take small doses daily on a permanent basis. There is no harm in doing so. As you will probably recognize from Chapter 11, which deals with our diet today, the nutrients in our food are often lost to us, therefore taking supplements in the long term as a general health aid may be a sensible move.

RESULTS OF CLINICAL TRIALS PERFORMED BY THE PRE-MENSTRUAL TENSION ADVISORY SERVICE

Name and type of product	Available from	Dosage given	Improved a lot	Improved slightly	No worse but no better
Optivite	Nature's Best	4 per day increasing to 8 per day pre-menstrually	71.5%	16.5%	12%
Optivite	Nature's Best	2 per day increasing to 4 pre-menstrually	65%	31%	6%
Evening primrose oil (Efamol)	Healthfood shops	8×500 mg capsules per day	64%	19%	17%
Femvite	Chemists, mail order (available from health-food shops in late 1994)	2 per day	84%	7%	7%
PMT	Australia New Zealand Singapore	2 per day	60%	30%	10%

Out of all the supplements available, only Optivite and Efamol have shown consistently significant results in clinical trials. For details of supplements available in Australia and New Zealand see Appendix 3.

WHAT ABOUT YOUR DRUGS?

If you are currently taking prescribed drugs from your doctor, I don't advise you to stop taking them or reduce them without his or her consent. Having said that, we do find that most women, once established on their nutritional programme, no longer feel the need for their tranquillizers, anti-depressants or sleeping pills.

Vitamins and minerals can be taken quite happily alongside most drugs. There are a few exceptions however. Any antibiotic in the tetracycline family should not be taken with minerals. Evening primrose oil should not be taken by anyone who has a history of epilepsy. When you feel the time has come to reduce your drugs, do go to see your doctor before taking any action, especially if you have been taking the drugs for a long period of time. Coming off drugs suddenly may bring on nasty withdrawal symptoms.

17

NUTRITIOUS RECIPES

Although this is not designed to be a recipe book, I felt it would be useful for you to have some guidelines to work with. It's better if you are not short of ideas to begin with: the more you like your new diet, the higher the chances of your sticking to it. In the Recommended Reading List on page 251, I have suggested many inexpensive recipe books which will give you further ideas. It might be an idea to visit a good bookshop and have a browse through the books, so that you can select those you find most suitable.

The recipes I have given cover breakfast, soups, lunch, dinner and sweets. All the recipes are suitable for those of you who are moderate sufferers. For those of you who suffer severely and therefore select a restricted diet, follow the recipes with a code beside them.

There are two codes:

G = Grain-free.
Y = Low yeast content.
No code = Suitable for all sufferers who are not on restricted diets.

Note: Imperial and American measures are given in brackets, where appropriate.
Use salt substitute, not salt.
Miso when not in brackets is soya.

BREAKFASTS

WHOLEWHEAT PANCAKES (CREPES)

110 g (4 oz/½ cup) wholemeal
  (wholewheat or buckwheat) flour
1 small egg

300 ml (10 fl oz/1¼ cups) skimmed
  (skim) milk
oil for cooking

Make a thin batter with the flour, egg and skimmed milk, whisking well. Use kitchen paper to wipe a small non-stick frying pan with oil and heat until it is smoking. Pour a generous 2 tablespoons of the batter into the pan and swirl it around to cover bottom as thinly as possible. Cook the batter for 60 seconds, then flip it over with a spatula and cook the other side for a few seconds only. If you are going to eat straight away, tip on to a heated plate – otherwise, stacked pancakes with cling film (plastic wrap) in between can be stored in the refrigerator. They can be easily reheated individually on a plate covered with foil over a pan of water, or in the microwave oven. SERVES 4

MUESLI

½ mug (½ cup) dried apricots
½ mug (½ cup) jumbo oats
½ mug (½ cup) barley flakes
¼ mug (¼ cup) large sultanas
  (golden raisins)

½ pint (1 cup) fresh orange juice
2 apples, grated
milk to mix
¼ mug (¼ cup) chopped mixed nuts
clear honey, to taste

Put apricots, oats, barley flakes, sultanas and orange juice in a mixing bowl. Cover and leave to soak overnight. Next morning, stir in the apple and sufficient milk to give a soft consistency. Spoon the muesli into dishes and top with chopped nuts and honey. SERVES 3–4

HOT FRUITY BREAKFAST

25 g (1 oz/2 tbsp) lightly crushed
  millet, toasted

150 ml (¼ pint/½ cup) milk
stewed fruit according to taste

Mix the millet and milk in a pan. Bring gently to the boil and simmer for 5 minutes, stirring occasionally. Put in a serving bowl, stir in 15–30 ml (1–2 tbsp) stewed fruit, and serve with extra milk substitute or a spoonful of sugar-free jam. SERVES 1

DRIED FRUIT CONSERVE   G

200 g (7 oz/1 cup) dried apricots
apple juice
Use one of the following flavourings:
5 ml (1 tsp) orange flower water

or
5 ml (1 tsp) grated orange peel
or
50 g (2 oz/½ cup) flaked almonds

Soak apricots overnight in water. Put the apricots into a saucepan and just cover them with apple juice, using the minimum amount to ensure a thick purée. Simmer them, uncovered, for about 30 minutes or until they are thoroughly cooked and soft. Cool and then thoroughly blend or sieve them until they have a smooth, thick consistency. Add one of the flavourings.

Purée will keep in refrigerator for about 10 days. SERVES 2

SOUPS

LENTIL AND VEGETABLE SOUP   G

15 g (½ oz) soft vegetable margarine
1 onion, chopped
1 garlic clove, crushed
2 large carrots, finely diced
2 sticks celery, sliced
2 tomatoes, skinned and chopped
50 g (2 oz/1 cup) mushrooms, chopped

100 g (4 oz) cabbage, shredded
100 g (4 oz/½ cup) continental lentils, pre-soaked
1 litre (1¾ pints) vegetable stock
bouquet garni (sprig parsley, thyme and bay leaf tied)
parsley
pepper

Melt margarine in a large saucepan and sauté the onion for five minutes without browning. Add garlic and rest of vegetables and cook gently for five minutes over the heat, then add the stock and bouquet garni, stir in extra parsley and season to taste with pepper. SERVES 4

BROCCOLI SOUP   G&Y

225 g (8 oz–1 lb) broccoli, chopped
1.7 litres (3 pints) vegetable stock
1.25 ml (¼ tsp) salt

30 ml (2 tbsp) semi-skimmed (skim)
   milk
pinch nutmeg
pinch cayenne pepper

Combine broccoli, stock and salt in large saucepan, bring to the boil. Reduce heat and simmer for 15 minutes. Remove from heat, blend mixture to purée with milk, nutmeg and cayenne. Return to pan, heat through, do not boil. SERVES 6

NUTTY PARSNIP SOUP   G

25 g (1 oz/1 tbsp) vegetable
   margarine
1 medium onion, chopped
300 g (10½ oz) parsnips, sliced
1 tbsp smooth peanut butter

dash shoyu (soya derivative, from
   healthfood shops)
1 vegetable stock cube
600 ml (1 pint) water
25 g (1 oz/¼ cup) peanuts, roasted

Melt the margarine in a deep pan. Sauté the onions and parsnips together until beginning to soften. Stir in the peanut butter to coat the vegetables. Add a little shoyu. Bring vegetable stock to the boil and add the water gradually, allowing the peanut butter to thicken slightly. Continue cooking until all ingredients are soft. Blend. Roughly grate the peanuts and scatter on the surface just before serving. (Hazelnuts and hazelnut butter can be used instead.) SERVES 4

FRESH AVOCADO AND TOMATO SOUP   G&Y

50 g (2 oz/¼ stick) butter/margarine
1 medium-sized onion, chopped
1 small potato, chopped
450 g (1 lb) tomatoes, quartered
2 garlic cloves

1 bay leaf
30 ml (2 tbsp) tomato purée (paste)
450 ml (¾ pint) vegetable stock
450 ml (¾ pint) milk
2 avocados (ripe)
pepper to taste

Melt the butter/margarine and sauté the onion until transparent. Add potato, tomatoes, garlic, bay leaf, tomato paste and stock. Cover and simmer for 20 minutes. Take off the heat, stirring in the milk and chopped avocado flesh. Remove bay leaf. Blend in small quantities in liquidizer goblet. Adjust seasoning to taste and reheat to serving temperature. SERVES 4–6

CHICKEN SOUP G&Y

1 chicken boned and cut into 2.5 cm
    (1 in) cubes
600 ml (1 pint) water
4 garlic cloves, sliced (optional, to
    taste)
2 sticks of celery, chopped

2 carrots, chopped
1 medium onion
50 g (2 oz) peas
50 g (2 oz) cooked brown rice
25 g (1 oz) parsley, chopped
herbs and seasoning to taste

Simmer chicken in water for 40 minutes. Add garlic, vegetables and rice and simmer for additional 20 minutes. Serve topped with scissor-snipped fresh parsley. Add herbs according to taste. SERVES 4

SALADS

Always use the very best and freshest ingredients.

BEANSHOOT SALAD G&Y

50 g (2 oz/½ cup) almond halves
1 tsp oil
¼ tsp salt

50 g (2 oz) carrots
2 bananas
300 g (8 oz) fresh beanshoots

Put the almonds, oil and salt in small ovenproof dish. Mix well, then roast in the oven at 200°C (400°F/Mark 6) for about 10 minutes until golden. Leave until cold. Grate carrots and slice the bananas, combine with almonds and beanshoots. SERVES 4

WALDORF SALAD G

4 sticks celery
50 g (2 oz/½ cup) walnuts
1 large dessert apple

150 g (6 oz) Cheddar cheese
salt and pepper
French dressing

Chop the celery and walnuts. Dice the apple and cheese. Mix all the ingredients together in a salad bowl. Add seasoning and dressing to taste. SERVES 4

BULGAR AND NUT SALAD

200 g (8 oz/1⅓ cups) bulgar
    (cracked wheat)
1 large sized onion, finely chopped
3 tbsp olive oil
100 ml (4 fl oz) tomato purée
    (paste)
60 ml (4 tbsp) dried mint

5 ml (1 tsp) ground cumin
5 ml (1 tsp) ground coriander
2.5 ml (½ tsp) ground allspice
110 g (4 oz/1 cup) walnuts and/or
    hazelnuts, very coarsely chopped
juice of 1 lemon

Soak the cracked wheat (available from healthfood shops) in plenty of fresh cold water for 15 minutes, drain it well and squeeze out as much of the water as you can. Fry the chopped onion in a tablespoon of oil, until very soft but not yet coloured. Mix all the ingredients in a large serving bowl and leave for about an hour for the bulgar to absorb the flavours and become plump and tender. SERVES 4

GRAPEFRUIT AND ORANGE SALAD   G&Y

1 whole grapefruit
1 orange
75 g (3 oz/½ cup) sunflower seeds

50 g (2 oz/½ cup) mixed nuts
    chopped
orange juice, freshly squeezed

Remove rind of grapefruit and orange and chop flesh, mix with sunflower seeds and nuts and a little orange juice. SERVES 4

ORANGE AND CUCUMBER SALAD   G&Y

2 oranges, divided into segments
½ cucumber, thinly sliced

1 small onion, thinly sliced into rings
½ small lettuce

Mix all ingredients together. SERVES 4

GREEN BEAN AND SWEETCORN SALAD   Y

200 g (8 oz) young French beans,
   topped and tailed
150 g (6 oz) can sweetcorn

2 spring onions (scallions), thinly
   sliced
2 tbsp French dressing (not for low
   yeast diet)

Cook the beans in slightly salted boiling water until tender. Drain, refresh in cold running water, leave to cool. Mix together the beans, sweetcorn and onions, Stir together with French dressing. SERVES 4

SALAD DRESSINGS

PEANUT AND CHILLI   G

25 ml (1 fl oz/2 tbsp) peanut oil
1 medium onion, thinly sliced
2.5 ml (½ tsp) chilli powder
5 ml (1 tsp) sugar/honey
5 ml (1 tsp) shoyu/tamari (soy
   sauce, from healthfood shops)
15 ml (1 tbsp) tomato purée (paste)
   (optional)

30–45 ml (2–3 tbsp) peanut butter
   (smooth)
3 cloves garlic, crushed or finely
   chopped
200 ml (7 fl oz/1 cup) water
200 ml (7 fl oz/1 cup) milk
dash of pepper

Heat oil gently and stir in onion, chilli, sugar/honey and shoyu, cook until onion is soft. Stir in tomato purée, peanut butter and garlic. Add water and milk and bring back to the boil, stirring regularly until mixture is smooth and not too thick. Season with pepper to taste.

It is important that the consistency is not too thick as it will become thick and lumpy if overcooked. MAKES 2½ CUPS

AVOCADO AND YOGURT DRESSING   G&Y

1 ripe avocado
½ lemon
400 ml (14 fl oz) yogurt

3 cloves garlic (crushed)
pinch of salt and pepper

Halve the avocado and scoop out the flesh, blend or mash immediately with lemon juice. Fold yogurt and garlic into avocado mixture until smooth. Season to taste, or season with chilli or cayenne pepper. MAKES 2½ CUPS

YOGURT HERB DRESSING   G

125 ml (5 fl oz/½ cup) natural
   yogurt
1 clove garlic, crushed
15 ml (1 tbsp) cider vinegar

5 ml (1 tsp) clear honey
15 g (½ oz) parsley
15 g (½ oz) mixed mint and herbs
pinch of salt and pepper

Place all ingredients except herbs in a bowl, adding salt and pepper to taste and mix thoroughly with a fork. Add herbs finely chopped and mix well or blend for 1–2 minutes. Chill until required. MAKES 1 CUP

CREAMY TOMATO DRESSING   G&Y

30 ml (2 tbsp) home-made
   mayonnaise
1 tomato, chopped

10 ml (2 tsp) lemon juice
2.5 ml (½ tsp) dried or 1 tsp fresh
   basil

Blend all the ingredients together on low speed. MAKES ABOUT ⅓ CUP

OIL AND FRUIT DRESSING   G

30 ml (2 tbsp) olive oil
15 ml (1 tbsp) sesame oil
5 ml (1 tsp) mayonnaise
5 ml (1 tsp) mustard

juice from a lemon or 15 ml (1 tbsp)
   wine vinegar
5 ml (1 tsp) concentrated apple juice
   (optional)
black pepper to taste

Blend all the ingredients together until smooth. This dressing keeps well in the fridge in a sealed container. MAKES 1 CUP

LUNCHES AND DINNERS

GRILLED (BROILED) SARDINES   G&Y

Wash and dry sardines, dust with peppered flour (non-wheat flour for restricted diets) and grill (broil) for 5–10 minutes depending on size, turning once.

or

Place sardines on the grill (broiler), sprinkle with pepper and olive oil and grill for 5–10 minutes depending on size, turning once.

STUFFED PEPPERS   G

1 medium onion	2.5 ml (½ tsp) yeast extract (Miso)
2 sticks celery	4 medium-size green or red (bell)
100 g (4 oz) mushrooms	peppers
1 large tomato	30 ml (2 tbsp) buckwheat or other
1 medium-sized carrot	grain-free flour
25 g (1 oz/½ stick) margarine	seasoning to taste
100 ml (5 fl oz/½ cup) water	100 g (4 oz) Cheddar cheese, grated
5 ml (1 tsp) tomato purée (paste)	

Chop the onion, celery, mushrooms and tomatoes and dice the carrot, melt margarine and fry onion, carrot, celery and mushrooms together for 5 minutes. Stir in the tomato, water, tomato purée and yeast extract. Cover and simmer for 10–15 minutes, until just tender. Meanwhile, halve peppers lengthways and remove the seeds, then steam for 10 minutes. Arrange in an ovenproof serving dish. Drain vegetables, reserving the cooking liquid. Fill the peppers with the vegetables. Sprinkle the flour into the vegetable liquid and bring to the boil. Adjust seasoning to taste. Pour over the peppers, sprinkle with the cheese and bake in the oven at 200°C (400°F/Mark 6) for 15 minutes. Serve at once. SERVES 4

SPANISH OMELETTE   G&Y

1 small onion, chopped	2 eggs
25 ml (1 fl oz/¼ cup) water	5 ml (1 tsp) butter
1 stick celery, chopped	2 tomatoes, chopped
1 green (bell) pepper	parsley (scissor-snipped)

Place the onions and water in a sealed pan over a medium heat. When water begins to boil reduce the heat to low. Add celery and green pepper and continue cooking until soft. Do not overcook. Beat eggs, melt butter in a medium frying pan over a low heat. Pour in beaten eggs and allow to cook gently. Strain vegetables, tip onto partly cooked omelette and add tomatoes. When cooked serve sprinkled with parsley. SERVES 1

STIR-FRY VEGETABLES   G†*

There are many different combinations of vegetable in season that can be used for stir-frying. You can use six or seven different vegetables or only two or three.

To obtain the best results, stir-fry vegetables should be cooked with the minimum oil at a high heat as rapid cooking seals in the flavour.

Here are some nice last-minute additions to your stir-fry. Experiment to find your favourite seasoning and flavouring. Less well-known ingredients are available from healthfood shops.

*Seasoning

Salt, pepper, chilli, grated ginger, five spice (use very moderately), sesame seeds (ground), fenugreek (ground), turmeric, coriander, paprika, nori seaweed (toasted and crumbled).

*Flavouring

Shoyu/tamari, Miso (all Japanese/Chinese condiments made from soya beans), sesame oil, tahini (sesame seed butter), sunflower oil, safflower oil, sherry, vermouth, lemon juice.

450 g (1 lb) fresh broccoli
225 g (8 oz) cauliflower
15 ml (1 tbsp) oil
2.5 cm (1 in) fresh ginger, sliced and
    finely shredded
2 large carrots, peeled and sliced

2.5 ml (½ tsp) sesame oil
225 g (8 oz) fresh bean sprouts
225 g (8 oz) Chinese leaves or white
    cabbage, shredded
2.5 ml (½ tsp) salt

Separate the broccoli heads into small florets and peel and slice the stems. Separate the cauliflower florets and slice stems. Heat oil in a large wok or frying pan. When it is moderately hot add ginger shreds. Stir-fry for a few seconds. Add the carrots, cauliflower and broccoli and stir-fry for 2–3 minutes then add sesame seed oil, bean sprouts and Chinese leaves or white cabbage. Stir-fry for further 2–3 minutes. Season to taste. Serve at once. SERVES 4–6

* † and Y if yeast-free flavouring selected

Ginger can be substituted for garlic and soy sauce can be added in final stage of frying before serving.

MACKEREL WITH HERBS (IN FOIL)   G&Y

4 medium-sized fresh mackerel,
    gutted
juice of one lemon
freshly ground black pepper

4 small bunches of 4 different fresh
    mixed herbs, e.g. tarragon, chives,
    parsley and sage
little olive oil

Preheat oven to 240°C (475°F/Mark 9). Wash mackerel and sprinkle insides with lemon juice. Add generous sprinkling of pepper. Put bunch of mixed herbs inside each fish and brush skin with oil to avoid sticking, wrap each fish individually in foil, quite tightly, bake for 10–12 minutes and serve. SERVES 4

STUFFED MACKEREL IN FOIL

2 large oranges
4 tbsp porridge (rolled oats)
1 medium-sized onion, finely chopped
1 tbsp parsley, finely chopped
1 tbsp raisins

1 apple, grated
pinch of salt
1 tsp dried rosemary or 4 sprigs fresh
    rosemary
4 medium-sized fresh mackerel,
    gutted

Grate zest of orange, chop flesh into small pieces, discarding pips and any tough pith. Mix the orange zest and flesh with oats, onion, parsley, raisins and grated apple and pinch of salt. Divide mixture into 4 and stuff mackerel loosely. Place rosemary in each fish. Bake in foil as above for about 40 minutes. SERVES 4

VEGETARIAN GOULASH   G

45 ml (3 tbsp) oil
1 medium onion, sliced
2 medium carrots, diced
2 medium courgettes (zucchini),
    sliced
½ small white cabbage, finely
    shredded
15 ml (1 tbsp) paprika

2.5 ml (½ tsp) caraway seeds
2.5 ml (½ tsp) mixed herbs
pinch of nutmeg
600 ml (1 pint) tomato juice
300 ml (½ pint) water
1 vegetable stock cube
142 ml (¼ pint) soured cream or
    natural yogurt

Heat oil in large saucepan and sauté the onion and carrot until the onion is transparent. Add courgettes and cabbage and cook over medium heat for 10 minutes, stirring frequently. Stir in paprika, caraway seeds, herbs and nutmeg, then add tomato juice, water and stock cube. Cover and simmer for about 20 minutes until the vegetables are just tender. Adjust seasoning with a small pinch salt and pepper. Serve each portion with a drop of soured cream or yogurt. Serve at once. SERVES 4–6

STEAMED FISH (WITH GARLIC, SPRING ONIONS [SCALLIONS] AND GINGER)   G&Y

350 g (12 oz) firm white fish fillets (cod, sole etc)

2.5 ml (½ tsp) salt

15 ml (1 tbsp) fresh ginger, finely chopped

30 ml (2 tbsp) spring onions (scallions), finely chopped

15 ml (1 tbsp) light soy sauce (not for yeast-free diet)

15 ml (1 tbsp) oil, preferably groundnut

5 ml (1 tsp) sesame oil

2 garlic cloves, peeled and thinly sliced

Rub cleaned and dried fish with salt both sides and leave for 30 minutes. Steam fish over simmering water until just cooked, covering steamer tightly. Sprinkle on the ginger, spring onions and light soy sauce. Heat the two oils together in small saucepan, when hot add garlic slices and brown. Pour the garlic oil mixture over the top of the fish. Serve at once. SERVES 4

SNOW PEAS WITH TIGER PRAWNS   G&Y

450 g (1 lb) snow peas (mange tout))

450 g (1 lb) uncooked tiger prawns

375 g (13 oz) uncooked broad oriental rice noodles

5 ml (1 tsp) finely chopped root ginger

45 ml (3 tbsp) sesame oil

30 ml (2 tbsp) oyster sauce

5 ml (1 tsp) sugar

15 ml (1 tbsp) sherry or white wine

fresh coriander to decorate

Top and tail the snow peas and wash them. Clean and wash the prawns and pat them dry with kitchen paper. Place the noodles in boiling water and simmer gently for 3 minutes, until slightly undercooked. Place the ginger and the oil in a wok and heat. Fry the snow peas briefly in the hot oil stirring constantly. Remove and place on a warmed dish. Place the tiger prawns in the wok and cook until they become pink. Drain the noodles and rinse with cold water to remove the starch. Return snow peas to the wok with the prawns, add the oyster sauce and the sugar, and simmer for another minute or two. Gently pour one tablespoon of sherry or white wine around the circumference of the wok, and then remove peas and prawns from the wok with a slatted spoon and transfer to a dish. Place noodles in the wok and quickly stir-fry them in the remaining oil turning constantly. Turn the noodles out onto a flat platter and place the snow peas and prawns on the top. Decorate with fresh coriander and serve immediately. SERVES 4

Variation If you like spicy food, before stir-frying the noodles mix 5 ml (1 tsp) chilli sauce with the hot oil and then place the noodles in the wok.

FRAGRANT LAMB G&Y

2–3 lb (900 g–1.3 kg) fillet joint of leg of lamb or 6 fillets of lamb	30 ml (2 tbsp) brandy
	45 ml (3 tbsp) white wine
45 ml (3 tbsp) sesame oil	black pepper to taste or a sprinkling
1 clove of garlic, chopped	of black peppercorns
1.25 cm (½ in) lump of root ginger, chopped	5 ml (1 flat tsp) cornflour
whole spring onion	8 large lettuce leaves to decorate the serving plate
45 ml (3 tbsp) light soy sauce	sprig of coriander

Seal the lamb by cooking in a little hot sesame oil for two minutes each side. Remove the lamb from the hot oil and place in a pressure cooker. Add the chopped garlic, chopped ginger, the whole spring onion, the remaining sesame oil, soy sauce, brandy, white wine, and black pepper or peppercorns. Put the lid on the pressure cooker and bring to the boil. Lower the heat, and cook at pressure for 35 minutes. Decorate a large serving dish with lettuce leaves ready to receive the lamb. Remove the pressure cooker from the heat and place under cold running water to cool. Place the lamb on a chopping board and slice into portions. Arrange the chops or the sliced lamb joint on the serving dish and place in the oven to keep warm whilst you prepare the sauce. Drain the juice and thicken with the cornflour, stirring constantly. Remove the serving dish from the oven, pour the sauce over the lamb and decorate with the coriander. Serve immediately. SERVES 6

LAMB PAPRIKA   G

2 onions, sliced
50 g (2 oz) mushrooms, sliced
2 carrots, sliced
4 lamb chops (lean)

30 ml (2 tbsp) paprika
450 ml (¾ pint) water
15 ml (1 tbsp) cornflour (cornstarch)
    (or alternative grain-free flour)

Mix vegetables together and place in casserole. Arrange chops on top. Stir paprika into water and pour over chops, cover and cook until chops are tender. Remove vegetables and chops and arrange on warm serving dish. Mix cornflour with a little cold water and use to thicken liquid from chops. Cook for 2–3 minutes, pour over chops. SERVES 2–4

LIVER WITH ORANGE   G

225 g (8 oz) lamb's liver
30 ml (2 tbsp) wholewheat flour (or
    alternative grain-free flour)
2.5 ml (½ tsp) dried thyme or basil
25 ml (1½ tbsp) sunflower oil

1 orange, peeled and sliced
grated orange peel
15 ml (1 tbsp) soy sauce
30 ml (2 tbsp) orange juice

Wash liver, slice thinly, pat dry with kitchen paper. Cut out and discard stringy pieces, coat in flour seasoned with herbs. Heat oil in a frying pan and fry liver pieces gently for 5 minutes, turning to cook evenly. Add orange slices and peel, soy sauce and orange juice. Heat through gently and serve. SERVES 2

NUT ROAST   G

1 medium onion
25 g (1 oz/¼ stick) butter/margarine
225 g (8 oz/2 cups) mixed nuts
100 g (4 oz/2 cups) cooked brown
    rice

200 ml (½ pint) vegetable stock
10 ml (2 tsp) yeast extract (Miso)
5 ml (1 tsp) mixed herbs
salt and pepper to taste

Chop onions and sauté in butter until transparent. Grind nuts in a blender or food processor until quite fine. Heat stock and yeast extract to boiling point, then combine all the ingredients including the cooked brown rice together and mix well until the mixture is a fairly slack consistency. Turn into greased shallow baking dish, level the surface, and bake in oven at 180°C (350°F/Mark 4) for 30 minutes until golden brown. SERVES 4–6

COLOURFUL LENTILS   G

60 ml (4 tbsp) oil
3 cloves garlic, crushed
4 carrots, chopped
1 green (bell) pepper, chopped
1 red (bell) pepper, chopped
5 ml (1 tsp) basil
3 sticks celery, chopped

15 ml (1 tbsp) brown rice miso
900 ml (1½ pints) hot water
675 g (1½ lb) tomatoes, skinned,
  seeded and chopped
280 g (10 oz) lentils, not presoaked
30 ml (2 tbsp) chopped parsley
seasoning to taste

Heat oil in a pan and add the garlic, carrots, green and red peppers, basil and celery. Cook until the ingredients are soft. Mix the brown rice miso with hot water and add this to mixture, together with the tomatoes. Stir in the lentils. Season to taste. Simmer for 1 hour. Serve, garnished with the chopped parsley. SERVES 4 OR 6 AS A STARTER

STUFFING FOR ROAST CHICKEN   G

1 stick celery, finely chopped
2 cloves garlic, crushed
30 ml (2 tbsp) sunflower oil
60 g (2 oz/¼ cup) uncooked long
  grain brown rice
150 ml (¼ pint) hot water

120 g (4 oz/2 cups) mushrooms,
  sliced
30 g (1 oz/⅙ cup) sultanas
60 g (2 oz/⅓ cup) dried apricots,
  soaked and chopped
30 ml (2 tbsp) tarragon

Fry the celery and garlic in the oil for 2–3 minutes. Add the rice and sauté for a few minutes. Pour in the hot water, stir, then simmer for 5–6 minutes until most of the water has been absorbed, but the rice is still hard. Remove from the heat and mix in the remaining ingredients. Allow to cool for a little, then use to stuff the chicken.

SWEETS

FRUIT JELLY   G

22 g (¾ oz) gelatine
600 ml (1 pint) unsweetened fruit
   juice
   e.g. apple, pineapple

Sprinkle the gelatine on 1 tbsp heated fruit juice and stir well until dissolved. Add the rest of the juice. Put into a wetted mould and chill until set. SERVES 4

DRIED FRUIT COMPOTE AND YOGURT   G

15 g (½ oz/1 tbsp) sugar
600 ml (1 pint) water
5–10 cm (2–3 in) stick of cinnamon

450 g (1 lb) mixed dried fruit e.g.
apple rings, peaches, apricots,
prunes, pears and sultanas

Dissolve the sugar in the water over a gentle heat, add the cinnamon. Place the dried fruit in a bowl and pour the syrup over. Cover and leave to soak overnight. If the soaked fruit is not tender, replace in the pan and simmer for a few minutes. Serve cold with yogurt. SERVES 4–6

RHUBARB FOOL   G&Y

25 g (1 oz/¼ stick) margarine
225 g (8 oz) rhubarb

12–25 g (½–1 oz) brown sugar
200 ml (7 fl oz) natural yogurt

Melt margarine in a pan. Add rhubarb and sugar and cook until tender. Purée rhubarb and yogurt together in a blender. Chill before serving. SERVES 4

STUFFED BAKED APPLES   G

4 good-sized cooking apples
1 tbsp honey/sugar-free jam

Stuffing suggestions:
Dates, cinnamon, raisins and honey

Core apples and slit skins in a ring round the middle. Stuff with chosen filling and honey. Bake until fruit is tender. Serve hot or cold. SERVES 4

CARROT CAKE   G

4 eggs
225 g (8 oz/1 cup) caster (superfine)
   sugar
grated rind of 1 lemon
225 g (8 oz/2 cups) ground almonds

225 g (8 oz) carrots, finely grated
25 ml (1½ tbsp) rice flour
5 ml (1 tsp) wheat-free baking
   powder

Preheat the oven to 180°C (350°F/Mark 4). Separate the eggs. Place yolks, sugar and lemon rind in a bowl or in a blender or food processor and beat together well. Add the almonds and carrots to this mixture. Stir well. Sift the flour and baking powder together then fold into mixture. In another bowl beat the egg whites until they are stiff, then fold them into the mixture. Grease an oblong baking tray 8×12×2 inches (20×30×5 cm). Spread the mixture out in the tray and bake for 45 minutes. Leave to cool in the tray, then cut into slices. MAKES 10 SLICES

BANANA CREAM   G

4 medium bananas
15 ml (1 tbsp) lemon juice

400 ml (15 fl oz/2 cups) yogurt
5 ml (1 tsp) honey

Place all ingredients in the blender and blend until creamy. Chill well before serving. SERVES 4

FRUITY CAKES   G

100 g (4 oz/1 stick) butter/margarine
100 g (4 oz) unrefined sugar
   (reduced to caster (superfine)
   sugar consistency in a blender or
   food processor)
2 eggs, beaten

200 g (5½ oz) Trufree No 7 self-
   raising (self-rising) flour, or other
   wheat-free flour
100–150 g (4–6 oz/¾–1 cup) mixed
   raisins, currants and sultanas
   (golden raisins)

Cream butter or margarine and sugar till light and fluffy. Add eggs gradually then fold in flour. Stir in mixed dried fruit. Put mixture into individual cake cases and bake at 190°C (375°F/Mark 5) for 15–18 minutes till risen and golden.

Alternatively place all the mixture in a 500 g (1 lb) loaf tin and cook at 180°C (350°F/Mark 4) for 20–25 minutes for a sweet fruit loaf. MAKES 10 CAKES

GINGER BANANAS   G

4 ripe bananas   25 g (1 oz) flaked almonds
small amount preserved ginger

Slice the bananas into individual dishes (one per person). Rinse the syrup from the preserved ginger and chop fairly finely. Sprinkle ginger over the bananas and top with a few almonds. SERVES 4

Variation Mix in a few drops of lemon juice and sprinkle with sunflower seeds.

EGG CUSTARD   G&Y

175 ml (6 fl oz/¾ cup) milk   a few drops of real vanilla essence
2 egg yolks   (optional)
mild honey to taste

Heat the milk to boiling point and add slowly to the well-beaten egg yolks. Return to the pan, preferably a double boiler, and stir over a gentle heat until the mixture thickens slightly. Sweeten to taste with honey and add a few drops of vanilla essence if liked. The custard will thicken as it cools. SERVES 2

CAKES, BISCUITS AND BREAD

BUCKWHEAT AND RICE BREAD

This makes brown bread which is crisp on the outside and soft on the inside.

300 g (12 oz) buckwheat flour   2.5–5 ml (½–1 tbsp) salt
150 g (6 oz) brown rice flour   340–360 ml (just over ½ pint)
1½ packets easy yeast   hand-hot water
5 ml (1 tsp) sugar   2 500 g (1 lb) loaf tins
15 ml (1 tbsp) oil

Mix together flours and easy yeast. Add sugar, oil and salt and mix to a thick batter with the hand-hot water. Grease and flour the two loaf tins.

Divide mixture between the two loaf tins, cover and leave to rise in a warm place for 20–30 minutes. Bake at 230°C (450°F/Mark 8) for 35–40 minutes. The bread will slightly contract from the side of the tins when it is cooked. Cool for 5 minutes in the tins and then turn out onto a wire rack. MAKES 14 SLICES (7 EACH LOAF)

POTATO AND RICE BREAD

This is a white bread which is delicious when freshly baked, and subsequently makes very nice toast. It tastes rather like crumpets.

250 g (10 oz) potato flour
200 g (8 oz) brown rice flour
1½ packets easy yeast
5 ml (1 tsp) sugar

15 ml (1 tbsp) oil
2.5–5 ml (½–1 tsp) salt
340–360 ml (just over ½ pint)
    hand-hot water
2 500 g (1 lb) loaf tins

Mix together flours and easy yeast. Add sugar, oil and salt and mix to a thick batter with the hand-hot water. Grease and flour the two loaf tins. Divide mixture between the two loaf tins, cover and leave to rise in a warm place for 20–30 minutes. Bake at 230°C (450°F/Mark 8) for 35–40 minutes. The bread will contract slightly from the side of the tins when it is cooked. Cool for 5 minutes in the tins and then turn out on to a wire rack. MAKES 16 SLICES (8 EACH LOAF)

POTATO SHORTBREAD

150 g (6 oz) potato flour
100 g (4 oz) margarine

50 g (2 oz) sugar
75 g (3 oz) ground almonds

Put all ingredients in to a food processor and beat together for 5–6 seconds. Scrape bowl and repeat the process until a ball of dough is formed. Put dough into a greased 7–8 in (17.5–20 cm) round sandwich tin and press down evenly. Mark out portions with a knife, prick all over and bake at 180°C (350°F/Mark 4) for 35–40 minutes. Cut into wedges and cool in tin. MAKES 8 SLICES

APPLE AND CINNAMON CAKE

4 large cooking apples
225 g (8 oz) brown rice flour
4 large eggs
100 g (4 oz) ground almonds
100 g (4 oz) caster sugar
100 g (4 oz) cooking flora
few drops of almond essence to
    flavour

15 ml (1 tbsp) cinnamon

To decorate:

approximately 16 apple slices
7.5 ml (½ tbsp) of cinnamon
15 ml (1 tbsp) of caster sugar

Grease a deep 8 in (20 cm) loose-bottomed circular baking tin. Pre-heat oven to moderate temperature, 150°C (300°F/Mark2). Peel, core and slice the apples and leave to soak in cold water. Place the flour, eggs, ground almonds, caster sugar, cooking flora and almond essence in the bowl of a mixer and beat until light and fluffy. Line the cake tin with approximately 1½ in (3.75 cm) of mixture. Place most of the apples in the tin and sprinkle with sugar and cinnamon. Spread the additional mixture on to the top of the apples and smooth off the top ready for the decoration. Gently push remaining apple slices into the top of the cake in a circle and sprinkle with cinnamon and sugar. Bake in a moderate oven for at least one hour, until cooked through. Cool briefly, then gently ease the cake out of the tin and onto a plate. Serve hot as a pudding or cold as a cake with whipped or pouring cream. MAKES 8 GOOD SIZED SLICES

ALMOND MACAROONS

2 large egg whites
150 g (6 oz) ground almonds

75 g (3 oz) caster sugar
18 almond halves

Put the unbeaten egg whites into a bowl with the ground almonds, and beat well adding the caster sugar 1 tablespoon at a time. Line biscuit trays with greaseproof paper. With moist hands roll the mixture into balls and flatten in the palm of your hand. Lay the flattened biscuits carefully onto the trays and place an almond half in the middle of each biscuit. Bake in a moderate oven at 180°C (350°F/Mark 4) for 25 minutes or until golden brown. Keep in an airtight tin, or freeze. MAKES 18 (9 PORTIONS)

COCONUT PYRAMIDS

4 egg yolks or two whole eggs
75 g (3 oz) caster sugar

juice and rind of half a lemon
250 g (8 oz) dessiccated (dried and shredded) coconut

Beat the egg yolks and sugar until creamy. Stir in the lemon juice, rind and coconut. Form into pyramid shapes, either with your hands or using a moist egg cup, and place on a greased baking tray. Bake at 190°C (375°F/ Mark 5) until the tips are golden brown. Keep in an airtight tin or freeze.
MAKES ABOUT 24 (12 PORTIONS)

18

STRESS OR DISTRESS?

Let's first take a look at the terms stress and distress. In my opinion a certain amount of stress in life gets the adrenaline going and can be both mentally stimulating and healthy. When the pressure rises to the point where it then becomes uncomfortable, you can rest assured that you've hit the band of distress.

Don't ever underestimate the power of distress on your physical and mental well-being. I've seen many a 'strong' person bite the dust when under incredible pressure. The classic case is a person who seems to cope amazingly well with a disaster or a near-tragedy. They sail through the event appearing cool, calm and collected. Then several months later get physically sick or become emotionally unbalanced. It is now understood that stress places extra nutritional demands on the body. And when we are feeling stressed we often don't eat as well as usual, which can make matters worse.

Part of the game is being able to identify the source of stress and admit honestly that you are finding it a strain.

When you are feeling on top of the world physically and mentally your tolerance of problems or particularly difficult situations may be higher. Whereas when you feel below par, extra problems often seem too much to bear.

Many a physical and emotional illness is precipitated by stress. The body's demand for B vitamins increases when under stress. Often, when people have severe problems, their diet suffers and they either eat insufficient food to meet their requirements or indulge in too much junk food and alcohol. You will have seen from Chapter 14 how deficiencies in B vitamins can lead to nervous and mental disorders. Food allergies are also often linked to distressing situations. These can affect the mind and the body. Migraine headaches, irritable bowel syndrome, agoraphobia, diarrhoea, depression, insomnia, nervous tension, mood swings, restlessness, etc. can all result from stress-induced food intolerance.

A PROBLEM SHARED IS A PROBLEM HALVED

There is no need to pretend you aren't suffering: it's far better to talk over your problems and frustrations, and even have a good cry if you feel like it. Crying can be very therapeutic. Once the problem has been talked through, you may find it gets put a little more into perspective. You may suddenly realize how to cope with the situation immediately, or in the long term. Support and reassurance are very comforting: having a friend to lean on at times of great need is a very valuable asset. There is no substitute for plenty of open, honest communication.

Try to stand outside the problem and examine it clearly. This often helps you to see things more clearly. Sometimes, being so involved in a situation means you can't 'see the wood for the trees'.

Most of all, take time out each day to get your attention off the problem. Consciously daydream, if you like, in a quiet room undisturbed, or go for a long country walk and observe the wonders of nature. Discipline yourself to do this regularly. You'll be surprised how therapeutic these activities can be.

HOW STRESS AFFECTS YOUR BODY

Pay attention to your body telling you it's not very happy. Look out for possible weak areas that are more susceptible to tension build-up. For example:

Forehead	Upper back
Face	Lower back
Neck	Hands
Shoulders	Legs

Clenched teeth, grinding teeth at night, headaches and eye strain are all signs of inner stress. Becoming aware of your weaknesses is half the battle. The stresses and strains of life do tend to build up in the body. We are each affected differently. Some people suffer backaches, whilst others get headaches. When the body becomes loaded with tension we tie up our energy to some extent. The energy flows become blocked and as a result symptoms like headaches and abdominal cramps are likely to become worse.

You can gently massage any tense areas or have someone do it for you, preferably each day. Also try to spend 10–15 minutes at the end of the day consciously relaxing your muscles, beginning with your face and working your way down to your toes.

A good massage is soothing. Yoga may help and it is easy to practise simple relaxing techniques at home. There are other suggestions to help you through difficult periods. Meditation, autogenic training and physical exercise seem to be beneficial for some people. It's really a question of choosing a method of relaxation which you are happy to practise regularly.

There are certain areas in your life which you might like to examine if you are feeling stressed.

- Have you taken on so many commitments that you aren't able to really enjoy life?

Some people just can't say 'No'. They have good hearts, and little appreciation of their actual working capacity. If you are guilty of this, do sit back and have a good think about it. Make yourself a work schedule and a leisure schedule and stick to it.

- Have you got any goals or aims in life you are pursuing? Having a strong sense of purpose in life is a great asset. Not having a purpose or direction can have repercussions on your mental well-being and subsequently affect your health. Without a desire to achieve something, life often becomes rather boring and meaningless.

- Have you got many unfinished projects on the go, and never seem to get around to finishing any one of them?

Knowing that you should have completed a project and didn't, especially if it's something promised to another, can be stressful. Make a list of any unfinished projects and then assign a regular time each week, to work through them gradually.

- Is your home and/or work environment tidy and in order, or have you allowed things to pile up around you?

It is difficult to thrive or relax properly in an area which is untidy, disordered or dirty. If you feel there is room for improvement, why not have a grand 'sort out' or clean up – I'll bet you feel better afterwards.

- Do you have plenty of interests and activities to pursue in your spare

216

time? It is healthy to maintain a wide variety of interests: perhaps some activities that you like to indulge in yourself, and also activities and interests you can share with other members of your family, friends and pets.

- Do you take regular exercise and set aside relaxation time for yourself? Exercise and relaxation are both extremely valuable pursuits and contribute greatly to health. The next chapter is on the subject of exercise and should help you to work out an activity plan.

19

THE VALUE OF EXERCISE AND RELAXATION

I can't emphasize strongly enough how important exercise and relaxation are in maintaining a healthy body. There have been several studies which demonstrated that exercise was a valuable tool in overcoming depression, and the PMS A symptoms of nervous tension, mood swings, irritability and anxiety.

If you don't like structural exercises you should at least take a brisk walk for half an hour a day. Personally I find swimming one of the most stimulating exercises, especially at the start of the day.

Beyond doubt, exercise raises energy levels, and your spirits. On a regular basis, it also speeds up the metabolism of the body. Although you may have to push yourself initially, I assure you it will pay dividends within a short space of time.

The mind and body work closely together. The mental stress of PMS will be reflected in the physical tension in your body. The muscular aches and pains of PMS such as headaches, neck pain and stiff joints, together with the more obvious low backache and abdominal cramps, all work to increase feelings of anxiety and depression. It's hardly surprising that the heart rate increases, as the nervous and physical tension increases, all adding to feelings of being 'wound up'.

Exercise may provide help for PMS sufferers more than just by acting as a general tonic. Recently, it has been shown that the level of a particular brain hormone, beta-endorphin, a hormone associated with a sense of well-being and pain relief, was found to be low in pre-menstrual sufferers in the few days before their period. The levels during the first phase of the menstrual cycle were normal when compared with healthy women who did not have PMS. Beta-endorphin is an important self-produced hormone, which may affect mood and well-being, and also influence the function of other hormones. Its level can be raised by regular and usually prolonged physical exercise. Potentially, it could also be influenced by dietary and nutritional factors.

Thus, regular physical exercise by stimulating the body's natural production of beta-endorphin might help to prevent the dip that occurs pre-menstrually in PMS sufferers. The value of exercise in PMS has been studied in two papers from North America. Both of these report a modest benefit of aerobic exercise on PMS, especially for mental symptoms. Breast tenderness was not helped very much by this approach. My own experience supports this. Other studies have shown that physical exercise can be of value in the treatment of depression.

However, you can have too much exercise as well. Analysis of a large group of sufferers contacting the WNAS revealed that the least symptoms were experienced by those who exercised three or four times per week. Those who exercised every day had as much PMS as other women but with a smaller degree of relief in the week after their period.

GENERAL ADVICE

- It is important to take time off to care for yourself.

- Ensure that exercise and relaxation become part of your daily lifestyle.

- Choose styles of exercise that suit your personality and lifestyle.

- Make an effort to slow down at the critical time and look to ways of calming your mind and body – particularly important if your coordination suffers and you become clumsy.

- Above all, take a programme of exercise that balances the 3 'S's with some 'R' – universally known as:

STRENGTH, STAMINA,
SUPPLENESS AND RELAXATION

Taking each of the elements in turn, I have highlighted the important factors.

S for Strength can be described as the maximum force needed by a muscle or group of muscles to overcome a resistance.

In everyday terms this means being able to push, pull, lift, climb and carry without injuring yourself. Strong back and abdominal muscles will help improve your posture and guard you from most lower back pain.

There is another important element of strength to consider and that is:

E for Endurance is the muscle's ability repeatedly to perform or maintain a task for a prolonged period of time.

There is also cardiovascular (heart and blood vessel function) training which partners muscular endurance training. Different forms of activity will improve the endurance qualities of different muscle groups. For example, running will train the leg muscles much more than the upper body and arms, while swimming will emphasize upper body endurance. Both, however, will increase cardiovascular endurance.

S for Stamina simply means being able to keep going; whether you're walking, swimming, running or cycling – and without stopping or becoming tired!

These types of activity are called 'aerobic' because of the increased need for oxygen by the working muscles. Remember, the heart is a muscle too and it needs exercise just as much as your legs or arms. The lungs are used to oxygenate the blood. With regular exercise, the heart and lungs become more efficient. The benefits of aerobic training mean you eventually achieve better results with less effort. Your heart and lungs will have to work less hard in daily life.

Experts disagree as to exactly how much aerobic exercise you need to benefit or gain from the training effect. It will also vary from person to person. A general rule of thumb is to aim for at least 20 minutes about three times a week.

S for Suppleness and flexibility: the ability to move your joints through their full range of movement. In other words, being able to bend, stretch, reach and turn to your fullest. Of all the fitness elements so far, flexibility must rate as the one most likely to affect your everyday life. It also means protecting your muscles and joints from injury and stiffness, as well as improving your circulation, posture and poise.

Improving your range of movement will also help to improve your performance in other activities. Correct stretching, when practised after your exercise session (as well as before), will help to minimize the likelihood of post-exercise soreness.

R for Relaxation is the art of letting go. Knowing how to let go and with confidence, is probably one of the most important elements of health and fitness. The ability to release unnecessary muscular tension and calm the mind is a wonderful resource to call upon. Tension is tiring and unproductive.

For some, exercise itself is a form of relaxation, while others might turn to a hobby or pastime.

Relaxation and breathing go hand in hand. Indeed, improving your breathing patterns during exercise is one of the keys to success. It also engenders a feeling of alertness and readiness to cope.

Over the weeks of a considered programme of exercise you will increase the efficiency of your heart and lung capacity with deeper breathing.

TIPS AND HINTS ON EXERCISING

To really ensure you gain the maximum benefit from your efforts, take a few moments to read the following tips and hints – they make all the difference to how you feel about your exercising.

- Remember, exercise should be fun and something you look forward to.

- It won't be if you push yourself fast and furiously, it will only leave you exhausted, sore and disappointed with your efforts.

- Really listen to your body. Believe it or not, it knows best!

- Take it slowly and gradually for longer-lasting results.

- Take time to work out your fitness aims and objectives – what do you want to achieve from your efforts? Finding and following the right programme for you is as vital as eating the right food.

- Decide which activity, or blend of activities, will suit you and help to realize your aims.

221

- Mix and match whenever possible. Avoid boredom by choosing from several activities you know that you will enjoy and stick at. Better still, are they convenient and can you enjoy the company of others at the same time?

- Try to combine some of your exercises with fresh air and sunlight, both of which have proven benefit in helping to relieve PMS symptoms.

- Balance is the key to successful exercising. Give upper and lower body the same amount of work and spread the load.

- Don't expect miracles overnight – be patient and persevere!

- Aim for quality of exercise, not quantity – look forward to it and enjoy it.

PRECAUTIONS

Most people do not need a full medical check-up before exercising, but if you answer YES to any of the following questions, or you are over 35 and a 'first timer', it's best to discuss your plans with your doctor.

Have you ever suffered from, or is there a family history of:

Chest pains or pain in the shoulders?
High blood pressure or heart disease?
Chest problems like asthma or bronchitis?
Back pain or joint pains?
Headaches, faintness or feelings of nausea?
Diabetes?
Are you taking any medication?
Are you recovering from illness or recent operations?
Are you very overweight?
Are you pregnant?

If you have a cold or sore throat, give exercise a miss until you feel better. When you do resume, take it slowly and build up to your pre-illness fitness level gradually. If you ever feel pain, dizziness, nausea or undue tiredness whenever or wherever you exercise, STOP immediately. Rest and wait.

Change your position or slacken off the intensity if relevant. Try again. If the complaint persists, stop and seek professional advice.

Posture pointers

- Stand in front of a full-length mirror with feet about hip-width apart and insteps lifted.

- Gently rock back and forth to find your balance and 'centred' position. Body-weight will feel evenly balanced between balls and heels, as well as inner and outer edges of feet.

- Line knees directly over ankles and gently pull up thigh muscles above the knees.

The standing position

Now stand sideways to the mirror. Push your bottom out and see and feel the lower back arch and tummy bulge. Correct this by pulling in the abdominal muscles and tucking the buttocks under you. See and feel the lower back lengthen as the pubic bone (pelvis) tilts up to the ceiling. This is the pelvic tilt.

- Keep hips level and maintain pelvic tilt as you turn to face mirror.

- Lift ribcage up and away from hips.

- Pull shoulders down from ears; keep them level and aligned over ankles.

- Let arms hang loosely.

- Lift head upwards from crown and feel the back of neck lengthen.

- Hold chin at right angle to ground.

- Feel entire spine lengthen.

Run through these posture pointers and the pelvic tilt frequently throughout the day, to maintain alignment and heighten your awareness.

Warm-up

Now you're ready to warm up. Never miss out this section as it prepares your body for the work to follow. Mobilizing and loosening exercises, plus some preliminary stretches, will help to improve your performance and skill by increasing the body temperature. A warm-up also helps to reduce the risk of injury and soreness. About 10 minutes is all most people need. Similarly, 'warm down' at the end of each session – no matter how rushed you are. End with some rhythmical exercises and slow holding stretches that taper down from more demanding ones. A warm-down will induce a feeling of relaxation and well-being. It will also help to reduce the likelihood of post-exercise stiffness and soreness.

Warm up by moving rhythmically for 10 minutes to your favourite piece of music, working from your feet upwards, gradually using your whole body.

During your warm-down, take it easy, hold your stretches and slow down gradually. This will minimize any soreness and stiffness.

Relieve the tension

This section takes a look at specific exercises and steps you can take to release tension associated with PMS, as well as improve posture and awareness.

Deeper breathing will be promoted, as well as relaxation and a feeling of calm.

Shoulders and neck

Tension and tightness generally collect at the base of the neck and across tops of shoulders. They are mostly due to the way we sit and stand, as well as being our natural reaction to stress – we slouch, so the neck collapses and the shoulders hunch. Not a pretty sight and often it leaves us with a headache due to the constriction of blood supply to and from the brain.

Take positive steps to ovecome these problems by loosening shoulders and paying more attention to posture. See posture pointers on page 223.

To start, stand or sit well with the head centred and breathe well as you:

1. Lift both shoulders up, pull them back and strongly down. Repeat several times.

Tip – Make sure you really squeeze into the upper back and keep chin held in.

2. Clasp hands loosely behind lower back and rest them just above buttocks.

Keep elbows bent and hands resting on body throughout.

Squeeze between the shoulder blades so the elbows draw together.

Hold and release slowly.

Repeat several times.

Feel the squeeze between the shoulder blades and the stretch across the chest.

Tip – Keep the shoulders down, head centred and lower back straight.

3. Turn head slowly to look over right shoulder while maintaining length in the neck and keeping shoulders still.

Return to centre and repeat to opposite side.

Repeat several times.

Return to centre and pull chin in to lengthen back of neck.

Tilt head slowly to right shoulder while keeping shoulders level.

Feel the stretch on the opposite side.

Return slowly to centre.

Tip – As you tilt head, imagine you are looking into a mirror to see both cheeks evenly.

Finally, return to centre, pull shoulders down and tuck chin in.

Tilt head gently forwards.

Feel the stretch along the neck.

Return to centre and repeat once more, breathing well.

Back and hips

1. Back strengthener

Lie on your front on either a mat or rug, with legs together, forehead on floor and chin tucked in.

Clasp hands loosely and rest them on lower back.

As you breathe out, contract abdominal and buttock muscles and squeeze between the shoulder blades.

Straighten arms down towards your feet and raise chest, shoulders and forehead off the floor to form one continuous line.

Lower slowly to the floor and repeat once more.

2. Back release

From the previous exercise, place hands under shoulders and gently push up onto your knees to lower your bottom back onto your heels.

Fold your body forwards to rest chest on thighs.

Tuck your head down and rest arms down by sides of body.

Tip – If you feel claustrophobic, stretch your arms out in front of you and rest forehead lightly on floor.

3. Pelvic tilt

Use the pelvic tilt as a back release as well as a preliminary movement to abdominal strengtheners.

Pelvic tilts can be done standing, sitting or lying. Take time to practise the movement, as getting it right makes all the difference to the safety and effectiveness of your exercising and alignment.

Start by lying back on a mat or rug.

Bend knees with feet hip-width apart and lengthen back of neck by tucking chin in.

226

As you breathe out, press lower back down on to mat and pull in abdominal muscles.

Feel the pubic bone tilt up to the ceiling and the lower back flatten down against the floor.

Practise several times until you feel confident of the movement.

4. Curl-overs to strengthen abdominal muscles

Strong abdominal muscles help prevent some lower back pain.

Start as for the pelvic tilt and rest hands on your thighs.

As you breathe out, pelvic tilt and curl head and shoulders slowly off the floor, sliding hands towards knees.

Hold for count of four with waist and lower back on floor.

Lie back slowly and repeat four times.

Let go!

Having the ability to release tension and calm the mind is a wonderful resource to call upon. Tension is tiring and wasteful. Knowing how to cope and apply positive resources is the key to successful relaxation. Adopt any position you find comfortable and supportive for your lower back and neck. It may mean sitting in a high-back chair, or lying back with neck supported by a cushion and legs resting on a chair or stool.

Use your breathing to enhance your relaxation and let your restorative side take over.

Remember to pull the shoulders well down from the ears and let arms rest heavily.

Take several deep breaths, feeling the ribcage move up and out like bellows as you breathe in, and downwards as you breathe out.

Your breathing will gradually become more rhythmical as you start to let go.

Run down your body and check where you feel tight.

Are your shoulders up round your ears? Pull them down. Are your hands clenched? Stretch them out and let the fingers curl.

What about your buttocks and lower back? Make an extra effort to relax and release – try the pelvic tilt to prevent back aching.

Concentrate on your legs, particularly ankles and feet. Let them go and feel the whole body soften.

Finally pay attention to your mouth and face. Soften the jaw and let the softness spread over your face – around the nostrils, between and over your eyes and across your forehead to your hairline.

Spend a few quiet moments with yourself.

When you feel ready, take a few deep breaths, have a good stretch and yawn before curling over to one side and sitting up slowly.

20

OTHER VALUABLE THERAPIES

As well as dealing with symptoms on a nutritional level it is important to make sure that your whole body is functioning at optimum level. The years during which you may have suffered nutritional deficiencies, while coping with stressful situations and pre-menstrual symptoms, may well have taken their toll on your body. The body is a very complicated, but delicate network of bones, muscles, ligaments, nerves, organs and blood vessels. Physical symptoms and nervous tension can affect the smooth running of the body processes. When you make a start on your nutritional programme, if your symptoms are intense, you might consider the value of osteopathy, cranial osteopathy, acupuncture, or acupressure. They are powerful tools and can help to bring about speedy relief of symptoms.

OSTEOPATHY

It is not uncommon, through the wear and tear of everyday life, for subtle back or neck problems to occur. I have seen many resistant, long-standing headaches cured by some good osteopathic manipulation. It is certainly worth having a check-up with a qualified osteopath if you feel tension building up in your back or neck, or if you suffer regular headaches.

Cranial osteopathy, or cranio-sacral therapy as it is known, is a specialized form of osteopathy. Unlike conventional osteopathy, it is a gentle yet potent form of therapy. The aim is gently to coax the muscles, tendons, joints and connective tissue to establish correct functions and release re-strictions, thus restoring normal circulation, flow of energy and glandular secretions.

The cranio-sacral mechanism is comprised of the cranium (the skull), the sacrum (the bone at the base of the spine), the membranes surround-ing the brain, the spinal cord and the fascia of continuous, clingfilm-like sheet that surrounds the muscles, organs, joints and bones. The tension of this fascia, the clingfilm-like lining, is all important. If you have ever worn an all-in-one pants suit that is too tight or too short in the body, you will have experienced some discomfort. If the tension in the body's fascia becomes too tight, you can't just take it off like an uncomfortable piece of clothing, and it is possible that body functions can be affected in the long term.

Cranial osteopaths claim a good success rate with women who have PMS and other menstrual disorders. You will find it very gentle treatment. Here are some experiences of a cranial osteopath who regularly treats women with PMS and menstrual problems. As well as her treatment she recommends that her patients take regular exercise and seek nutritional advice.

Case history 1

The patient experienced migraine and PMS for five to six days prior to each period. She had some lower back strain, reduced mobility in her upper neck and some pelvic congestion. Her neck was treated and normal function restored. As a result, the congestion and strain within the skull were reduced, the migraines were instantly alleviated, and the PMS symp-toms reduced. The patient then received nutritional advice and her PMS reduced further.

Case history 2

This patient was a woman aged 44 who suffered with severe PMS, and backache before and during her period. She was very tall and had poor posture. When examined, she had restricted movement in the lower back and pelvic congestion. After treatment over a period of two months she became 90 per cent better.

It is certainly worth finding a local practitioner if you feel the need is there. (See page 254.)

ACUPUNCTURE AND ACUPRESSURE

It is worth mentioning the contribution made by traditional Chinese medicine in the treatment of female health problems. According to the severity of the problem, there are two levels at which treatment can be taken. The first level is appropriate for severe symptoms and involves consulting an acupuncturist. Many of the problems mentioned, including PMS, painful periods, irregular periods, fluid retention and distension, pelvic inflammation, migraines, backache, morning sickness and other troubles of pregnancy, menopausal symptoms, depression, anxiety and insomnia may all respond to treatment by acupuncture. If you feel your complaint is too serious or persistent to cope with by yourself, acupuncture is worth considering as a possible option.

Of course you should always ensure that you get help from a properly trained and registered practitioner. You can usually obtain information from your public library or Citizens Advice Bureau. A register is published by the Council for Acupuncture, listing all members of the four recognized and affiliated professional bodies.

As we are concentrating on aspects of self-help, it is worth considering a second level of treatment, more appropriate to the minor or occasional problems which you can sometimes alleviate by self-assessment and treatment at home. This can be done through Shiatsu, the Japanese finger pressure method (sometimes called acupressure). In this system the body is influenced in various ways by stimulating key points, found along the course of energy channels circulating near the skin surface. These are the same as acupuncture meridians, but the points are stimulated by pressure rather than needles.

For Shiatsu to be effective it is important to give the right kind of pressure, for an appropriate length of time. It is no good pushing pressure points like 'magic buttons' and it is important to recognize by the feel whether what you are doing is correct. Provided you adopt the right approach, Shiatsu may be very helpful, whether you enlist the help of a friend or perform it on your own (self-Shiatsu).

Here is a summary of the method and a description of how to find just a few of the most useful points for some of the troubles mentioned.

Pre-menstrual depression/anxiety

First, try working along the inner leg. Also, two inches above the wrist, in between the tendons at the centre of the inner arm, there is a good point to press firmly. Breathing is very important to get your energy flowing smoothly, so try this simple exercise. Kneel on a cushion or carpeted floor and join your hands together with the fingers back to back while pointing the fingertips towards your own upper abdomen. Let your relaxed fingers press into the centre, below the ribs but above the navel. As you do this lean gently forward and exhale. The pressure should lend a little force to the exhalation. Wait for the inhalation to come naturally and raise yourself back again to the upright kneeling position while breathing in. Go gently at first, repeating the action with every breath, leaning a bit further on to your fingers each time. The abdominal muscles may seem tight or tender but try to relax fully at the end of each breath while leaning forward. Only do this 10 times. You may move your fingers up and down or a little way along the ribs to explore for any tension. Afterwards sit quietly for a minute. You may feel like a good stretch before getting up.

Insomnia/headaches

Work with your own fingertips along the base of the skull behind the head where it joins the neck. Feel for any sensitive hollows where the muscles meet the bony ridge and, leaning your head back, let your fingers penetrate and hold for a few breaths. (If you do this for a friend, support her forehead with one hand and use your other hand to find points with finger and thumb on either side of her neck, pressing inward and upward.) For frontal headaches lean forward, letting your fingertips support the forehead just below the eyebrows – it may feel tender, but breathe and relax for several seconds. Also, work generally along the inside edges and soles of the feet, pressing especially around the inside ankle area. Another useful point for headaches can be found by pressing hard into the fleshy area between your finger and thumb – press towards the edge of the bone on the forefinger side.

Period pains

Get comfortable. Feel for sensitive points along the inside of the lower leg between the edge of the bone and the calf muscle. Hold any points with sustained thumb-pressure to the limit of comfort for five or six seconds or longer. You should try to breathe easily in a relaxed way and maintain the pressure until the sensation diminishes a little. To make it easier, reinforce one thumb with the other while pressing. Ask a friend or partner to lean with their thumbs into the area of the sacrum (triangular bony part at the base of your spine between the buttocks), they could explore a little way each side of centre, pressing firmly but gently any tender spots they find (you should say if it is too strong).

If this approach really interests you, there are two particularly good books you could read which are mentioned on the Reading List on page 251. You could also look for Shiatsu classes in your area. If you do not know of any, write to the secretary of the Shiatsu Society whose address is listed in Appendix 5 at the back of the book, page 254. The Society will send you a list of qualified teachers.

Whatever you do, it is important to ensure that you put yourself in the hands of a qualified practitioner. These days all the recognized alternative therapies have official associations. These bodies keep registers of qualified practitioners. It is best to check up as there are, sadly, quite a few non-qualified practitioners who are not to be recommended.

21

OTHER
RELATED PROBLEMS

By now you should have a good idea of what may be causing your pre-menstrual symptoms and how you can treat them successfully by changing your diet, taking some nutritional supplements and doing some moderate exercise. Very often PMS exists together with other health problems. This may be by chance, but sometimes there is a dietary connection. In this chapter I want to take a brief look at some common health problems and situations that can occur alongside PMS.

PAINFUL PERIODS

Painful periods are particularly common in young women, especially before they start child-bearing. Period pains are not actually part of PMS, and anyone who experiences severe pain should check with their doctor as there may be an underlying problem such as fibroids in the womb or ovar-ian cysts.

Often, however, there is no problem with the anatomy and you may need to try some self-help measures. There are various options available, from pain-killers to more natural remedies.

Aspirin, paracetamol and ibuprofen can all be effective, and another pain-killer that I referred to earlier, mefenamic acid, may also help asso-ciated PMS. This pain-killer is only available from your doctor.

A more natural treatment which can sometimes be helpful is the mineral magnesium, according to one small study from France. This is worth considering in view of the benefit that magnesium can bring to PMS as well. Also, changing your diet, taking other supplements and regular exercise might improve your body's chemistry in a way that reduces the level of chemicals that are associated with painful periods. Practically all the women who have been through our programme, who had painful periods initially, noticed that their period pain disappeared.

Heat is helpful, too, as it helps to relax the muscles. The WNAS has discovered a wonderful thermal heat pad that tucks inside your clothes, and helps to soothe away the pain. These pads are especially comforting in winter, and are available by mail order from the WNAS (see page 254).

HEAVY PERIODS

Excessive loss of blood is a problem for up to 10 per cent of menstruating women and is the main factor that leads to iron deficiency and anaemia in women of child-bearing age. Periods tend to get a little heavier with increasing age and with increasing weight, but there are other factors too. It is quite difficult for women to judge accurately just how heavy their periods are, so if your periods seem heavy it would be useful for you to have a blood test to check for anaemia or mild iron deficiency. A serum ferritin test is often the best as it detects low iron stores more accurately than the haemoglobin test.

It is also wise to have a check for gynaecological abnormality, but more often than not none will be found. If you are contemplating the oral contraceptive pill as a means of contraception, you are likely to find that it lessens the menstrual flow. Having said that, we have a great deal of success with regulating the timing and the flow of periods just by improving each individual's nutritional state.

Eating a healthy diet rich in iron and B vitamins, losing weight if you are overweight, and taking specific nutritional supplements is certainly worth a try.

IRREGULAR PERIODS

Irregular periods, especially those that are infrequent, can either be due to being too thin, or can occur in association with being overweight and developing excessive hair growth. This latter situation can be due to cysts on the ovaries (polycystic ovaries), a condition which results in hormone imbalances and can aggravate PMS.

Though polycystic ovaries can be treated by powerful hormonal drugs, they have been shown recently to respond extremely well to a weight-reducing low-fat diet. By losing only a stone in weight, the periods can become more regular, and there can be a reduction in excessive body and facial hair and an improved chance of becoming pregnant.

Being underweight due to illness or a poor diet, as in anorexia nervosa, can also result in irregular or absent periods. This is particularly likely to lead to a serious fall in the level of oestrogen and as a result premature thinning of the bones – osteoporosis. This process can be further accelerated if there is also an excessive amount of exercise, as in some performance athletes or ballet dancers.

PREGNANCY

This is still the best treatment for PMS! But, alas, is not the solution. However, a sound nutritional state during pregnancy is of paramount importance, and it therefore deserves a mention.

Since December 1992 the recommendation of the Chief Medical Officer of the Department of Health in the United Kingdom has been that all women who are intending to become pregnant or who are likely to should eat a healthy diet *before* they conceive. This is to ensure that they receive enough Folic acid, one of the B group vitamins, adequacy of which helps guard against the risks of spina bifida or other damage to the brain and nervous system. If the prospective mother is not eating a diet rich in Folic acid, i.e. fresh vegetables, fruit, oranges, orange juice and fortified breakfast cereals, then she should take a supplement providing 400 mcg per day.

Conversely, too much vitamin A may lead to other problems in pregnancy. Consequently, pregnant women are also advised not to take any vitamin preparations containing animal vitamin A-retinol or to eat liver, which may contain particularly large amounts of this nutrient. This means that if you are taking multi-vitamins, cod liver oil or Optivite you should stop these if you become pregnant. Do not exceed the recommended amount for these or any other vitamin preparations. The risk from excess vitamin A in tablets is mainly theoretical, but that provided by a single serving of liver is many times that to be found in the usual dosage of most vitamins.

POST-NATAL DEPRESSION

The association between depression after childbirth and pre-menstrual problems has been known for many years and was used as evidence that both conditions were due to a lack of the hormone progesterone. This has

proved not to be the case in PMS. There is evidence that both conditio.
may reflect a vulnerability of the body to hormonal changes, and that the
ability to tolerate this may in turn be due to both nutritional and social
factors. For example, there is now good evidence that post-natal depression is more likely to occur in women with a history of depression or who
lack adequate social support to cope with a new-born babe.

Some workers have related post-natal depression to changes in blood
calcium or a lack of vitamin B. A healthy diet, plenty of rest, sleep and a
supportive and loving environment seem to be good treatment for both
post-natal depression and PMS. It is noteworthy that during pregnancy
and whilst breastfeeding, the demands for calcium, magnesium and the B
vitamins are very high and a lack of most of these can cause changes in
mood.

During pregnancy and breastfeeding, the good nutrients go sailing
across the placenta or out through the breast milk to the baby. If the
nutrients are not replaced in adequate quantities it stands to reason that at
the end of the day it is the mother who will end up a depleted heap! I often
hear from mothers who suddenly develop severe PMS symptoms after pregnancy or breastfeeding, especially after the birth of a second child, which
often seems to be the straw that breaks the camel's back.

STERILIZATION

Female sterilization is most often achieved by cutting or clipping the Fallopian tubes that normally carry the eggs released from the ovary to the
womb. By preventing the union between the egg and the sperm a high
degree of protection against pregnancy is achieved. The operation, which
is usually performed under general anaesthetic, can cause a few minor
changes in hormone balance but these usually settle down within six
months. Though it is not officially recognized as being a factor in the production of PMS, my experience is that for a few women it appeared to be
an important and unwelcome influence as borne out by Jane's testimony.

'Ever since I was sterilized I had PMS symptoms. I never had any kind of
PMS or period problems before. I went back to the doctor who sterilized
me when I started to get these symptoms every month. He just turned
around and said, "You women are all the same. You don't want any
more babies, we sterilize you and then you come back and complain."
The doctor assured me that sterilization had nothing to do with the
symptoms I was getting now, but I insisted that before the sterilization I

...OK, terrific every month and did not have any PMS ...tsoever. I was very annoyed by his reaction.'

...ms suddenly arrive is not really understood, although it is bei... ...ogesterone levels drop for a while after sterilization. However, we have managed to eliminate the symptoms once again with the nutritional programme. Obviously, much more research is needed into the whole issue of the implications of nutritional deficiencies.

THE MENOPAUSE

For most women, PMS should be diminishing at the time of the menopause. This is certainly true for many, as numerous surveys have shown that the peak age for experiencing PMS symptoms is mid-thirties with a fall off thereafter. However, for some women PMS symptoms may worsen as the menopause approaches, and the two can blend together. The symptoms are quite different. At the menopause, which is characterized by the cessation of periods, there are symptoms of oestrogen deficiency such as vaginal dryness and shrinkage of breast tissue. The hot flushes and sweats are due to surges of other hormones from the pituitary gland at the base of the brain which is trying to persuade the failing ovaries to carry on working. Again, as in menstruation itself or post-delivery, there is considerable variation in individual women's ability to tolerate these hormonal changes.

Associated symptoms such as depression, mood changes, weight gain, fatigue and insomnia are not characteristic of the menopause, but do genuinely appear more frequent at this time. Changing your diet as if to combat PMS is as effective at this time of life. Magnesium and the essential fatty acids appear to be important in the normal functioning of the ovaries. Making sure that there is an adequate supply of these and other nutrients may help ease the passage of menopausal symptoms.

Interestingly, in the Orient menopausal symptoms are less of a problem than they are in the West, and this has been attributed to the effects on hormone metabolism of a diet low in fat, high in fibre and plentiful in fresh fruit and vegetables.

Thinning of the bones leading to osteoporosis is particularly likely to accelerate around menopause with the loss of protective oestrogen. Calcium and exercise can limit this process and a specialized supplement rich in magnesium and multi-vitamins, Gynovite, may also help improve bone density. Many women are unable to take hormone replacement therapy (HRT), either for medical reasons, or because they experience side-effects. For example, it is thought that one-third of women on HRT experience symptoms of PMS, and of course they continue to have a monthly bleed. For the last eight years the WNAS has been providing a programme for women experiencing menopausal symptoms with a great deal of success.

Hormone replacement therapy has become very popular in the US and is being greeted with much enthusiasm in many quarters of the UK. It can be taken in the form of pills similar to oral contraceptives, as an implant inserted under the skin or as a patch applied to the skin of the abdomen or buttock. Some women swear by it, and others cannot tolerate it, so there has to be a natural alternative.

In my experience over the last 10 years, finding the right diet to suit your body, taking specific nutritional supplements in the short term and moderate regular exercise can only serve to improve your general well-being. Once you have learned what your body requires, not only do you stand a good chance of overcoming your symptoms, but you will be far more likely to improve your quality of life, and improve your chances of avoiding the illnesses that can occur later in life, like heart disease, mental illness, or cancer.

22

MEN WHO NO LONGER SUFFER

I didn't feel that the book would be complete without giving a voice to the men in our lives. I have concentrated so far on how women suffer with PMS. But it's not just women who suffer, let's face it, the men are very definitely on the receiving end! Women who have supportive partners have a far easier time on the programme than those whose partners refuse to acknowledge the condition and instead of being understanding, just simply fight back and turn off.

I have had the good fortune to hear from many men who were deeply concerned about the welfare of their women, once they understood that PMS was a real condition, which would respond to treatment.

I think it's important for women to stand back and examine some of the viewpoints, in retrospect, of men who have lived with PMS sufferers before, during and after their nutritional programme. I'm happy to say they can mostly look back and laugh, probably with relief, for the storm is over.

Tom Moor, Jane's husband, is relieved to say that he got back the girl he married.

'Jane was very irritable, she couldn't hold a conversation without snapping. I couldn't touch her for two weeks before her periods as her breasts were so sore and tender. She rarely wanted to go out and would make excuses to stay at home. When she had PMS she changed from being very happy-go-lucky to being bitchy, irritable and tired.

When she was pre-menstrual I used to keep out of her way. I still

240

showed her that I loved her and waited patiently for her one good week each month. We were hoping for an early menopause.

The nutritional programme has made a tremendous difference to our lives. We are able to lead a normal life again. My wife laughs and jokes and she is popular at work.

My advice to other men is to seek help as it is available. Once their partner is on a nutritional programme, help her to persevere, as it will pay dividends in the long run. I feel that more education for men is necessary, more widespread information directed at couples. I, like most men, was totally baffled as to what the cause of the problem was.'

Don, June Garson's husband couldn't imagine what the consequences might have been had she not received help.

'Generally speaking I am a calm, tolerant person. I tried to make allowances, but I didn't understand the problem. It was like living with a "time bomb" not knowing when it was going to go off! June was permanently "uptight" and tearful pre-menstrually. She was unable to cope with life or deal with the children rationally.

Once on the nutritional programme an immediate improvement was noticeable. Her new-found state of mind and feeling of well-being turned the clock back to the time when we met, prior to our children being born. She reverted back personality-wise to the girl I fell for. I no longer dread the time of the month.

My advice to other men is as follows:

Be totally committed to discussing the subject in detail with your partner, read extensively on the subject and INSIST on her seeking help, not only for her sake, but for the rest of the family. Ignorance of the subject is the major hurdle to overcome.

I found your literature and your "cure" very interesting as I employ 150 people, many of them women. As a result of my experience with my wife I was able to realize that a staff problem affecting many employees was due to the PMS of a particular female employee. I have been able to discuss her problem sympathetically and we hope to solve the unrest in the office, as on my recommendation she has written to you for your help.'

Nadine's boyfriend felt that the biggest change for him was that he no longer had to duck to avoid the flying saucepans!

'Nadine's hysterical and often violent acts of throwing objects did cause anger, but more usefully, it improved my reaction time and my catching abilities no end!'

Life was difficult to cope with for Nadine. There were times of great frustration when new remedies for PMS failed to work. Since introducing the nutritional programme into her life, the quality of life for Nadine and her partner has increased enormously.

'I think the key to coping with PMS is to be patient and caring. If her irritability makes you irritable, then feel it, but don't show it. If her hysteria is frightening then allow yourself to be afraid, but be bigger than your fear, and calm her down. Be practical, do the cooking or take over the task she is finding difficult to cope with. Give up your time because you can bet she's feeling worse than you've ever done, and deserves your understanding and a shoulder to lean on. Tell her you love her and reassure her, and most of all, mean it.'

This bittersweet excerpt is from a letter written by the husband of one of our patients:

'I am Dodd, a roofing contractor with eight children and a wife with severe PMS symptoms. She was a complete Jekyll and Hyde character when her PMS struck.

Knowing what divorce can do to a family, I had to have the patience of Job with Eleanor. But after violent attacks (both on myself and the children), outrageous outbursts, locking herself into hotel rooms, insults, screams of rage, alienation from reality, a suicide attempt, and jealous behaviour I had had it. Bearing in mind that for most of the month she was warm, affectionate and everything a wife should be.

The worst of it all was after an attack when the illness had left her and she would creep back to me. Then I had to play the part of the caring husband again.

How can you expect a young couple with two children to come to terms with this terrible PMS problem when there is nowhere to go, nobody to see them? PMS is a dreadful affliction. It is self-destructive, life-threatening and family-life threatening. When I was a child, I would go to see a horror film and on it would be a pit of snakes – provided you did not disturb them they left you alone but woe betide you if you disturbed them. It was the same with Eleanor if she stuck to the diet or went on a binge.

Women are such beautiful creatures, advanced both mentally and physically from the male. More adaptable, stronger, philosophical, and yet they have to cope with some of the most awful female problems. Is this the price a woman has to pay for her beauty?

Eleanor is now cured of her PMS symptoms. I know she is cured and the WNAS has been responsible. The reason (after trying everything else) I know they have hit the nail on the head is because if complacency sets in and she starts pinching sweets, eating curries and drinking, I can guarantee by the end of her monthly cycle she will be going through agony. I am eternally grateful.'

His advice to other men is as follows:

1. A woman has to realize that she has a problem and that it is not everybody else around her that is wrong, but herself.

2. If and when she realizes this, she is 49% there.

3. She has to get the husband to realize (buy him a dummy to suck; he will need it to bite hard on). You are then 98% there.

4. The last 2% is really just the beginning. When it has been realized, you still have an awful long way to go. But it is like everything else in life, you do not get owt for nowt. This now is when you really have to work hard. It is just like any other illness – if left untreated, it just gets worse.

Isn't that great? What wonderful understanding! The common factor for most men who are supportive, seems to be that they were educated on the subject of PMS. When they don't understand what's going on, they obviously find it more difficult to be supportive in the long term, which is quite understandable.

On behalf of PMS sufferers I would like to thank the supportive men of the world for being willing to share the problem. With more education, communication and understanding in the future on the subject of PMS, far fewer lives will be needlessly disrupted.

1 DICTIONARY OF TERMS

Abbreviations used

g = gram, mg = milligram (100 mg = 1 g), mcg = microgram (100 mcg = 1 mg), iu = international unit, kj = kilojoule

ADRENAL GLANDS. The adrenal glands are two small glands situated at the top of the kidneys. They produce several different hormones, most of which are steroid hormones. Hormones from the adrenal glands influence the metabolism of sugar, salt and water and several other functions.

ALDACTONE. This is a diuretic drug which helps fluid retention. It inhibits the action of aldosterone, a hormone from the adrenal glands. It is also known as spironolactone.

ALDOSTERONE. This is a steroid hormone produced by the adrenal glands which is involved in salt and water balance. When it is produced in excess it causes the body to hold water and sodium salt.

ALLERGY. An unusual and unexpected sensitivity to a particular substance which causes an adverse reaction. Foods, chemicals and environmental pollutants are common irritants and they may cause a whole range of symptoms including headaches, abdominal bloating and discomfort, skin rashes, eczema and asthma.

AMENORRHOEA. A complete absence of periods.

AMINO ACIDS. Chains of building blocks which combine together to form the proteins that make living things. There are some 20 or more amino acids, some of which are essential and some non-essential.

ANTI-DEPRESSANTS. These are drugs used to suppress symptoms of depression.

BROMOCRIPTINE. A powerful drug, used to suppress the hormone prolactin. Further details of this can be found in Chapter 12, on conventional remedies. It is occasionally used in the treatment of PMS.

CARBOHYDRATES. Carbohydrates are the main source of calories (kjs) in almost all diets. *Complex carbohydrates* are essential nutrients and occur in the form of fruits, vegetables, pulses and grains. They are important energy-giving foods. There are two sorts of complex carbohydrates: the first are digestible, such as the starches, and the second are not digestible and are more commonly known as 'fibre'.
Refined carbohydrates. These consist of foods that have been processed and refined. White or brown sugar and white flour have, in the process of refining, had many of the vitamins and minerals present in the original plant removed. Further details on this may be found in Chapter 11.

CERVIX. The neck of the womb which projects downwards into the vagina.

CORPUS LUTEUM. Literally, a little yellow gland or body. It is the part of the ovary that remains after the egg has left. It produces two hormones, oestrogen and progesterone, during the second half of the menstrual cycle.

DAY 1 OF CYCLE. The first day of the menstrual bleeding, the day the period arrives, is the first day of the menstrual cycle.

246

DEFICIENCY. A lack of an essential substance, e.g. a vitamin.

DIURETICS. Drugs which cause an increased production of urine by the kidneys. They are used to treat fluid retention.

DOPAMINE. Dopamine is a brain chemical affecting mood. It has a sedating effect.

DYSMENORRHOEA. This is a term used to describe pain occurring during periods.

ENDOCRINE GLANDS. Glands that secrete hormones and regulate other organs in the body. The thyroid and the pituitary glands are endocrine glands.

ENDOMETRIOSIS. A condition in which the lining of the uterus begins to grow outside the uterus in the abdominal cavity. It is usually a painful condition and can be a cause of infertility.

ENDORPHINS. Hormones from the pituitary gland and fluid in the spine which are believed to help control moods, behaviour and part of the workings of the pituitary gland itself. They may also have an effect on how sugar is used in the body, and on other amounts of hormones released from the pituitary gland and the ovaries. If this is so, the production of oestrogen and progesterone could be affected by endorphins.

ESSENTIAL FATTY ACIDS. One of the essential groups of foods which we need to eat to remain healthy. These are essential fats that are necessary for normal cell structure and body function. There are two: linoleic and linolenic acids. They are called 'essential' as they cannot be made by the body but have to be eaten in the diet.

FALLOPIAN TUBES. A pair of slender tubes through which the egg passes on its way from the ovary to the uterus. Fertilization occurs in the Fallopian tubes. Very rarely the egg remains in the tube and grows: this is called an ectopic pregnancy, and is a medical emergency accompanied by severe abdominal pain.

FOLLICLE. A small sac in the ovary containing an egg (ovum). After release of the egg at mid cycle the follicle becomes a corpus luteum.

FOLLICLE STIMULATING HORMONE (FSH). A hormone of the pituitary gland which stimulates the growth of the follicles in the ovaries.

FOLLICULAR PHASE. The first half of the menstrual cycle when an egg is growing in the ovary. The egg is surrounded by cells which produce the hormone oestrogen and which thus prepares the uterus for conception. The egg and surrounding cells are called a follicle.

GLUCOSE. A form of sugar, found in the diet or released by the liver into the bloodstream, which is then used by the brain for energy. This is the only source of energy usable by the brain.

GRAAFIAN FOLLICLE. A mature egg which is surrounded by a bag of fluid within the ovary.

HORMONES. Substances formed chiefly in the endocrine glands, which then enter the bloodstream and control the activity of an organ or body function. Adrenaline and insulin are hormones, as are oestrogen and progesterone.

HYPERHYDRATION – too much water present. This is a term used to describe water retention in the body.

HYPOGLYCAEMIA – LOW BLOOD SUGAR. This is a condition in which there is a deficiency of glucose in the bloodstream, often caused by an excess of insulin or a lack of food. As glucose is required for normal brain function, mental disturbance can occur as can other symptoms: headaches, weakness, faintness, irritability, palpitations, mood swings, sweating and hunger. One of the commonest contributing factors is an excess of refined carbohydrates in the diet.

HYPOTHALAMUS. The region of the brain controlling temperature, hunger, thirst and the hormones produced by the pituitary gland.

HYSTERECTOMY. A surgical procedure to remove the womb and the Fallopian tubes. Sometimes one or more ovaries are also removed.

LUTEAL PHASE. The time after the egg has left the follicle in the ovary, and the follicle then becomes a gland known as the corpus luteum. The corpus luteum produces progesterone.

LUTEINIZING HORMONE (LH). The pituitary hormone which fosters the development of the corpus luteum.

MENORRHAGIA. An excessive loss of blood during each period.

MENSES. The discharge of blood and tissue lining from the uterus, which occurs approximately every four weeks between puberty and the menopause.

MENSTRUAL CYCLE. The monthly cycle involving the pituitary gland, ovaries and uterus in which an egg is produced ready for conception to take place. In each cycle an egg in the ovary is released and the lining of the womb develops ready for conception and implantation of the fertilized egg. If this does not occur, the lining of the womb is shed and a period occurs.

MENSTRUAL SYMPTOMATOLOGY DIARY. A chart which is a daily record of all symptoms that occur throughout the menstrual cycle.

METABOLISM. The process by which the body maintains life. It is the cycle of nutrients being broken down to produce energy, which is then used by the body to build up new cells and tissues, provide heat, growth, and physical activity. The metabolic rate tends to vary from person to person, depending on their age, sex and lifestyle.

MITTELSCHMERZ. Pain associated with ovulation. It occurs usually at the time of ovulation, about halfway through the cycle. Translated, it means 'middle pain'.

NUTRITION. The British Society for Nutritional Medicine's definition is 'the sum of the processes involved in taking nutrients, assimilating and utilizing them'. In other words, the quality of the diet and the ability of your body to utilize the individual nutrients and so maintain health.

OESTROGEN. A steroid hormone which is produced in large quantities by the ovaries, and in smaller amounts by the adrenal glands. It is responsible for the development of breasts and other sexual characteristics at puberty. Oestrogen is also responsible for the production of fertile cervical mucus, the opening of the cervix, and building up of blood in the lining of the uterus, preparing for a fertilized egg.

OVARIES. A pair of glands situated on either side of the uterus, in which eggs and sex hormones, including oestrogen, are produced.

OVULATION. The release of the ripe egg (ovum) from the ovary. The two ovaries ovulate alternately every month. Occasionally, the two ovaries ovulate simultaneously, in which case the result may be twins.

OVUM. The egg which is released from the ovary at the time of ovulation.

PALPITATIONS. The heart beating too fast and sometimes irregularly.

PITUITARY GLAND. A small gland situated at the base of the brain, which produces many hormones, among which are those which stimulate the ovary and the thyroid.

PRE-MENSTRUAL. A term used to describe the time before the arrival of a period.

PRE-MENSTRUAL SYNDROME. This is the name given to a collection of mental and physical symptoms which manifest themselves before the onset of a period.

PRE-MENSTRUAL TENSION. This was the name first given to the symptoms detected before a period in 1931 by Dr Frank. Now the correct name is Pre-Menstrual Syndrome. However, many women still prefer to call the condition PMT – Pre-Menstrual Tension.

PROGESTERONE. A hormone secreted by the corpus luteum of the ovary during the second half of the menstrual cycle. Some studies have shown that a deficiency in progesterone may be responsible for some PMS symptoms. Progesterone is an important hormone during pregnancy.

PROGESTOGENS. A group of synthetic hormones, with actions similar to progesterone.

PROLACTIN. The hormone secreted by the pituitary gland which is involved in milk production. It is also known to affect water and mineral balance in the body, and in some women may play a part in the changes pre-menstrually.

PROSTAGLANDINS. Hormone-like substances found in almost every cell in the body, which are necessary for the normal function of involuntary muscles, including the heart, the uterus, blood vessels, the lungs and the intestines.

Prostaglandins are sometimes regarded as health controllers, as they seem to play an important part in the controlling of many essential functions in the body. They do not come directly from the diet, but are made in the body itself. Because of this, the body relies on a good diet in order to produce prostaglandins. The special substances that the body needs to make these hormones are called essential fatty acids.

SEROTONIN. A brain chemical that influences mood.

STEROIDS. Substances which have a particular chemical structure in common. All the sex hormones, such as oestrogen, progesterone, etc are steroids.

THYROID GLAND. A gland situated in the neck, which produces the hormone thyroxine. The thyroid gland regulates metabolism.

TRANQUILLIZERS. A group of drugs which artificially sedate the body. They may be useful in the short term, but in the long term they can have addictive qualities.

UTERUS (WOMB). A sac-like organ which is located in the abdomen of a woman, and designed to hold and nourish a growing child from conception until birth.

VAGINA. The passage that leads from the uterus to the external genital organs.

2   FOOD ADDITIVES

There are many types of food additives. Most of them are denoted by a number prefixed by E. The E stands for EEC, as the European Community Regulations state that, since 1 January 1986, all foods containing additives, except for flavourings, must have an E number, or the actual name, in the list of ingredients. Some food additives are natural, vegetable-derived compounds, or even vitamins, and are perfectly harmless. However, these are not used frequently. The following additives can be associated with the exacerbation of certain medical problems:

Azo-dyes E102, E104, E107, E110, E122, E123, E124, E128, E131, E132, E133, E142, E151, E154, E155, E180
Benzoates E210–E219
Sulphur dioxide and sulphites E220–E227
Nitrites and nitrates E249–E252
Proprionic acid and propionates E280–E283
Anti-oxidants, BHA & BHT E320 and E321
Monosodium glutamate (MSG) and related compounds E621–E623

Many food allergy associations now give details of suppliers of foods suitable for people who suffer from allergies. Some of these are mentioned on page 253. Many supermarkets will now provide lists of their products which are free from additives, milk, wheat, eggs, etc. For those who wish to request further details, it is suggested that you contact the customer relations department of the appropriate supermarket chain.

The Ministry of Agriculture, Fisheries and Food has produced a booklet explaining what the 'E' numbers mean. There is also the excellent book 'E for Additives' by Maurice Hanssen, which is readily available. An organization called 'Foresight', The Association for the Promotion of Pre-Conceptual Care, have produced a handbag-sized booklet based on the information from the book 'E for Additives'. They have marked additive numbers with a colour code, red for danger, and they specify precisely why, orange for those additives on which conflicting reports still exist, and green for those about which there are no known side-effects. This booklet is immensely valuable as it takes the confusion out of shopping. You will find the Foresight address in Appendix 5 should you wish to obtain a copy.

3 NUTRITIONAL SUPPLEMENT SUPPLIERS

1.	Efamol	Boots, chemists, healthfood shops and Nutritional Health (mail order)*
2.	Femvite	Nutritional Health (mail order)*. Available from chemists and healthfood shops in late 1994.
3.	Linusit Gold	Healthfood shops.
4.	Magnesium Hydroxide Mixture	Boots and other chemists.
5.	Optivite	Boots, chemists, healthfood shops and Nutritional Health (mail order)*
6.	Natural Vitamin E	Healthfood shops and Nutritional Health (mail order)*
7.	Sugar Factor/Normoglycaemia	Nutritional Health (mail order)*

*Mail Order Address
Nutritional Health Ltd
PO Box 926
Lewes, East Sussex
BN7 2QL

Australia

NNFA (National Nutrition Foods Association)
PO Box 84, Westmead, NSW 2145. Tel: 02 633 9913
The NNFA have lists of all supplement stockists and retailers in Australia, if you have any difficulties in obtaining supplements.

New Zealand

NNFA (National Nutrition Foods Association)
c/o PO Box 820062, Auckland, New Zealand.
Again the NNFA have lists of all supplement stockists and retailers in New Zealand, if you have any difficulties in obtaining supplements.

4 RECOMMENDED READING LIST

NOTE
UK, USA and A denotes the following books are available in Great Britain, United States and Australia.

GENERAL HEALTH

1. *Pure, White and Deadly* by Professor John Yudkin (a book about sugar) price £9.95 (published by Viking). **UK A**
2. *Coming off Tranquillizers* by Dr Susan Trickett, price £1.99 (published by Thorsons). **UK USA A** (Lothian Publishing Co).
3. *The Migraine Revolution – The New Drug-free Solution* by Dr John Mansfield, price £4.99 (published by Thorsons). **UK USA A** (Lothian Publishing Co).
4. *Understanding Cystitis* by Angela Kilmartin, price £4.99 (published by Arrow Books). **UK A**
5. *The Book of Massage*, price £9.99 (published by Ebury Press). **UK**
6. *Do-it-yourself Shiatsu* by W. Ohashi, price £5.50 (published by Unwin). **UK**
7. *Candida Albicans: Could Yeast Be Your Problem?* by Leon Chaitow, price £3.99 (published by Thorsons). **UK USA A** (Lothian Publishing Co).
8. *Candida Albicans* by Gill Jacobs, price £6.99 (published by Optima). **UK USA A**
9. *Nutritional Medicine* by Dr Stephen Davies and Dr Alan Stewart, price £7.99 (published by Pan Books). **UK A**
10. *The Y Plan Countdown*, price £6.99 (published by Hamlyn). **UK**
11. *Bone Boosters – Natural Ways to Beat Osteoporosis* by Diana Moran and Helen Franks, price £9.99 (published by Boxtree Limited). **UK**
12. *The Migraine Handbook* by Jenny Lewis, price £6.99 (published by Vermilion). **UK A**
13. *The Book of Yoga*, Sivananda Yoga Centre, price £9.99 (published by Ebury Press). **UK A**

DIET

1. *The Vitality Diet* by Maryon Stewart and Dr Alan Stewart, price £4.99 (published by Optima). **UK A**
2. *Good Food Gluten-Free* by Hilda Cherry Hills, price £9.99 (published by Keats). **USA**
3. *The Wheat and Gluten Free Cookbook* by Joan Noble, price £8.99 (published by Vermilion). **UK A**
4. *The New Why You Don't Need Meat* by Peter Cox, price £10.99 (published by Bloomsbury). **UK A**
5. *Beat Sugar Craving* by Maryon Stewart, price £7.99 (published by Vermilion). **UK A**
6. *The Allergy Diet* by Elizabeth Workman SRD, Dr John Hunter and Dr Virginia Alun Jones, price £3.99 (published by Martin Dunitz). **UK USA**
7. *The Candida Albicans Yeast-Free Cook Book* by Pat Connolly and Associates of the Price Pottenger Nutrition Foundation, price £6.95 (published by Keats Publishing Inc). **UK USA**

8. *The Cranks Recipe Book* by David Canter, Hay Canter and Daphne Swann, price £1.85 (published by Grafton). **UK**
9. *The Food Intolerance Diet* by Elizabeth Workman SRD, Dr Virginia Alun Jones and Dr John Hunter, price £3.95 (published by Martin Dunitz). **UK USA**
10. *Raw Energy* by Leslie and Susannah Kenton, price £6.99 (published by Vermilion). **UK A** (Doubleday Publishing Co).
11. *The Reluctant Vegetarian* by Simon Hope, price £8.95 (published by William Heinemann). **UK**
12. *The Salt-Free Diet Book* by Dr Graham McGregor, price £3.95 (published by Martin Dunitz). **UK USA**
13. *Gourmet Vegetarian Cooking* by Rose Elliot price £2.95 (published by Fontana). **UK A**
14. *Healthy Cooking*, price 0.99 from Tesco Stores. **UK**
15. *Food Allergy and Intolerance* by Jonathan Brostoff and Linda Gamlin, price £4.99 (published by Bloomsbury). **UK A**
16. *The Gluten-free and Wheat-free Bumper Bake Book* by Rita Greer, price £2.95 (published by Bunterbird Ltd). **UK**

STRESS

1. *Self-Help for your Nerves* by Dr Clair Weekes, price £5.95 (published by Angus and Robertson). **UK USA** (Hawthorn Publishing Co).
2. *Stress and Relaxation Self-Help Techniques for Everyone* by Jane Madders, price £6.99 (published by Optima). **UK USA A**
3. *Lyn Marshall's Instant Stress Cure*, price £8.99 (published by Vermilion). **UK A**

GENERAL
1. *How to Stop Smoking and Stay Stopped for Good* by Gillian Riley, price £5.99 (published by Vermilion). **UK A**
2. *Getting Sober and Loving It* by Joan and Derek Taylor, price £7.99 (published by Vermilion). **UK A**
3. *The National Childbirth Book of Breast Feeding* by Mary Smale, price £7.99 (published by Vermilion). **UK**
4. *Tired all the Time* by Dr Alan Stewart, price £6.99 (published by Optima). **UK USA A**
5. *Memory Power* by Ursula Markham, price £7.99 (published by Vermilion). **UK A**
6. *Alternative Health Aromatherapy* by Gill Martin, price £5.99 (published by Optima). **UK USA A**
7. *Alternative Health Acupuncture* by Dr Michael Nightingale, price £5.00 (published by Optima). **UK USA A**
8. *Alternative Health Osteopathy* by Stephen Sandler, price £5.99 (published by Optima). **UK USA A**

5 USEFUL ADDRESSES

GREAT BRITAIN

British Acupuncture Register and Directory
34 Alderney Street, London SW1V 4UE.   Tel: London (071) 834 1012.

The Council for Acupuncture
Suite 1, 19a Cavendish Square, London W1M 9AD.   Tel: London (071) 409 1440.

Alcoholics Anonymous (AA)
General Services Office, PO Box 1, Stonebow House, Stonebow, York YO1 2NJ.
Tel: York (0904) 644026.

Action Against Allergy
23–24 George Street, Richmond, Surrey TW9 1JY.

National Society for Research into Allergy
PO Box 45, Hinkley, Leicestershire LE10 1JY.   Tel: 0455 851546.

Anorexia and Bulimia Nervosa Association
Tottenham Women's and Health Centre, Annexe C, Tottenham Town Hall, Town Hall
Approach, London N15 4RX.   Tel: London (081) 885 3936 (Wednesdays
6–8.30 pm only)

International Federation of Aromatherapists
4 Eastmearn Road, West Dulwich, London SE21 8HA.
Letters only enclosing a sae.

British Pregnancy Advisory Service
7 Belgrave Road, London SW1V 1QB.   Tel: London (071) 222 0985.

Brook Advisory Centre
Head Office, 153a East Street, Walworth, London SE17 2SD.   Tel: London
(081) 708 1234.

CLEAR (Campaign for Lead Free Air)
3 Endsleigh Street, London WC1H 0DD.   Tel: London (071) 278 9686.

Hyperactive Children Support Group
59 Meadowside, Angmering, Littlehampton, West Sussex BN16 4BW.
(Postal enquiries only.)

ASSET
The National Association for Health and Exercise Teachers
202 The Avenue, Kennington, Oxford OX1 5RN.   Tel: Oxford (0865) 736066.

The Sports Council
16 Upper Woburn Place, London WC1H 0QP.   Tel: London (071) 388 1277.

Medau Society
8b Robson House, East Street, Epsom, Surrey KT17 1HH.   Tel: Epsom
(03727) 29056.

Endometriosis Society
35 Belgrave Square, London SW1X 8QB.   Tel: London (071) 235 4137.

Food Watch International
Butts Pond Industrial Estate, Sturminster Newton, Dorset DT10 1AZ.
Tel: Sturminster Newton (0258) 73356.

Foresight
Association for the Promotion of Pre-Conceptual Care
The Old Vicarage, Church Lane, Whitney, Godalming, Surrey GU8 5PN.
Tel: Wormley (042879) 4500.

Friends of the Earth Ltd
26–28 Underwood Street, London N1 7JQ.   Tel: London
(071 490 1555.

Migraine Trust
45 Great Ormond Street, London WC1 3HD.   Tel: London (071) 278 2676.

National Childbirth Trust
Alexander House, Oldham, London W3 6NH.   Tel: London (081) 992 8637.

The European School of Osteopathy
104 Tonbridge Road, Maidstone, Kent ME16 8SL.   Tel: Maidstone (0622) 671558.

The British School of Osteopathy
Little John House, 1–4 Suffolk Street, London SW1 4HG.   Tel: London
(071) 930 9254.

Patients Association
18 Victoria Park Square, Bethnal Green, London E2 9PF.   Tel: London
(071) 981 5676.

Action on Phobias
c/o Shandy Mathias, 8–9 The Avenue, Eastbourne, East Sussex BN21 2YA.
Letters only enclosing a sae.

The Women's Nutritional Advisory Service
PO Box 268, Lewes, East Sussex BN7 2QN.   Tel: Brighton (0273) 487366.

Association for Post-Natal Illness
7 Gowan Avenue, London SW6 6RH.   Tel: London (071) 731 4867.

Release
388 Old Street, London EC1V 9LT.   Tel: London (071) 729 9904.

Samaritans
10 The Grove, Slough SL1 1QP.   Tel: Slough (0753) 532713.

The Shiatsu Society
Elaine Liechti, 19 Langside Park, Kilbarchan, Renfrewshire PA10 2EP.
Tel: Kilbarchan (050 57) 4657.

The Henry Doubleday Research Association
Ryton Gardens, National Centre for organic gardening, Ryton on Dunsmore, Coventry
CV8 3LG.   Tel: Coventry (0203) 303517.

The Soil Association
86–88 Colston Street, Bristol BS1 5BB.   Tel: Bristol (0272) 290661.

Both these organizations advise on all aspects of non-chemical agriculture, give advice to amateur and professional organic growers, and have a constantly updated list of sources of organic produce.

Ash (Action on Smoking and Health)
5–11 Mortimer Street, London W1N 7RH.   Tel: London (071) 637 9843.

Tranx (UK) Ltd
National Tranquilliser Advice Centre, Registered Office, 25a Masons Avenue,
Wealdstone, Harrow, Middx HA3 5AH.   Tel: (client line) (081) 427 2065 [24-hour answering service] (081) 427 2827.

AUSTRALIA

Blackmores Limited
23 Roseberry Street, Balgowlah, NSW 2093.   Tel: (02) 949 3177.

Royal Society for the Welfare of Mothers and Babies
2 Shaw Street, Petersham, NSW 2049.   Tel: (02) 568 3633.

Childbirth Education Association of Victoria
21 Greensborough Centre, 25 Main Street, Greensborough, Victoria 3088.

Women's Health Advisory Service
187 Glenmore Road, Paddington NSW 2021.   Tel: (02) 331 5014.

Liverpool Women's Health Centre
26 Bathurst Street, Liverpool NSW 2170.   Tel: (02) 601 3555.

Adelaide Women's Community Health
64 Pennington Terrace, Nth Adelaide SA 5006.   Tel: (08) 267 5366.

PMT Relief Clinic
Suite 6, 32 Kensington Road, Rose Park, South Australia 5067.   Tel: (08) 364 2760.

NEW ZEALAND

Papakura Women's Centre
4 Opaneke Road, Papakura, Auckland.   Tel: 299 9466.

Whakatane Women's Collective
PO Box 3049, Ohope.   Tel: (Whakatane) 076 24757.

Health Alternative for Women
Room 101, Cranmer Centre, PO Box 884, Christchurch.   Tel: 796 970.

Women's Health Collective
63 Ponsonby Road, Ponsonby, Auckland.   Tel: 764 506.

West Auckland Women's Centre
111 McLeod Road, Te Atatu, Auckland.   Tel: 8366 381.

Tauranga Women's Centre
PO Box 368, Tauranga.   Tel: 783 530.

The Alice Bush Family Planning Clinic
214 Karangahape Road, Auckland.   Tel: 775 049.

Family Planning Clinic
Arts Centre, 301 Montreal Street, Christchurch.   Tel: 790 514.

USA AND CANADA

National Institute of Nutrition
1565 Carling Avenue, #400, Ottawa, Ontario K12 8R1.

The American Academy of Environmental Medicine
PO Box 16106, Denver, Colorado, 80216.

Optimox Inc
PO Box 3378, Torrance, California 90510–3378.   Tel: (800) 223 1601.

6 CHARTS
AND DIARIES

SYMPTOMS	WEEK AFTER PERIOD (Fill in 3 days after period)				WEEK BEFORE PERIOD (Fill in 2-3 days before period)			
	None	Mild	Moderate	Severe	None	Mild	Moderate	Severe
PMS – A								
Nervous Tension								
Mood Swings								
Irritability								
Anxiety								
PMS - H								
Weight Gain								
Swelling of Extremities								
Breast Tenderness								
Abdominal Bloating								
PMS - C								
Headache								
Craving for Sweets								
Increased Appetite								
Heart Pounding								
Fatigue								
Dizziness or Fainting								
PMS - D								
Depression								
Forgetfulness								
Crying								
Confusion								
Insomnia								
OTHER SYMPTOMS								
Loss of Sexual Interest								
Disorientation								
Clumsiness								
Tremors/Shakes								
Thoughts of Suicide								
Agoraphobia								
Increased Physical Activity								
Heavy/Aching Legs								
Generalized Aches								
Bad Breath								
Sensitivity to Music/Light								
Excessive Thirst								

Do you have any other PRE-MENSTRUAL SYMPTOMS
not listed opposite? Use this page to make a note of these.
'Weight Gain' in the chart opposite refers to the amount
you put on before your period.

MENSTRUAL SYMPTOMATOLOGY DIARY

Month:_____

GRADING OF MENSES	GRADING OF SYMPTOMS (COMPLAINTS)

GRADING OF MENSES

0–none   3–heavy
1–slight   4–heavy and
2–moderate   clots

GRADING OF SYMPTOMS (COMPLAINTS)

0–none
1–mild–present but does not interfere with activities
2–moderate–present and interferes with activities but not disabling
3–severe–disabling. Unable to function.

Day of cycle																														
Date																														
Period																														

PMS - A

Nervous tension																														
Mood swings																														
Irritability																														
Anxiety																														

PMS - H

Weight gain																														
Swelling of extemities																														
Breast tenderness																														
Abdominal bloating																														

PMS - C

Headache																														
Craving for sweets																														
Increased appetite																														
Heart pounding																														
Fatigue																														
Dizziness or faintness																														

PMS - D

Depression																														
Forgetfulness																														
Crying																														
Confusion																														
Insomnia																														

PAIN

Cramps (low abdominal)																														
Backache																														
General aches/pains																														

NOTES:

MENSTRUAL SYMPTOMATOLOGY DIARY

Month:_____

GRADING OF MENSES | GRADING OF SYMPTOMS (COMPLAINTS)

0–none   3–heavy
1–slight   4–heavy and
2–moderate   clots

0–none
1–mild-present but does not interfere with activities
2–moderate-present and interferes with activities but not disabling
3–severe-disabling. Unable to function.

Day of cycle																													
Date																													
Period																													

PMS - A

Nervous tension																													
Mood swings																													
Irritability																													
Anxiety																													

PMS - H

Weight gain																													
Swelling of extemities																													
Breast tenderness																													
Abdominal bloating																													

PMS - C

Headache																													
Craving for sweets																													
Increased appetite																													
Heart pounding																													
Fatigue																													
Dizziness or faintness																													

PMS - D

Depression																													
Forgetfulness																													
Crying																													
Confusion																													
Insomnia																													

PAIN

Cramps (low abdominal)																													
Backache																													
General aches/pains																													

NOTES:

7 REFERENCES

Below is a list of some of the more important references relating to studies detailed in this edition of the book. The WNAS has endeavoured over the years to keep details of most of the important studies on the causation and treatment of PMS. A copy of these references and other information on PMS can be obtained from the WNAS by sending £3 in postage stamps to The Women's Nutritional Advisory Service, PO Box 268, Lewes, Sussex BN7 2QN.

Chapter 1

1. Green R., Dalton K. The Pre-Menstrual Syndrome. British Medical Journal. May 9, 1953. P1007–1014.
2. Abraham G.E. Nutrition and the Pre-Menstrual Tension Syndromes. Journal of Applied Nutrition. 36:103–124. 1984.
3. Morton J.H., Additon H., Addison R.G., Hunt L., Sullivan J.J. A clinical study of Pre-Menstrual Tension. A.M.J.Obstet.Gynecol. 55:1182–1191. 1953.

Chapter 2

1. Abraham G.E. Management of the Pre-Menstrual Tension Syndromes: Rationale for a Nutritional Approach. In: A Year in Nutritional Medicine, Second Edition 1986. Ed. by Bland J. Keats Publishing, Inc. New Canaan, Connecticut: 125–166. 1986.
2. Munday M.R., Brush M.G., Taylor R.W. Correlation between Progesterone, Oestradiol and Aldosterone Levels in the Pre-Menstrual Syndrome. Clinical Endocrinology. 14:1–9. 1981.
3. Watts J.F.F., Butt W.P., Logan Edwards R., Holder G. Hormonal Studies in Women with Pre-Menstrual Tension. British Journal of Obstetrics and Gynaecology. 92:247–255. 1985.
4. Dalton M.E. Sex Hormone-Binding Globulin Concentrations in Women with Severe Pre-Menstrual Syndrome. Post-Graduate Medical Journal. 57:560–561. 1981.

Chapter 3

1. Moos R.H. Typology of Menstrual Cycle Symptoms. American Journal of Obstet.Gynec. 103:390–402. 1969.

Chapter 4

1. Dalton K. Pre-Menstrual Syndrome and Progesterone Therapy. Second Edition. William Heinemann Medical Books Limited London. 1984.
2. Hargrove J.T., Abraham G.E. The Incidence of Pre-Menstrual Tension in a Gynaecologic Clinic. The Journal of Reproductive Medicine. 27:721–724. 1982.
3. Hargrove J.T., Abraham G.E. The Ubiquitousness of Pre-Menstrual Tension in a Gynaecologic Practice. The Journal of Reproductive Medicine. 28:435–437. 1983.

Chapter 5

1. Yudkin J. Pure, White and Deadly. Viking Press. London. 1986.
2. Royal College of General Practitioners. Alcohol – A Balanced View. Report from General Practice 24. RCGP London. 1986.
3. Drug Abuse Briefing. Institute for the Study of Drug Dependents. London. 1986.
4. Abraham G.E. Nutrition and the Pre-Menstrual Tension Syndromes. Journal of Applied Nutrition. 36:103–124. 1984.

5. Ashton C.H. Caffeine and Health. The British Medical Journal. 295:1293–4. 1987.

Chapter 6

1. Boyle C.A. et al. Caffeine Consumption and Fibrocystic Breast Disease: A Case-Control Epidemiologic Study. JNCI. 72:1015–1019. 1984.
2. O'Brien P.M.S, Selby C., Symonds E.N. Progesterone, Fluid and Electrolytes in Pre-Menstrual Syndrome. The British Medical Journal. 10 May 1980: 1161–1163.
3. MacGregor G.A. et al. Is 'Idiopathic' Oedema Idiopathic. The Lancet 1:397–400. 1979.
4. O'Brien P.M.S., Selby C., Symonds E.M. Progesterone, Fluid and Electrolytes in Pre-Menstrual Syndrome. The British Medical Journal. 280:1161–3. 1980.

Chapter 7

1. Yudkin J. Pure, White and Deadly. Viking Press. London. 1986.
2. Morton J.H., Additon H., Addison R.G., Hunt L., Sullivan J.J. A clinical study of Pre-Menstrual Tension. A.M.J.Obstet.Gynecol. 55:1182–1191. 1953.

Chapter 8

1. Abraham G.E. Nutrition and the Pre-Menstrual Tension Syndromes. Journal of Applied Nutrition. 36:103-124. 1984.
2. Dalton K. Pre-Menstrual Syndrome and Progesterone Therapy. Second Edition. William Heinemann Medical Books Limited London. 1984.

Chapter 9

1. Dalton K. Pre-Menstrual Syndrome and Progesterone Therapy. Second Edition. William Heinemann Medical Books Limited London. 1984.

Chapter 10

1. Pre-Menstrual Syndrome – Proceedings for Workshop held at the Royal College of Obstetricians and Gynaecologists. London, 2nd December 1982. Ed. Taylor. R.W. Medical News – Tribune Limited. London. 1983.
2. Sampson J.A. Pre-Menstrual Syndrome: A Double-Blind Control Trial of Progesterone and Placebo. British Journal of Psychiatry. 135:209–215. 1979.
3. Dennerstein L., et al. Progesterone and the Pre-Menstrual Syndrome: A Double-Blind Cross Over Trial. British Medical Journal. 290:1617–1621. 1985.
4. Magos A., Studd J. Progesterone and the Pre-Menstrual Syndrome: A Double-Blind Cross Over Trial. British Medical Journal. 291:213–214. 1985.
5. O'Brien P.M.S. The Pre-Menstrual Syndrome: A Review of the Present Status of Therapy. Drugs 24:140–151. 1982.

Chapter 11

1. Modern Nutrition in Health and Disease. Ed: Goodhart R.S., Shils M.E. Sixth edition Lea and Febiter, Philadelphia. 1980.
2. Nutritional Medicine. Davies S., Stewart A. Pan Books London. 1987.
3. Lewis J., Buss D.H. Trace Nutrients 5. Minerals and Vitamins in the British Household Food Supply. British Journal of Nutrition. 60:413–424. 1988.
4. Spring J.A., Robertson J., Buss D.H. British Journal of Nutrition. 41:487–493. 1979.
5. Gregory J., Foster K., Tyler H. and Wiseman M. The Dietary and Nutritional Survey of British Adults. HMSO. London 1990.
6. Committee on Medical Aspects of Food Policy. Dietary Reference Values for Food Energy and Nutrients for the United Kingdom. HMSO. London 1991.

Chapter 12

1. Piesse. J.W. Nutrition Factors in the Pre-Menstrual Syndrome. International Clinical Nutrition Review. 4:54–81. 1984.
2. Hargrove J.T., Abraham G.E. Effect of Vitamin B6 on Infertility in Women with Pre-Menstrual Syndrome. Infertility 2:315–322. 1979.
3. Abraham G.E., Hargrove J.T. The Effect of Vitamin B6 on Pre-Menstrual Symptomatology in Women with Pre-Menstrual Syndrome: A Double-Blind Cross Over Study. Infertility. 3:155–165. 1980.
4. Gunn A.D.G. Vitamin B6 and the Pre-Menstrual Syndrome. In Vitamins-Nutrients as Therapeutic Agents. Ed: Hanck A., Hornig D. Hans Huber Publishers. Bern. 1985. P213–224.
5. Stokes J., Mendels J. Pyridoxine and Pre-Menstrual Tension. The Lancet 1:1177–1178. 1972.
6. Abraham G.E. Magnesium Deficiency in Pre-Menstrual Tension. Magnesium Bulletin 1:68–73. 1982.
7. Abraham G.E., Lubran M.M. Serum and Red Cell Magnesium levels in patients with Pre-Menstrual Tension. The American Journal of Clinical Nutrition. 34:2364–2366. 1981.
8. Sherwood R.A., Rocks B.F., Stewart A., Saxton R.S. Magnesium in the Pre-Menstrual Syndrome. Ann. Clin. Biochem. 23:667–670. 1986.
9. Pre-Menstrual Tension: An Invitation a Symposium. Ed. Abraham G.E. Journal of Reproductive Medicine. 28:7 & 8:433–538. 1983.
10. Fushs N., Hakim M., Abraham G.E. The Effect of a Nutritional Supplement, Optivite, for Women with Pre-Menstrual Tension Syndromes. 1. Effect of Blood Chemistry and Serum Steroid levels during the mid-luteal phase. The Journal of Applied Nutrition. 37:1–11. 1986.
11. Chakmakjian Z.H., Higgins C.E., Abraham G.E. The Effect of a Nutritional Supplement, Optivite, for Women, on Pre-Menstrual Tension Syndromes: 2. The effect of Symptomatology, using a Double-Blind Cross-Over Design. The Journal of Applied Nutrition. 37:12–17. 1986.
12. London, R.S. et al. The Effect of Alpha-Tocopherol on Pre-Menstrual Symptomatology: A Double-Blind Study. Journal of the American College of Nutrition. 2:115–122. 1983.
13. London, R.S. et al. The Effect of Alpha-Tocopherol on Pre-Menstrual Symptomatology: A Double-Blind Study 2. Endocrine correlates. Journal of the American College of Nutrition. 3:351–356. 1984.
14. O'Brien P.M.S. Pre-Menstrual Syndrome. Blackwell Scientific Publications, Oxford, 1987.
15. Stewart A.A. Rational Approach to Treating Pre-Menstrual Syndrome. WNAS publication, 1989.
16. Stewart A. Clinical and Biochemical Effects of Nutritional Supplementation on the Pre-Menstrual Syndrome. The Journal of Reproductive Medicine. 32:435–441. 1987.
17. Boyd E.M.F. et al. The effect of a low-fat, high complex-carbohydrate diet on symptoms of cyclical mastopathy. The Lancet. 2:128–132. 1988.
18. Freeman E., Rickels K., Sondheimer S.J. and Polansky M. Ineffectiveness of Progesterone Suppository Treatment for Pre-Menstrual Syndrome. Journal of the American Medical Association. 264:349–53. 1990.
19. Kleijnen J., ter Riet G. and Knipschild P. Vitamin B6 in the Treatment of Pre-Menstrual Syndrome: A Review. British Journal of Obstetrics and Gynaecology. 97:847–852. 1990.
20. London R.S., Bradley L. and Chiamori N.Y. Effect of a Nutritional Supplement on Pre-Menstrual Symptomatology in Women with Pre-Menstrual Syndrome: A Double-Blind Longitudinal Study. Journal of the American College of Nutrition. 10:494–499. 1991.

Chapter 14

1. Yudkin J. Pure, White and Deadly. Viking Press, London. 1986.
2. Royal College of General Practitioners. Alcohol – A Balanced View. Report from General Practice, 24. RCGP. London 1986.
3. Health Education Council. That's The Limit – Booklet. HEC, 78 New Oxford Street, London EC1A 1AH.
4. Nutritional Medicine by Dr Stephen Davies and Dr Alan Stewart. Pan Books. 1987.
5. Which? Troubled Waters, Which? November 1986. P494–497.
6. Spring J.A., Robertson J., Buss D.H. Trace Nutrients 3. Magnesium, Copper, Zinc, Vitamin B6, Vitamin B12 and Folic Acid in the British Household Food Supply. Br.J.Nutr. 41:487–493. 1979.
7. Victor B.S., Greden J.F., and Lubetsky, M. Somatic Manifestations of Caffeinism. J.Clin Psychiat. 42:185–8. 1981.
8. Disler P.B. et al. The Effects of Tea on Iron Absorption. Gut 18:193–200. 1975.
9. Tonkin S.Y. Vitamins and Oral Contraceptives. In Vitamins in Human Biology in Medicine. Ed: Briggs M.H. CRC Press, Boca Raton, Florida. P29–64. 1981.
10. Walters A.H., Fletcher, J.R., Law S.J. Nitrate in Vegetables: Estimation by HPLC. Nutrition and Health. 4:141–149. 1986.
11. Mount J.L. The Food and Health of Western Man. Charles Knight & Co Ltd, London. 1975.
12. The Booker Health Report – A Survey of Vitamin and Mineral Intakes within Certain Population Groups. Booker Health Foods. 1986.

Chapter 19

1. Chuong C.J., Coulam C.B., Kao P.C., Bergstalh J., Go V.L.W. Neuropeptide levels in Pre-Menstrual Syndrome. Fertility and Sterility. 44:760–765. 1985.
2. Prior J.C., Vigna Y. and Alojada N. Conditioning Exercise Decreases Pre-Menstrual Symptoms. European Journal of Applied Physiology. 55:349–355. 1986.

INDEX

abdomen:
  bloating, 13, 17, 40-6, 171, 180
  curl-over exercises, 227
  pain, 15
Abraham, Dr Guy, 3, 16, 120, 131,
    162, 190
aches, generalized, 13
acne, 13, 133, 144, 184
acupressure, 231-3
acupuncture, 231
additives, food, 96, 106, 131, 251
adrenal glands, 10, 11
adrenaline, 47, 214
advice lines, 247
aerobic exercise, 219, 220
aggression, 21
agoraphobia, 13, 74-80, 214-15
alcohol, 48, 106, 143, 169, 214
  and clumsiness, 71
  consumption levels, 95-6, 97
  effects of, 108-9
  vitamin and mineral deficiencies,
    133, 134-5
allergies, 94, 116, 187, 214-15
  to grains, 171-80
  to yeast, 180-3
almond macaroons, 212
aluminium, 105, 106
amino acids, 10, 98, 124
anaemia, 48, 132, 133, 144, 235
ankles, swollen, 13
anorexia nervosa, 236
antacids, 106
anti-anxiety drugs, 115-16
antibiotics, 96, 103, 116, 192
anti-depressants, 115, 192
anxiety, 13, 17, 19, 20, 116, 120,
    218, 231-2

appetite, increased, 17, 48
apples:
  apple and cinnamon cake, 212
  stuffed baked apples, 208
apricots:
  dried fruit conserve, 195
ascorbic acid see vitamin C
aspirin, 234
asthma, 13, 106
Ativan, 97
autogenic training, 216
avocados:
  avocado and yogurt dressing, 200
  fresh avocado and tomato soup,
    196-7

back, tension-releasing exercises,
    226-7
backache, 13, 215, 218, 229-30
bad breath, 13
baking powder, 173
bananas:
  banana cream, 209
  ginger bananas, 210
barley, 171, 176
batter, grain-free, 173
beanshoot salad, 197
benzodiazepenes, 97
beta-carotene, 127
beta-endorphin, 218-19
beverages, 147, 150, 178
  see also alcohol; coffee; tea
biscuits:
  almond macaroons, 212
  grain-free, 173, 174
  potato shortbread, 211
Biskind, Dr, 2

blackcurrant seed oil, 121
bloating, 13, 17, 40-6, 171, 180
blood sugar levels, 47-8
boils, 13
bones, osteoporosis, 11, 236, 238
borage oil, 121
brain:
  control of hormones, 10-11
  food cravings, 47
  glucose and, 126
  menstrual cycle, 7
bran, 131
bread:
  buckwheat and rice bread, 210-11
  grain-free, 171-2, 176
  potato and rice bread, 211
breadcrumbs, grain-free, 173
breakfast:
  menus, 145-6, 176
  recipes, 194-5
breakfast cereals, 172
breast-feeding, 129, 131, 237
breasts:
  cancer, 95, 130
  lumps, 15
  swollen, 13, 40
  tenderness, 13, 15, 17, 42, 114,
    115, 121, 125, 185, 188
  breathing, 20, 221, 227
broccoli soup, 196
Bromocriptine, 114
buckwheat and rice bread, 210-11
bulgar and nut salad, 198

caffeine, 19-20, 48, 107, 108, 167
cakes:
  apple and cinnamon cake, 212
  carrot cake, 209
  coconut pyramids, 213
  fruity cakes, 209
  grain-free, 173-4, 176
calcium, 105, 106, 109, 130-1, 153-4,
    167, 237, 238
cancer, 93-4, 95, 96, 105, 127, 130
Candida albicans, 116, 180, 181

carbohydrates, 41, 125-6
cravings, 47-54
carbon dioxide, hyperventilation, 20
cardiovascular disease, 93
carotene, 94
carrot cake, 209
cars, driving ability, 91-2
case histories:
  Anita Walker, 53-4, 63-9, 84,
    90, 158, 161, 182
  Dee, 43-4
  Geraldine Ellis, 48-53, 73-4,
    84-5, 136, 183
  Ifey, 88
  Jane Moor, 75-80, 237-8, 240-1
  Judith, viii
  June Garson, 241-2
  Liz, 86-7
  Nadine Morris, 34-9, 242
  Pauline Solent, 22-8, 70
  Penny, 85-6
  Rebecca Harley, 44-6, 138
  Ruth Sears, 28-34, 92
  Sally Noone, 58-63, 89-90
  Sandra Patterson, 137
cereals:
  nutritional content, 149-51, 153,
    154
  pesticides, 96
  sensitivity to, 171-80
cervix, 6, 7, 9
charts, 157-63, 256-9
chicken:
  chicken soup, 197
  stuffing for roast, 207
chilli:
  peanut and chilli dressing, 199
chocolate, 47, 48, 49, 50, 53-4, 95
cholesterol, 104, 125, 126
chromium, 101, 130, 134-5, 154-5,
    183
cigarette smoking, 48, 71, 96, 104,
    135, 143, 144, 169
clumsiness, 13, 71-2
coconut pyramids, 213

cod liver oil, 236
coffee, 19-20, 41, 48, 71, 95, 107, 110, 133, 136, 143, 164, 167
coffee substitutes, 147
colourful lentils, 207
Committee on the Medical Aspects of Food, 99
confusion, 13, 18
constipation, 13, 126, 171, 175
contraceptive pill, 97-8, 113, 235
convenience foods, 131, 132
cooking methods, 102
copper, 101, 105, 106, 130
corn, 176
corpus luteum, 9
cramps, 13, 215, 218
cranial osteopathy, 229-30
cravings, 13, 17, 47-54, 134, 183-4, 190
crime, 80-2
crying, 13, 18, 215
cucumber:
    orange and cucumber salad, 199
curl-overs, 227
custard, egg, 210
Cyclogest, 112
cystitis, 13, 180, 181
cysts, ovarian, 234

dairy produce, 131, 143, 150, 167
Dalton, Dr Katharina, 2-3, 13, 56, 58, 81
Danazol, 114
dandelion coffee, 167
dandruff, 185, 188
daydreaming, 215
Department of Health, 99
depression, 13
    acupressure, 231-2
    exercise and, 218, 219
    menopause, 238
    oral contraceptives and, 97
    PMS D (depression), 18, 55-70, 144, 161, 190
    post-natal, 49, 236-7

stress and, 215
    yeast sensitivity and, 180, 181
desserts, recipes, 208-10
diabetes, 126
diaries, 161-3, 256-9
diarrhoea, 13, 122, 171, 215
diet and nutrition:
    additives, 96, 106, 131, 251
    allergies, 94, 116, 171-83, 186, 214-15
    ancestors' diet, 103
    carbohydrates, 41, 125-6
    cholesterol, 104, 125, 126
    choosing a nutritional plan, 142-55
    cooking methods, 102
    effects on menstrual cycle, 10-11
    essential fatty acids, 125, 185, 238
    fats, 19, 95, 103-4, 125, 155
    fibre, 19, 126
    habits, 109-10
    nitrates, 96, 105
    nutritional content, 149-55
    and oestrogen levels, 19
    organic produce, 103, 145
    pesticides, 96
    phosphorus, 95, 130-1, 168
    polyunsaturated fats, 103, 125, 155
    processed food, 102, 168, 214
    proteins, 124-5, 170
    salt content, 40-1
    saturated fats, 95
    and stress, 214
    sugar content, 104
    tailor-made nutritional programme, 156-92
    treatment of PMS, 118-22
    twentieth-century changes, 95-6
    vegetarian and vegan, 129, 133, 170
    water, 126-7
dinner:
    menus, 146, 177
    recipes, 201-7
disorientation, 13

distress, 214
diuretics, 115, 132, 133
dizziness, 13, 17, 48
Doxycycline, 116
dressings see salad dressings
dried fruit:
    dried fruit compote and yogurt,
        208
    dried fruit conserve, 195
driving ability, 91-2
drugs, 97, 192
    treatment of PMS, 115-17
dydrogesterone, 112-13

ECT (electroconvulsive therapy), 26
eczema, 13, 106, 121, 125, 133, 184,
        185, 190
Efamol, 125, 191
eggs:
    egg custard, 210
    nutritional content, 150, 151, 154
    Spanish omelette, 201-2
eggs (ova), 6-9, 237
Ellis, Geraldine, 48-53, 73-4, 84-5,
        136, 183
emotional stress, 11
endometriosis, 113, 114
endometrium, 6
endurance, muscular, 220
epilepsy, 122, 192
essential fatty acids, 125, 185, 238
evening primrose oil, 118, 121, 122,
        125, 137, 191, 192
exercise, 11, 143-4, 216, 217, 218-28
eye strain, 215

facial hair, 15, 236
fainting, 13, 17, 48
Fallopian tubes, 7, 237
fatigue, 13, 17, 48, 171, 184, 238
fats, in diet, 19, 95, 103-4, 125, 155
Femvite, 122, 188, 191
fertilization, 7
fertilizers, nitrate, 96, 105
fibre, dietary, 19, 126

fibroids, 234
fish:
    fish oils, 143, 155
    grilled (broiled) sardines, 201
    mackerel with herbs (in foil), 203
    nutritional content, 149-51, 153-4
    steamed fish with garlic, spring
        onions and ginger, 204
    stuffed mackerel in foil, 203
flatulence see wind
flours, grain-free, 173
fluid retention, 40-2, 115, 127, 132
folic acid, 99, 129, 236
follicles, 7-9
food see diet and nutrition
Food and Drug Administration
        (USA), 99
food additives, 96, 106, 131, 251
food cravings, 13, 17, 47-54, 134,
        183-4, 190
food sensitivity, 186
    to grains, 171-80
    to yeast, 180-3
fool, rhubarb, 208
forgetfulness, 18
fragrant lamb, 205
Frank, Dr Robert T., 2, 12
Freeman, Dr, 112
fructose, 125
fruit, 96, 98, 105
    dried fruit compote and yogurt,
        208
    dried fruit conserve, 195
    fruit jelly, 208
    fruity cakes, 209
    hot fruity breakfast, 194-5
    nutritional content, 149, 150,
        152-5
    see also apples, bananas etc.

gallstones, 126
gamma-linolenic acid, 121
Garson, Don, 241-2
Garson, June, 241-2
ginger bananas, 210

glucose, 47, 125, 126
goals, 216
goulash, vegetarian, 203-4
grains, sensitivity to, 171-80
grapefruit and orange salad, 198
green bean and sweetcorn salad, 199
green leafy vegetables, 169
Greene, Dr Raymond, 3
growth hormones, 96
Gynovite, 238

hair, facial, 15, 236
hair problems, 184, 185
Harley, Rebecca, 138
Harris, Dr, 2
hayfever, 13
headaches, 13, 15, 17, 183, 218
   acupressure, 232
   caffeine and, 20
   cravings and, 48
   oral contraceptives and, 97, 113
   osteopathy, 229-30
   pain-killers, 115
   stress and, 214-15
heart:
   exercise, 220
   heart disease, 93, 95, 103-4, 119,
      126
   palpitations, 20
   pounding, 13, 17, 48
heat therapy, 235
herbal teas, 108, 147, 167
hives, 13
honey, 168
hormones:
   causes of PMS, 3, 19
   cholesterol and, 125
   effect on mood and behaviour,
      9-10
   and exercise, 218-19
   hormone replacement therapy
      (HRT), 238-9
   menstrual cycle, 7, 9
   treatment of PMS, 111-14
   see also oestrogen; progesterone

hostility, 13
hyperactivity, 106
hyperventilation, 20
hypoglycaemia, 47
hypothalamus, 10-11

ibuprofen, 234
implants, hormonal, 113. 114, 239
infertility, 184
insomnia, 13, 18, 20, 116, 190, 215,
      232, 238
iron, 100-1, 130, 170
   deficiency, 48, 132-3, 134-5, 137,
      184, 235
   sources of, 151-2
   tea and, 108
   vitamin C and, 129
irritability, 13, 17, 19, 20-1, 218
irritable bowel syndrome, 34-9, 171,
      214-15
Israel, Dr, 2
IUDs (coils), 184

jelly, fruit, 208
joints:
   problems, 13, 218
   suppleness, 220-1
'junk food', 168, 214

Kelly, Donna, 81
kidneys, 126-7
Kimberly-Clark, 89

lactose, 125
lamb:
   fragrant lamb, 205
   lamb paprika, 206
lead pollution, 105, 106
legs, aching or restless, 13
leisure activities, 216-17
lentils:
   colourful lentils, 207
   lentil and vegetable soup, 195
libido, 72-4
light sensitivity, 13

linoleic acid, 125
linolenic acid, 125
linseed, 175
lithium, 116
liver, functions, 124, 125, 126
liver (in diet), 236
   liver with orange, 206
Lovell, Debra, 81
Lubran, Dr, 120
lunch:
   menus, 146, 177
   recipes, 201-7
lungs, exercise, 220

macaroons, almond, 212
McCance, Dr, 2
mackerel:
   mackerel with herbs (in foil), 203
   stuffed mackerel in foil, 203
magnesium, 11, 41, 105, 130
   alcohol and, 109
   and anxiety, 19
   dairy products and, 143
   deficiency, 100, 131-2, 134-5
   and depression, 55
   diuretics and, 115
   and fatigue, 48
   and the menopause, 238
   and painful periods, 234-5
   and post-natal depression, 237
   side-effects, 122
   sources of, 149-50
   treatment with, 119-20
   and vitamin B6, 128
manganese, 101
marijuana, 48
massage, 216
meat, 145
   fat content, 103
   nutritional content, 149-54
   pesticides in, 96
meditation, 216
mefenamic acid, 115, 234
men, living with PMS sufferers,
   240-4

menopause, 5, 238-9
menstrual cycle, 5-11
mental illness, 94
menus, 145-8, 176-80
mercury, 105
metabolism, 123-4, 218
migraine, 13, 97, 113, 115, 183,
   214-15, 230
milk, 96
minerals, 98, 130-5
   deficiencies, 134-5, 188, 189
   supplements, 187, 188, 190-2, 252
   toxic, 105-6
Mogadon, 97
mood swings, 13, 17, 19, 20, 56,
   215, 218, 238
Moor, Jane, 75-80, 237-8, 240-1
Moor, Tom, 240-1
Morris, Nadine, 34-9, 242
mouth:
   cracking at the corners, 180, 184
   ulcers, 13
mucus, cervical, 6, 7
muesli, 194
multi-vitamins, 120-1, 188, 236
muscles, 123
   endurance, 220
   relaxation, 216
   strength, 220

nail problems, 184
Naltrexone, 116
neck, tension-releasing exercises,
   224-5
nerve damage, 122
nerves, 123
nervous tension, 13, 17, 19, 20-1,
   190, 215, 218
nicotinamide see vitamin B3
nicotinic acid see vitamin B3
nipples, discharges, 15
nitrates, 96, 105
noise sensitivity, 13
noodles:
   rice, 172

snow peas with tiger prawns,
204-5
Noone, Sally, 58-63, 90
norethisterone, 113
nutrition *see* diet and nutrition
nuts:
nut roast, 206-7
nutritional content, 149-54
nutty parsnip soup, 196

oats, 171, 176
obesity, 126
oestrogen:
causes of PMS, 2, 19
effect on mood and behaviour, 9
menopause, 238
menstrual cycle, 7, 9
the Pill, 97, 113
and suicidal feelings, 57
treatment of PMS, 113
oil and fruit dressing, 200
oils, 153
fish, 143, 155
vegetable, 143
vitamin E content, 153
omelette, Spanish, 201-2
Optivite, 120-1, 122, 188, 190-1, 236
oral contraceptives, 19, 97-8, 113,
235
oranges:
grapefruit and orange salad, 198
liver with orange, 206
orange and cucumber salad, 199
organic produce, 103, 145
osteopathy, 229-30
osteoporosis, 11, 236, 238
ovaries:
cysts, 234
false menopause, 114
hormone production, 7-9, 10, 11,
112
magnesium and, 55
menopause, 238
menstrual cycle, 6-9
polycystic, 235-6

overweight, 42-3, 55, 139, 235-6
ovulation, 6-9
Owen, Nicola, 81

pain:
abdominal, 15
period, 14, 113, 115, 190, 232,
234-5
pain-killers, 115
palpitations, 20, 190
pancakes:
grain-free, 173
wholewheat, 194
panic attacks, 19
paracetamol, 234
parsnip soup, nutty, 196
pasta, grain-free, 172
patches, hormonal, 113, 239
Patterson, Sandra, 137
peanut and chilli dressing, 199
pelvic tilt, 223, 226-7
peppers:
Spanish omelette, 201-2
stuffed peppers, 201
periods:
heavy, 15, 113, 114, 133, 144, 184,
235
irregular, 15, 235-6
painful, 14, 113, 115, 190, 232,
234-5
pessaries, progesterone, 112
pesticides, 96
phosphates, 131
phosphorus, 95, 130-1, 168
phytic acid, 131
the Pill, 97-8, 113, 133, 182, 235
pituitary gland, 7, 10-11, 114, 138,
238
pollution, 96, 106
polycystic ovaries, 235-6
polysaccharides, 126
polyunsaturated fats, 103, 125, 155
post-natal depression, 49, 236-7
posture, 223
potassium, 41, 115, 130, 132, 168

potatoes:
  potato and rice bread, 211
  potato shortbread, 211
prawns:
  snow peas with tiger prawns,
    204-5
Pre-Menstrual Syndrome (PMS):
  drug treatment, 115-17
  hormonal treatment, 111-14
  incidence, 93-5
  nutritional treatment, 118-22
  PMS A (anxiety), 17, 19-39, 144,
    145, 160-1, 190
  PMS C (carbohydrate craving),
    17, 47-54, 144, 145, 161, 190
  PMS D (depression), 18, 55-70,
    144, 161, 190
  PMS H (hydration), 17, 40-6,
    144, 161, 190
  sub-groups, 17-18
  symptoms, 12, 13-14, 16-18
Pre-Menstrual Tension (PMT), 12
pregnancy, 9, 129, 131-2, 236, 237
preservatives, 106
processed food, 102, 168, 214
progestagens, 112-13
progesterone:
  causes of PMS, 2, 3
  effect on mood and behaviour, 9
  menstrual cycle, 7, 9
  and post-natal depression, 236-7
  and sterilization, 238
  treatment of PMS, 112-13
prolactin, 114
proteins, 124-5, 170
psoriasis, 133
pulses, nutritional content, 149-51,
  154
pyridoxine see vitamin B6

raising agents, 173
raw food, 169
recipes, 193-213
relationships, 83-7
relaxation, 216, 217, 218-19, 221,
  227-8

religion, 1
restlessness, 13
retinol, 127, 236
Reynolds, Anna, 81
rhubarb fool, 208
riboflavin see vitamin B2
rice:
  buckwheat and rice bread, 210-11
  potato and rice bread, 211
  rice noodles, 172
running, 220
rye, 171, 176

salad dressings:
  avocado and yogurt, 200
  creamy tomato, 200
  oil and fruit, 200
  peanut and chilli, 199
  yogurt herb, 200
salads, 143, 169
  beanshoot, 197
  bulgar and nut, 198
  grapefruit and orange, 198
  green bean and sweetcorn, 199
  orange and cucumber, 199
  Waldorf, 197
salt, 40-1, 95, 115, 126-7, 132, 143,
  167-8
sardines, grilled (broiled), 201
saturated fats, 95
schizophrenia, 58
Sears, Ruth, 28-34, 92
sedatives, 115-16
selenium, 101, 130
sensitivity see food sensitivity
sex drive, 13, 72-4
sex hormones see oestrogen;
  progesterone
Shiatsu, 231-3
shortbread, potato, 211
shoulders, tension-releasing
  exercises, 224-5
skin problems, 185, 190
sleep see insomnia
sleeping tablets, 97, 115-16, 192
smoking, 48, 71, 96, 104, 135, 143,
  144, 169

snacks, 146-7, 174, 177-8
snow peas with tiger prawns, 204-5
sodium, 130, 132
    see also salt
Solent, Pauline, 22-8, 70
soups:
    broccoli, 196
    chicken, 197
    fresh avocado and tomato, 196-7
    lentil and vegetable, 195
    nutty parsnip, 196
Spanish omelette, 201-2
sperm, 6, 7
Spironolactone, 115
sponge cakes, 173
stamina, 220
standing position, 223
starflower oil, 121
sterilization, 237-8
stir-fry vegetables, 202-3
strength, 220
stress, 11, 58-9, 94, 214-17
Studd, John, 113
stuffing for roast chicken, 207
sucrose, 125, 126
sugar, 125-6
    consumption of, 95, 104, 142-3,
        168-9
    cravings, 13, 47-54, 134-5, 183-4,
        190
    and fluid retention, 41
suicidal feelings, 13, 56-70
supplements, 188, 190-2, 252
suppleness, 220-1
sweetcorn:
    green bean and sweetcorn salad,
        199
sweets, recipes, 208-10
swimming, 218, 220
swollen extremities, 13, 17, 42
symptoms:
    of PMS, 12, 13-14, 16-18
    withdrawal, 164, 192

tea, 19-20, 41, 48, 71, 95, 108, 133,
    135, 143, 164, 167

teeth, signs of stress, 215
tension:
    exercises to release, 224-8
    nervous tension, 13, 17, 19, 20-1,
        190, 215, 218
testosterone, 114
tetracycline, 192
thiamin see vitamin B1
thirst, 13
thrush, 97, 116, 133, 136, 180, 181,
    182-3
thyroid gland, 10, 11, 48, 138
tocopherol see vitamin E
tomatoes:
    creamy tomato dressing, 200
    fresh avocado and tomato soup,
        196-7
tongue, sore, 184
toxic minerals, 105-6
trace elements, 101, 130
tranquillizers, 97, 192
tremors, 13
tryptophan, 128

urination, frequency of, 20
urine, 126
uterus:
    fibroids, 234
    menstrual cycle, 6, 7, 9

vagina, 6
    discharges, 15
    infections, 116
    soreness, 15
Valium, 97
varicose veins, 126
vegan diet, 170
vegetable oil, 143
vegetables, 143, 169
    lentil and vegetable soup, 195
    nutritional content, 149-55
    stir-fry vegetables, 202-3
    toxins, 96, 105
    vegetarian goulash, 203-4
    vitamins and minerals, 98
vegetarian diet, 129, 133, 170

vegetarian goulash, 203-4
violence, 21, 80-2
vitamins, 10, 98, 127-30
  deficiencies, 134-5, 188
  multi-vitamins, 120-1, 188, 236
  supplements, 188, 190-2, 252
  vitamin A, 94, 127, 236
  vitamin B complex, 2, 19, 55, 99-100, 105, 122, 127-9, 181-2, 214, 237
  vitamin B1 (thiamin), 109, 128, 134-5
  vitamin B2 (riboflavin), 106, 128
  vitamin B3 (nicotinic acid), 128
  vitamin B6 (pyridoxine), 11, 99, 100, 109, 118-19, 122, 128-9, 133-5, 137, 149
  vitamin B12, 129
  vitamin C, 94, 105, 106, 108, 129, 133, 134-5, 152-3
  vitamin D, 109, 125, 130
  vitamin E, 94, 119, 129-30, 153

Waldorf salad, 197
Walker, Anita, 53-4, 63-9, 84, 90, 91, 158, 161, 182
walking, 144, 215, 218
walnuts:
  bulgar and nut salad, 198

warming-up exercise, 224
water, 104-5, 126-7
water filters, 105-6
water retention, 40-2, 115, 127, 132
water tablets, 115, 132, 133
weight gain, 13, 15, 17, 40-6
weight loss, 15, 42-3, 139
wheat, 171, 175-6
wholefoods, 143
wholewheat, 171
wholewheat pancakes, 194
wind, 13, 171, 180, 181
withdrawal symptoms, 164, 192
womb see uterus
work, productivity and efficiency at, 87-90

yeast sensitivity, 180-3
yoga, 216
yogurt:
  avocado and yogurt dressing, 200
  banana cream, 209
  dried fruit compote and yogurt, 208
  yogurt herb dressing, 200

zinc, 11, 101, 105, 109, 130, 133-5, 137, 150-1, 170, 184

FURTHER HELP

If you would like information on the WNAS programme for pre-menstrual syndrome, or want to let me know about your success using the recommendations in this book, you can write to me at the following address.

If you require information, a large (A4) stamped, self-addressed envelope will guarantee you a reply; please state particularly that you are interested in receiving information on PMS, as we help women with all sorts of other conditions as well (see below).

Women's Nutritional Advisory Service
PO Box 268
Lewes
East Sussex BN7 2QN.

ADVICE LINES
FROM THE WNAS

OVERCOME PMS NATURALLY	0839 556600
THE PMS DIET LINE	0839 556601
OVERCOME MENOPAUSE NATURALLY	0839 556602
THE MENOPAUSE DIET LINE	0839 556603
BEAT SUGAR CRAVING	0839 556604
THE VITALITY DIET LINE	0839 556605
OVERCOMING BREAST TENDERNESS	0839 556606
OVERCOME PERIOD PAINS NATURALLY	0839 556607
GET FIT FOR PREGNANCY AND BREASTFEEDING	0839 556608
SKIN, NAIL & HAIR SIGNS OF DEFICIENCY	0839 556609
IMPROVE LIBIDO NATURALLY	0839 556610
BEAT IRRITABLE BOWEL SYNDROME	0839 556611
OVERCOME FATIGUE	0839 556612
BEAT MIGRAINE NATURALLY	0839 556613
OVERCOME OVULATION PAIN	0839 556614
DIRECTORY	0839 556615